Cambridge IGCSE™

ICT

STUDENT'S BOOK

T0370999

Paul Clowrey

William Collins' dream of knowledge for all began with the publication of his first book in 1819. A self-educated mill worker, he not only enriched millions of lives, but also founded a flourishing publishing house. Today, staying true to this spirit, Collins books are packed with inspiration, innovation and practical expertise. They place you at the centre of a world of possibility and give you exactly what you need to explore it.

Collins. Freedom to teach.

Published by Collins
An imprint of HarperCollins*Publishers*
The News Building, 1 London Bridge Street, London, SE1 9GF, UK

HarperCollins*Publishers*
Macken House, 39/40 Mayor Street Upper,
Dublin 1, D01 C9W8, Ireland

Browse the complete Collins catalogue at
www.collins.co.uk

10 9 8 7 6 5 4

ISBN 978-0-00-843092-4

British Library Cataloguing-in-Publication Data
A catalogue record for this publication is available from the British Library.

Author: Paul Clowrey
Previous edition author: Colin Stobart
Publisher: Elaine Higgleton
Product manager: Alex Marson
Proofreader: Alison Bewsher
Image researcher: Alison Prior
Cover designer: Gordon MacGilp
Typesetter: Jouve UK LTD
Production controller: Lyndsey Rogers

Printed in India by Multivista Global Pvt. Ltd.

MIX
Paper | Supporting
responsible forestry
FSC™ C007454
FSC
www.fsc.org

This book contains FSC™ certified paper and other controlled sources to ensure responsible forest management.

For more information visit: www.harpercollins.co.uk/green

The publishers gratefully acknowledge the permission granted to reproduce the copyright material in this book. Every effort has been made to trace copyright holders and to obtain their permission for the use of copyright material. The publishers will gladly receive any information enabling them to rectify any error or omission at the first opportunity.

Cambridge International copyright material in this publication is reproduced under licence and remains the intellectual property of Cambridge Assessment International Education.

Exam-style questions [and sample answers] have been written by the authors. In examinations, the way marks are awarded may be different. References to assessment and/or assessment preparation are the publisher's interpretation of the syllabus requirements and may not fully reflect the approach of Cambridge Assessment International Education.

Third-party websites and resources referred to in this publication have not been endorsed by Cambridge Assessment International Education.

The external web links have been included for the convenience of users and were checked at the time of publication, but the Publisher is not responsible for the content of external sites and cannot guarantee that links continue to work or that the quality of the content has been maintained. The links are not intended to form part of the product and have been included purely for educational purposes. It is the user's responsibility to ensure the external web links meet their requirements.

Contents

Introduction

Welcome to your new textbook for the Cambridge IGCSE™ and IGCSE (9-1) Information and Communication Technology syllabuses (0417/0983) for examination from 2023. This book and digital download have been produced to provide support for all students studying this syllabus.

An integrated approach to ICT

The Cambridge IGCSE™ Information and Communication Technology syllabus has been designed to provide you with an **integrated** understanding of ICT. In short, this means learning about how the different areas of ICT are connected. For example, learning about the internet involves learning about computer networks, different types of hardware and software, how to create websites and how ICT is used in businesses. When you learn about ICT you can also apply it to all the other subjects that you are studying.

The Cambridge IGCSE™ Information and Communication Technology exams are made up of three papers: one paper for the theory side of the syllabus and two papers for the practical side. This book explores how the theory and practice of ICT are integrated.

We need to learn about different devices, applications and systems, how they have developed and their advantages and disadvantages – this is the theory. But knowing this helps us to understand how to use hardware and software, and how to develop our skills – this is the practice. And of course we need to know how all of this links to the real world; how you can use ICT in your school and home life and how people and businesses all over the world use ICT.

How this book works

This book is divided into eight main units that interweave all twenty one topics of the Cambridge IGCSE™ Information and Communication Technology syllabus by linking the theory content of the syllabus with the practical elements of the syllabus.

The eight units include sessions that cover the theory (for example, *The main components of a computer*) followed by sessions that cover the practical skills (for example, *Creating a newsletter*). Each unit starts with an introduction to the topic, and outlines a practical task that makes a connection between what you will learn in the theory and the practical skills that you will be developing. For example, in Unit 2 you will learn about input and output devices in the theory sessions. In the practical sessions you will focus on creating presentations. Your practical task in this unit is to create an electronic presentation for an animation company to explain how different input and output devices are used in the business.

How the pages work

The theory and the practical sessions both contain a variety of useful features to help you through the book.

- Session opener – introduces the topic.
- Language boxes – help you with any difficult or confusing terminology.
- Glossary terms – highlighted in blue, the definitions can be found at the back of the book.
- Activities – each session contains several activities. In the theory sessions these help reinforce what you've learnt and in the practical sessions they test your skills.
- Review and revise – A recap of what you should have achieved by the end of each session.
- Screenshots – used throughout the practical sessions to illustrate skills.*
- Tip boxes – additional support, from keyboard shortcuts to revision tips.
- Real world boxes – explain the significance of ICT in the real world.

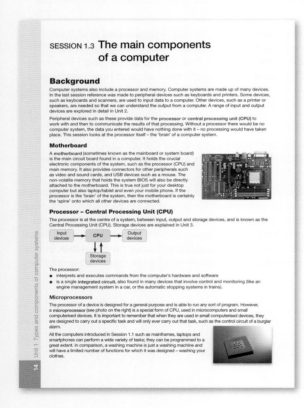

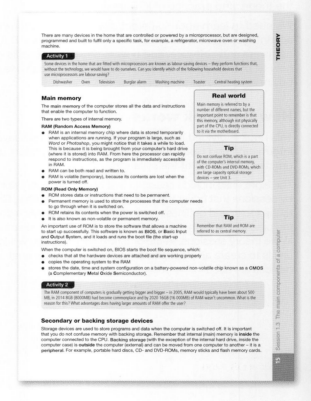

*We have used some popular software packages for illustration. But you should be able to follow the practical sessions in this book with the operating systems or software packages you use at school or at home.

SESSION 4.3 The internet and intranets

Background

The internet is an **inter**national **network** of computers that allows users to use email, browse the World Wide Web or to chat either by text or by voice.

Schools, banks and other organisations often restrict access to the internet, but want to provide internet-type resources and experiences to their users. They do this by setting up an intranet, best thought of as an **internal** restricted access **network**.

The internet

Websites

Internet browsers accessing the World Wide Web allow us to visually access some of the information stored on the internet through websites. As of 2014 there are well over one billion websites, each containing any number of webpages.

Webpages	Websites
Documents that can be seen on a computer screen. May contain: • text • animations • images • video • sound.	Lots of webpages that are linked together by hyperlinks. Clicking on a hyperlink allows a user to navigate between webpages in the website. They also allow you to move to other websites.

Each webpage has a unique address. This address helps web browsers to find them. The address is known as the **U**niform **R**esource **L**ocator or **URL**. This is how a URL is made up:

https://www.harpercollins.co.uk/corporate/about-us/

Protocol	Host name	Domain name			File path	Filename
		Second level domain (SLD)	Sub domain	Top level domain (TLD)		
https://	www	.harpercollins	.co	.uk/	corporate/about-us/	

Activity 1

Look at the following web addresses. Break them down into their component parts. The first one is done for you.

• http://images.example.com
• http://www.examples.gov.za/example/page1
• http://examples.mycompany.org/in/example/page5

Protocol	Host name	Domain name			File path	Filename
		Second level domain (SLD)	Sub domain	Top level domain (TLD)		
http://	images	.example		.com		

Language

The World Wide Web is also referred to as www, or the web.

Tip

It is important that you know that the World Wide Web is part of the internet. You access the web by using a web browser like Mozilla Firefox, Google Chrome, Safari (Apple) or Microsoft Edge.

Real world

You can recognise hyperlinks easily. Hyperlinks are normally shown in blue underlined text and can link to a webpage, image or any other computer file. When the mouse pointer hovers over them, it will either change to a small hand or a box will appear providing a URL to click and follow.

Real world

You will notice the example given doesn't have a filename as part of the address. The way websites are structured, some will show a file name (such as index.html .htm or .php) and some will only display a file path.

Accessing the internet

Users access the internet through an Internet Service Provider (ISP). There is usually a fee for this service. Users are allocated login details when they sign up to an ISP, including a username and a password.

Each time a user logs in, the ISP can monitor how they are using the service. In many countries, ISPs are required to keep records of the webpages, websites and emails that users access and create.

There are three main methods of connecting to the internet:

Method of internet access	Equipment required	Advantages	Disadvantages
Dial-up	Dial-up modem	Usually very cheap. Only requires access to a telephone line.	Slowest connection – 56 kbps. Telephone line tied up while the modem is in use.
Fibre optic cable	Cable modem	Very fast, stable connection, does not tie up telephone line. Cable network supplier can also offer other internet-based streaming services.	Often only available in cities and towns.
Broadband (Digital Subscriber Line – DSL)	ADSL modem	Fast connection. Always on – does not tie up the telephone line. Uses traditional copper-wire infrastructure.	Heavy users can find download and upload limits to be too restrictive. Areas with multiple subscribers will suffer from lower download speeds.
Mobile broadband (via dongle or tethering)	Mobile phone with mobile data access	Mobile access, available anywhere a mobile data signal is available.	Can be very expensive Mobile download speeds can be slower Not suitable for multiple devices

The internet and networks

Networks often have many users. In order for multiple users on a network to access the same internet connection, a **proxy server** is used. A proxy server acts as a gateway between network users and the internet by submitting all the internet requests for those users and then returning to them the results of their requests and the information received. You can see in the diagram below that users access the internet through the proxy server.

The proxy server:

• submits just one request for all the users to the router
• can also store copies of webpages for easy access
• restricts access to some users
• checks the source or destination of a data packet and allows or refuses access.

Access to the internet is often managed by a **firewall** to protect users from hackers. A firewall is software that prevents unauthorised communication to or from the network, usually placed between the internal network and an external network, like the internet. A firewall restricts access to identified computers by noting and blocking specific **IP addresses** or blocking certain types of internet traffic.

Language

Proxy means 'stands in for' – so a proxy server stands in for all the users.

Real world

In some organisations, like schools, there are restrictions on the webpages students are allowed to see.

SESSION 3.5 Adding text and images to a document

Background

In this session you will build upon and discover the following skills:
• accurately adding and formatting text
• using tables
• inserting images in a document.

Adding and formatting text

Typing text straight into a word processed document is the simplest way to add information, and there are a variety of formatting tools to help you to present it in the most suitable way.

Text formatting

Below are a selection of fonts, styles and sizes.

The **Font** window shown above can be found on the main menu or **Formatting toolbar**. The font, style and size of any selected font can be changed to suit the requirements of the document. **Bold** or underlined headings, for example, are a good way of highlighting important information. Additional font effects include superscript, adding very small letters above the line of text and subscript, small letters just below.

Text alignment

The text on the right has been added to a document with two columns. The four paragraphs are aligned to the left margin, the right margin, centrally and fully justified (which means the text is spaced to meet both the left and right edges of the text area).

Tip

A standard selection of fonts is installed on every computer but new ones can be installed and different computers may not have the same fonts. This should be considered when transferring work from one machine to another.

Language

Serif and sans-serif fonts. When describing fonts, a serif typeface has detailing at the ends of strokes in letters, while sans-serif fonts do not. Serif fonts are normally thought of as being traditional styles, such as Times New Roman, while sans-serif fonts like Arial are considered more modern.

Activity 1

Create a new word processing document and type the name of the organisation in this unit – Abacus International Bank – six times on the page. Using different fonts and styles, create what you think are three modern headings and three more traditional ones. Share your ideas with a partner and discuss which would be most suitable for this type of business.

Bulleted and numbered lists

Bullet points or numbered lists are useful for displaying different points of information. They can be accessed from the main menu or by right clicking within a text area. Right clicking a bullet point or number will allow you to format it using the options shown.

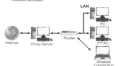

Paragraph formatting

The space before and after paragraphs, line spacing, and tab settings can be edited to suit the style of document. The **Paragraph** dialogue box and settings can be found by selecting **Layout** from the ribbon bar.

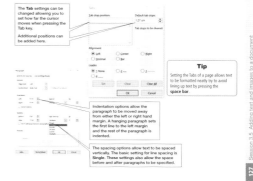

The **Tab** settings can be changed allowing you to set how far the cursor moves when pressing the Tab key.
Additional positions can be added here.

Indentation options allow the paragraph to be moved away from either the left or right hand margin. A hanging paragraph sets the first line to the left margin and the rest of the paragraph is indented.

The spacing options allow text to be spaced vertically. The basic setting for line spacing is **Single**. These settings allow the space before and after paragraphs to be specified.

Tip

Setting the Tabs of a page allows text to be formatted neatly try to avoid lining up text by pressing the **space bar**.

Theory and Practical review

- What have you covered? – a recap of each unit's sessions.
- Different question types – from simple multiple choice questions to those that ask you to describe an answer to show your knowledge.
- Numbered steps – guide you through the necessary steps to a finished document relevant to the skills in each unit.
- Session references – these let you know which sessions to refer back to for help with the question.
- Progress check – a useful guide to what you'll need to know to make good and excellent progress.

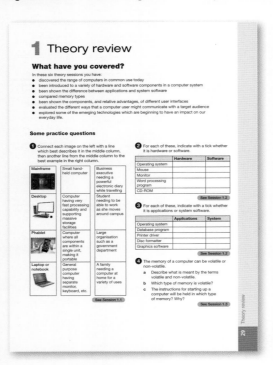

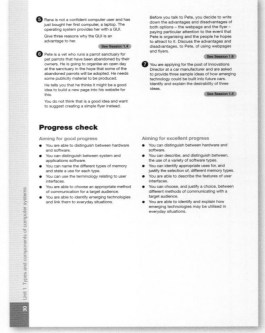

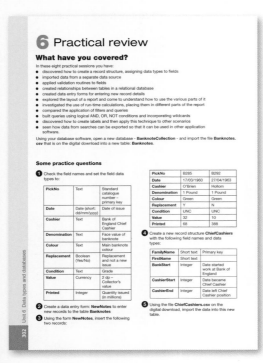

Practice questions

Each unit consists of ICT theory and practical skills-based sessions. At the end of each are review sections containing practice questions to test what you have just learned in the unit. Your teacher will have access to the answers to these questions. See page 3 for an overview of features for these pages.

The digital download that accompanies this book contains practice tests made up of exam-style questions. The best way to use these tests is to try to answer them yourself, either in class or as homework within a set time.

The digital download

The digital download that accompanies this book has two main useful parts:

1. source files
2. practice test questions.

Source files

Some of the practical tasks you have to do require you to use files that we have already prepared for you. We recommend that you copy all of these files to your own – or your school's – computer at the start of the course.

Extra support

The extra support folder contains some useful information sheets relating to website authoring and spreadsheets.
It is indicated in the book when you might want to refer to these.

Microsoft Office, Open Office and other Software

In the preparation of the practical tasks throughout this book we have relied heavily on Microsoft Word, Excel, PowerPoint and Access for our illustrations. It is recognised that centres may use a number of other software packages such as Open Office. Wherever there are significant differences between how to perform a specific spreadsheeting task, for example a function's use in Excel or Calc, we have included information about how you may tackle the task in other software. The nature of word processing software makes it more difficult to offer specific, or even general, alternative advice for locations of various menu, or drop down list, items. Any required item, such as creating a header/footer, are described in such a way as to make it easy for you to search and locate that menu/drop down list item in your own software and apply it appropriately. Often we also give an indication of the group or family of items that the required one may be a part of, enabling you to locate them more easily. If you are a user of software other than Microsoft Office you are not at any disadvantage and can successfully complete any task in this book, as indeed many before you already have.

1 Types and components of computer systems

Why this unit matters

ICT influences what we do, how we travel, what we listen to, how we shop and how we communicate. In offices and classrooms people are using computers. While on the move, smart phones, watches and wearable technology go with us. You may notice goods being scanned at the supermarket, or a car attached to a computer that will monitor, analyse, and improve the performance of its engine.

All Computers Inc. is a large computer supply company. They supply everything from small hand-held computers right up to big computer systems for banks and insurance companies. Many customers find it difficult to make a choice when it comes to buying a computer. This is what some of their customers have said:

There are so many types of computers here. They all seem to do the same thing but some are faster than others, some have keyboards and mice, some are voice controlled. I can't tell the difference between a computer costing $200 and one costing $2000.

If I buy a computer, what else will I need to get? I've heard that I need to buy hardware and software. What does that mean, and how will I know the difference?

I've been looking at the labels that describe the computers. They're a bit complicated. I don't understand what CPU, RAM or ROM are. I need to know about operating systems. I don't know which one I should choose.

Your practical task

All Computers Inc. has decided that it would be helpful if the company had some simple information sheets to describe:

- the advantages and disadvantages of different operating systems
- the different types of computers that are available to buy
- the different types of computers they sell, to help customers decide which is the best computer for them
- the different components of a computer: CPU, screen, keyboard, printer, and external hard drive.

They have asked you to produce this information by creating and editing the contents, appearance and layout of documents.

What this unit covers

THEORY

Sessions

PRACTICAL

Sessions

PRACTICAL REVIEW

By the end of the theory sessions you will be able to:

- identify the different types of computers
- describe a range of emerging technologies
- define what is meant by hardware and software and give examples
- identify the main components of a general purpose computer
- identify operating systems, including those which contain a graphical user interface or a command line interface
- show an understanding of a range of documents that communicate knowledge and ideas.

In your practical work you will develop and apply skills in:

- creating, formatting and opening documents using information from different sources
- combining text, images and numeric data in your work
- formatting texts in lists and tables
- saving and printing your work
- communicating using email
- using the internet as a source of information
- performing a mail merge.

Types of computers

Background

There are many different kinds of computer systems. Some computer systems are very big because they are used to carry out large and complex tasks. Others are small and portable – small enough to put in your pocket – even to wear around your wrist or as a pair of glasses. This session will look at the ways in which various types of computer are used, as well as their characteristics.

Desktop computers

When describing a computer, it is typically a desktop computer that comes to mind. Most desktop computers have common components such as a tower, monitor, keyboard and mouse (although some desktops combine the tower and monitor, see Session 1.2 for more detail). Some users create and store documents, some play games, others create music, video and photographic content; the applications are endless. When a computer is being used by only one person at a time, controlling the **application software** being used, providing any required data and using the processed results with no connection to any other resource, the computer and its use is referred to as being **standalone**. The computer and any related resources, such as a printer, are being used as an isolated workstation.

Often these computers will be connected together in order to share data, programs and other resources such as a printer, application programs or an internet connection. In these cases, the computers are considered to be **networked**. Just think of the computers in your school ICT suite and how resources can be shared. It would be crazy for each computer to have its own printer, or that you always had to work on the same computer because your files were only on that computer's hard drive. The sharing of any information resource and devices means that any user is able to provide information to many other users as well as being able to access a wealth of information from someone in the next room, a nearby town or a different country.

In Unit 4 you will discover the advantages of networking a computer and various ways to do this.

Mobile computers

Not limited to a particular location, mobile computing allows the user to work in almost any location. Modern mobile computers come in a variety of formats.

Laptop computers

Laptop computers are many people's preferred choice of computer because they can offer the same processing capabilities as a desktop computer but are portable. Many families choose to buy a laptop instead of a desktop computer because they take up so little space, can be moved around the house depending on who is using it, and can be packed tidily away. A laptop computer has an inbuilt screen, keyboard and mouse pad, making it completely self-contained. Some people may choose to connect an external keyboard or mouse but leave them at home when using their laptop when they are out. Because a laptop is carefully designed to

minimise necessary (physical) space, one problem is the ability to upgrade or add extra components.

Tens of thousands of people carry laptops around every city, every day; business people and students. Like desktop computers, laptops can be used as standalone computers or as networked computers. If you take your laptop to school with you, the Wi-Fi system can connect you to all the school resources and its internet connection. The same is true if you are in a cafe or similar public space with Wi-Fi access; providing access to the internet.

Tablet computers

Tablet computers are portable computers with slightly smaller screens than an average laptop. Their defining characteristic is that user interaction is all through touch. There is no mouse or keyboard. Users can swipe, pinch, drag and rotate icons on the screen to activate tasks, using the position of their finger as a cursor, and input data. The use of solid-state flash memory (see Unit 3) means that these devices switch on and are ready for use very quickly.

Tablets take advantage of Wi-Fi and cellular data technology because they are devices that many people will use for entertainment while on the move: reading newspapers and magazines; internet browsing; playing games; and watching TV programmes or films. This means that tablets need the fast internet connection that downloading/streaming video content demands. Tablets can run the same applications as laptops, so it would be possible to work on a word-processed document or a spreadsheet for example. However, the virtual keyboard can be difficult to use for these tasks and some users will still connect a Bluetooth keyboard and mouse.

Smartphone

Designed to fit in a pocket and be used on the move, smartphones are quickly becoming one of the most common devices across the globe. In a similar way to the tablet, smartphones are designed around a touchscreen interface and combine the use of specially designed applications, or apps, with a mobile cellular connection that provides access to voice calls and the internet almost anywhere. The worldwide boom in social networking use is linked directly to the increase in smartphone accessibility and development.

Phablet

A combination of the words phone and tablet, a phablet is a device that combines elements of both. With a screen size larger than a regular smartphone but smaller than a tablet, these devices are popular for creative applications, often using a stylus, as well as reading, gaming and entertainment. As the screen size of many modern smartphones increases, many manufacturers offer the same product in both smartphone and phablet sizes.

How computers are used

From smartphones to desktop computers, many of their uses are now crossing devices and only limited by computing power.

- Office and business management includes the use of computers for office-based applications, data analysis and communication through email, voice and video-based platforms. Network compatibility, leading to Internet and cloud-based systems, covered in Unit 4, now links users together across the globe.
- Computers in education allow students to research, present and create computer-based work, and to access online lessons, tutorials and videos.
- Gaming continues to develop on all computer platforms, from gaming-specific consoles to expansive desktop computer games and multiplayer smartphone apps. As CPU computing power is beginning to level out across devices, the same games are being developed as cross-platform products, able to connect gamers no matter which type of computer they are using.
- Entertainment has embraced the rise in video streaming platforms, as well as video and audio sharing platforms, to expand entertainment from traditional television and radio to include all computing devices.
- Remote controlled devices take advantage of network, **Wi-Fi** and **Bluetooth** connectivity to allow one computing device to control another. This might be controlling a drone with a smartphone, a technician remotely controlling a computer to repair a problem or using a tablet to control a robot in a dangerous situation.

Types of computers

Type of computer	Description	Advantages	Disadvantages
Mainframe or Server	These are extremely large computers used in organisations (such as banks and government departments) where very large amounts of data are processed.	• Capable of large scale **processing** which makes use of increased storage capacity and fast processor speeds. • Capable of complex problem-solving that would take smaller computers much longer to do.	• Mainframes are so large that they take up almost a whole room. • Complex to set up. • Expensive to operate and maintain and they require specialist staff to operate them.
Desktop or Personal computer (PC)	This is a general purpose computer made up of separate components: • monitor • keyboard • mouse • processor and **storage**.	• Spare parts are often cheap because they are standardised. • They often have faster processors than laptop computers for the same price. • Components can be replaced or upgraded, improving its lifespan.	• Lack of portability – heavy and separate components are connected by wires. • **Files** have to be copied and stored on portable **disks**, especially if you need to take them with you.
Laptop or Notebook	This is a computer where all the components are together in a single unit. This means that they are portable; unlike desktop computers, they can be moved from one work area to another.	• Portability. • Users can work anywhere, especially if they can access **Wi-Fi** or mobile cellular networks (see Unit 4) and link to other media.	• Loss and theft are key disadvantages. • Battery life is limited. • Keyboards and **pointing devices** are not as flexible as those on a desktop. • Laptops are more compact, so overheating can be a problem. • Lower specifications may mean some graphics-heavy gaming applications may not run.
Tablet	Like a laptop this is a small portable computer but the biggest difference is that its user interface is all through touch.	• Portable and easy to use. • Quick to switch on. • Thousands of downloadable applications available.	• Not all have mobile cellular access. • Touch-screen typing can be difficult. • Not all have ability to make phone calls.

Type of computer	Description	Advantages	Disadvantages
Phablet	Combining the functionality of a smartphone and a tablet, these touch-screen devices provide more productivity than a standard smartphone due to the increased screen size.	• More portable than a standard tablet. • Includes mobile cellular access for mobile Internet applications. • Larger screen aids communication applications.	• Larger size means it may not fit in the pocket, unlike a smartphone. • Less practical for phone calls due to size, may require headphones.
Smartphone	This is an advanced mobile phone that combines voice and messaging with mobile computing applications. Features include: web browsers, high resolution touch screens, GPS navigation, digital camera and video, social networking, office productivity and gaming.	• Mobile online access to data. • Portable, affordability and easily accessible across the globe. • Just one device can accomplish many tasks at work or at home. • Contacts' details and phone numbers can be integrated into communication applications.	• Increased size and shorter battery life over a traditional mobile phone. • Data usage costs vary across the globe and younger users can accidently run up large bills. • Some webpages may not display or function entirely as the web designer expected.

Activity 1

Look through the list of computer types and think about where you have seen them being used. Discuss with a partner and decide on three reasons why a student might choose a laptop computer rather than a general purpose desktop computer.

You can see in the table above that the devices described become physically smaller. However, many tablets and smartphones have similar processing capabilities to much larger general purpose computers. Advances in technology mean that smaller devices are increasingly capable of better performance.

Activity 2

We all know that you can make phone calls with a smartphone, but it can do so much more. It adds in features that not too long ago you would have found only on a laptop or a computer; such as the ability to send and receive email, edit documents and play games. Do some research and determine:
- how a smartphone is different from a conventional mobile phone
- a clear definition of a smartphone
- from a computing perspective, what can a smartphone be used for?
- what is it that makes it smart?

Review and revise

You should now be able to:
- identify different types of computers including the mainframe, desktop and laptop computers, tablets, phablets and smartphones.

SESSION 1.2 Hardware and software

Background

Computer systems are made up of **hardware** and **software**. Computer hardware is made up of the parts of the computer that you can touch: its physical components. Software is the programs, instructions and data that controls the operation of a computer and enables the computer to carry out a task.

Hardware

When you look at a computer and all the **peripheral devices** that are attached to it, you can see examples of hardware such as:

- monitor
- keyboard
- mouse
- printer
- speakers
- scanner
- webcams
- headphones

Some peripheral devices have more than one function. Many people now choose to have their scanner, photocopier and printer together in one device, which are widely known as All-In-One printers. Touch-sensitive screens allow us to use them as input devices as well as output devices (see Session 2.1, page 62).

Having an external hard drive is an excellent way of giving yourself extra portable storage space as well as providing a backup facility.

Activity 1

Can you identify each of the seven examples of hardware listed in this picture?

Of course, there are other examples besides the hardware that can actually be seen. There is other hardware that is built into, or inside the computer case (or tower) including:

- **Internal memory** (RAM and ROM – see Session 1.3)
- Central Processing Unit (CPU) (see Session 1.3)
- A **motherboard** (see Session 1.3)
- Graphics cards (note the connection sockets such as VGA, HDMI, DVI)
- Sound cards (note the sockets for such hardware as headphone and microphone)
- Internal hard disk drive
- Network Interface Cards (NIC) (See Unit 4)

There is also computer hardware in devices like mobile phones, **satellite navigation** systems, automatic washing machines and even in car engines.

Software

There are two types of software that are used to operate a computer.

System software	These are **programs** and files that make up the computer's **operating system**.
	Examples of **system software** include the software to connect with the printer, that controls the way the screen appears, the software that deletes a file or a folder. These run invisibly in the background so that you can do your work effectively.
Applications software	Also known as **applications programs**. These programs allow users to write letters, solve problems, perhaps using spreadsheet and database software, or to play games.

Real world

VGA (Video Graphics Adapter) and DVI (Digital Video Interface) allow the transmission of video from a desktop computer or laptop to a monitor or projector.

Although similar, HDMI allows the transmission of video and audio, making it idea for modern entertainment devices such as connecting a TV to a games console or satellite system.

Examples of system software

System software generally runs in the background but examples that might be running on your computer might include:

- compilers that convert user-written high-level code into machine code only a computer can understand
- linkers that take individual compiler outputs and convert them to a single program
- device drivers for peripheral devices
- operating systems
- utilities that protect your computer from malware.

Examples of applications software

If you look at your computer screen, you should see that there are many different kinds of applications software. You might see examples of the following software (you are likely to have many more):

- word processing
- spreadsheet modelling
- database management
- device control
- measurement and sensor recording
- applets and apps
- video, graphics and audio editing
- computer aided design (CAD)

Activity 2

Complete the following table by deciding whether the listed software is either applications or system software and then give a description of what it does. You might need to search for some answers on the internet.

Software for...	Applications/System	What does it do?
Word processing	Application	Creation of reports/letters/posters/flyers
Anti-virus software		
Spreadsheet		
Operating system		
Internet browser		
Photo-editing software		
File manager		
The programming language 'Scratch'		
Printer driver		

Review and revise

You should now be able to:

- identify a variety of hardware components
- describe the key elements of hardware and the difference between hardware and software
- describe the difference between system and applications software
- give examples of applications software.

Tip

See Session 1.8 for information and advice about internet research.

Tip

When referring to applications software, it is better if you can describe what the software does rather than just knowing the name of the software.

The main components of a computer

Background

Computer systems also include a processor and memory. Computer systems are made up of many devices. In the last session reference was made to peripheral devices such as keyboards and printers. Some devices, such as keyboards and scanners, are used to input data to a computer. Other devices, such as a printer or speakers, are needed so that we can understand the output from a computer. A range of input and output devices are explored in detail in Unit 2.

Peripheral devices such as these provide data for the **processor** or **central processing unit (CPU)** to work with and then to communicate the results of that processing. Without a processor there would be no computer system, the data you entered would have nothing done with it – no processing would have taken place. This session looks at the processor itself – the 'brain' of a computer system.

Motherboard

A **motherboard** (sometimes known as the mainboard or system board) is the main circuit board found in a computer. It holds the crucial electronic components of the system, such as the processor (CPU) and main memory. It also provides connectors for other peripherals such as video and sound cards, and USB devices such as a mouse. The non-volatile memory that holds the system BIOS will also be directly attached to the motherboard. This is true not just for your desktop computer but also laptop/tablet and even your mobile phone. If the processor is the 'brain' of the system, then the motherboard is certainly the 'spine' onto which all other devices are connected.

Processor – Central Processing Unit (CPU)

The processor is at the centre of a system, between input, output and storage devices, and is known as the Central Processing Unit (CPU). Storage devices are explained in Unit 3.

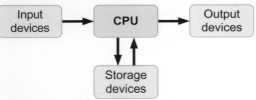

The processor:

- interprets and executes commands from the computer's hardware and software
- is a single **integrated circuit**, also found in many devices that involve control and monitoring (like an engine management system in a car, or the automatic stopping systems in trains).

Microprocessors

The processor of a device is designed for a general purpose and is able to run any sort of program. However, a **microprocessor** (see photo on the right) is a special form of CPU, used in microcomputers and small computerised devices. It is important to remember that when they are used in small computerised devices, they are designed to carry out a specific task and will only ever carry out that task, such as the control circuit of a burglar alarm.

All the computers introduced in Session 1.1 such as mainframes, laptops and smartphones can perform a wide variety of tasks; they can be programmed to a great extent. In comparison, a washing machine is just a washing machine and will have a limited number of functions for which it was designed – washing your clothes.

There are many devices in the home that are controlled or powered by a microprocessor, but are designed, programmed and built to fulfil only a specific task, for example, a refrigerator, microwave oven or washing machine.

Activity 1

Some devices in the home that are fitted with microprocessors are known as labour-saving devices – they perform functions that, without the technology, we would have to do ourselves. Can you identify which of the following household devices that use microprocessors are labour-saving?

Dishwasher   Oven   Television   Burglar alarm   Washing machine   Toaster   Central heating system

Main memory

The **main memory** of the computer stores all the data and instructions that enable the computer to function.

There are two types of internal memory.

RAM (Random Access Memory)

- RAM is an internal memory chip where data is stored temporarily when applications are running. If your program is large, such as *Word* or *Photoshop*, you might notice that it takes a while to load. This is because it is being brought from your computer's hard drive (where it is stored) into RAM. From here the processor can rapidly respond to instructions, as the program is immediately accessible in RAM.
- RAM can be both read and written to.
- RAM is volatile (temporary), because its contents are lost when the power is turned off.

ROM (Read Only Memory)

- ROM stores data or instructions that need to be permanent.
- Permanent memory is used to store the processes that the computer needs to go through when it is switched on.
- ROM retains its contents when the power is switched off.
- It is also known as non-volatile or permanent memory.

An important use of ROM is to store the software that allows a machine to start up successfully. This software is known as **BIOS**, or **B**asic **I**nput and **O**utput **S**ystem, and it loads and runs the boot file (the start-up instructions).

When the computer is switched on, BIOS starts the boot file sequence, which:

- checks that all the hardware devices are attached and are working properly
- copies the operating system to the RAM
- stores the date, time and system configuration on a battery-powered non-volatile chip known as a **CMOS** (a **C**omplementary **M**etal **O**xide **S**emiconductor).

> **Real world**
>
> Main memory is referred to by a number of different names, but the important point to remember is that this memory, although not physically part of the CPU, is directly connected to it via the motherboard.

> **Tip**
>
> Do not confuse ROM, which is a part of the computer's internal memory, with CD-ROMs and DVD-ROMs, which are large capacity optical storage devices – see Unit 3.

> **Tip**
>
> Remember that RAM and ROM are referred to as central memory.

Activity 2

The RAM component of computers is gradually getting bigger and bigger – in 2005, RAM would typically have been about 500 MB, in 2014 8GB (8000MB) had become commonplace and by 2020 16GB (16 000MB) of RAM wasn't uncommon. What is the reason for this? What advantages does having larger amounts of RAM offer the user?

Secondary or backing storage devices

Storage devices are used to store programs and data when the computer is switched off. It is important that you do not confuse memory with backing storage. Remember that internal (main) memory is **inside** the computer connected to the CPU. **Backing storage** (with the exception of the internal hard drive, inside the computer case) is **outside** the computer (external) and can be moved from one computer to another – it is a **peripheral**. For example, portable hard discs, CD- and DVD-ROMs, memory sticks and flash memory cards.

Storage devices are sometimes called:
- backing/backup storage or backing/backup store
- **secondary storage**
- external storage.

Why have internal *and* external storage?

It is important to realise that the computer is more efficient, and therefore faster, when instructions and data are immediately accessible to the processor. If the processor continually had to transfer instructions and data to and from external devices, such as a hard drive, and RAM, it would slow down processing tremendously. That is why computers have RAM in increasingly large capacities.

External storage is still needed though. RAM is volatile storage and its contents are lost when the computer is switched off. We need to store that data or those programs somewhere safe. There are also many times when we need to take a file and use it on another computer – you may use a pen drive to work on files at school and then take them home to complete for homework. You could not do that if the files were stored in the computer at school – you would also always have to work at the same computer and the computer could never be turned off!

Input and output devices

You will learn more about input and output devices in Unit 2, but it is useful be able to identify the differences. The peripheral devices you have learnt about so far can be divided into two categories:
- Input devices are those that are used to put information into the computer.
- Output devices are those that take information from the computer for other uses.

Some examples of input and output devices are listed below:

Input devices: keyboard, mouse, webcam, scanner

Output devices: monitor, printer, speakers, headphones

Activity 3

Give a brief explanation of the type of input and output that each of the devices above are used for. For example: *A webcam inputs moving images of the person using the computer for video or video messaging.*

Review and revise

You should now be able to:
- describe the main components of a typical computer system: motherboard, central processing unit (CPU), main/internal memory (including ROM and RAM), input devices, output devices and secondary backing storage
- explain the difference between internal and backing storage.

SESSION 1.4 Operating systems

Background

Operating systems are made up of software that allows users to interact with the computer system. Operating systems have a number of key functions:

- controlling the input, output and backing storage devices
- loading, running and storing applications programs
- handling errors that occur in applications programs
- maintaining the security of the computer system
- keeping a log of computer usage
- managing the **user interface** so that the user can communicate with the computer system.

User interfaces

A user interface allows the user to interact effectively with the computer system. There are four main types of user interfaces:

- **Command Line Interface** – CLI
- **Graphical User Interface** – GUI
- Dialogue (or voice) based interface
- Gesture (or touch) based interface

Command Line Interfaces

CLIs are often seen in specialist systems, where users type instructions for activities like opening or saving a file. Users have to learn and remember commands that have to be typed in for even the simplest of actions. Using a PC with the Windows 10 operating system, you can access the CLI by following the menu options: **Windows Systems > Command Prompt**, alternatively search for **Command Prompt** in the search bar. If using MAC OS, access the Applications folder and choose **Utilities > Terminal**, or search for **Terminal** using the Launchpad menu.

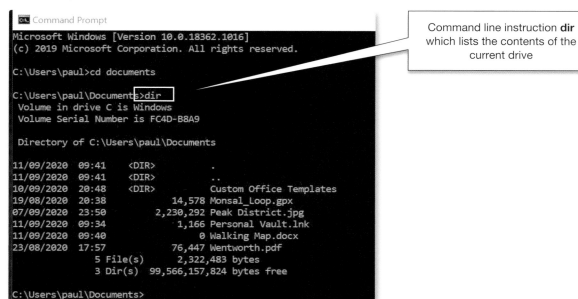

Command line instruction **dir** which lists the contents of the current drive

Advantages of CLIs are that the user communicates directly with the computer and can make decisions about exactly what they want to see happen.

Disadvantages of CLIs are that typing in commands can be very slow and relies on the user remembering the way that commands have to be given to the computer. They can be difficult to edit or change.

Graphical User Interfaces

GUIs use pictures and symbols rather than having to type in a number of commands. All the commands that would have been typed in using a CLI are already programmed into the GUI. This means that users do not have to learn and remember a lot of commands – they just need to know what actions the **icons** represent.

You can see GUIs on your gaming devices, digital cameras and mobile phones as well as on your computers. The type of GUI will depend on the device you are using.

One of the most common GUIs is the **WIMP** interface. WIMP stands for Windows, Icons, Menu and Pointing device. It uses a mouse (or similar device) to control a cursor, which can be used to select icons that open and run programs. Many programs can be selected to run at the same time.

To make it easy to find programs that are open and running, the operating system places each file in a separate **window**. Many windows can be displayed at the same time. This might make it difficult to work with, so it is possible to 'minimise' a window to the area at the bottom of the screen: the program stays open, but you can choose when to bring the window up on the screen again.

> **Language**
>
> Symbols in a GUI are also known as icons.

In this example of a GUI, you can see the following:

Along the bottom toolbar:
- A launch button
- A search box, to search for files or applications
- Program icons, used to launch applications and display those running.
- Technical icons, including Wi-Fi connections, power options and the time.

Along the left hand side:
- Operating system shortcuts, links to fixed drives, system options, network connections, user files and the recycle bin.

Along the top of the screen:
- Customisable shortcuts to either commonly used applications, files, folders and even website addresses.

Dialogue based interfaces

Voice control has been available on desktop computers and mobile devices for many years but prone to mistakes with commands misheard and dictation recording the wrong words. In recent years, as smart devices have become commonplace, the creation of internet-linked intelligent voice assistance has led to the widespread introduction of voice control. Within the home, commands can be linked to lighting, heating, entertainment and even shopping choices.

Gesture based interfaces

There are other GUIs that do not rely on a cursor to select an icon. You have probably seen, and used, a touch-screen device to select icons, open programs and change the layout. This operation is known as post-WIMP interaction, because it was developed after WIMP.

Touch-screen devices are newer, allowing users to scroll, pinch (choose and resize) and rotate images and documents using fingers and thumbs to create gestures the device can understand. This type of action would be difficult using a simple mouse. Touch screens are a common feature of smartphones and tablets but they are now becoming more popular on desktop and laptop computers, smart home devices and even automobile dashboards.

Key differences between interfaces

CLIs tend to be used by technicians and specialists who need access to all areas of the computer. Knowing the different commands enables technicians to look after the computer system, and to make changes.

Because GUIs use icons, users need only limited knowledge to carry out complex activities. GUIs have been developed in such a way so that young children can use them. However, users can only access programs or carry out activities that have icons allocated to them; without a visible icon in a GUI, users will not know how to access it. Gesture and dialogue based systems add another level of user-friendly access meaning very little, if any, training is required to use these systems. CLI and GUI systems are still required for those users wanting direct computer access and the ability to used advanced software or write computer code.

Activity 1

There are many operating systems in use. *Windows*, *Linux* and *MAC OS X* may be familiar to you, but there are others that are in everyday use on mainframe computers and the latest smartphones.

Create a table like this:

Operating system	Computer type/size		
	Mainframe	Desktop	Smartphone
Windows			
macOS			
Ubuntu			
Linux			
Unisys OS 2200			
Android			
z/OS			
iOS			

Find out what type and size of computer the listed operating systems are designed for and place a tick in the appropriate column. Find one more operating system for each computer type/size.

Review and revise

You should now be able to:
- understand the function of an operating system
- describe the difference between interface systems.

SESSION 1.5 The impact of emerging technologies

Background

General developments, such as increased storage capacity and processor speeds and the miniaturisation of technology, advance our devices but the way we interact with technology largely remains the same. It takes a real innovation to shift the way technology is used. For example, in the late 2000s the introduction of capacitive touch technology changed the way in which we interact with, and therefore control, technology.

The idea of being able to touch/swipe/pinch our way through a TV listing, an email, a webpage or a photograph album would have been an extraordinary idea before the Apple iPhone hit the stores in 2007 (although touch-screen technology had been around for a number of years before that). Similar devices from other manufacturers and the evolvement of tablet computers have shifted our use of technology.

This session will explore some of the emerging technologies that are breaking into, and having an impact on, our everyday life.

Security

All students entering examination halls may soon find themselves submitting to technology applying the latest in **artificial intelligence biometrics**. A few examination boards already use fingerprint recognition devices to identify students in the examination room. If a student needs to leave the room, to use the bathroom for example, their fingerprint is recorded as they leave and then again as they re-enter – to make sure the person who left is the same as the one entering. Finger and palm print recognition door locks do exist not just in major organisations. Soon you may be able to open your house front door or the family garage simply by placing a finger over a special scanner built into the door handle. Many people quickly pass through airport controls because they have had the iris in their eye scanned. This could be used to manage access to restricted areas of not just buildings, but also our streets and cities.

It is not difficult to see the use of these technologies becoming more common-place. Imagine never having to carry a front door key around in your bag, or your parents not needing car keys anymore, because there are small fingerprint scanners built into door handles, or eye scanners built into door frames or the steering wheel.

Activity 1

Research the development of *Facial Recognition Systems*. How do they work? Where are they being used in the world right now? Might there be an issue with people's privacy?

We are all used to checking that certain websites such as ones used for shopping are secure. We expect that all information transferred is safe. The process of 'scrambling' and 'descrambling' a message (encrypting and decrypting) is called **cryptography**. This process is based on mathematical **algorithms** which use a 'scrambling' **key**, with the sender and receiver of the message knowing what combination of keys to use. Without the proper key, it's virtually impossible to decipher an encoded message. The ability to protect stored files or email attachments with encryption is now commonplace in business. It is the introduction of end-to-end encryption messaging apps that really highlighted the advantages, and disadvantages of private world-wide communication. As people became concerned with social media platforms profiting from the content of their posts, the desire for messaging systems that couldn't be read by any organisation or government increased.

Text translation

Computer-assisted translation is language translation in which a person translates with the aid of computer (application) software or an online translation service. The person carrying out the translation can use a variety of software including: monolingual and bilingual dictionaries, parallel texts, translation memory, and language search engines.

The increased reliability of translation systems has led to increased popularity in education and tourism. Students can check pronunciations and translations when away from their teacher or classroom and smartphone apps allow the instant translation of signs, menus and the user's voice when travelling in a foreign country.

Many companies require websites that are multilingual, and brochures for products and services may be required in different languages. For example, if your school is bilingual or international, many of your publications will be in two or more languages, and the school website may also offer pages of translated text. With companies and markets developing and moving ever faster the need for accurate and consistent translation is paramount.

Vision enhancement

When illumination is inadequate for a person to see clearly, vision enhancement devices enable images to be formed by intensifying or enhancing the low level of light that exists. The image many of us have of this technology is of night-vision scopes, which exist either to be mounted on vehicles, weapons or worn by a person as a pair of goggles. Age-related night vision problems make it difficult for people who drive at night for a living, such as truck drivers, taxi drivers, police officers, ambulance drivers, firefighters, and other public safety officers. A second way that an image can be enhanced is by capturing infrared light and producing on screen a thermal image. Infrared images are used for a wide variety of forensic and industrial purposes, because they can reveal chemical compositional differences not evident in visible light. These technologies are being used in the development of autonomous vehicles with the need to 'see' in all conditions.

Activity 2

The use of 3D imaging in medicine to enhance CT, MRI and ultrasound scans is providing a wealth of extra, detailed information for medical procedures. What is holography? Is there a connection between 3D imaging and holographic imaging? Identify three possible uses for this technology.

Augmented and virtual reality

Virtual reality (VR) is a computer-generated recreation of a user's field of view, through a VR headset, making them feel like they are in an environment different to their own. Combining this with audio and a controller to navigate the virtual world has been thought of as the next level in gaming for many years.

Augmented reality (AR) plays computer generated imagery on top of the user's field of view. This may be used to provide information, a heads-up display for a driver or pilot for example, or interactive elements. Mobile smartphone games are taking advantage of AR, combined with the smartphone's **GPS** and gyroscopic functionality, to create games that seem to take place in the real world.

Activity 3

Many of us still only associate virtual and augmented reality with gaming and experimental, fictional worlds, but these products are now commonly used by many companies, from visualising products and user interaction to the remote operation of surgical equipment in an operating theatre by a surgeon on the other side of the world. Choose an area of society you are interested in and identify some of the latest ideas using this technology.

New technology, new applications and new generations of users combine to push our use of ICT into many new areas of medicine, travel, shopping, warehousing/retailing, industry and entertainment. Unit 5 considers the effects of using ICT in many situations.

Review and revise

You should now be able to:
- describe how emerging technologies are having an impact on everyday life.

Activity 4

You should be familiar with images of robots working in industrial settings, but robots are being developed for use in many different settings: there is an experimental robot on the International Space Station; exoskeletons have been developed to help those working to clean up areas after natural and industrial disasters; Unmanned Aerial Vehicles are given a variety of roles. Choose an area such as medicine, the home, space or commerce, and find out what you can about the most recent developments in robotics in that area.

SESSION 1.6 Using a computer system to communicate

Background

A range of ICT applications are used in our everyday lives and the way you communicate is influenced by the technology and software applications available to you. This session will look at the software opportunities and considerations for a range of communication forms including:

- newsletters and posters
- websites
- multimedia presentations
- audio
- video
- media streaming
- e-publications.

Newsletters and posters

Newsletters are information sheets that are distributed within organisations or communities to keep them up-to-date with the latest news that affects or interests them directly. Your school may have its own newsletter. Newsletters can be produced using **desktop publishing** software, but in the practical sessions of this unit you will be learning how to produce them using **word processing** software.

Posters can also be produced quickly and easily using word processing or desktop publishing software. As with newsletters, they can include photographs and images. Posters are usually one-page documents, designed to present information in a clear, but attention-grabbing way. A poster may be advertising an event, film or product release and would normally include:

- the title of the event or product
- important dates
- key product, location or contact details

Activity 1

What would a poster advertising a new takeaway restaurant need to include?

Producing documents using a computer

Producing documents to communicate on a computer has a number of advantages:

- They are cheaper to produce compared to using a professional designer.
- An organisation can print as many documents as they need.
- Previous versions, newsletters for example, can be stored electronically.
- They can be distributed as paper copies or electronically.
- Physical copies can be printed onto different types and sizes of paper and printed on one side or both to form a leaflet or magazine.
- Correcting errors is quick and easy – the inbuilt dictionary highlights spelling and grammatical errors, offering suggestions where potential errors are highlighted.
- Formatting documents to meet the needs of the audience is also straightforward and can include features such as:
  - columns to structure text
  - **white space** to draw the eye to key areas

- pictures, diagrams and other images such as photographs
- changing the Size and CASE of text to emphasise headings
- suitable fonts, such as Calibri or Times New Roman or **Comic Sans**
- *italics*, <u>underlining</u>, **bold** or other special effects to add emphasis
- bullet points and indentations – just like this list
- multimedia presentations which are themed and animated using pre-built templates
- video and audio editing software purchased at a much lower cost, or even free, compared to a few years ago
- online platforms which allow us to upload our own streaming content and publications to share around the world.

Activity 2

Find examples of the software used in your school to create communication documents.

The importance of a corporate style and software choice

Later in this unit you will find discussion about corporate image and the importance of image and styling, along with a practical exercise.

A corporate house style is a set of rules that any communication document produced by an organisation should follow. This can include the following:

- choice of text, graphic and background colours
- choice of font and text styles
- use of a specific logo and associated graphics
- consistent styling in any photographs
- use of approved and appropriate language.

In order to produce professionally styled corporate documents, videos, websites and presentations, organisations will often move away from standard office-based software and use specifically designed software.

You made have heard of some of the following:

- Adobe Creative Suite, including Photoshop and InDesign: Used to edit photos, create newsletters and posters and edit broadcast quality video.
- The CorelDraw graphics and image editing suite: Used to create original vector graphics, photo editing and document layouts.
- QuarkXpress: Used to create print and web-based promotional material.

What these products offer, by themselves or in combination, is the ability to produce material of a high, professional standard. Here are some possible scenarios that might require such software:

- Controllable image resolution; you do not want a school brochure that has grainy or pixelated images!
- The colour in photographs might need to be manipulated, the images used may need to 'bleed', or run off the page without leaving a coloured border.
- Text might need to creatively wrap around part of an image.
- Colours might need to be matched exactly with the corporate style guide/template.

In Session 6.11 you will see how a database program can be used to create business cards, but this is not a sophisticated and graphically interesting solution. Ideally you would set up a template with a desktop publishing package. This would adhere to company corporate style guidelines and save the document/file to a high-resolution industry standard format that can be sent to a printing house for commercial printing.

Activity 3

Look through this book and pick out the elements that contribute to the corporate style. What are the styles of the main headings, sub-headings and body text? Can you see columns on the pages? Now imagine how you would go about creating a similar document.

Websites

In many respects, websites are electronic versions of newsletters and posters. There are many software packages for creating webpages and websites, known as **web authoring** software.

Websites offer the owners, producers and users of the websites a number of advantages:

- Rather than just having text and images, websites can have sound, video and animation.
- Buttons, images and highlighted text can encourage the reader to focus on specific aspects – and can be used to **link** directly to other webpages.
- Websites can be viewed all over the world and on any smart device with internet connectivity.

Of course, there are also disadvantages:

- Websites can be illegally altered without the knowledge or authorisation of the producer. It is difficult for a user or reader to know if unauthorised changes have been made.
- You cannot usually see a website unless you have access to the **internet**.
- A website needs to be updated regularly to keep it up-to-date. People expect the page they see to contain the latest information.

Tip

The syllabus doesn't specify specific software. It is important you choose the most appropriate software package to meet the needs of the end user.

An example of a website

Activity 4

Connect to the internet:

1 View the BBC news website: www.bbc.co.uk/news. When was this site last updated? How often is it updated? How can you tell?

2 Visit the Cambridge Assessment International Education home page at www.cambridgeinternational.org. When was this page last updated? How do you know?

3 Why do you think there is a difference between the 'update cycles' of the BBC and Cambridge websites?

Tip

You'll learn more about web authoring software and how to create webpages in the practical sessions of Unit 4.

Multimedia presentations

Like websites, multimedia presentations engage the audience, often showing and explaining to them the content of a topic by using not just text, but images, charts and diagrams, sound, video and animation. There are many software packages designed to produce simple and complex multimedia presentations. Presentations come in many forms and for different purposes.

Advantages of multimedia presentations:

- A good presentation (using sound, animation and video) helps to focus the audience's attention on the key points being made.
- Presentations can be interactive – links to different presentation slides, new information, even to websites, can be included.

Disadvantages of multimedia presentations:

- You cannot usually run a presentation for an audience without a computer system and a projector, which can be very expensive.
- If links to websites are included, the presentation will be limited to locations with an internet connection.
- A poorly produced presentation, perhaps with too much text on a slide, or too many animations, will lose its impact because the audience may not be able to recognise the key points.

Tip

You'll learn more about creating and producing multimedia presentations in the practical sessions of Unit 2.

An example of multimedia presentation slides

The head teacher of your school has some important information about changes to subjects to give to parents, and she is wondering how to communicate this. She has invited you (as Head of ICT) and the Head of English to a meeting. The Head of English thinks that the information should go out in a newsletter. You believe that there should be a parents' meeting where the head teacher explains the changes with the aid of a presentation. Compare and contrast the two types of document for this task.

Audio

Using audio to communicate opens up a range of possibilities. Audio editing software allows the combination of recorded voice, sound effects and music to create the following:

- audio advertising
- downloadable recordings (or Podcasts) which can be downloaded to portable devices
- audio books and magazines.

Advantages of audio:

- Users can listen to a broadcast whilst doing something else.
- Production costs are lower than video.
- Audio can be listened to on the move.

Disadvantages of audio:

- It is a purely descriptive media, no images.
- There is so much choice available, finding new listeners can be difficult.

> **Tip**
>
> You'll learn more about some of the benefits of mobile technology in Session 4.6

Video

Using video to communicate takes the potential of audio recordings and adds moving images, photographs, visual effects and text. The opportunities offered includes:

- video advertising
- broadcast or internet-based content.

Advantages of video:

- Videos can be written to optical discs and distributed as physical products.
- Video can be downloaded, or streamed from the internet (See Media Streaming).
- Video can be added to Multimedia presentations.
- Original film can be combined with stock footage from around the world.
- Many of us now carry smartphones with video functionality in our pockets.

Disadvantages of video:

- Editing and producing professional video requires specialist equipment and software.
- Poor quality video production will struggle to attract viewers.
- There is so much choice, finding new viewers can be difficult.

Media Streaming

Streaming is the process of watching online video or listening to audio without having to download the entire file before accessing it. This allows video, music, radio and podcasts to be accessed instantly and the user can jump to any point in the stream without waiting.

Advantages of media streaming:
- Content doesn't need to be downloaded before viewing.
- Mobile internet connectivity means content can be streamed anywhere.
- Streaming video game services offer the chance to play high quality games on any device.

Disadvantages of media streaming:
- The quality of the stream depends on the available internet connection.
- Streaming platforms need to ensure their system can keep up with demand.
- Compared to broadcasted TV and Radio, there are very few rules in respect to content and appropriateness.
- Users don't own a physical copy of the media they have streamed.
- If the platform stops working, what happens to the media that has been bought?

e-publications

This is the process of traditional style magazines, newspapers, books and comics creating electronic versions that can be viewed on specialist e-readers or handheld smart devices.

Advantages of e-publications:
- E-readers using e-paper use very little power and can store thousands of books.
- Users can read in any location and in any language.
- Larger smart devices with colour screens can show comics and magazines.

Disadvantages of e-publications:
- Traditional publishers are concerned about the sales of paper-based books.
- Owners don't own a physical copy of a book they buy online.
- If the platform stops working - will we still have access to the ebooks that have been bought?

Analysing the needs of the audience

When designing any ICT-based document or communication it is essential to consider the audience of the product.

The following audience characteristics should be taken into account:
- Age: this will influence the style, content and reading level.
- Gender: the gender of the audience, especially for products aimed at a specific gender, may influence the content and design.
- Interests: the theme and therefore interests of the audience will dictate the content and design.
- Location and language: specific languages and locations around the world often have visual styles and even guidance on content that should be considered.
- Income: the income of the audience may influence the content and style.

The audience is the end user of the product and asking the following questions during the design process should ensure their needs are fully met:
- In what form will they be accessing the communication? On paper, screen or via audio?
- Is the language used suitable and at the correct level for the target audience?
- Can any special needs be met? Subtitles, audio descriptions and clear media descriptions, for example.

Failure to consider the needs of the audience means they are unlikely to engage, read or get involved with the communication or ICT product.

Activity 6

For each of the scenarios below, decide which of A-E is the best way to communicate the information. Give reasons for your choices.

A   a newsletter

B   a video

C   a poster

D   a website

E   a multimedia presentation

	Scenario	A B C D E	Reason
1	Amika is in charge of preparing a document that is to be sent to all the parents of pupils in Excelsior School. The document will include news about recent events, sporting results and a quiz.		
2	Douglas Cheung has been asked to share some sales information within his company, with a very large audience, at the same time and in the same place.		
3	The school theatre group is presenting their own version of *Romeo and Juliet*. They would like to be able to show it to those not able to attend.		
4	The headteacher has decided that a school newsletter should be more widely available. She knows that there are former pupils in Egypt, the USA, Dubai and the Caribbean.		
5	Junaid of All Computers Inc. wants as many people in the local area as possible to see an advertisement for a half-price sale on laptops and netbooks.		

Review and revise

You should now be able to:

- describe a range of communication applications such as:
  - newsletters and posters
  - websites
  - multimedia presentations
  - audio
  - video
  - media streaming
  - e-publications.
- discuss the need for software that professional, corporate publications require.
- describe the importance of analysing the needs of the audience when designing solutions.

1 Theory review

What have you covered?

In these six theory sessions you have:
- discovered the range of computers in common use today
- been introduced to a variety of hardware and software components in a computer system
- been shown the difference between applications and system software
- compared memory types
- been shown the components, and relative advantages, of different user interfaces
- evaluated the different ways that a computer user might communicate with a target audience
- explored some of the emerging technologies which are beginning to have an impact on our everyday life.

Some practice questions

1 Connect each image on the left with a line which best describes it in the middle column, then another line from the middle column to the best example in the right column.

Mainframe	Small hand-held computer	Business executive needing a powerful electronic diary while travelling
Desktop	Computer having very fast processing capability and supporting massive storage facilities	Student needing to be able to work as she moves around campus
Phablet	Computer where all components are within a single unit, making it portable	Large organisation such as a government department
Laptop or notebook	General purpose computer having separate monitor, keyboard, etc.	A family needing a computer at home for a variety of uses

See Session 1.1

2 For each of these, indicate with a tick whether it is hardware or software.

	Hardware	Software
Operating system		
Mouse		
Monitor		
Word processing program		
CD-ROM		

See Session 1.2

3 For each of these, indicate with a tick whether it is applications or system software.

	Applications	System
Operating system		
Database program		
Printer driver		
Disc formatter		
Graphics software		

See Session 1.2

4 The memory of a computer can be volatile or non-volatile.

a Describe what is meant by the terms volatile and non-volatile.

b Which type of memory is volatile?

c The instructions for starting up a computer will be held in which type of memory? Why?

See Session 1.3

5 Rana is not a confident computer user and has just bought her first computer, a laptop. The operating system provides her with a GUI.

Give three reasons why the GUI is an advantage to her.

See Session 1.4

6 Pete is a vet who runs a parrot sanctuary for pet parrots that have been abandoned by their owners. He is going to organise an open day at the sanctuary in the hope that some of the abandoned parrots will be adopted. He needs some publicity material to be produced.

He tells you that he thinks it might be a good idea to build a new page into his website for this.

You do not think that is a good idea and want to suggest creating a simple flyer instead.

Before you talk to Pete, you decide to write down the advantages and disadvantages of both options – the webpage and the flyer – paying particular attention to the event that Pete is organising and the people he hopes to attract to it. Discuss the advantages and disadvantages, to Pete, of using webpages and flyers.

See Session 1.6

7 You are applying for the post of Innovations Director at a car manufacturer and are asked to provide three sample ideas of how emerging technology could be built into future cars. Identify and explain the desirability of three ideas.

See Session 1.5

Progress check

Aiming for good progress

- You are able to distinguish between hardware and software.
- You can distinguish between system and applications software.
- You can name the different types of memory and state a use for each type.
- You can use the terminology relating to user interfaces.
- You are able to choose an appropriate method of communication for a target audience.
- You are able to identify emerging technologies and link them to everyday situations.

Aiming for excellent progress

- You can distinguish between hardware and software.
- You can describe, and distinguish between, the use of a variety of software types.
- You can identify appropriate uses for, and justify the selection of, different memory types.
- You are able to describe the features of user interfaces.
- You can choose, and justify a choice, between different methods of communicating with a target audience.
- You are able to identify and explain how emerging technologies may be utilised in everyday situations.

Document production: Entering and editing data from different sources

Background

Every day you are likely to come into contact with documents, posters, letters, leaflets, books and other printed materials that were prepared using software that enables users to develop and edit text-based documents. In this session, you will be looking at how to create and open documents using information from different sources. The examples here are from *Microsoft Word*, but you can use any word processing software to complete the tasks and activities.

Locating and recognising file types

As part of your practical work, you will need to be able to open and edit work that has been prepared for you. People do not always work using the same types of text editing software, so there are various 'generic' file types that all computer systems will recognise.

> **Language**
>
> Generic file types means that you will be able to work with them regardless of the software packages that you are using.

Activity 1

Open the digital download folder titled Session 1.7 within the Unit 1 source files and look at the file types that are there.

You should see that there are three types of generic files. You can recognise them by their extensions (the letters that come after the dot). These are listed in the table below.

Format	Meaning	Description
.csv	comma separated values	This data contains data items that are separated by commas. When imported into text editing software (a word processing program, for example) the data can be formatted as a table. Often, .csv files are used as source data for spreadsheets and databases as the data can be read by any appropriate software.
.rtf	rich text format	Text files, which keep some of the formatting that was in the original file.
.txt	text file	.txt files contain text. All the formatting is removed. .txt files can be opened in any text editing or word processing program.

Opening documents and importing data from existing files

When you create the documents for your practical work, you can use many different types of document formats as part of your work. As well as the generic file types you could include:

.doc	A document file created in *Microsoft Word 2003* or earlier
.docx	A document created in *Microsoft Word 2007* or later
.odt	A document created in *Open Office Writer*

Follow the steps below to:
- create a new document
- open a document
- import text
- save as a *Word* document.

Open your word processing software, for example, *Microsoft Word*. You need to open the document called **ComputerTypes.rtf**, that you found in the Session 1.7 folder of the digital download. You need to select **File > Open**. This will open a new window. You need to browse the folder for the document.

> **Real world**
>
> Portable document format (.pdf) files are another 'generic' file type, a universal document file format. Although specific to the Adobe Acrobat system, the Adobe Reader is widely and freely available. When you convert documents, forms, graphics, and web pages to PDF, they look just like they would if printed. pdf files are especially useful for documents such as magazine articles, product brochures, or flyers. Portable document format files have become the standard for transferring documents between different computer platforms when you want to preserve the original graphic appearance and can be opened on any computer platform as long as you have downloaded Adobe Reader.

ComputerTypes is an .rtf file. Double click on **ComputerTypes.rtf** to open it. This will open the file in *Word* and you can now begin to improve the way the document looks, and to format and edit the text.

Before you do anything with the text the file needs to be saved in a new format, as a word processed file. Click on, or select the option to **Save As**. Save the file as: **ComputerTypes** with the file type .doc, .docx, odt or whatever your software uses.

Page layout

The layout of the pages in your document needs to be considered very carefully. Each time you import text, or open a document that someone else has created, you may be dealing with the page settings that were set when the document was created. This can have an impact on the layout of your document, and can lead to poor quality printing.

Look carefully at the length of ComputerTypes. It should be three or four pages long in your word processor.

In your word processing program select **Page Layout** and open the **Page Setup** dialogue box by clicking the icon at the bottom right.

From here you can change:

- the orientation of the page (landscape or wide, portrait or tall)
- the size of the paper
- the layout of the page
- the size of the margins.

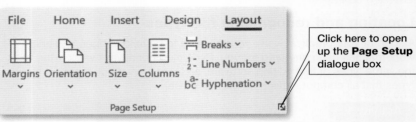

Click here to open up the **Page Setup** dialogue box

Real world

The **gutter** that you can see in the **margins** menu refers to part of the page outside the margins. This is important if the pages are to be bound. The gutter leaves space for staples or binding, and means that the text on the page is printed with enough space around it to make reading easier. Most of the time, the gutter is set to 0 cm. The gutter position can be set to: Top (top of the page) or, more usually, to: Left.

Activity 2

How is **ComputerTypes** laid out? Using the **Page Setup** dialogue box that you have just opened, use the tabs that are available to find out the answers to these questions:

1. What is the orientation of the page?
2. How big are each of the margins: left, right, top, bottom?
3. What is the paper size?

Activity 3

These settings are not convenient. You need the orientation to be portrait and hopefully fit everything onto a single page. Open up the **Page Setup** dialogue box again. Using the tabs change the page settings so that the document has:

1. a page size of A4
2. a page orientation of portrait
3. all 4 margins set to 2 cm

Save the document.

The document should fit onto one page and the top of it should look like this:

Look through the text that is now on your one page. It looks quite messy. The words are different sizes in different paragraphs, some paragraphs are over to the right, some centred and the style of type is different. You need to tidy it up.

Font type

The type of a font can be described as being either **serif** or **sans-serif**.

The difference is very easy to see:

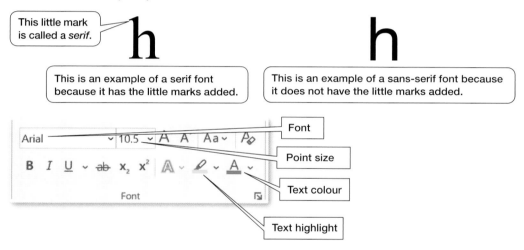

Changing the font, size and colour is very easy. You have a panel that allows you to work with fonts. Can you work out what the **B**, *I* and U icons will do?

Paragraph alignment

The next layout problem concerns the paragraphs. Some are over to the left, some centred and some to the right. This is known as paragraph **alignment**, and you may hear this referred to as *justified*. Some paragraphs are left aligned (or left justified), some centred and some right aligned (or right justified). Changing the alignment is very easy. There is a panel that allows you to change the alignment with just a click of the mouse.

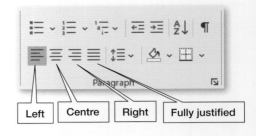

| Left | Centre | Right | Fully justified |

Click anywhere in the first paragraph and the left alignment button should be highlighted. Click anywhere in the third paragraph and see that the right alignment button is highlighted, and the fourth and fifth paragraphs are centred.

With the left mouse button, click at the very start of the first word of the second paragraph (not the heading), hold down the mouse button and drag the cursor to the very end of the second paragraph. Let go of the mouse button and the text of the paragraph will be highlighted. Click on the fully justified button to see what effect this has – both left and right margins are straight, like you see in a newspaper or magazine.

Click and highlight the very first heading, Now click on the **bold** and <u>underline</u> icons in the font panel (**B** and <u>U</u>). The first paragraph should look like this:

<u>Mainframe computer</u>
These are extremely large computers used in organisations (such as banks and government departments) where very large amounts of data are processed. They are capable of processing very big jobs which make use of their large memories and fast processor speeds. They are also capable of complex problem-solving that would take smaller computers much longer to do. However, mainframes are so large that they take up almost a whole room and are very complex to set up. Mainframe computers are expensive to operate and maintain and they require specialist staff to operate them.

```
Laptop or notebook
This is a computer where all the components are together in a single unit. This means
that they are portable; unlike desktop computers, they can be moved from one work area
to another. Because of this portability, users can work anywhere, especially if they can
```

Copying and pasting text from another document

The document is missing any text to do with Desktop or Personal Computers. A friend has prepared some for you. It is saved as **DesktopComputer.txt** on the digital download. Locate and open the file in your word processor.

Click on the first letter of the text and highlight all the text. Find an icon or menu item that allows you to copy text. The icon might look like this:

Click on this item and then return to **ComputerTypes**. Move down the document and click in the space between the first and second paragraphs. Now find the paste icon (right), or menu item, which will be in the same place that you found copy.

The paragraph from **DesktopComputer.txt** is now pasted into **ComputerTypes** to become the second paragraph. Save the document **ComputerTypes** and close **DesktopComputer.txt**.

Activity 5

Check through **ComputerTypes** so that:
- all paragraphs are fully justified (both the left and right margins are aligned).
- each heading is left aligned.
- each heading (there are six) is bold, underlined and highlighted yellow.
- each heading is a sans-serif font (use the same font for each heading).

Save the document.

Click to the left of the first heading and then press the ⌷Enter⌷ key to make a couple of blank lines and then click in the empty top line. You are going to give the document a title.

Activity 6

1   Type in: **Computer Types**.
2   Make this title a sans-serif font.
3   Change the size of the title to 20.
4   Make the heading bold and centre aligned.

Save the document.

Headers and footers

Sometimes titles are put at the top of the page as you have done. Important information can also be put in the **header** and **footer** areas of a document. They can also be used to provide information about the document that will appear on every page.

The header is at the top of the page. It can be used to insert the title of the document. The footer is at the bottom of the page. It is often used to print the page number of the document. This is really important when you have documents that include lots of pages. Page numbers help readers to find their way around a document, and to check the order of printed pages.

You are going to put a header in the document – your name, and a footer – today's date. There is no need to enter page numbers in this document.

Double click in the space just above the heading **Computer Types** and the header space will open up:

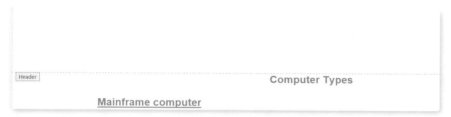

In the top of the window you will also be presented with a range of options such as adding date, time, or page numbers. All you are interested in is adding your name so click on the tab or menu to go back to the panels, which have the options for changing font, size and paragraph alignment.

Type in your name in a serif font size 10 and make it italic, left aligned. Double click back in the main body of the page. You have now created a header and it should be visible to you, but as a faint grey colour.

Activity 7

1   Double click in the space at the very bottom of the page to open up the footer area. Find the options panel for inserting automated objects. It may look like this:

2   Place the date in the footer, as an automatically updated field, left aligned.
3   Place the full file path in the footer, as an automatically updated field, after the date, separated by a comma
4   Make the footer items: serif font, size 10, italic
5   Double click in the main body of the text and save the document.

Real world

Data items such as: date, time, page numbers, are often placed in footers and headers. These are automated – they are placed as fields in the document and will update with current data, if required. If you insert a date field, it will always display todays date when you view or print the document, unless you have deselected the 'update automatically' option. The same is true of the time field, it will display the current time when the document is opened or printed.

Tip

Make sure you know the difference between 'File name' and 'File path'.

Review and revise

You should now be able to:

- load data from an existing file
- copy and paste text from another document
- open documents of *.txt* and *.rtf* file types, saving each as a word processed format
- use headers and footers, with automated fields
- set specific fonts and sizes, knowing the difference between serif and sans-serif font types
- emphasise text
- align text paragraphs
- adjust page orientation, page size and margins.

SESSION 1.8 Internet research

Background

A good newsletter requires relevant information and images that are suitable for the intended audience and purpose. The internet provides access to millions of pages, documents, images and descriptions that can help when researching any project, but deciding where to start looking and what key words to use can be daunting.

All Computers Inc. requires a newsletter containing information about the peripherals that are needed to connect to a desktop computer. In order to create this newsletter you will need to search the internet for images and technical information. In this session you will look at the following:

- carrying out an internet search
- how search engines respond to a search
- how to evaluate search engine responses
- how to evaluate website content
- recording the URLs of useful websites
- downloading text and images.

Search engines

There are many search engines available, but they all perform a similar task – searching for content based on the words you enter.

A typical search engine will help to target your results by allowing you to choose the type of information you require.

www.google.com

Targeted searches can be carried out without extra search terms.

Specific areas that can be searched range from images, news and shopping to videos and books.

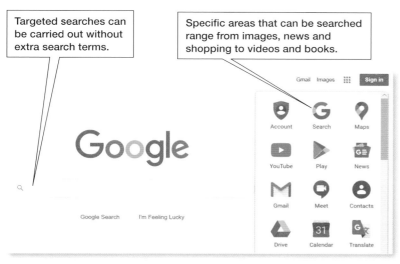

www.yahoo.com

www.duckduckgo.com

Activity 1

The search engines Google, Yahoo and DuckDuckGo are mentioned above, but there are many others. How many different search engines can you find? Make a list and then compare your list with others in your group. Does it seem like you all use the same ones? Are some search engines designed for specific tasks? Can you work out or find out which are the most popular and why?

Carrying out an internet search

Modern search engines are designed to respond to keywords: the more keywords we use, the more specific the results. As you will learn, a search engine will respond with what it thinks you would like to find. You will need to be careful in your searches and learn how to evaluate the results and the content the results link to. In the production of your newsletter you need to find images and text that you can copy, edit and paste into your newsletter.

Using **mouse** as an example, the first couple of results refer to the small mammal. Instead, let us try a more specific search: **computer mouse**. The results are now a combination of shopping sites selling computer hardware and the following Wikipedia article on the history and technical specifications of a standard computer mouse.

How search engines respond to a search

In the early days of internet searching, before broadband connections, search engines would provide the number of potential results and the amount of time it took to respond. The time taken using older 'modem-based' internet connections became an important consideration for users. The number of results, often in the millions, would also guide users into thinking about a more specific search.

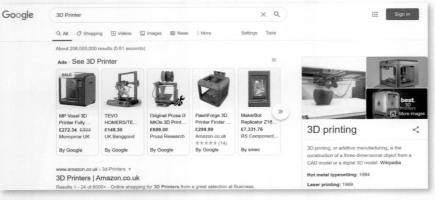

Using **3D Printer** as an example, over 200 million responses are provided in 0.7 seconds. To narrow this down, let's consider a budget 3D printer and the results have dropped to around 15 million and 0.5 seconds.

Evaluating search engine results

It is important not to simply click the first result when carrying out an internet search. Consider the following before making a choice and this applies to text, image and video searches:

● Is the link an advertisement? Many search engines allow commercial companies to pay for their content to appear at the top of any search made. These are usually identifiable by the short-hand **Ad**.

- How many of the links are simply shopping sites? You may wish to outline the key features of a computer mouse, not find the cheapest one on the market.
- Do you recognise the website listed in the results? You will be aware of worldwide news, information and encyclopaedia sites, but if the result has a very strange web address it might be one to avoid.
- Is the result from an organisation or user-generated content from an individual? This individual may be an expert in their field or someone simply telling a story in a blog. This doesn't mean user-generated content should be avoided, just be aware and try and double check any information you use.

Evaluating website content

Having chosen a search engine result, it is still important to look at the website content provided carefully. Consider the following questions and make a judgement on whether the information provided is trustworthy or not:

- Why has the content been created? Is this a reputable site known across the world? Is it impartial or **biased**? Is the site purely commercial, which means it may have been paid to promote a certain product or theme.
- When was the site last updated? If a site is out of date, the information it holds may be out of date.
- Is the information provided correct? If it is factual data, try and find a second or third source to confirm it. If the site is based on user-generated content, consider the authors and their knowledge on the topic.

Boolean operators

It is possible to use Boolean operators when using a search engine. Combining keywords with operators allows a more specific search. The example below shows how to specifically search for a computer mouse.

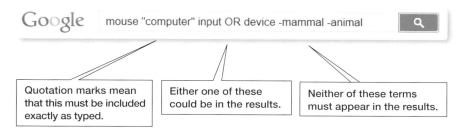

Activity 4

Try experimenting with Boolean operators to search for examples of computer-related devices.

Locating information from a specific website

Many large websites contain their own search functions that allow you to search within them. The following website **URLs** all have internal search facilities:

- **www.wikipedia.org**
- **www.bbc.co.uk**
- **www.ted.com**
- **www.nationalgeographic.com**
- **www.pixabay.com**

Activity 5

Using the website **www. pixabay.com**, enter the key word Games controller into the search window. If you are successful, try further ICT terms.

Downloading and saving information

Images or files relevant to any project can be **downloaded** onto a computer so that they become available as a local resource (this means that these files can be accessed again without the internet).

Before you download any information or images from the internet, it will be useful for you to create a folder within your work area, which you will use to collect together the resources that will be going into the newsletter.

Create a folder called NEWSLETTER.

The steps below show how to download an image from the internet.

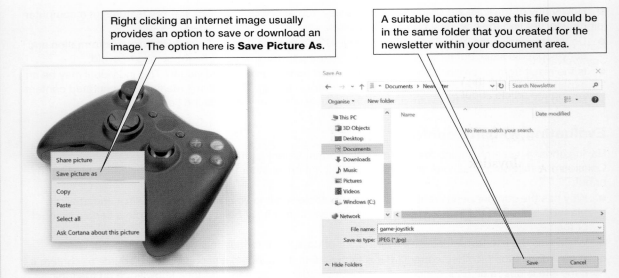

Right clicking an internet image usually provides an option to save or download an image. The option here is **Save Picture As**.

A suitable location to save this file would be in the same folder that you created for the newsletter within your document area.

Recording research results

When carrying out research it is important to record the addresses of useful websites, especially the URL of specific pages that contain information that you have decided to use, or of images that you have downloaded. Creating a word processed document of URLs that can be referred back to again is a useful way of recording them and this document can then be shared with others to help them with a similar task.

In your word processor software open a new document. Save this document as **NewsletterURLs**. Switch back to your internet browser and the image of the joystick from the save image task above.

> ### Real world
>
> A URL (Uniform Resource Locator) is the long string that refers to a web address, usually starting with www. This indicates to your web browser on which server, and stored in which folder, the page or image can be located.

Copying and pasting URLs

Click once in the address bar and the URL will be highlighted. Now hold down the $\boxed{\text{Ctrl}}$ (or Control) key on your keyboard and then press the $\boxed{\text{C}}$ key once. This is an instruction to copy whatever has been highlighted.

Switch to the document **NewsletterURLs** and click in the top line of the page. Hold down the $\boxed{\text{Ctrl}}$ key again but this time press the $\boxed{\text{V}}$ key once. This is an instruction to paste whatever has been copied. The URL from the browser is pasted into the document. You might want to type in some headings to help you remember what the URL was pointing to.

Newsletter research

The newsletter you are going to produce will contain the following input and output devices.

Input devices: keyboard, mouse, scanner, joystick.

Output devices: TFT monitor, Inkjet printer.

> ### Activity 6
>
> Using the search methods described so far, find and download images for each of the six devices, saving them into your NEWSLETTER folder. Do not forget to copy and paste the image URLs into the **NewsletterURLs** document. Remember that you are collecting images suitable for a professional-looking newsletter. Save **NewsletterURLs**.

Saving text from the internet

Of course the newsletter is not just going to be full of images, it will also need text alongside each image to explain what the device is needed for.

You can locate text about anything, just as easily as you can for images. It is tempting to copy lots of text and include it in your newsletter but you need to remember that material created by someone else might be copyright protected. Session 5.5 explains the issue of copyright fully for you. For now, you need to be aware that the people or organisations who post information on a website may not want anybody else to copy and use it.

There is nothing wrong, of course, with saving text that you will refer to later on. You need to remember that any information that you copy and paste should only be used to *help* you put together the newsletter.

Now, go back to your search engine and (making sure you are searching for websites and not images) type in **Joystick for PC**.

High on the list will be the Wikipedia website. Click on the link and you should see an image of a joystick illustrating the article about joysticks, which is similar to this:

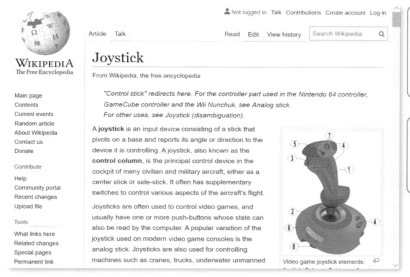

Tip

Beware, websites change all the time and the results in this screenshot may have changed.

Reading through the text you might decide that the second paragraph is the one with the better information for your needs.

Click at the start of the second paragraph and, without releasing the left mouse button, drag the cursor to the end of the paragraph. Release the left mouse button and the text of the second paragraph will be highlighted.

A **joystick** is an input device consisting of a stick that pivots on a base and reports its angle or direction to the device it is controlling. A joystick, also known as the **control column**, is the principal control device in the cockpit of many civilian and military aircraft, either as a center stick or side-stick. It often has supplementary switches to control various aspects of the aircraft's flight.

Joysticks are often used to control video games, and usually have one or more push-buttons whose state can also be read by the computer. A popular variation of the joystick used on modern video game consoles is the analog stick. Joysticks are also used for controlling machines such as cranes, trucks, underwater unmanned vehicles, wheelchairs, surveillance cameras, and zero turning radius lawn mowers. Miniature finger-operated joysticks have been adopted as input devices for smaller electronic equipment such as mobile phones.

As you did with the URL, press Ctrl + C to copy the text.

Select the document **NewsletterURLs** and click in the next available line of the page and press Ctrl + V to paste the text from the website into your document.

Now copy and paste the Wikipedia page URL into the document as well so that you know where this text came from.

Activity 7

Using the method described for locating, copying and pasting text, find text that could be used as background information for each of the six devices and copy and paste it (and the URL) into the **NewsletterURLs** document. Save the document **NewsletterURLs**.

You now have a document that contains all the URLs of images that you want to use in the newsletter, along with suitable background text and their URLs. Additionally, in the folder NEWSLETTER you have six images that are going to be used.

These images and the text will be used in the next session to create the newsletter itself.

Downloading tables and charts

There will be times when researching information that you find either a table or a chart that you want to download. Downloading a table is a case of copying and pasting the information as you would some text, while a chart can be saved just as you saved images in Activity 6. It is important to credit the source of information in the table if you use it directly – tell the readers of your document where the data came from.

Open your web browser, search for The CIA World Factbook and open the website.

Here you will find data from around the world on a range of topics. This page lists the latitude and longitude of places in the world.

Let's say you would like to copy a selection of this table in a document.

Simply highlight the data you wish to use, press Ctrl + C to copy, and then move to your document and press Ctrl + V to paste. You will then get the table as it appeared in the website in your document. Remember to reference its origin. With constantly changing data such as this it is also a good idea to date it although in this case the date is within the copied data.

When carrying out research, you may come across a chart or graph that you would like to insert into a document.

Where a chart is provided as an image, this can be saved in the same way as an image and inserted into a document.

Once saved in your work area it can be imported/inserted into your document as you have with other images.

Review and revise

You should now be able to:

- choose and use an internet search engine to locate relevant text or images
- compare and evaluate search results and linked content.
- use the search facilities within specific websites
- record the URLs of useful websites
- insert objects from online sources.

SESSION 1.9 Creating a newsletter

Background

All Computers Inc. requires a newsletter containing information about the peripherals that are needed to connect to a desktop computer. You have already downloaded the images and text that you think will provide a professional and informative newsletter.

In this session you will be guided through the process of combining your images and text in order to create the newsletter. To achieve this you will:

- create a document where the information is presented in columns
- stretch and crop images
- arrange text around the images.

If you have not had access to images or text you can use **NewsletterText.rtf** and the images: **Keyboard.jpg**, **Mouse.jpg**, **Scanner.jpg**, **Joystick.jpg**, **LCDMonitor.jpg**, **InkjetPrinter.jpg** that are on the digital download.

Importing text

The first task is to set up the text in the document in the style that you require. In your word processing software open either the **NewsletterURLs** document that is in your folder NEWSLETTER, or **NewsletterText. rtf** from the digital download.

If you are using your own text then carry out these steps:

1   Open a new document in your word processor.
2   In **NewsletterURLs** highlight and copy all your saved text that will be used in the newsletter.
3   Switch to your new document and paste the text onto the page.

No matter where your text has come from, save your document of text as a word processed document called **Newsletter**.

Activity 1

The page layout needs some work. Using **Page Setup**, change **Newsletter** so that:
- the page orientation is Landscape
- all four margins (top, right, bottom and left) are 2 cm
- the page size is A4
- you have a header with the text: **All Computers Inc.**
- the text of the header is a sans-serif font, size 16, bold and is centred
- the footer is 2 lines. The first line has the text: **Date created:** followed by today's date. A second line has the text: **Date/time last printed:** followed by an automatically updated day/time field
- the text in the footer is a sans-serif font, size 8, italic and right aligned.

Save **Newsletter**.

Creating columns

The body of the text now needs to be arranged into two columns.

In the area of your word processor where you accessed the Page Layout panel you should also find an icon or menu item that allows you to select columns. To arrange text into columns only takes a few steps.

1   Highlight the whole of the first paragraph and click on the icon for columns.
2   You will be asked how many columns are needed – select two.

Your text should now be looking like this:

All Computers Inc.

Keyboard
Used to enter text into a computer. The advantages of using a keyboard are: it is designed for long-term repetitive use and widely available; most people are familiar with them; wireless versions are now available. However, data can only be input as fast as it can be typed and people with physical disabilities may struggle to use them. Another problem is that there is a danger of repetitive strain injury after long continuous use.

Scanner
Allows hard copies of images (such as drawings or photographs) or text to be transferred to a computer. Images can be scanned at a high resolution. Flat-bed scanners are quite common and often built into printers. Unfortunately, high-resolution scanning produces large file sizes, and this can be a very time-consuming process.

Activity 2

Make the following changes:

1   Arrange the second paragraph (about scanners) into three columns.
2   Arrange the third paragraph into two columns.
3   Highlight the fourth paragraph. Click on the columns icon but now select the option for **More Columns**.
4   Enter **4** as the number of columns and **1** for the spacing between the columns, and click **OK**.
5   Save the document.

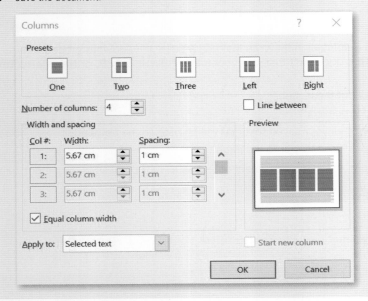

You should now have a document where the first four paragraphs look like this:

All Computers Inc.

Keyboard
Used to enter text into a computer. The advantages of using a keyboard are: it is designed for long-term repetitive use and widely available; most people are familiar with them; wireless versions are now available. However, data can only be input as fast as it can be typed and people with physical disabilities may struggle to use them. Another problem is that there is a danger of repetitive strain injury after long continuous use.

Scanner
Allows hard copies of images (such as drawings or photographs) or text to be transferred to a computer. Images can be scanned at a high resolution. Flat-bed scanners are quite common and often built into printers. Unfortunately, high-resolution scanning produces large file sizes, and this can be a very time-consuming process.

Mouse
Used to control the position of the pointer on the screen in any computer system. Its advantages are that: it directly transfers physical movement into the computer system; it is designed for long-term repetitive use and widely available; on-screen menus can be accessed quickly/more easily; wireless versions are now available; they are easier to use than a keyboard for those with limited finger movement. The disadvantages of using a mouse are that it requires a flat surface to work on and that the ball mechanism in older mice can stop working.

LCD Monitor
The successor to the CRT tube; thinner, lighter but serves the same purpose. Used in home and office computing they have replaced traditional CRT monitors and can easily be wall mounted. Power requirements are low, so they have lower running costs. Modern screens can also incorporate touch technology. A disadvantage is that early models had a limited viewing angle and could blur when showing fast-moving images.

Now go through the entire document and change all six paragraphs back to a single column and save the document again.

Activity 3

All Computers Inc. have decided that their newsletters and other customer information sheets should always be in a serif font and be size 11.

1 Change all the body text (everything except the headers and footers) to size 11 and a serif font.

2 Change all six headings to a sans-serif font, size 12 and bold and underlined.

3 Highlight all the text and set to two columns.

4 Save the document.

Inserting images

Now the images need to be placed. Click before the first word in the first paragraph. Find the icon or menu item, which allows you to insert an image.

You are going to insert a picture so click on the Picture icon.

You will be asked where the picture is coming from. Navigate through your folders until you find your NEWSLETTER folder where you saved your six images. You want the keyboard picture first so select this to be inserted.

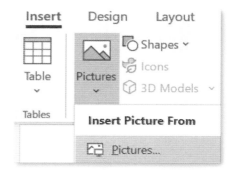

The picture is retrieved and inserted into the text where the cursor was at this point will be far too big for the newsletter.

Notice the small points on each corner of the image and at the side half-way points. These are also known as 'resizing handles'. If you do not see these, click once on the image.

Resizing an image

You need to resize the image as it is far too big. Click and hold down the left button of the mouse when the cursor is over the top right point of the image. Drag the cursor toward the middle of the image. You should see either the outline or the image shrinking:

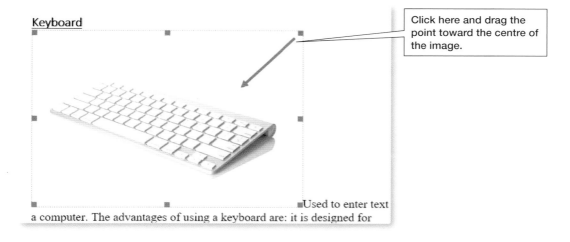

Click here and drag the point toward the centre of the image.

When you have shrunk the outline of the image to a size you think is suitable, let go of the left mouse button. The image is resized. It may look like this:

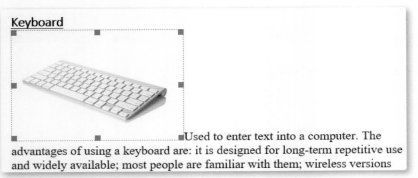

Keyboard

Used to enter text into a computer. The advantages of using a keyboard are: it is designed for long-term repetitive use and widely available; most people are familiar with them; wireless versions

Save the document. The keyboard image is a little tall for the space you are using so you will shrink it down a little more.

Cropping an image

Click and drag the middle point in the top edge of the image to flatten it. This does not look good. All you have done is squash the image. This is an important lesson to learn. When you resize an image you should always try and preserve the **aspect ratio**. This means that when resized you have kept all the dimensions in proportion. In word processing software, when you click and drag on any of the corner sizing points, the aspect ratio will be preserved, when you click and resize on any of the mid-side resizing point you will only succeed in squashing the image somehow.

To get the image back to its proper aspect ratio, you can either:

- reopen the document as it was before you squashed the keyboard
- click and drag the image back to its original size
- press Ctrl + Z to undo the last thing you changed.

What you really want to do is **crop** the image – cut away the part you do not want. Click on the image again and look for the icon that allows you to crop. It may look something like this:

> **Tip**
>
> Using Ctrl + Z can be very useful as it works with many different software programs, not just word processing.

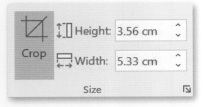

Click on this icon and move back over the image. Now click on the top middle resizing point and drag down into the image. There is a line showing you where the new side will appear, but this time when you let go the area that you dragged over will be cut away.

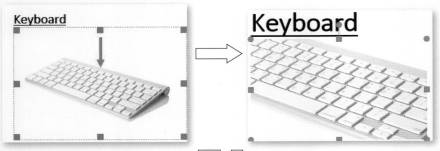

If you are unhappy with it then press Ctrl + Z to undo the cropping and try again. Resize and crop until you are happy with the resulting image size.

Text wrapping

The final adjustment to make now is with getting the text to flow around the image. This is called **text wrapping**. You may have already seen an icon for this, as shown below.

Click on the keyboard image and then click on the Text Wrapping icon and choose **Square** from the list. Immediately you will see a difference. The text is now wrapping around the image. This makes a great difference to the appearance of the newsletter.

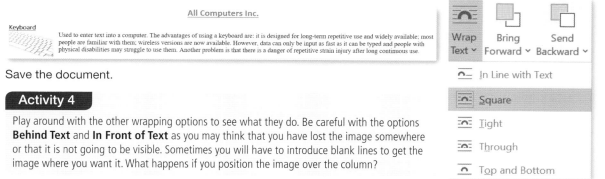

Save the document.

Play around with the other wrapping options to see what they do. Be careful with the options **Behind Text** and **In Front of Text** as you may think that you have lost the image somewhere or that it is not going to be visible. Sometimes you will have to introduce blank lines to get the image where you want it. What happens if you position the image over the column?

Open the document you saved before Activity 4. Now you need to complete the newsletter. You have a number of tasks to do.

Activity 5

1   Change all the body text to be fully justified.
2   Insert the other five images into their correct places in the text.
3   Resize and crop each image so that it appears exactly as you want it to be.
4   Apply text wrapping to all the images.
5   Adjust either the image size or your cropping so that everything remains on one page.
6   Save the document.

The top of the completed document might look like this:

There is a document, **Newsletter.pdf**, on the digital download that shows a finished example.

Review and revise

You should now be able to:
- create a document where the information is presented in columns
- resize and crop images, maintaining their aspect ratio
- manage text wrapping around images.

SESSION 1.10 Communication

Corporate style

All Computers Inc. has a corporate style guide. This is a very important policy document and will make clear a wide variety of things such as:

- the way standard letters should be laid out
- the size and font face to use for various elements of a document (headings and paragraphs for example)
- the format of dates
- where a company badge or image should be placed
- the specific colours that must be used (the hexadecimal numbers for a web page background, or text for example).

These guides are produced to ensure consistency across a range of publications.

Generally, the larger and more widely recognisable the organisation is, the stricter the corporate visual guidelines.

Which font for which audience?

There is a great deal of debate about what type of font face is best for a particular purpose, depending on the target audience and on the medium used, for example the printed page or the computer screen. Different fonts can also be used to give a particular impression of the type of organisation.

Language

For a reminder about the differences between serif and san-serif fonts look back at Session 1.7.

Serif fonts generally provide an invisible line that the eye can follow, improving reading speed and decreasing eye fatigue. Most books, newspapers, and magazines use a serif font, often because they give a more traditional feel, especially for established organisations with an older audience. Many books and other resources printed for a younger audience are printed in sans-serif fonts (such as this book) because the simplicity of the letter shapes make them more recognisable. The cleaner, minimalist feel of a sans-serif font could be favoured by a younger, more modern organisation.

So while a popular choice might be to send out a sales letter or brochure in the mail set in a serif font, you might want to consider other factors – who is going to read the document?

On screen, the convention seems to be to use a sans-serif font. Firstly, sans-serif fonts are cleaner or neater, given the small space that a pixilated letter is created within, and the serifs can make letters blur together. Secondly, with smartphones and other small devices having small screens but still accessing large volumes of text, the idea of clean and neat characters is important when screen resolution in these devices is not high. This is especially true with today's users rapidly zooming in and out when reading content and text has to be clear and easily read at any size.

Activity 1

Open the document **ComputerTypes** from Session 1.7.

Create a style for **AllComputerHeading** with the following definition:

- a sans-serif font, size 12, bold, dark green
- spacing before to be 0 point, after, 8 point
- left justified.

Apply this style to all six headings in the document.

Create a style for **AllComputerText** with the following definition:

- a serif font, 9.5 point size, dark blue
- spacing before to be 0 point, after, 8 point and line spacing to be multiple at 1.15
- fully justified.

Apply this style to all the body text of the document.

Create a style for **AllComputerTitle** with the following definition:

- a serif font, size 17, dark blue
- spacing before to be 0 point, after, 8 point
- centred.

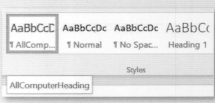

The top of the document may look like this:

Computer Types

Mainframe computer

These are extremely large computers used in organisations (such as banks and government departments) where very large amounts of data are processed. They are capable of processing very big jobs which make use of their large memories and fast processor speeds. They are also capable of complex problem-solving that would take smaller computers much longer to do. However, mainframes are so large that they take up almost a whole room and are very complex to set up. Mainframe computers are expensive to operate and maintain and they require specialist staff to operate them.

Save this new document as: **ComputerTypesCorporate**.

Using emails to send attachments

Email is an electronic method of sending and receiving text messages from one computer to another over a network – either local – or wide – area. An attachment is an electronic copy of a file (which can be anything that converts into a digital copy, such as an image, a document, a video or sound clip) which is sent with the message.

You should be very familiar with sending and receiving emails. To be able to send a file as an attachment it must be available to you, since you need at attach it to your email before you can send it. This means you have either created and saved it, or downloaded it, into a local folder.

Activity 2

In your email software click to open a new email message. Look around the window to find an option to add an attachment. A symbol often used is a paperclip, or there might simply be the words **Add attachment** or **Add file**. You will need to know where the file to be attached is saved, because when you click the button to add an attachment, you will be given a dialogue box to navigate through your folders in order to locate it. Search through your folders until you find the **Newsletter** you saved in Session 1.8. Select it for attachment by clicking on the file name, and then on **Open** (or maybe you have **Insert**).

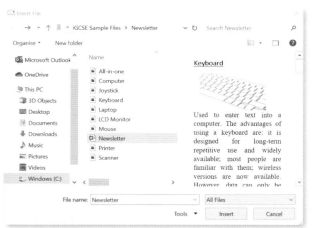

Here is a typical screen layout when composing a new email with an attached file:

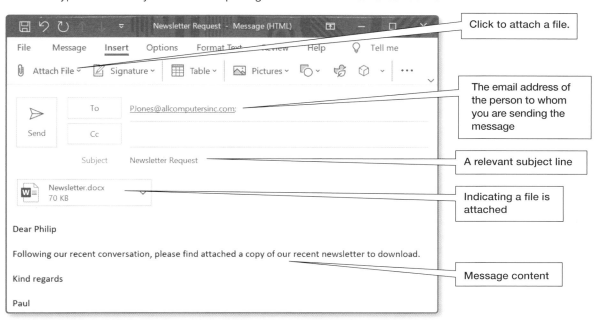

Click to attach a file.

The email address of the person to whom you are sending the message

A relevant subject line

Indicating a file is attached

Message content

In this case clicking on the 'Send' button will send the message and the attached file (Newsletter.docx) to Philip Jones (PJones@allcomputersinc.com).

Close the email message without sending it.

If you had multiple files to attach, you would simply click on the paperclip icon, browse and attach each file in turn. Your email software may allow you to browse folders and make multiple selections in one browsing action.

Receiving and downloading an email attachment

When you receive an email with an attachment, it will be displayed in the message and can then be downloaded and stored in a suitable location.

However, on receiving an email with an attachment do not automatically download and save it. You need to be constantly thinking about the dangers of downloading a file that contains malicious software (.zip and .exe files are potentially the most dangerous – although some email software will not allow these to be sent/downloaded). You need to ask yourself: Do I know the person who has sent this email? Am I expecting an attachment from them? What kind of file is the attachment? Do I trust the person who has sent this attachment? Be aware of potential dangers.

Activity 3

The file **Newsletter** is one that needs to be emailed to one of your work colleagues at All Computers Inc. Ask a friend to act as the colleague at All Computers Inc. and send them an email with your newsletter as an attachment.

Real world

Once all the attachments are added, check that you have:

- the correct email address of the person to whom you are sending the message
- an informative subject line
- a clear and instructive message to the person.

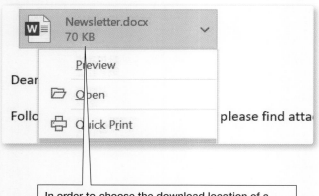

In order to choose the download location of a file attachment, right click the mouse on the link and select **Save File** or **Save File As**. You will be given a standard file window to choose the location of the download.

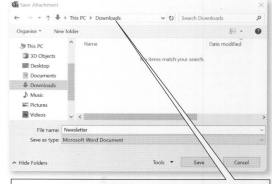

Clicking on the filename of the attachment or the download button will send the file to your default download area. The could be a folder name DOWNLOADS in the MY DOCUMENTS area, or the location where you last saved something

Activity 4

Reverse the previous activity and ask a friend to send you a copy of their presentation. Download it to a sensible location and open it.

Using Cc and Bcc

The standard way to add an address to an email is using the **To** option. However, there are occasions when the **Cc** (carbon copy) and **Bcc** (blind carbon copy) options can be used. Adding an address or addresses to the Cc window, in addition to the **To** window, will result in that person also receiving a copy of the message sent. All those involved will be able to see all addressees.

Real world

Cc and Bcc are normally positioned under the **To** option. However some email programs have the Bcc option disabled by default, as it often associated with spam and junk mail, so you may need to re-enable it before it can be used.

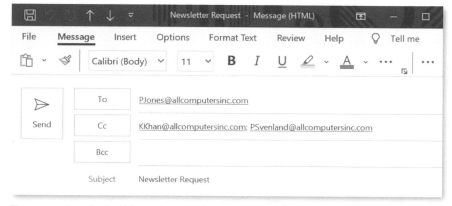

For example, Khaled Khan also requires a copy of the newsletter for filing purposes. It's not directly for him to work with; he just needs to be kept up-to-date with what is happening with various publications. Petra Svenland of the printing department also needs a copy so that she knows what printing is about to be requested. In this case you would Cc Khaled and Petra. Philip Jones would be aware that Khaled and Petra had also received the email and attachment.

There are occasions when it is polite not to let everyone who receives an email, know the email addresses of everyone else who has received the email. This would not necessarily happen when sending emails within an organisation – many organisations actively encourage an openness about communication and require everyone's email address to be visible on a message.

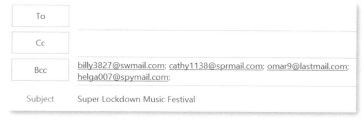

For example, you may have signed up to a music festival news website. An email newsletter may be sent out to all the people on the group's email list. As a matter of privacy it would be essential that you did not see everyone else's email address and you would be upset if you knew that your email address had been given to many other people without your permission. This is achieved is by using Bcc.

In this case **the website owner** has written to Billy, Cathy, Omar and Helga – and anyone else on the mailing list. When Billy receives the email he will see that it has come from the music festival website but will not see any other email addresses – it will seem as though he is the only recipient.

Using email contacts

As has been mentioned, when contacting friends or colleagues using email, their address must be exactly right; one single character error and the message will not be received. Being able to save email addresses as contacts is an essential feature of any email software program or web-based email provider.

Web-based and software email packages may appear to be different but each will have some way of storing contacts and each person (just like an entry in a database) can have a number of different pieces of information (or fields) linked to them.

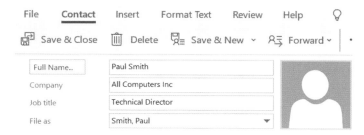

This example of an address book entry shows the sort of information that can be saved. This may include:

- name
- contact email(s)
- job title
- company
- telephone number
- addresses
- photo.

For the purpose of this activity, only the name and email addresses need to be accurate, the other details can be invented.

To add a contact to the address book click on an icon or a tab that indicates **Add New Contact**. You may have buttons such as these:

Clicking on Contact brings up the panels where you can add the details of the person to be added as a contact to your address book.

Once the details for a new contact have been entered they need to be saved.

Eventually you will have built up a contact list like this:

Contact groups/distribution lists

So far you have added the names and contact details of people who will eventually be a part of your complete address book. You need these specific contacts to be grouped so that you can refer to them all by a single name. This would enable us to send an email to a group instead of a list of individuals. Your email software might refer to Distribution Lists, as in the example below rather than Groups.

The first step to creating a group is by naming one. Click on the **New Group** (or **Distribution list**) button or icon in your software and name the group **AllComputersInc**.

Save the group.

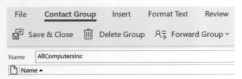

Here the steps would be:

- select the contact (Philip)
- choose to **Add** Philip to the group
- click and add the other four employees to the group
- click 'OK' to save these employees into the group.

In some software, once a group is created, members can be added from your existing address book by selecting **Add Members** from a main menu. A **Remove Member** option will take that person out of the group but will not remove the person from the address book.

In the example above, selecting the person in the list and then clicking on 'Delete' will remove the person from the list.

Selecting just that group (All Computers Inc) will result in just those contacts who belong to that group being displayed:

Sending a message to a contact group

After choosing to create a new message all that is necessary is to click on 'Send To:' and then select the group from the list of available contacts:

To	⊞ **AllComputersInc**;
Cc	
Bcc	

Activity 8

You need to send the Newsletter to all the people in the group **AllComputersInc**.

Create a new email message that:

- will be sent to the members of the group **AllComputersInc**
- has your own email address as a Bcc
- has the subject line: **Requested newsletter attached**
- has the message: **Hello everyone, Further to the recent request for the latest version of the newsletter, please find it as an attachment. Download and save to an appropriate folder. Kind regards.**

Send the email.

- Make sure that all your friends who are on the list received the email.
- Make sure that you (as a Bcc) also received the email.
- Save the attachment in your **Downloads** folder.

Acceptable language, guidelines, netiquette and security

Whenever you are using email, you need to be aware of issues surrounding your use of it. The country that you are emailing from, or even into, may have strong filtering and censorship policies in place that need to be considered. Therefore, it is vital that in composing emails you avoid contentious or inflammatory vocabulary or content. Not only may this be inappropriate for the audience, but it may also be picked up by filtering systems that will block, or treat as spam, your email, meaning that your email does not get delivered. The following pieces of advice should be followed when using email.

Language
- Do not use offensive language, slang or terms that may cause offence.
- Think about the age of the person you are talking to.

Guidelines

Many organisations will have a set of rules, including schools, that must be followed when using email. Failure to do this can lead to disciplinary action. These guidelines, or policies, might include:

- Ensuring all messages are encrypted.
- Requiring passwords to open important documents sent as attachments.
- Making sure messages and attachments are work or school related.

Activity 9

Do you have a school email address? If so, find out what/if any rules are in place which govern your use of language, including slang abbreviations, common text speak abbreviations or emoticons/emojis. Does your school email system have strong filtering based on vocabulary in the subject line/the text of the message?

Netiquette

Internet etiquette describes commonly accepted practices when working online, with a focus on being polite, respecting other people's views and being considerate of those you communicate with. Here are some common practices:

- Avoid WRITING IN CAPITALS, as it appears you are shouting.
- Don't pass on personal information that doesn't belong to you.
- Avoid forwarding SPAM (also covered in Session 8.2), advertising emails or copyrighted work.
- Remember anything you send could be posted publicly, consider privacy.

Security

One of the most common ways to spread a computer virus is through email. The dangers of malware are discussed in Session 8.2, but the following considerations relate to email:

- Use encryption (Session 4.7) to ensure messages can't be intercepted and read.
- Be careful when attaching and downloading attachments.
- Password protect attachments that may contain sensitive data, a job application for example.

Review and revise

You should now be able to:

- create documents using multiple data sources
- describe why corporate style guides are important
- to create and apply styles in a document
- create, send and receive an email message that has an attachment, and download the attachment
- use Cc, Bcc, Reply and Forward appropriately
- create and use an email group
- discuss the issues surrounding the constraints affecting the use of email.

1 Practical review

What have you covered?

In these four practical sessions you have:
- created new documents from external data and amended this text
- explored the use of footers and headers
- practised creating and applying styles, including font face, size, bold, underline, italic, alignment
- imported images, clip art and charts, resizing and cropping them
- practised adjusting the page layout: orientation, margins, columns
- practised sending a document as an attachment
- learned how to use advanced searching techniques to locate images and textual information on the internet
- practised copying/downloading images, text, charts and tables from websites
- practised working with templates and source data for a mail merge.

Some practice questions

You are going to edit a document, which is to be included as a review in a travel guide published by Compass Adventure Holidays.

1 Add the following contact for the Cycling Editor at the publishers, to your address book:

Cycling Editor   My.Name@abc.com

(*where* My.Name@abc.com *is **your** email address*)

2 Using a suitable software package, load the file **IndochinaByBicycle.rtf**.

3 Save the text as a word processing document with the name: **IndochinaArticle**.

4 Set the page size to A4.

5 Set the page orientation to landscape.

6 Set the top, bottom, left and right margins to 1.5 cm.

7 In the footer of the document place:
- an automated date, centre aligned.

8 In the header of the document place:
- an automated page number, right aligned.

Make sure that the header and footer are displayed on every page and that the alignments match the page orientation and margins.

9 Insert this heading at the start of the document:
Across Indochina by Bicycle

10 Create a style **IndochinaHeading** with these settings:
- centre aligned
- a sans-serif font
- bold
- size 28 point.

Apply this style to the heading.

11 Format the body text into two equally spaced columns, with a 1 cm gap between the columns.

12 Create a style **IndochinaText** with these settings:
- be a sans-serif font
- be fully justified
- have one and a half line spacing
- have a font size of 11 points.

Apply this style to the text in the body of the document.

13 Identify the three subheadings and make them *bold italic*.

14 The main image for the article is to be a picture of the Victory Gate at Angkor Thom, in Cambodia, as shown here.

Use a search engine to find an image of this gate. If you are unable to, there is an image on the digital download.

Download and save this image into the same folder as you have saved **IndochinaArticle**.

15 Insert this image into **IndochinaArticle** so that it is centred, spanning the two columns on the first page. Use the text wrapping options to help with this.

Crop and resize the image so that it is the height of the column on the page (about 15 cm) and maintain the aspect ratio.

The first page should look like this:

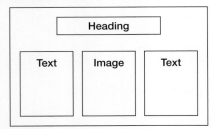

16 Save the document with a new name.

17 Prepare an email message:
- to be sent to the **Cycling Editor** (from your contacts list)
- with the subject **Indochina part 1**.

The body of your message should have the text:

Attached is the first section of the Indochina article.

18 Attach the document you saved at step 16 to this email.

Send the email.

Progress check

Aiming for good progress

With your word processing software you:
- can import text from .rtf and .txt file types into your word processing application
- can import images, charts or clip art into a document, resizing and cropping as necessary
- can adjust page settings: orientation, size, margins, two columns and place data in footers and headers.

You can also:
- search the internet for images, download and save them to your computer
- copy text from webpages to place in a document of your own.

Using your email software you:
- can compose a message with an attached file
- can use the Cc, Reply and Forward options as appropriate
- can add a person's email details to a contact list.

Aiming for excellent progress

With your word processing software you:
- can confidently import text from a variety of file types into your word processing application
- can import images, charts or clip art into a document, resizing and cropping as necessary
- are confident with page settings: orientation, size, margins, multiple columns and also using footer and headers.

You can also:
- search the internet for images, download and save them to your computer
- copy text and tables from webpages to place in a document of your own.

Using your email software you:
- can compose a message with an attached file
- can use the Cc, Bcc, Reply and Forward options as appropriate
- can set up and use contact lists and contact groups.

2 Input and output devices

Why this unit matters

Computers process information. We enter information into a computer system (input), where it is processed, and then we receive back a useful response (output).

Typing on a keyboard, taking a digital photo and listening to music are all examples of where input and output devices are essential. They allow us to collect information from the world around us, process it and then have it returned to us in a suitable format.

As well as physically interacting with input devices there are many devices that can collect data directly and feed it into a system. These can scan and interpret information from a range of sources, from our handwriting, an exam paper or a credit card.

Every day I check in and check out hundreds of books and journals. I use input devices to scan ISBN barcodes and identity cards. I use output devices to print overdue notice letters and display book searches. (Librarian)

We use lots of different input and output devices at the bank. We use devices for processing cheques and cash, and setting up customers with new bank cards. And don't forget we provide access to the internet and telephone banking – which means more devices! (Banker)

I work in an automated greenhouse. We use a computer system to monitor conditions and adjust the temperature. The input and output devices that make up this system include sensors, motors, heating and lights. (Plant scientist)

Your practical task

Imagine that during your holidays you are helping at a company called True to Life Studios that makes animated films – both traditional cartoons and modern **computer generated** films. The building has offices, canteen facilities and a small shop. New members of staff and volunteers like yourself are always surprised by the huge range of different input and output devices and systems used – from using graphics tablets to draw characters, and sound systems for testing effects, to building alarm systems and even the kitchen facilities.

All new staff members follow tours and training sessions on their first day, and you have been asked to create an electronic presentation to explain how different input and output devices are used throughout the business.

The **animation studio** described above (True to Life Studios) is one that you will revisit throughout this unit. However, it could easily relate to any of the situations above, all of which use the same devices and systems described in this unit, but in different ways.

What this unit covers

THEORY

Sessions

Theory review

PRACTICAL

Sessions

Practical review

By the end of the theory sessions you will be able to:

- describe the various types of input, direct data and output devices, the different forms they take and examples of how they are used in the wider world – for example, in different industries, banks and design studios

- identify and explain the advantages and disadvantages of different input and output devices in relation to their purpose

- understand how systems are used in practical situations and describe the most suitable input and output devices for each, based on user needs.

In the practical sessions you will develop and apply skills in:

- communicating using presentations

- using the internet as a source of information

- combining text, images and graphical elements in your work

- designing and presenting for a specific audience

- using suitable animation effects and transitions

- using master slides to set the style and layout of a presentation

- saving and printing your work.

SESSION 2.1 **Input devices**

Background

Input devices are the means of entering information into a **computer system**. This information may be simple numeric data typed into a keyboard, sound picked up by a microphone, a digital image generated by a camera or scanner, or environmental data picked up by a sensor.

How data is processed

The diagram below represents any computer-based system. Data is input into the system, it is processed and an output is produced. For example, a letter is typed into a computer using a keyboard (input) and it is saved onto the hard disk (storage). The letter can then be printed using a printer (output), but a copy is still saved on the disk.

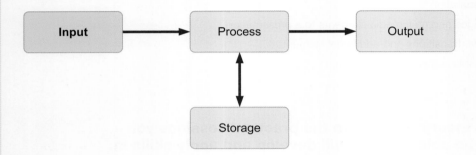

Input devices used in organisations

The animation studios use graphic tablets and scanners to digitise sketchwork, and models, webcams and microphones to video conference with clients around the world. In the shop, barcode and magnetic stripe readers are used when selling food. These are the sorts of input devices that would be found in any business or organisation, from a hospital to a bank or factory.

Analogue and digital data

Computers process digital information in binary, using the numbers 0 and 1. This allows different digital devices across the world to communicate. Analogue data is based around changing values over time in a physical way, such as the movement of a clock hand or expansion and contraction of mercury in a thermometer. Modern input and output devices use digital data, but some devices are still based on analogue systems and require a converter. Examples of systems requiring a converter are sensors for temperature, pressure, light and measure scale (°C for temperature, for example).

An analogue to digital converter (**ADC**) converts this analogue value to a digital binary value a computer can process. ADCs are found in pressure and temperature sensors, computer microphones and photographic scanners.

In contrast, a digital to analogue converter (**DAC**) converts a digital signal into an analogue one. Examples include converting a digital voice recording to an analogue loudspeaker in our television or telephone and the control of mechanical devices using an **actuator**. See Session 5.7 for more information on the use of actuators.

> ### Real world
>
> The cloning of bank cards and the information on their magnetic stripes was reduced by new cards that use the **Chip and PIN system** (see page 67); over 50 countries now use this technology. Despite these new measures, ATMs are still used to commit fraud, often by thieves fitting false fronts to machines.

Input devices and their advantages and disadvantages

Input device	Advantages	Disadvantages
Keyboards: used to enter text into a computer.	• Designed for long-term repetitive use and widely available. • Wireless versions reduce desktop clutter and connect either via Bluetooth to the computer or radio frequencies to a USB dongle. • Function keys can be set to perform tasks or open specific programs. • Alternative keyboard layouts to suit all languages and typing styles are available.	• Data can only be input as fast as it can be typed. • People with physical disabilities may struggle to use them. • Danger of repetitive strain injury after long periods of continuous use. • Wireless versions require an internal power supply.
Numeric keypad: used where only numerical information needs to be entered.	• Simple to use. • Ideal for banking or mathematical systems. • Saves space.	• Limited to numerical data only.
Mouse: used to control the position of the pointer on the screen in any computer system.	• Directly transfers physical movement into the computer system. • Designed for long-term repetitive use. • On-screen icons, menus and sub-menus can be quickly accessed using customisable click buttons. • Wireless versions reduce desktop clutter and connect either via Bluetooth to the computer or radio frequencies to a USB dongle. • Easier to use than a keyboard for those with limited finger movement. • Handheld wireless presentation pointer versions using gyroscopic sensors to control the curser.	• Requires a flat surface on which to work. • The operation of optical or laser mice can be affected by reflective desk surfaces. • Some versions are designed only for right-hand use. • The ball mechanism in older mice can stop working. • Wireless versions require an internal power supply.
Touch / track pad: an alternative to a mouse, built into most laptops but also available as a separate device.	• Removes the need for a separate mouse. • Functions can be assigned to different areas of the pad or to multi-finger gestures. • Requires less movement space than a traditional mouse.	• Requires fine finger control. • Can become uncomfortable after prolonged use.
Tracker ball: an alternative to a mouse, useful for children or for those who have limited movement in their hands; also used in design applications.	• Requires very little space to operate. • Easier to control than a mouse for those with limited hand movement.	• The tracker ball is often removable and can be lost. • Not as widely used as a mouse and therefore more expensive.

Input device		Advantages	Disadvantages
	Remote controls: held in the hand and used to control TVs, PCs, home entertainment systems, projectors, etc.	• Devices can be controlled from a short distance. • Each button can carry out a different function. • Multiple devices can be assigned to a single remote control.	• Devices can be difficult to use if remote control is lost. • Often limited to a direct line of sight to function correctly.
	Scanners: allow hard copies of images (such as drawings or photographs) or text to be transferred to a computer.	• Images can be scanned at very high resolution. • Often built into printers to create multi-functional devices.	• High-resolution scanning produces large file sizes. • Time-consuming. • Large amount of desk space required, functionality is often now replaced by smartphone applications.
	Joysticks / Gamepads: used in computer games and real-world machinery and vehicles to control movement.	• Commonly used and recognisable across the world and requires little training in its use. • Machinery can be controlled remotely. • Easy to use as there are very few buttons. • Can be controlled with one hand.	• Limited to directional control. • Limited to thumb and first finger buttons; additional functions may require additional devices.
	Steering wheel: used in desktop computers, game consoles and simulators to control a virtual vehicle.	• Accurately represents the steering wheel just like in a real vehicle. • Force feedback can be added to provide road resistance.	• Limited to driving specific applications. • Adding mechanical elements such as force feedback and gear levers increases manufacturing costs. • Requires additional elements such as foot pedals to create a fully immersive experience.
	Touch screens: removes the need for a keyboard, allowing a user simply to choose options on screen. Common place in smart hand-held devices but also used in public information kiosks.	• Often added as additional functionality to laptops and desktop computers. • Screen can be cleared easily, making it ideal for weather resistant devices and public access terminals. • Options and menus can be accessed quicker than using a mouse.	• More expensive than a standard display. • Finger-based systems can lack precision control.

Input device		Advantages	Disadvantages
	Digital still / video cameras: used to take high-quality photographs or video that can be viewed immediately on a display and directly uploaded to a computer or printer.	• Resolution is much higher than traditional film. • Storage capacity can be expanded using memory cards. • There are no development costs providing you have access to a computer. • Many cameras now include GPS technology to tag location data and wireless connectivity to upload media online. • Locations and buildings can be remotely monitored.	• The higher the **resolution**, the more memory is needed to store it. • Editing high definition 4K stills and video requires a computer with a powerful processor. • Some cameras compress the images, reducing quality. • Require regular charging or battery replacement. • As more additional features are being added, battery life often suffers as a result. • Many people now use a mobile smart phone as a replacement for a digital camera or camcorder.
	Microphones: used to input sounds and voices.	• These can be used with computers with voice recognition software to control systems. • Used to enable chat facilities on computers and other devices. • Extremely common and inexpensive. • Used to input voiceovers for multimedia presentations.	• **Voice command** software often must be taught to recognise a user's voice. • Digital audio files can take up a lot of space. • Need to be quite near the sound source in order to work correctly.
	Temperature sensor: used to input temperature readings to a microprocessor or computer. Used in microprocessor-controlled washing machines, computer-controlled greenhouses and microprocessor-controlled central heating systems.	• Much more accurate than traditional thermometers and able to detect very small temperature changes. • Data does not need to be read manually; the microprocessor does it automatically.	• An additional analogue to digital (ADC) convertor is required to input the signal into a computer to process.
	Pressure sensor: used to input pressure readings to a microprocessor or computer. Found in computer-controlled burglar alarm systems, automatic doors, weighing scales, automatic washing machines, robotics and production line control.	• Much more accurate than traditional weighing devices; able to detect very small changes in pressure. • As with other sensors, data does not have to be read manually.	• Any object of a suitable weight can incorrectly activate them. • As with other sensors, an ADC converter is required.

Input device	Advantages	Disadvantages
Light sensor: used to input light readings to a microprocessor or computer. Used in automated street lighting (turning lights on at night and off during the day), photography and space telescopes (to measure light levels and adjust the image accordingly).	• Able to detect very small changes in light levels. • As with other sensors, data does not have to be read manually.	• As with other sensors, an ADC converter is required. • Can be activated incorrectly with artificial light.
Graphics tablet: used to input freehand drawings using a connected pen, or stylus.	• Can be used to input much more natural drawings than can be achieved with a mouse. • Unlike a mouse click, graphic tablet pens are often pressure sensitive, allowing for variations in line thickness and shade.	• Requires space and practice to use. • Becomes impossible to use if the stylus or pen is lost.
Webcams: attached to PCs, laptops and mobile phones to capture still and moving images. Used in **video conferencing** and to record video messages.	• Integrated into the majority of smartphones, tablets and laptops. • Allows people to chat face-to-face across the world from their own homes. • Inexpensive to produce, compared with video cameras, and widely used in many different devices.	• Usually only designed for **streaming** video online and do not normally have internal storage. • Camera built into devices do raise security concerns related to external access.
Light pens: used to draw or control elements directly onto a computer display. Used in **CAD** and manufacturing systems.	• Precise inputs can be made faster than using a mouse or keyboard. • Data can be 'written' onto the screen.	• Requires practice and a steady hand to use. • Rarely used today due to the introduction of touch screens.

Activity 1

Write a list of five input devices you have recently used in your home and school life and describe briefly why you have used them.

Evaluating input devices

Webcams, video cameras, scanners and digital cameras can all capture images, but it is the purpose behind capturing the image that influences the decision about which one to use. The diagram on the right illustrates the main considerations that need to be taken when choosing a suitable input device.

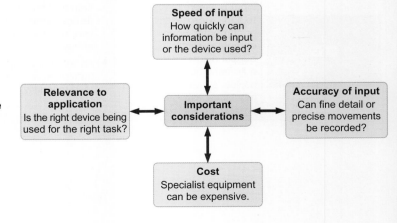

Speed of input
How quickly can information be input or the device used?

Relevance to application
Is the right device being used for the right task?

Important considerations

Accuracy of input
Can fine detail or precise movements be recorded?

Cost
Specialist equipment can be expensive.

Activity 2

Consider the following types of organisations and their requirements:

- the animated film studio outlined in this session
- manufacturing
- a hospital
- your school.

List and describe four input devices you might find in each organisation. State their advantages and disadvantages.

Review and revise

You should now be able to:

- correctly identify a variety of input devices
- consider the impact of input devices in your own life and the world around you
- describe suitable uses for each, depending on the organisation's requirements
- discuss how the same input device can be used for a variety of purposes
- state the difference and explain the need for conversion between analogue and digital data.

Direct data entry devices

Background

The majority of the input devices in Session 2.1 rely on physical interaction, but the following devices read data from the source provided, such as a bank card or written document, and transfer it directly to its associated computer system.

Direct data devices and their advantages and disadvantages

Direct data devices	Advantages	Disadvantages
Magnetic stripe readers: used to read data from magnetic stripes on identity and banking cards.	• Information can be input into a system quickly. • More accurate than typing data manually. • Data is hidden from sight within a stripe, so is more secure than a printout or screen.	• They are not as secure as data stored on a chip, for example. • Very limited storage capacity in the stripes.
Chip and PIN readers: used to read data from chips on bank cards and confirm purchases using a pin code.	• More secure than magnetic stripe systems. • Chips can hold lots of data or information, from personal details to images. • Data can be encrypted. • Data can be protected with a private Personal Identification Number (**PIN**).	• Not all countries have adopted this system, which could cause access issues. • Unable to use if the PIN number is forgotten or lost.
PIN pads: used to enter data into Automated Teller Machines (**ATM**), Electronic Funds Transfer at Point Of Sale (**EFTPOS**) systems, entry doors and handheld devices.	• **PIN** codes help to prevent unauthorised access. • Secure entry doors can be accessed without the need for a physical key or card.	• People can be seen entering the PIN code. • Anyone with the correct code can use the device. • PIN numbers can be forgotten.
Radio Frequency Identification (RFID) readers: used to read data wirelessly from RFID chips, or tags, using an electromagnetic field. Tags can be attached to any object and are used in stock control, commercial outlets and medical applications.	• It enables credit and debit cards and smartphones to make contactless payments. • Data chips can be read within a specified area, without a line of sight. • Important information can be easily added to any object, or person. • Can be used to store secure data on a passport, personal identification or car key, allowing access based on chip data. • Retail industries can monitor stock levels very accurately.	• Higher initial investment compared to barcodes for example. • Chips can be damaged, colliding with other objects. • Security concerns; chips could be illegally accessed and data compromised. • Data could be accidently read multiple times, providing inaccurate results.

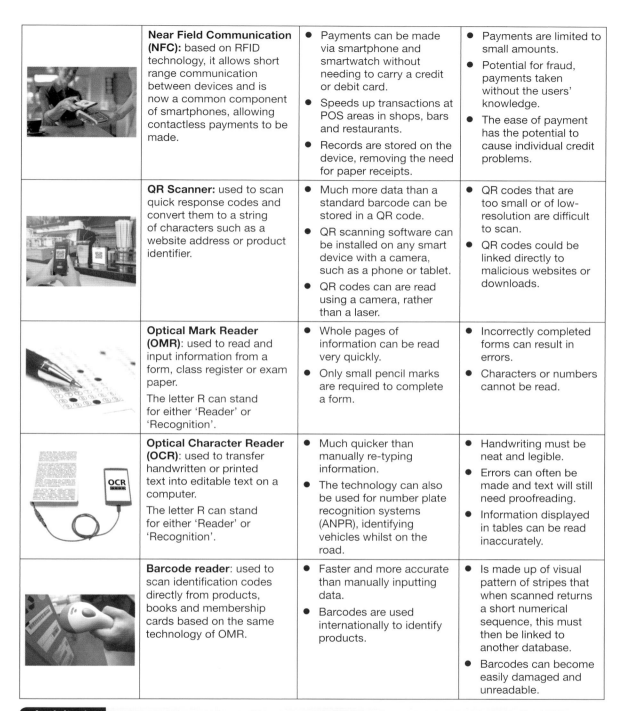

	Near Field Communication (NFC): based on RFID technology, it allows short range communication between devices and is now a common component of smartphones, allowing contactless payments to be made.	• Payments can be made via smartphone and smartwatch without needing to carry a credit or debit card. • Speeds up transactions at POS areas in shops, bars and restaurants. • Records are stored on the device, removing the need for paper receipts.	• Payments are limited to small amounts. • Potential for fraud, payments taken without the users' knowledge. • The ease of payment has the potential to cause individual credit problems.
	QR Scanner: used to scan quick response codes and convert them to a string of characters such as a website address or product identifier.	• Much more data than a standard barcode can be stored in a QR code. • QR scanning software can be installed on any smart device with a camera, such as a phone or tablet. • QR codes can are read using a camera, rather than a laser.	• QR codes that are too small or of low-resolution are difficult to scan. • QR codes could be linked directly to malicious websites or downloads.
	Optical Mark Reader (OMR): used to read and input information from a form, class register or exam paper. The letter R can stand for either 'Reader' or 'Recognition'.	• Whole pages of information can be read very quickly. • Only small pencil marks are required to complete a form.	• Incorrectly completed forms can result in errors. • Characters or numbers cannot be read.
	Optical Character Reader (OCR): used to transfer handwritten or printed text into editable text on a computer. The letter R can stand for either 'Reader' or 'Recognition'.	• Much quicker than manually re-typing information. • The technology can also be used for number plate recognition systems (ANPR), identifying vehicles whilst on the road.	• Handwriting must be neat and legible. • Errors can often be made and text will still need proofreading. • Information displayed in tables can be read inaccurately.
	Barcode reader: used to scan identification codes directly from products, books and membership cards based on the same technology of OMR.	• Faster and more accurate than manually inputting data. • Barcodes are used internationally to identify products.	• Is made up of visual pattern of stripes that when scanned returns a short numerical sequence, this must then be linked to another database. • Barcodes can become easily damaged and unreadable.

Activity 1

Write a list of three direct data entry devices you or your family have used and describe briefly how they were used.

Evaluating direct data input devices

It is important to choose the best device, based on the users' needs, and consider the advantages and disadvantages of each. The choice of direct data device depends on the specific type of information being read, be it text or graphical. The diagram below illustrates the main considerations that need to be taken when choosing a direct data entry device.

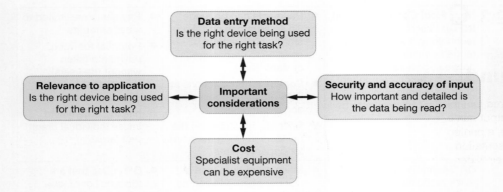

Data entry method
Is the right device being used
for the right task?

Relevance to application
Is the right device being used
for the right task?

Important
considerations

Security and accuracy of input
How important and detailed is
the data being read?

Cost
Specialist equipment
can be expensive

Activity 2

Consider a banker like the one on page 60 that has to process cash requests and provide new cards to customers. List the direct data entry devices a bank may use and describe how they would be used.

Review and revise

You should now be able to:

- correctly identify a variety of direct data entry devices
- consider the impact of these devices on your life and the world around you
- describe suitable uses for each, depending on the organisations requirements
- describe the key differences between magnetic and chip reading devices and the advantages and disadvantages of each
- identify the security dangers of chip and PIN systems and describe how can users protect themselves.

SESSION 2.3 Output devices

Background

Once data is entered into a system, it is processed and an output is produced. This output can be presented to the user in a variety of ways: for example, a printed document, a receipt from a shop till or a **multimedia** presentation. In this session, you will look at different output devices, their wider-world uses and their suitability for different tasks.

The input, process and output cycle

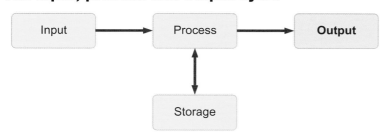

Output devices used in organisations

At the animated film studio, as in many other organisations, you will find visual and printed displays, speaker systems, automatic doors and building alarm systems.

Output devices and their advantages and disadvantages

Output device		Advantages	Disadvantages
	Cathode Ray Tube (CRT) Monitor: presents text and graphics visually using a cathode ray tube but being gradually replaced by LCD and LED based screens.	• Bright, clear display. • Low initial cost. • Can display text, graphics, photos and videos. • Reading documents on screen saves paper. • A wide viewing angle.	• Unpopular due to weight and size. • Difficult to recycle, large cause of e-waste. • Unsuitable for those with visual disabilities. • Use lots of power, increasing running costs.
	Thin-Film-Transistor/ Liquid Crystal Display (TFT/LCD) Monitor: used in home and office computing and gradually replacing CRT monitors.	• Lighter and thinner than CRT monitors and becoming cheaper. • Uses very little power, so lower running costs. • Modern screens can also incorporate touch technology. • Can be wall-mounted.	• Early models had a limited viewing angle and could blur when showing fast-moving images. • Due to their thinner bodies, they can be damaged easily.

Output device		Advantages	Disadvantages
	Light Emitting Diode (LED) Monitor: an LCD based monitor that uses light emitting diodes rather than florescent lighting to backlight the screen.	• Lower energy consumption. • Improved image quality and contrast, compared to older LCD screens. • Can be wall-mounted and incorporate touch screen technology. • Becoming the standard in televisions, portable devices and computers. • Organic LED (OLED) screens can have even greater contrast and be thinner in design.	• Newer technology can be more expensive. • Not as effective on very large screens.
	Touch screen: can serve as an input and output device as user input can instantaneously be shown on the screen.	• Interaction can be instantly seen on the screen. • Users can quickly change the information being displayed.	• Displays can be blocked by fingers using the screen. • Marks from physical interaction can affect the view.
	Multimedia projector: can be connected to a computer, television or **media player** to present information to a large audience. Used in schools, universities and business conferences.	• Portable. • Able to produce a larger display than monitors. • Smaller, lighter LED based versions can be used for home entertainment.	• Although portable, still requires an external power source. • Requires a darkened room to produce bright images. • Space is needed to project upon and for the projector to be positioned at a suitable distance. • Lamps are very expensive to replace.
	Laser printer: used in organisations to print text, graphics and photos quickly and with high quality. Ideal for colour reports, newsletters or posters.	• Prints high-quality images very quickly. • Toner cartridges are designed to print thousands of pages. • Very little noise compared to other printers. • No danger of spillages due to powder-based cartridges.	• Both printer and cartridges are more expensive than inkjet printers. • Without regular servicing and good ventilation, ozone emissions can reach dangerous levels.
	Inkjet printer: often used in the home to print high-quality text, graphics and photos. Used to print digital photography and small documents (a few pages).	• Printers and cartridges are cheap to purchase and run for light or medium use. • Modern printers often include built-in scanners and card readers. • Capable of photo-quality images and high-quality graphics.	• Ink costs can be expensive for printing large numbers of pages. • Slower than laser printers. • Ink cartridges run out quickly. • Only really suitable for home or small office use. • Output quality depends on the type of paper used.

Output device		Advantages	Disadvantages
	Dot matrix printer: uses a printer head and ribbon to generate characters on continuous stationery. Still used in industry to print payslips, labels and invoices.	• Ideal for repetitive printing tasks, where speed, noise and quality are not an issue. • Running costs are very low. • Hard-wearing; suitable for factory environments. • Suitable for use with No Carbon Required (NCR) or carbonless paper to create two copies of the same document without re-printing.	• Noisy and slow to print. • Limited graphics resolution and colour options compared to inkjet or laser printers. • More prone to jamming than other printers due to the feed mechanism. • Expensive to buy.
	Wide format printer: used to print large banners, posters and signs, and normally use rolls rather than individual sheets of paper. Often used to produce large technical or engineering drawings.	• Cost effective for one-off or short runs of large-scale printing compared to batch production. • Versatility, from CAD drawings to long photographic banner prints.	• Ink-intensive, cartridges may need to be regularly replaced. • Expensive initial outlay costs.
	3D Printer: converts a computer generated 3D model into a physical object by printing multiple layers of material from a computer controlled printing head. From initial manufacturing applications, 3D printing is now becoming commonplace in hospitals, classrooms, design studios and the home.	• Ideal for one-off test models and prototyping applications. • Provides small-scale manufacturing processes to remote parts of the world. • Costs continue to fall every year – making home 3D printing possible. • Ability to create extremely complex and moving parts.	• Taking work away from skilled manufacturers. • Potential for printing dangerous items. • Unregulated, ideas can be stolen and copied. • Printing materials are still limited.
	Speakers: output audio information to a user as speech, music or sound effects. Used in many devices such as radios, televisions, music centres, computers and headphones.	• Available in many different shapes and sizes, from personal headphones to music concert speakers. • Able to output information to very large audiences. • Long lasting due to their simple construction.	• Unsuitable for those with hearing difficulties. • Potential noise pollution and disturbance to those nearby. • High quality headphones and speakers can be expensive.
	Plotter: unlike traditional printers, plotters create line-based graphics by drawing directly on the paper using a computer controlled pen.	• Ideal for large scale CAD or technical drawings. • Use less ink than other large-format printers. • Multiple coloured pens can be used.	• Take up more space than standard printers. • Unable to create high quality graphics or photos. • More expensive than other printers.

Output device		Advantages	Disadvantages
	**Actuator:** describes any device that is able to convert computer-based instructions into real-world physical motion or controlled movement; from switches to robotic arms.	• Can be replaced as part of a larger system if damaged. • Complex actuators can be programmed to complete a range of actions. • Repetitive tasks can be repeated over and over without the need for breaks.	• Size is determined by function and movement requirements. • Devices often need protecting from the environment. • Devices are often limited to one function.

Control devices

Motors are used in computer-controlled doors, windows, and robot arms to create movement.
- They are widely available and used in many industries.
- They are very accurate and able to repeat the same action indefinitely.
- They can be used to drive larger equipment such as cranes and robots.

Buzzers provide an audible signal or alarm like that in a mobile phone, oven or smoke detector.
- They are very simple to produce and widely available.
- Small buzzers can be fitted easily to a wide range of devices.
- They are instantly recognisable as a warning sound or siren.

Heaters are used in computer-controlled greenhouses, automatic washing machines and computer-controlled central heating systems.
- Heaters and cooling systems can be used to maintain a constant room or building temperature.
- They can create a suitable habitat for plants in a greenhouse.

Lights and lamps are used to illuminate spaces, such as streets, offices, the home and stadiums.
- They extend what we can do during the day beyond daylight hours.
- They can be used as an alarm or with a siren on an ambulance.
- They can act as a replacement for sunlight in automated greenhouses.

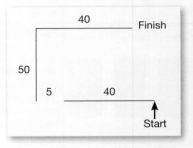

Turtle graphics

Used as an introduction to programming devices, turtle graphics allow a user to program a series of commands based on distance and direction from a start position (move forwards, backwards; turn left, right, etc.). This can be used to control a computer cursor or an actual floor-based robot ('turtle'). Using distance and rotation, a graphical image or pattern can be created either onscreen or physically on the ground with a pen attached to the robot.

The diagram and table on the right show a floor turtle following these instructions:

PENDOWN, LEFT 90, FORWARD 40, PENUP, FORWARD 5, PENDOWN, RIGHT 90, FORWARD 50, RIGHT 90, FORWARD 40.

Instruction	Meaning
FORWARD n	Move n mm forward
BACKWARD n	Move n mm backward
LEFT t	Turn left t degrees
RIGHT t	Turn right t degrees
PENUP	Lift the pen
PENDOWN	Lower the pen

Activity 1

Describe as many situations as you can where output devices like the ones in this session could be used, either to prevent danger or to rescue people from danger.

Evaluating output devices

The format of any output needs to be appropriate to the user and its environment (a warning buzzer in a noisy factory would serve little purpose), so the advantages and disadvantages of each device need to be considered. It is also important to remember the following considerations from the previous session: speed, relevance, quality and cost.

Activity 2

Write a list of five output devices you have used in your home and school life and describe briefly why you have used them.

Activity 3

Consider the following two groups of devices and compare them in terms of speed, relevance, quality and cost. Refer again to the diagram on page 70.

Group 1: CRT Monitor, LED Monitor, multimedia projector

Group 2: Inkjet printer, laser printer, dot matrix, large-scale printer

The continuing advancement of technology

It is important to be aware that technology is constantly developing and that some technologies are replacing others. CRT technology and dot matrix printers for example are very rarely used nowadays. 3D has once again being promoted in cinema and home theatre equipment, although the use of 3D glasses isn't as popular as manufacturers had hoped, leading to newer displays being developed that remove the need for them. One of the fastest moving technologies is that of 3D printing, allowing users to create their own individual products at home.

Activity 4

Consider the following types of organisations:
- the animated film studio outlined in this session
- a bank
- a hospital
- your school.

List and describe four output devices you might find in each organisation. State their advantages and disadvantages.

Real world

Robots are now regularly carrying out jobs that are considered too repetitive or dangerous for humans. Many of these jobs are in the production lines of the automotive industry, but they are also being used in other roles. Robots have been introduced for simple medical procedures, remotely controlled by a doctor where space is limited or the doctor is unable to travel to the patient. Military robots are used to investigate unsafe areas or devices, keeping people at a safe distance.

Real world

Immersive displays: Although virtual reality headsets had been available for many years, recent developments in lightweight, high-resolution displays and complex 3D modelling has meant they are being re-introduced. Immersive gaming is thought to be a large potential market, allowing gamers to feel like they are completely inside a 3D world, or an augmented version of our own world.

Review and revise

You should now be able to:
- correctly identify a variety of output devices
- consider the impact of output devices in your own life and in the world around you
- describe suitable uses for each that depends on an organisation's requirements
- discuss how the same output device can be used for a variety of purposes
- describe the advantages and disadvantages of different output devices while always considering their use.

How organisations use input, direct data and output devices

Background

During a typical day, you may encounter a number of devices: taking a hot shower, printing a homework report or booking tickets for the cinema. At school you may have a vending machine, where money is put into the machine, your choice is selected, and a snack is dispensed.

Common uses of input and output devices

A burglar alarm

Sensors constantly monitor the conditions within a building, feeding back data to a microprocessor. If the sensor detects the movement or warm body of a potential burglar moving through the building then the alarm is activated by the microprocessor, triggering lights and buzzers.

Input devices: sensors, a keypad (to set the alarm), remote control.
Output devices: buzzers, bells, lights.

Shopping using a debit or credit card

When you buy an item in most shops, a barcode scanner inputs the item's product code into the computer system. The product code is used to find the price of the product in the stock database and the price is shown on the till display. A card payment is made, using the Chip and PIN system or a magnetic stripe reader, and money is transferred electronically from the consumer to the shop's bank account. The item is then removed from the stock database and a receipt is printed.

Input devices: till keypad.
Direct data entry device: barcode scanner, Chip and PIN or magnetic card reader, RFID reader.
Output devices: receipt printer, till LCD display, buzzer.

A school registration system

As well as each student's name, address and family information, the school database will also include their timetable, their teachers' names and exam information. This information can then be processed to produce a variety of outputs, from personalised letters for the home, to printing a specific class group of photographs for a new teacher, or following a student's test results on-screen from one year to the next.

Input devices: keyboard, digital camera, mouse.
Output devices: inkjet or laser printer, CRT or LCD monitor.

A medical research centre

Many research centres are now taking advantage of recent advances in 3D scanning and printing technology. 3D models can be designed to individual requirements, printed and tested within a short space of time, saving time and money. Many of these examples are still in development and many more are being considered:

- Prosthetics: A prosthesis can be designed to the exact requirements of the patient, removing the need for adapting mass-produced models. The portability of 3D printing equipment means parts can be made anywhere in the world, in places without easy access to hospitals. This could also be expanded to operating theatre tools.
- Tissue engineering: The introduction of bioinks into the field of 3D printing is leading to advances in printing artificial live tissue based on the donor's own cells; engineered as a scaffold for repairing or replacing our bodies.

- Artificial blood vessels: The ability to print blood vessels, designed for a specific patient and purpose has a great many potential uses, especially treating patients with cardiovascular disease.
- Customised medicines: If a mass-produced medicine isn't suitable, the ability to print a tablet specifically designed to meet a patient's requirement, customised for a particular dosage or avoid a particular side effect for example would be of great benefit.

Input devices: keyboard, digital camera, mouse, scanners, drawing tablets.
Output devices: 3D printer.

Activity 1

During your day, you might have come into contact with the following systems. For each one, write the input and output devices associated with them.

1 Taking a bus, train or taxi.

2 Printing out a homework report.

3 Watching a documentary film at school.

Language

Any electronic device that you can pick up and hold in your hand is classed as hardware. For example, a printer, a webcam or a speaker. If it only exists within computer storage, then it is software.

Systems like these can be easily represented by simple diagrams. The following system is displayed in this way:

Borrowing a book from the library

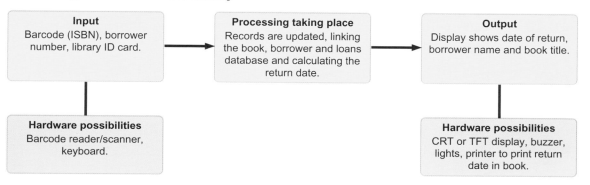

Input
Barcode (ISBN), borrower number, library ID card.

Processing taking place
Records are updated, linking the book, borrower and loans database and calculating the return date.

Output
Display shows date of return, borrower name and book title.

Hardware possibilities
Barcode reader/scanner, keyboard.

Hardware possibilities
CRT or TFT display, buzzer, lights, printer to print return date in book.

Activity 2

1 Using the diagram above as a guide, create similar diagrams of the following systems relating to the animated film studio.

2 Describe the required input and outputs, suitable devices and the processing that takes place in between.

   a Using a microwave oven to have a snack in the kitchen.

   b Paying for a drink or snack from the shop with a debit or credit card.

   c Booking cinema tickets online at a local cinema where employees receive a discount.

   d Creating a hard-drawn cartoon figure to be input into the computer.

Review and revise

You should now be able to:

- describe a wide range of systems that use input and output devices
- consider the types of information that is input, processed and output within these systems
- select the most suitable device for any system, but also taking into consideration that there are often alternatives.

2 Theory review

What have you covered?

In these four theory sessions, you have:

- Been introduced to a wide variety of input, direct data entry and output devices.
- Considered the advantages and disadvantages of using each of them.
- Identified and described input, direct data entry and output devices that can be found in specific situations.
- Evaluated the usefulness of a range of devices in specific situations.
- Considered the range of input and output requirements for a range of everyday systems.
- Considered and compared the processing requirements of a system, and matched input, direct data entry and output devices to these requirements.

Some practice questions

1 Name the devices A, B, C, D, E, F, G and H, using the words from the list.

Speakers	Webcam	Trackerball	Pin pad
Laser printer	Mouse	Microphone	Joystick
TFT screen	Scanner	Plotter	3D printer
RFID reader			

A B C

D E F

G H

See Sessions 2.1, 2.2 and 2.3

2 For each of the devices in the table, indicate with a tick whether it is an input or an output device:

Device	Input	Output	Direct data entry
Keyboard			
Digital camera			
Buzzer			
OMR			
Motor			
Chip and PIN reader			

See Sessions 2.1, 2.2 and 2.3

3 The director of a film that is being produced by True to Life Studios has gone abroad to choose filming locations. She needs to arrange a video conference with the studio chairperson. List the input and output devices she will need in order to hold this conference.

See Sessions 2.1 and 2.3

4 A friend of yours has just bought a new tank in which to keep some pet tropical fish and he has all the components spread out on a large table.

He shows you a water heater and a temperature sensor. Explain how these two devices will work together to keep the water in the fish tank at the right temperature.

See Sessions 2.1 and 2.3

5 A patient at a hospital has been connected to a computer device that is monitoring her heart rate and blood pressure. If either measurement drops below acceptable levels, a buzzer will sound to alert a member of the medical team. Give three reasons why a computer is used to monitor the patient rather than using humans.

> **See Sessions 2.1, 2.2, 2.3 and 2.4**

6 A group of students have started to produce a school magazine, which contains a mixture of calendar/diary items, reports, reviews and general news. The magazine will contain photographs as well as text. The students estimate that they will need 100 copies a month.

The students' teacher asks them what type of printer is needed. The three choices are a dot matrix printer, an inkjet printer and a colour laser printer.

a Give one advantage and one disadvantage of using each of these printers.

b From your answers to a, which printer would you recommend the teacher buys?

> **See Session 2.3**

7 Multiple-choice answer sheets can be marked by computer.

a The pre-printed information, such as the student's name and number, the school centre number and syllabus code, can be read by what optical device?

b The student's answers marked in pencil are read by what device?

> **See Session 2.1**

8 You have a loyalty card for a CD/music store. When you purchase something at the store, the card is inserted into an input device to read your details. There are three ways that this information can be read: by a *magnetic stripe reader*, by a *Chip and PIN device* or by a *barcode reader*.

a Describe each of the three terms in italics.

b Choose the most appropriate device for this situation and give reasons for your answer.

> **See Session 2.2**

9 A security firm has been to your house in order to advise on a setup for a burglar alarm system. They send you a report that contains this paragraph:

There are a number of ways of entry into the house. We recommend that (_____ ____) are placed behind every door and under each window to detect when someone steps into the house. A (___ ___) will be located in the kitchen so that the alarm can be set and deactivated. A (___ ___) can be installed at the bottom of the stairs, which lead to the upper floor so that our team in the city can see what is happening in the house when the alarm sounds. There will be a small (___ _____) within the control and communications panel in the kitchen so that you have face-to-face contact with us. If the alarm is set off, there will be (_____) outside so that passers-by can hear that something is wrong. (_____) will be activated, inside and out, if it is night-time.

Fill in the blank spaces with the names of input and output devices that have been mentioned throughout this unit.

> **See Sessions 2.1, 2.2, 2.3 and 2.4**

Progress check

Aiming for good progress:

- You are able to identify a range of input, direct data entry and output devices.
- You can choose input, direct data entry and output devices that are suitable to particular applications.

Aiming for excellent progress:

- You are able to identify a range of input, direct data entry and output devices.
- You can choose input, direct data entry and output devices that are suitable to particular applications.
- You are confident in explaining how a device can be used in a specific situation.
- You can compare the suitability of devices for an application, justifying your choice of preferred device.

SESSION 2.5 An introduction to presentations

Background

Presentation software is commonly used to present ideas to large audiences. In the following sessions you will be asked to create a presentation for the animation studio described in the introduction.

In this session you will find out how to do the following:

- become familiar with a common presentation software package
- use common presentation terms and phrases
- create a simple presentation combining text and graphics.

Real world

Where considering presentation software, there are many choices. Popular packages designed for office-use are normally paid for and licensed commercially, but becoming more and more popular are **Open-Source** packages. These are created and distributed free of charge with many of the features and regular updates of commercial software.

Activity 1

Using the internet if required, look at how many presentation-based packages there are currently available. These may be on Windows, Apple or Linux-based systems. Consider both commercially paid for and open-source products and discuss the common features between them and list their possible uses in the business world.

Presentation software layout

Below is a typical presentation authoring package, labelled to show the key features.

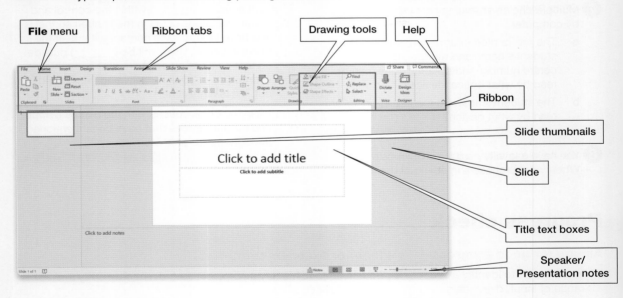

Activity 2

Examine the presentation software you are using, and if it is different to the one shown, discuss the similarities and differences.

Presentation terminology

Terminology	Example
Slide: each page within a presentation is called a slide. They are designed to completely fill the screen when presenting to an audience so that menus and buttons are not a distraction.	
Animation: these are visual effects that can be applied to any object within a presentation to provide movement or emphasis. It is really important when using animation to consider the audience when choosing animation effects. Having text and images whizzing around the screen will entertain young children but may look unprofessional to older audiences.	
Transition: the movement of one slide to another using an effect. These range from fades to star-wipes. Just like the use of animation effects, transitions should be used appropriately. Flashy transitions can distract the audience and look less professional than intended.	
Slide Master: the ability to create a template slide. The font, style, colour and graphics choices that are made can then apply to every new slide.	
Design Themes: pre-defined styles that set the background, layout and colours of a presentation. The choice of theme is the best way to promote your presentation in a certain way to the audience. Think carefully when choosing fonts, styles, colours and backgrounds to ensure you select the most appropriate.	

Terminology	Example
Slide Layout: pre-defined layouts for arranging content on slides. Ranging from a title slide to ones with space for a chart or video.	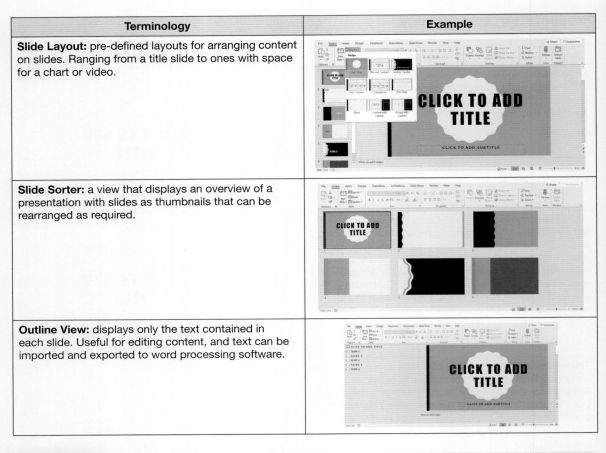
Slide Sorter: a view that displays an overview of a presentation with slides as thumbnails that can be rearranged as required.	
Outline View: displays only the text contained in each slide. Useful for editing content, and text can be imported and exported to word processing software.	

Having read through each of the terms on the previous pages, experiment with your presentation software so you are familiar with the location of each feature.

Creating a basic slide

When starting with any presentation software you are normally shown a new blank slide. If not, select **File > New Presentation**.

Adding and formatting text

A new basic slide normally appears with space for a title and subtitle. These text boxes can be typed into directly and the text then formatted to suit your needs.

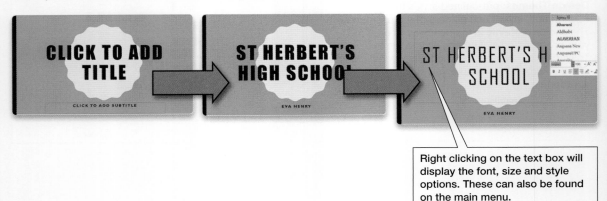

Right clicking on the text box will display the font, size and style options. These can also be found on the main menu.

Activity 4

Add your name and the name of your school to your slide. Try and make the font and style look similar to the one your school uses.

Tip

Once inserted, the required position of the image can be precisely adjusted using the keyboard's cursor keys. This applies to all office-based or image editing software.

Adding a graphic or object

Most office-based programs have the ability to add basic shapes and graphics. These can be used to create diagrams, a logo or simply make a slide look more attractive. The following steps will show you how to add basic shapes.

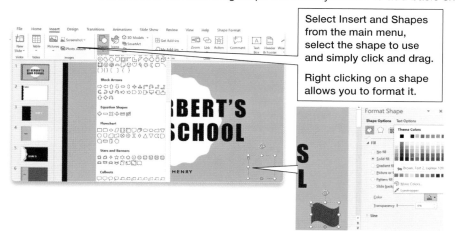

Select Insert and Shapes from the main menu, select the shape to use and simply click and drag.

Right clicking on a shape allows you to format it.

Adding alternative text to an object

Alternative text (alt-text) can be added to images, shapes or other objects. It provides a description for screen readers; providing additional support for those with a visual impairment.

To add alternative text, select the object and either right click and select **Edit Alt Text** or choose **Shape Format** from the ribbon and click the **Alt Text** button.

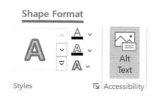

Activity 4

Create a simple logo using shapes. This may be for your school, yourself or a logo with which you are familiar. Try to combine different shapes, colours and use the Alt Text tool to add a useful description.

Slide navigation and external links

Navigation within a presentation allows the user to move from one slide to another in a non-linear way. This can be achieved using either an action button, assigning a specific action to an object, or by adding a hyperlink. A hyperlink is a link to another file address. When using presentation software this could be to another slide within a presentation, an external website or document, or an email address.

To add an action button, select **Shapes** from the **Insert** menu ribbon and a selection of pre-defined action buttons are available at the bottom of the list.

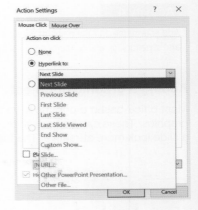

A specific action can be chosen, such as next or previous slide, and a shape drawn to represent it. Choosing a blank action allows any action to be attached to it. A blank button will still need an outline and a colour to be chosen afterwards.

To add a hyperlink, select the object in your presentation you wish to link from and select **Link** from the **Insert** menu ribbon. You are then provided with a number of options.

This will add a text comment to a hyperlinked object when the mouse hovers over it in presentation view, it might describe the function of the hyperlink or its destination.

This provides a direct link to a specified slide within that presentation or assign an action such as first, last or next slide.

Tip

Action buttons and hyperlinks within a presentation are designed to work when in full-screen presentation view, they will not activate when editing the presentation.

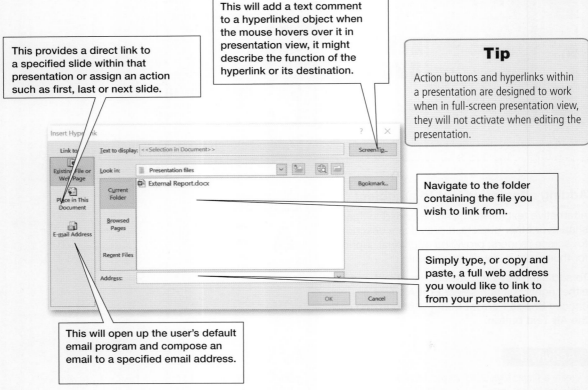

Navigate to the folder containing the file you wish to link from.

Simply type, or copy and paste, a full web address you would like to link to from your presentation.

This will open up the user's default email program and compose an email to a specified email address.

Activity 6

Experiment with adding the following functions within a practice presentation:
- action buttons that can move forwards and backwards through a slideshow
- a hyperlink to an external website or document of your choice
- an email to your school email address.

Review and revise

You should now be able to:
- describe the purpose and common uses of presentation software
- describe the common terms and phrases used in creating presentations
- format the look of a slide and add text and basic graphics for different audiences
- use action buttons and hyperlinks to add additional functionality and navigation.

SESSION 2.6 Presentation preparation

Background

Working for the animated films company called True to Life Studios, you have been asked to produce a presentation using suitable presentation software. This will inform new staff all about input and output devices, as well as how ICT is used outside of the offices, in building control systems and in the company's canteen and shop.

In this session you will find out how to do the following:

- create a new presentation
- design a suitable master slide in keeping with the company's house style
- create the first slide of your presentation
- save your work in a suitable format and location.

House style

Every large organisation will use a **house style**. This simply means having a set of rules to make sure that documents are consistent in the way they present information.

Audience

It is really important that the audience is considered in any presentation. The staff at True to Life Studios will be primarily young adults so consider the following and what choices will appeal to them:

- the language style and vocabulary used
- the quality of images and graphics
- the impact of animation styles and transitions.

Activity 1

Discuss how this project may have been tackled differently if you were going to create the same presentation for the following audiences:

- students that are younger than yourselves
- older adults who had have had little experience of using computers.

Create a new presentation

Below is a typical presentation authoring package. Select **File > New** and you will get the following screen:

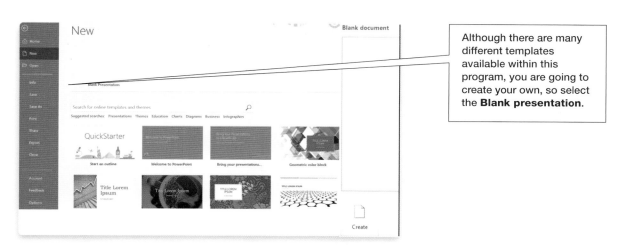

Although there are many different templates available within this program, you are going to create your own, so select the **Blank presentation**.

Saving and file location

It is important that the file you have created has a suitable filename and location. This means that you can regularly save your work as you progress and you will easily be able to find your work at a later date.

Activity 2

Set up a folder on your computer and save a new presentation within it, using suitable file and folder names.

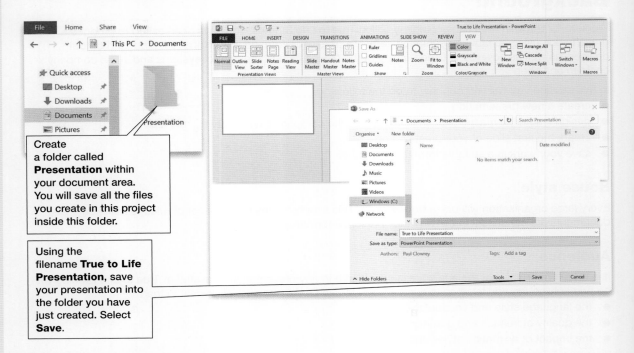

Create a folder called **Presentation** within your document area. You will save all the files you create in this project inside this folder.

Using the filename **True to Life Presentation**, save your presentation into the folder you have just created. Select **Save**.

Creating a master slide

A master slide can be used to set the house style for a presentation by selecting suitable standard colours, fonts and backgrounds for slides. Any drawing objects or design on a master slide will appear on all the slides that use it.

The following steps will show you how to create a suitable master slide for your presentation.

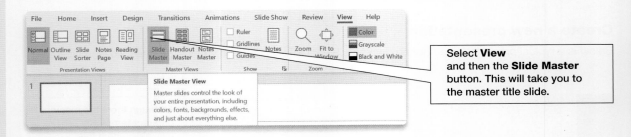

Select **View** and then the **Slide Master** button. This will take you to the master title slide.

Editing the master slide

Editing the master slide allows you to change the look of a presentation before adding content. This needs to match the sort of business or organisation for which the presentation is intended.

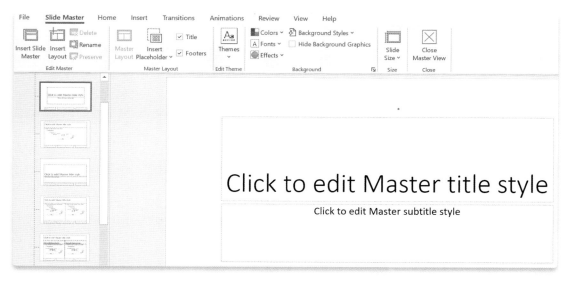

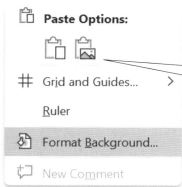

To change the background, right click and select **Format Background** from the options that appear. This will allow you to set the background colour using one of the following options:

● fill using a solid colour
● fill using a gradient (an effect where one colour blends to another)
● a stored picture or texture fill
● a pattern fill (made up of simple lines).

Texture fill

Solid colour fill

Gradient fill

Pattern fill

Edit your master slide. Experiment with background colours and fills and decide on a suitable background for your training presentation for True to Life Studios.

Tip

Formatting options are found in the formatting toolbar or by right clicking selected text.

Fonts, styles, colours and text alignments

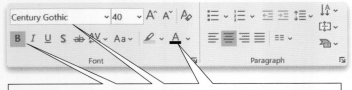

Click to edit Master title style

- Click to edit Master text styles
  - Second level
    - Third level
      - Fourth level
        » Fifth level

The font, size and style of the title have been changed and the alignment has been set to centre, placing it centrally on the slide in a bold style.

The main body text has the same font to keep consistency but it is slightly smaller, right aligned and in black.

• Click to edit Master text styles • Second level • Third level • Fourth level • Fifth level	1. Click to edit Master text styles 2. Second level 3. Third level 4. Fourth level 5. Fifth level

Bullet points can be added to any title, sub heading or piece of text and the points themselves can be changed to a variety of shapes.

Automatic numbering can be added to lists of text within textboxes and can be set as consecutive numbers or letters.

Experiment with the options shown and then choose suitable fonts, styles, sizes and alignments for your training presentation. Make sure that you save your work at regular intervals. Remember, this is a modern international business, so try to choose colours and fonts that reflect this and aren't too distracting or old-fashioned.

Header and footer

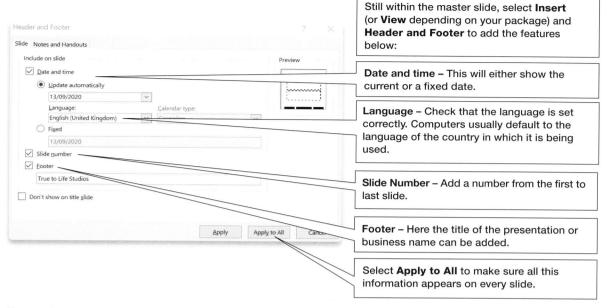

Still within the master slide, select **Insert** (or **View** depending on your package) and **Header and Footer** to add the features below:

Date and time – This will either show the current or a fixed date.

Language – Check that the language is set correctly. Computers usually default to the language of the country in which it is being used.

Slide Number – Add a number from the first to last slide.

Footer – Here the title of the presentation or business name can be added.

Select **Apply to All** to make sure all this information appears on every slide.

Remember, any header, footer, text box, graphic or image can be selected and dragged to any position. Do not assume that the **default** position of these elements is the most suitable for your presentation.

Activity 5

Still within the master slide, add relevant information to the header and footer of your presentation. This might include the date, slide number and company name.

Adding graphical elements to the master slide

ClipArt, **WordArt**, text boxes and shapes are all useful for creating simple logos and graphics. When you add these to the master slide, they will appear on every slide.

WordArt: A set of pre-formatted title styles that uses different fonts, styles and effects to create eye-catching titles. After selecting a suitable style, the text can be edited by double clicking on it.

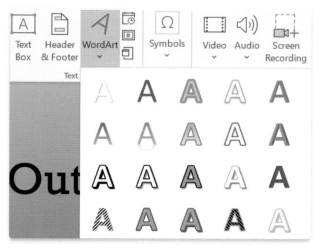

Tip

Many newer office-based packages no longer use contain 'ClipArt' graphical images as they can be easily found online.

Text boxes: Selecting **Insert > Text Box** will allow you to click and drag a text box of any size. Once it is complete, you can add text, which can be styled using the methods already described for other text on a slide.

ClipArt: Type in a word that matches the sort of image you would like to find. The computer will search for a suitable graphical image. Images often come packaged with presentation software and using these can save time.

Shapes: The **Shapes** (or **Autoshapes**) button provides a range of graphics built into the software. Once you have selected what you want, clicking and dragging with the mouse will create that shape of any size. Double clicking the shape will show options for fills and line styles.

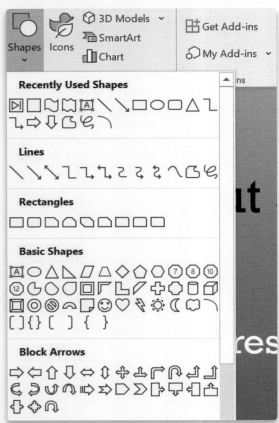

Tip

ClipArt, WordArt, text boxes, shapes and images can be resized and reshaped using the resizing handles around each object when selected. This applies to objects in most office based software.

Grouping

Text, images and shapes can be combined to create complex logos or graphics.

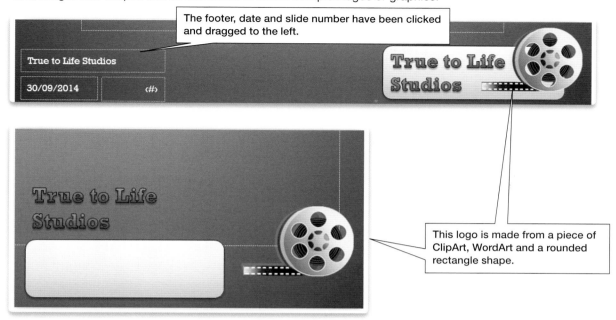

The footer, date and slide number have been clicked and dragged to the left.

This logo is made from a piece of ClipArt, WordArt and a rounded rectangle shape.

To create the logo, the three objects were arranged as required, selected and then grouped, by right clicking the selected objects and selecting **Group**, or selecting **Group** from the **Drawing Tools** menu. Once grouped, the graphic can be moved as one object.

Before creating a group, the order of the objects can be edited using the **Order Objects** menu. This allows one object to be placed over another if the text is being obstructed by the shape for example.

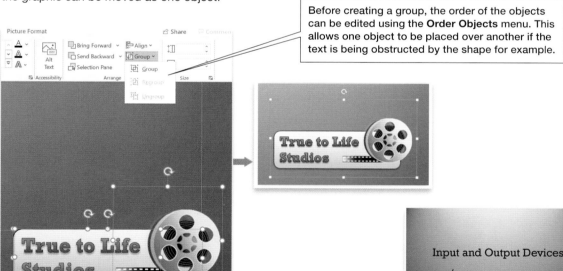

Activity 6

Add additional elements to your slide master; these may include a logo similar to the one shown, or more graphics in keeping with the style of the presentation. Make sure the graphics will not cause problems, such as overlapping with the rest of the information on your slides when you create them.

Title

Subtitle

Creating the title slide

Now the master slide is complete, you can select the **Close Master View** button and return to the normal slide view. A suitable title and subtitles can now be added, using the title slide that appears or by creating text boxes in a similar style to that shown to the right.

Activity 7

Add a suitable main heading and subtitle before moving on to the next session.

Review and revise

You should now be able to:

- create a new presentation document and save it with a suitable filename in a suitable location
- create and edit a master slide in order to set styles
- insert, edit and move text and objects within the master slide
- use bullets and numbering to help display lists within a slide.

SESSION 2.7 Adding text, images and multimedia elements to a presentation

Background

The presentation you are creating for True to Life Studios will provide on-screen information, images, text and speaker notes to help the presenter. In this session, you will find out about the following skills:

- adding new slides
- inserting images into a presentation
- editing, positioning and adjusting text and images
- adding text to a presentation
- adding speaker notes.

Tip

Remember all of the options and skills in this section can also be applied when using master slides as outlined in the previous session.

Adding new slides

Look at the following two slides, which demonstrate how space, size and the balance of text and imagery must be considered.

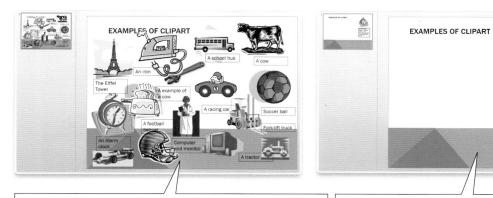

This slide has too much information. The images and text boxes clash and it would be difficult to read during a presentation.

This slide has too little information and lots of white space. To cover all the devices in your presentation in this way would take too many slides.

Activity 1

Add six pieces of ClipArt or Internet sourced graphics, and a short description of each to a new blank presentation slide. Choose three static and three animated images before carrying out the following:

- Experiment with the position and size of your text and graphics. When you are happy that a large audience could read the slide easily, compare with a friend and discuss.
- Discuss the differences between the animated and static graphics. Which would be the most appropriate for the presentation you are creating?

Presentation authoring software allows the creation of new slides based on the layout of content that will be added. You must decide which layout is the most appropriate.

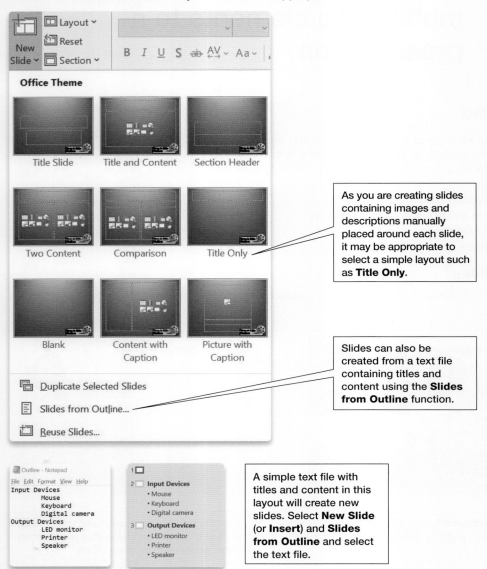

As you are creating slides containing images and descriptions manually placed around each slide, it may be appropriate to select a simple layout such as **Title Only**.

Slides can also be created from a text file containing titles and content using the **Slides from Outline** function.

A simple text file with titles and content in this layout will create new slides. Select **New Slide** (or **Insert**) and **Slides from Outline** and select the text file.

Activity 2

Open the presentation you've started for True to Life Studios. Each input and output device needs an image and a basic description, with the advantages and disadvantages included as speaker notes. Look again at the devices listed in Sessions 2.1 and 2.2. Decide how many slides you think you will need and create them within your presentation.

Activity 3

Before adding images to your presentation you need to research, download and save images for each of the devices listed in the theory sessions of this unit. Refer back to the guides on internet searches in Unit 1; some of the websites you researched then will be a good place to start.

Inserting images into a presentation

Images can be inserted into a presentation from many different sources. They may be stored on a CD-ROM of images, saved into a document area or imported directly from a digital camera or scanner. Select **Insert > Picture**.

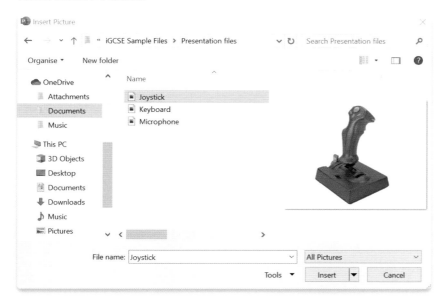

Activity 4

Insert your images of input and output devices onto the slides you created. You will need to consider the following when doing this:

- How many images can be placed on each slide without overcrowding it?
- Each image will need a title and short description, so leave space for this.
- Make sure the images do not overlap with the title, footer or any other graphics within the master slide.
- Make sure you keep saving your work as you progress through the project.

Editing, positioning and adjusting text and images

Presentation authoring software will normally include options to crop, resize and adjust the colour of an image. These options can be found by selecting an image and then **Picture Format** option from the ribbon menu. Alternatively right click on an image and select **Format Picture**.

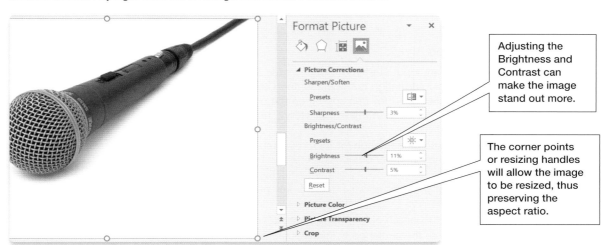

Adjusting the Brightness and Contrast can make the image stand out more.

The corner points or resizing handles will allow the image to be resized, thus preserving the aspect ratio.

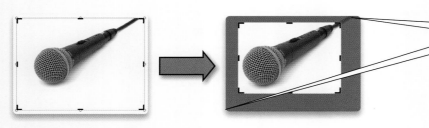

By dragging the corner crop points, unwanted areas can be removed.

The **Crop** tool can normally be found within the Format Picture toolbar or with the formatting toolbar.

Adding text to a presentation

Text is normally added using text boxes, which are created in the same style as the master slide created in Session 2.5. Depending on the slide layout of each slide, a text box for the title and main content may have already been created. The **Text Box** tool is used to create extra boxes that can be manually placed on the slide; to hold a short description, for example.

Adding speaker notes

Speaker (or presenter) notes are input at the bottom of a slide and are intended to provide additional information to the presenter. These do not appear to the general audience – they can appear on the presenter's own computer if the presentation is run in **Presenter view**. They might contain the following information:

- introductory notes about the presentation for the presenter, perhaps about the venue, or personal information about the presenter or the audience
- background information or prompts about images or key phrases shown to the audience
- timings for each topic, or the length of the whole presentation
- 'thank you' notes specific to the audience or information that must be passed on at the end.

The following two slides are examples of how speaker notes can be used. The slide above looks cluttered, while the slide below it looks more like the title slide of a presentation.

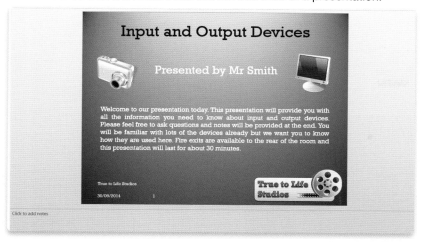

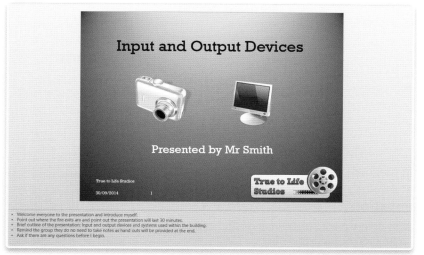

Activity 6

Using the information provided in this unit and additional information found using the internet, add speaker notes to describe the advantages and disadvantages of each device.

Adding video to a presentation

A video can be inserted into a presentation in a similar way to an image but there are few considerations to make before adding the video:

- The video file must be saved onto your computer and saved in the same file location as your presentation, this is because the presentation only links to the video placed upon the slide and it can disappear if the presentation and video are separated.
- Presentation software will often only accept certain video file types, so make sure you check which ones can be used.
- Does the video have sound? This should be considered as this can be a distraction and your presentation should be planned to accommodate it.

Tip

The following multimedia file types can be imported into a presentation:

Images: jpg, tiff, bmp, png, gif

Video: avi, mp4, mov, mpg, wmv

Sound: wav, mp3, mp4, aiff, midi, wma

Animated files: animated gif

Tip

Video editing and manipulation software is usually used to prepare videos before adding them to a presentation, as they often need to be trimmed to a certain length or screen size to fit appropriately into the presentation. Longer videos can also take up a large amount of file space.

Activity 7

Select two devices in your presentation that you could add a video for; a 3D printer would be a good example, and carry out the following:

- Investigate which video file formats your presentation package can accept.
- Come up with a list of sources you could use in order to find or create suitable videos.
- Add two videos to your presentation; these could replace the device images you have already found.

Adding sound to a presentation

Sound or music can be a good way to compliment a presentation and can be added to either play on its own within a slide or to accompany an animation or transition effect.

Activity 8

Add two sound effects to your presentation, the first should be a short music clip to play at the start of your first slide, the second should be a sound to accompany your slide transitions.

- Investigate which sound file formats your presentation package can accept.
- Come up with a list of sources you could use in order to find or create suitable audio files.
- Add the two sound effects using the notes in this session.

Review and revise

You should now be able to:

- add additional slides to a presentation based on the information required to be displayed
- insert, position and format multimedia objects into a presentation
- add, position and edit text boxes within a presentation
- use speaker notes to add additional written information about the contents of a slide.

SESSION 2.8 Adding animation, transitions and additional elements

Background

In this session, you will be shown the following skills:

- using shapes and lines to create graphics and diagrams
- adding a chart to a slide
- adding animation to images, text and other objects
- using slide transitions
- how to set up a presentation.

Creating graphics and additional elements

Using simple diagrams and text, you have been asked to explain the following:

- the building's alarm system
- how to input hand-drawn cartoon figures, colour them using the computer and present them to a project director
- how items are paid for at the company's own snack shop.

Activity 1

Sketch on paper three diagrams for these three systems, using the example shown in Session 2.3 as a guide. Discuss the variety of input and output devices that could be used.

Combining shapes and text

Simple shapes can also contain text, which is ideal for diagrams. Simply right click a shape and select **Edit Text**. You can then type within the shape, as you can in a text box.

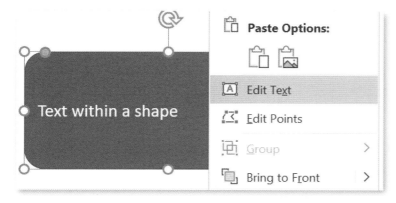
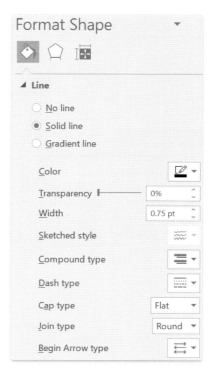

Using lines and arrows

A range of shapes and line drawing tools can be found by selecting **Insert** and then **Shapes** from the main ribbon. Having drawn a shape or line, the style can be adjusted via the right click menu and selecting **Format Shape**.

Using the tools demonstrated, create new slides in your True to Life Studios presentation to show the three diagrams you sketched in Activity 1. Each diagram should include text, shapes, lines and arrows.

Adding a chart

Most presentation packages will also allow a chart to be added, similar to the type produced in a spreadsheet application (see Session 3.6). Selecting **Insert > Chart** from the main menu will display the following options:

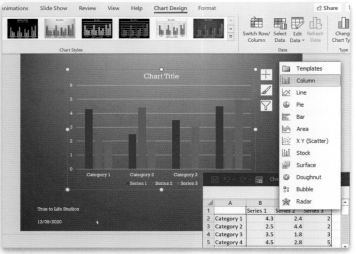
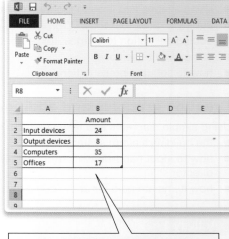

The sample data can be edited to use values and headings that are more relevant to your presentation.

The chart can then be customised by right clicking on any element. The following options are available:

- changing chart colours
- editing axis and segment labels
- editing or adding a title
- editing the original data.

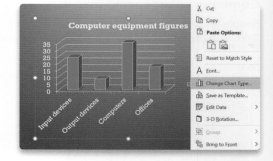

Activity 3

Add a chart to your True to Life Studios presentation, either using the data provided in Sampledata.csv on the digital download or by adding data of your own choice. Suggestions for charts might be:

- information about the company (for example, department and staff numbers)
- employee satisfaction results
- company sales figures.

Custom animation

Most presentation authoring packages offer a choice of built-in animations that can be applied to an object, image, shape or block of text. Most custom animations fall into the following categories:

- **Entrance:** The selected animation starts the moment the object appears.
- **Emphasis:** The animation runs while the slide is being shown on the screen.
- **Exit:** The selected animation is carried as the object disappears.
- **Motion Paths:** The chosen object follows a set path around the slide.

The following steps demonstrate the process of adding animation to objects. The process is the same for any object or style of animation.

Select an object and select **Animations** or **Add Animation** from the main menu. Then select a style of animation from four main categories. The following example shows an entrance animation being added to a simple car graphic. Once an animation style is selected, the Animation Pane will appear.

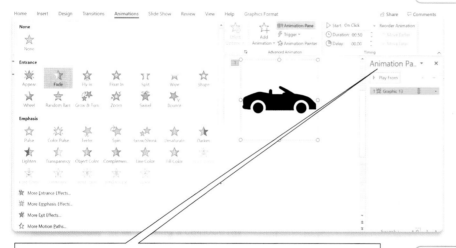

The following options are available when setting an animation:

- **Start:** selects whether the animation starts after the previous slide or following a key stroke
- **Direction:** changes the direction in which the car will appear
- **Duration:** sets the speed of the animation
- **Text Animation options:** allowing text to appear one line at a time.

Activity 4

Experiment with the following animation options, using the images and text you have already added to your presentation:

- Entrance effects such as Fly In or Fade
- Emphasis effects like Spin or Grow/Shrink
- Exit Effects like Split or Random Bars
- Timing options such as Mouse click and Delay
- Text animation on titles and bulleted text.

Working with a partner, discuss which styles of animation would be the most suitable for a business presentation.

Language

The word 'animation' in ICT means making an object change shape or move on-screen and can be used in many situations. Some examples are listed below.

Presentation software: Adding movement to objects and text when displayed to an audience.

Film making: Creating computer-generated characters in a three-dimensional environment.

Website design: Creating moving advertisements, menus and animated graphics.

Computer aided design (CAD): Manufacturers often create computer models of products, from automobiles to houses, and animate them to see what they would look like before building prototypes.

Slide transitions

The way one slide advances to the next on screen is called the transition. In a similar way to custom animation, most packages have a range of transition options, which can be selected from the **Transitions** menu.

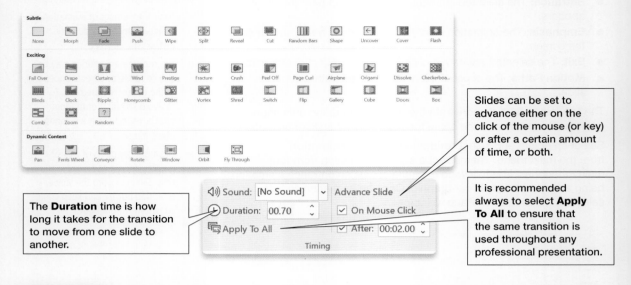

The **Duration** time is how long it takes for the transition to move from one slide to another.

Slides can be set to advance either on the click of the mouse (or key) or after a certain amount of time, or both.

It is recommended always to select **Apply To All** to ensure that the same transition is used throughout any professional presentation.

Activity 5

1 Experiment with the following transitions for your presentation:
   - Fades
   - Wipes
   - Star or shape transitions
   - Random settings.
2 Working with a partner, discuss which you think would be the most suitable for a business presentation.

Previewing effects

Although most presentation packages will preview effects as you add them, if you wish to view them as a complete slideshow, select **View Show** from the **Slide Show** menu or choose one of the options shown. At any time, press Esc to leave preview mode.

Suitability and consistency

Most authoring packages contain a wide selection of animation and transition effects. However, it is important to consider the audience for any presentation and to make choices that are consistent and do not distract from the information in the slides.

Activity 6

Experiment with transitions and animation and then choose a single transition to apply throughout. Add a small selection of animation effects that complement your work and will make it stand out when previewed.

Tip

A professional presentation should consider the following to maintain consistency when using transitions:

- Use only one transition style throughout the presentation so that it does not distract the viewers.
- Appropriate transition effects are fades, simple page wipes and dissolves. Try to avoid spinning or random effects.

Sorting slides into the right order

After having created a number of slides, it often becomes apparent that they are either in the wrong order, there is one slide too many or one has been missed. The **Slide Sorter** view within most presentation packages quickly allows changes to be made to a whole presentation.

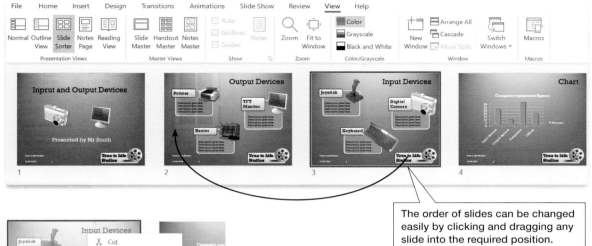

The order of slides can be changed easily by clicking and dragging any slide into the required position.

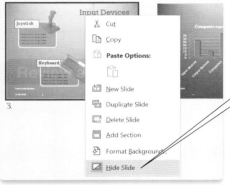

Occasionally, a slide might need to be hidden and restored at a later date. This can be achieved with the **Hide Slide** option.

Activity 7

Check the order of the slides you have created so far by using the **Slide Sorter** view. If possible, ask a friend to check the order as well.

Setting up a slide show

A range of options are available before presenting to an audience. Selecting **Slide Show > Set Up Slide Show** from the main menu will provide the following options.

Tip

If there are many different slides in the presentation, it is a common mistake to present them in the wrong order. This can confuse an audience and distract the presenter. Always check the order using the **Slide Sorter** view. If required, new slides can be added and unwanted ones deleted using the right click menu.

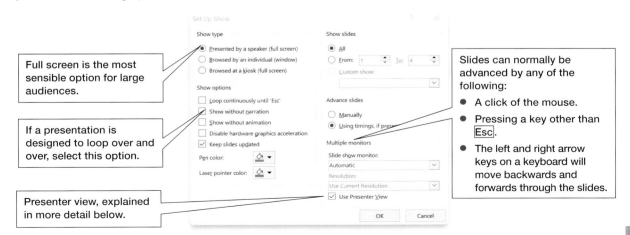

Full screen is the most sensible option for large audiences.

If a presentation is designed to loop over and over, select this option.

Presenter view, explained in more detail below.

Slides can normally be advanced by any of the following:

- A click of the mouse.
- Pressing a key other than Esc.
- The left and right arrow keys on a keyboard will move backwards and forwards through the slides.

Presenter view

Presenter view is used when connecting to an external display such as a projector or large additional monitor. It allows the main presentation to be displayed to the audience while the presenter sees a more detailed view that includes:

- any speaker notes that have been written for each slide
- how the current slide fits into the whole presentation
- any rehearsed or set timings.

Review and revise

You should now be able to:

- create custom graphics using lines and shapes
- add a chart to a presentation
- add suitable animation and slide transitions to a presentation
- set up a presentation based on presenter and audience requirements.

SESSION 2.9 Finalising and displaying your presentation

Background

Having completed your presentation for True to Life Studios, you will need to make final checks before you deliver it. In this session, you will find information on the following:

- checking the completed presentation for spelling and graphical errors
- saving your work in a suitably compressed format
- printing notes for the audience, taking into account the needs of the audience of any presentation.

Checking for errors

Spelling errors

Most presentation authoring packages have the ability to check for spelling errors. These can then be corrected automatically or manually edited, depending on the type of error. Spell checks can be carried out by looking for the **Spelling icon** shown or right clicking with the mouse on errors that will appear as underlined.

Graphical errors

Graphical errors are not automatically picked up, so it is important to check a presentation visually before presenting it as complete. Many errors come from the way text, graphics and images are arranged on-screen, but these can be easily rectified by **proofreading** your work.

The following example shows objects overlapping each other.

Selecting each object and right clicking the mouse on it allows the order to be changed using the **Bring to front** and **Send to back** options.

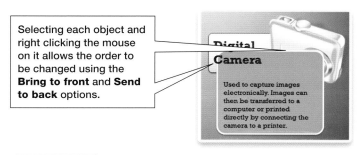

Activity 1

Do a spelling check on your presentation and then proofread it for any graphical errors. Make any changes that are needed until all errors are removed.

Saving a presentation

A **multimedia** presentation (containing text, images, music, sound and animation) can result in a larger-than-average file that can be difficult to email or transfer using portable storage devices. The **file size** can be made slightly smaller by using file **compression** software or by lowering the **resolution** of the images used. Images used in presentations are often larger than they need to be for a screen-based presentation.

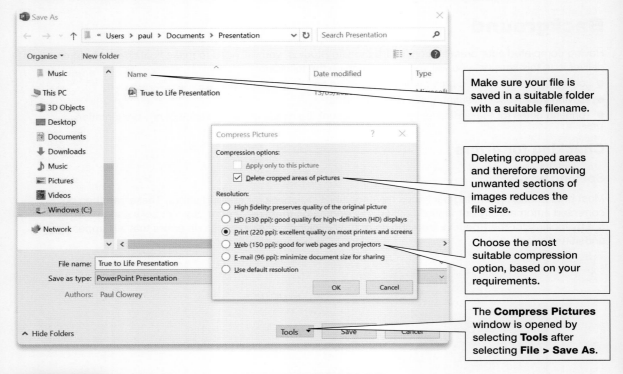

Make sure your file is saved in a suitable folder with a suitable filename.

Deleting cropped areas and therefore removing unwanted sections of images reduces the file size.

Choose the most suitable compression option, based on your requirements.

The **Compress Pictures** window is opened by selecting **Tools** after selecting **File > Save As**.

Activity 2

Check the order of the slides you have created so far by using the **Slide Sorter** view. If possible, ask a friend to check the order as well.

Printing audience notes

Selecting **File > Print** will present a number of printing options.

Although a presentation is normally designed to be displayed on a screen, there are times when a paper-based version is appropriate and there are a number of options available. Most presentation authoring packages can print slides in the following ways:

● Print each complete slide to one page.
● Print multiple slides to one page: usually 2, 3, 4, 6 or 9.
● Print single slides with speaker notes printed beneath them.

Tip

Remember that once a presentation has been compressed, this cannot be undone. Therefore, if a high-quality version of the file is needed for printing, you should save an original copy and compress a duplicate of it.

Language

Image compression settings often use 'ppi', which stands for Points Per Inch and refers to the number of pixels an image is made up of. The higher the ppi value, the more detailed the image.

3 Slides: Useful for annotating a presentation, either during or afterwards. Each slide has space for notes at the side; this could be used to describe animation in a school project or for making extra notes during a presentation.

4 to 9 Slides: Generally used as a quick paper copy of a presentation. Useful for presentations containing multiple slides.

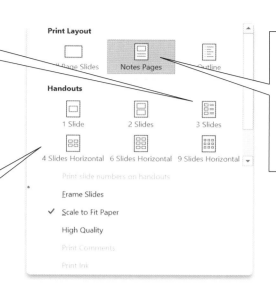

Notes Pages: Produces a single slide per page with any speaker notes written about it below. Useful for handing out copies after a presentation to an audience who would benefit from reading the extra notes.

Activity 3

Your presentation is also to be handed out as a guide and the extra speaker notes would be useful to staff. Choose the most appropriate options and print your presentation.

Review and revise

You should now be able to:

- check a completed presentation for spelling and graphical errors
- save a presentation with and without the images compressed
- print audience notes in a variety of formats, including notes and handout view, to meet the needs of the audience.

2 Practical review

What have you covered?

In these five practical sessions, you have:

- discovered how to create a new presentation
- practised designing a suitable master slide, in keeping with the companies house style and considering the needs of the audience
- created (and inserted) slides in your presentation
- practised combining text/images/sounds/video/animation/charts/speaker notes/shapes/lines to create visually attractive functional slides within your presentation
- investigated the use of animation on objects and transitions on slide changes
- saved your work in a suitable format and location
- compared different ways of producing audience notes, such as printing one or more slides per page or with presenter notes.

Some practice questions

You are going to create a short presentation for a vet who runs a parrot sanctuary.

1 Copy into your presentation authoring software the five blocks of text from the file **PeteParrot.rtf**.

You should have five slides, including one with bullet points.

2 Set the master slide as follows:

- background – dark blue
- heading font – pale blue, serif font, 40 point, bold, centred
- first level text font – white, serif, 28 point
- bullet points – white, serif, 20 point
- remove date (if automatically inserted)
- slide numbers – white, serif, 10 point, bold, displayed in the bottom centre of the slide
- your name should be in a separate text box in the bottom right corner – size, colour and style of your choice.

3 Insert a new slide before slide 1. Use a layout of title and subtitle for this slide. Ensure that the background, slide numbers and your name all match the master slide settings.

4 Add the Title: **Pete's Parrot Sanctuary**.

Add the Subtitle: **Looking after abandoned parrots**.

The title and subtitle should be in a sans-serif font, an appropriate size and red.

5 Place the picture **BlueGoldMacaw.gif** in the centre of the slide behind the titles.

Enlarge the image so that it is not less than 75 per cent of the height of the slide and make sure the aspect ratio is maintained.

6 Move slide 6 to be 3.

7 Delete the slide that is now number 6.

8 Insert a pie chart below the text on slide 3. If you know how, you can alter the data to make the chart more relevant to the presentation (using the data in the file **GeographicalArea.rtf**). However, it is not essential as you'll learn more about this in the following unit.

9 Apply animation to the bullet points on slide 4. They are to appear one at a time on the click of the mouse.

10 Change the format of slide 5 to have text on the left and space for an image on the right.

11 Place the picture **patagonian.jpg** to the right of the text in slide 5.

Enlarge the image so that it is about 50 per cent of the height of the slide and make sure that the aspect ratio is maintained.

12 Insert a new slide at the end of your presentation and remove all the layout boxes other than the title. Add the Title: Typical parrot habitat and insert the video Typical Habitat. mp4 and position it below the title. Set the video to launch as soon as the slide is opened.

13 Insert the sound effect Squark.mp4 to play on the first slide as the image of the BlueGoldMacaw appears.

14 Insert the animated image world.mp4 to the slide containing the chart in a suitable location and size it appropriately.

15 Choose a transition style and apply it to movement between all slides.

16 Check the consistency of formatting between all slides.

17 Save the presentation as **Pete's Parrots Presentation**.

When answering this type of question, it is important that you pay attention to the instructions, particularly:

- the position of the components on the master slide

- font, style and size: serif or sans-serif
- the consistency of formatting across all slides, especially if text is imported from another source.

Progress check

Aiming for good progress

- You are confident in setting up a master slide with all the standard features: slide numbering, consistent font, style, size and colour.
- You are able to import text or slides from another source into your presentation.
- You are able to import an image to a slide, being careful about its position.
- You are able to import a sound file or effect into your presentation.
- You can apply appropriate animation that takes place on a mouse click.
- You can print slides, one to a page.
- You can add transition effects that appear when you click to change slides.

Aiming for excellent progress

- You can confidently set up a master slide with required features, including images, shapes and lines.
- You can adjust the automatic settings so that, for example, the page number does not appear on the first slide.
- You can apply appropriate animation that can take place after a set time, not just after mouse clicks.
- You can apply appropriate and consistent transitions between slides, including timings if required.
- You ensue that the slide content is consistent across all slides and the content is not just checked for accuracy but appropriate for the audience.
- You can change the layout of slides and hide slides if necessary.
- You can import images, sound, video, animated files and charts into your slides, being careful about position and size.

3 Storage devices and media

Why this unit matters

Every year we save more and more information on computer systems and the need for data storage capacity keeps increasing. Data files, records, pictures, music, films, games and applications all require storage space. A few years ago, we only kept a few files on our computers, but we are now using computers at home, work and school.

I use a high-resolution digital SLR camera for still images and a dedicated high definition video camera for video. Both of these devices capture imagery at very high resolution, providing lots of detail but creating very large computer files. I need high capacity memory cards and computer drives to store and access my work. (Professional digital photographer)

From high resolution X-rays to patient records and training documents, lots of information is now stored on computers, making information easier to access from anywhere in the hospital. This information must be electronically secure from unauthorized access and backed up. If any of the original computer information is lost, another copy must be made available quickly. (Hospital worker)

Customers are often unsure about how much storage they need and want advice on the best way to back up their files. The advice we give must be based on the needs of the user. For example, a young family with a computer full of photos, videos and games will need more storage capacity than an author writing a book using a word processor. (Computer store manager)

Your practical task

You work for a new international bank called Abacus. The business prides itself on using the latest technological advances and incorporating them into its high street branches all around the world. You are responsible for making sure that computer information is stored and backed up at each branch and for ensuring that all staff are kept up-to-date with the methods used. Banking information is highly confidential and the risks to security, should any data be lost, are taken very seriously. Employees must use storage and backup methods correctly, and training documents are regularly produced.

You have been asked to:
- produce a training document for staff involved with storing and backing up data; it explains the different devices, media and methods available
- create a simple spreadsheet and chart that compares the storage capacities of different devices
- create an additional leaflet explaining electronic banking methods to new employees.

What this unit covers

THEORY

Sessions

3.1   Storage devices and media

3.2   The importance of data backup

3.3   Banking facilities today

Theory review

PRACTICAL

Sessions

3.4   Document preparation

3.5   Adding text and images to a document

3.6   Creating a simple data model and chart

3.7   Final document checks and presentation

Practical review

By the end of this unit you will be able to:

- describe a variety of storage devices and media, together with common uses for each
- explain the advantages and disadvantages of different methods in terms of speed, access, use and cost
- understand the importance of regularly backing up data
- describe the various electronic methods and communication systems used in banking today.

In your practical work, you will develop and apply skills in:

- communicating using document production skills
- document creation; combining text, images and graphical elements in your work
- creating and using a simple spreadsheet model
- saving, checking and printing your work
- using file compression to assist with storage and electronic transmission.

SESSION 3.1 Storage devices and media

Background

In this session, you will look at the many different storage devices and media used today, as well as their uses, capacities and differences.

The difference between storage devices and media

A storage device is something that has the ability to read and write information to and from storage media, for example, a CD/DVD writer or tape drive. The components that store the information, such as CD/DVDs, hard disks and memory cards, are storage media.

Storage technology

The technology used in modern storage devices and media comes in three varieties, each with its own characteristics.

- **Magnetic:** stores data in tiny magnetic dots on a disk or tape, organised to store binary data.
- **Optical:** uses a laser to read, and write, a binary dot pattern on a spinning disc.
- **Solid State:** uses non-volatile memory chips to store data electronically with no moving parts.

> **Activity 1**
>
> Write a list of all the things at home – not just computers – that you think can store electronic information. Compare and discuss your answers with a friend.

Storage devices and media: their advantages and disadvantages

Description		Advantages	Disadvantages
	Fixed magnetic hard disks: found in most computers as the main storage device. Use complex magnetic components. **Storage device using direct access**	• Their capacity is constantly increasing as prices are decreasing. • Fast access; data can be read from any part of the disk (this is known as random access).	• Due to their mechanical complexity, physical errors are extremely difficult to fix. • Limited life span; data should be transferred every few years. • Slightly slower to access than internal memory.
	Portable magnetic hard disk drives: a portable version of the hard disk. Ideal for transferring data from one computer to another and also used to increase a system's storage capacity. Also known as a removable hard disk drive. **Storage device using direct access**	• They can often be powered using the connecting USB cable. • Portable hard disk drives add extra storage capacity to a computer without having to open the computer casing.	• Similar to a larger hard disk; difficult to repair and a limited life span. • Slightly slower to access than internal memory. • Capacity is not as large as a standard hard disk.
	Magnetic tapes: used most commonly for large scale data storage and backup. **Storage media using serial or sequential access**	• A low cost way of storing hundreds of gigabytes of data. • Information can be set to back up overnight or outside of office hours. • Tapes are portable and can be stored safely.	• A special drive is required to read and write data to them. • Access is much slower than a normal hard drive. (Serial access, see page 112) • Not really practical for day-to-day storage and retrieval.

Description		Advantages	Disadvantages
	Optical CD/DVD: optical disk, normally used in retail for music releases and films to be played on home entertainment systems. **Storage media using direct access**	• Low cost due to mass production. • A world-wide standard; both CD and DVD players are widely available. • No moving parts and require no power supply. • Long lifespan if stored carefully.	• Scratches can make them unreadable. • Information is read-only.
	CD/DVD-ROM: optical disk, used to store commercial computer software such as an encyclopaedia, game or installation disk. **Storage media using direct access**	• Similar to that of CD/DVD disks. • Large software packages can be easily distributed.	• Similar to that of CD/DVD disks. • If damaged, software must usually be purchased again.
	CD/DVD-R (Media): optical disk that can be written with data or media files once only. Used for backups and writing music CDs. **Storage media using direct access**	• Low cost due to mass production. • Most computers have the ability to read and write disks. • A long lifespan; some manufacturers claiming at least 50 years. • Disks can be left open and added to until they are full.	• Similar to that of CD/DVD disks. • Errors can occur during writing, making the disk unusable. • Data cannot be erased.
	CD/DVD-RW: optical disk that can be written with computer or media files, erased and used again. **Storage media using direct access**	• Similar to that of CD/DVD-R disks. • Each part of the disk can be erased and rewritten hundreds of times.	• Lifespan is thought not to be as long as other optical disks. • Disks may stop working due to repetitive erasing and rewriting. • Not all disk players can play rewritable disks.
	DVD-RAM: similar to a DVD-R but designed to be more robust, with quicker access. **Storage media using direct access**	• Rewritable and protected from damage in a plastic case. • Designed and manufactured to a higher standard than standard CD/DVD-RW to last longer.	• More expensive than standard optical disks. • Less compatible with household players. • Slower to write than standard writable disks.
	Blu-ray: a high-capacity optical disk used for high-definition movies, computer and console games, and data backup. **Storage media using direct access**	• Able to store full-length high-definition films and modern computer and console games. • Up to 10 times the capacity of DVD disks. • Disks very difficult to copy, preventing piracy.	• Writable Blu-ray disks are expensive and require a Blu-ray compatible drive. • Commercial usage limited to entertainment media. • Blu-ray content more expensive than standard DVDs. • Already being replaced by Ultra HD Blu-ray.

Description		Advantages	Disadvantages
	Solid state memory: uses microchips to store information with no moving parts; found in portable drives and memory cards. **Storage media using direct access**	• Less susceptible to shock and damage. • Silent. • Faster read and write times than standard hard disks. • Used as a high-speed replacement for magnetic storage. • Ideal for portable devices.	• Practically impossible to repair if damaged. • Lower storage capabilities than hard disks. • Price per gigabyte of storage is higher than hard disks. • Vulnerable to electrical or magnetic interference.
	Pen drives: extremely portable solid state memory storage devices; designed to plug into the widely used USB port. **Storage media using direct access**	• Ideal for pocket and key-ring size devices. • USB sockets are found on the majority of computers. • Require no additional power.	• Similar to that of all solid state drives. • Can be easily misplaced or lost.
	Flash memory cards: used to expand storage in smart devices, games consoles and digital still/video cameras. **Storage media using direct access**	• Thumbnail-sized cards becoming common place. • Cost-effective way of adding additional storage to devices with limited storage. • Common standards include SD, MicroSD, xD and CFast.	• Smaller micro-style cards are easy to lose. • Many different models, each with slightly different connectors.

Describing storage devices and media

Different devices access and use memory in different ways. The following terms may be referred to when describing storage devices and media.

Main or internal memory: Memory used by a computer system when processing or storing information. Random Access Memory (RAM) can be read and written to while using programs; the more RAM a system has, the faster it will run. Read Only Memory (ROM) holds permanent data that cannot be changed; it is normally used to store the essential program drivers (or firmware) needed to start your computer.

Backing storage: Any type of data storage device apart from RAM or ROM. This includes the hard disk drive found inside most PCs and normally used to store data permanently, even when the computer is turned off.

Serial or sequential access: Data is stored in a sequential sequence so that information stored can only be accessed by scanning through the data to that point. Tapes are an example of this type of storage.

Direct/random access: Any piece of information stored on a random access device can be accessed without having to scan through its whole contents. This is much faster than serial access.

Connectivity: Many computers may use an internal drive to read storage media, but external devices can also be connected by USB, USB-C, FireWire, Ethernet cables or by using Wi-Fi networking.

Access speeds: This is how quickly a user can access the information on any storage device. Access speeds are measured in 'bytes per second' (Bps) with slower devices measured in thousands (KBps) and faster devices using millions (MBps). A user's choice of device may depend on how quickly they need to access data. Individual device speeds vary but generally speaking the following is true:

- **Magnetic tape drives:** Slow to access as the drive has to fast-forward or rewind to the required section.
- **Optical storage:** A modern compact disk will have an access speed of about 8 MBps, DVD about 20 MBps and Blu-ray disks 18 MBps.

Real world

The lifespan of any new technology is notoriously difficult to predict, as long-term tests are rarely done before it is put on sale. If a device has only been around for a few years, it is not certain how long it will work or keep the information that it stores. One thing that is agreed upon is that no one method should be relied upon as a permanent solution. A DVD-R can hold seven times the amount of data as a CD-R, and Blu-ray disks can store 10 times that of a DVD. Who knows what the next development will be?

- **Magnetic hard disk storage:** Modern drives can have access speeds of around 200 MBps.
- **Solid state based storage:** As there are no moving parts and flash based memory is much quicker to read and write, access speeds of over 500 MBps are possible.

Storage capacity

The table below provides some typical capacities, but it should be noted that hard disks and solid state drives are constantly increasing in storage capacity.

Storage device or media	Typical capacities (at the time of publication)
CD*	700 megabytes (MB)
DVD*	4.7 or 8.54 gigabytes (GB) (single or dual layer)
DVD RAM*	4.7 or 9.4 GB (single or dual layer)
Blu-ray*	25 or 50 GB (single or dual layer)
Pen drive**	2–64 GB
Flash memory cards**	2–64 GB
Portable disk drive**	320 GB–4TB
Solid state drive**	500 GB–2 TB
Magnetic disk drive**	1–8 TB
Magnetic tape**	500 GB to 5 TB

* Generally fixed manufacturing standards

** These capacities are constantly being increased as manufacturing techniques develop.

File sizes

When matching usage to storage devices, it is important to consider approximate sizes for different types of files.

8 bits	1 byte
1024 bytes	1 kilobyte (KB)
1024 kilobytes	1 megabyte (MB)
1024 megabytes	1 gigabyte (GB)
1024 gigabytes	1 terabyte (TB)

Word processed document	100 KB
eBook	500 KB
Mp3 track	5 MB
Digital photo	3 MB
Film	1.2 GB

THEORY

Real world

Every year we increase the amount of data we store; documents, photos, videos, games and music. This means file compression, using ZIP and RAR utilities is increasingly useful for storing and archiving files or reducing file sizes when emailing.

Language

Pen drives are sometimes referred to as **USB** or memory sticks.

Real world

There are many types of memory cards available today, and different manufacturers often create their own for a specific type of device. Look at the devices that you and your friends own, from cameras to mobile phones and portable gaming machines – how many different types of memory card do you use?

Activity 2

1 Create a short survey and ask classmates or friends to estimate how many of each of the following types of files they own electronically:

music tracks, **eBooks**, films, digital photos, office documents.

2 Combine your survey results with the approximate sizes above to estimate how much information the people you surveyed own. Which devices would be the most appropriate to store the data they own?

sl

Evaluating storage devices

It is important to choose the best device, based on the users' needs and considering the characteristics, advantages and disadvantages of each. The diagram below illustrates the main considerations when choosing a suitable storage device.

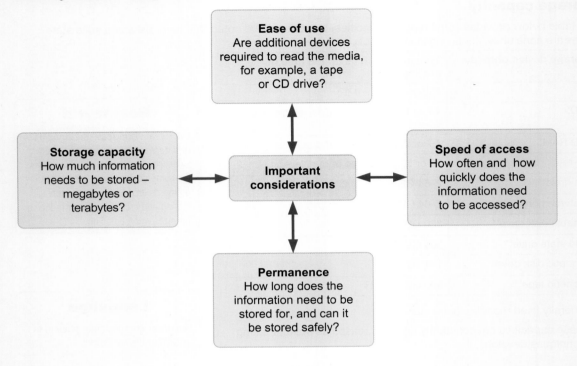

Ease of use
Are additional devices required to read the media, for example, a tape or CD drive?

Storage capacity
How much information needs to be stored – megabytes or terabytes?

Important considerations

Speed of access
How often and how quickly does the information need to be accessed?

Permanence
How long does the information need to be stored for, and can it be stored safely?

Activity 3

Using the storage considerations diagram as a guide, discuss in small groups the following situations, and decide on the best storage options.

1   Taking a report home to work on.
2   In an architect's office, using **CAD** to create building plans and graphics software to see what new buildings might look like.
3   In a music recording studio, using computers to record and then edit multiple audio tracks, from singers to instruments and percussion.

Review and revise

You should now be able to:

- describe the most common forms of storage devices and related media
- identify common uses for storage devices, including types of access and access speeds
- consider the different capacities available and define the difference between main/internal memory and storage
- explain the advantages and disadvantages of different methods in terms of speed, access, use and cost.

SESSION 3.2 The importance of data backup

Background

The phrase 'backing up' essentially means making an extra copy of computer information so that, in the event of a problem, loss of the original file, or damage to the computer, the backup copy can be used as a replacement. This session will look at the importance of backing up data and the various methods available.

What should be backed up?

In an ideal world, if the cost of storage space was no object, every system would be backed up. A backup copy of your home computer would include the **operating system**, program files, personal documents, device drivers and everything else on your computer. Unfortunately this is not always possible, so a choice has to be made about what to back up. Operating systems can be re-installed from disks and programs can be downloaded again, but photographs of your holiday or that last school report you wrote could not be replaced without being re-created.

This is even more important for organisations. Hospitals and banks, for example, store important, private information – and if that information became lost or **corrupted**, then lives and businesses could be at risk.

> **Activity 1**
>
> Think about the main computer in your home, or in a family member's home. What kind of important information is stored on it? Create a list of what you come up with and then, in a small group, discuss what might happen if that information were suddenly lost.

> **Activity 2**
>
> Create a table with the following headings:
> - School
> - A graphic designer
> - Designing the pages of a popular newspaper
> - Hospital
>
> For each heading, write a list of all the information you think would be important to back up, and describe what would happen if it were lost.

Backup models

The following are popular methods for backing up information.

- Manually choosing a selection of files to be saved onto a disk. This is useful for backing up a small selection of essential files. It is known as 'an unstructured backup'.
- Creating a copy of every file, both personal documents and system files, stored on a computer hard drive in case of a serious failure. This is often called creating an 'image' of a computer. There are software tools that can do this, but it does take time, which means it isn't suitable for regular use. This is referred to as 'a full system backup'.
- After a full system backup, backups are made at regular intervals of whatever has changed since the initial and following backups. This means that only small amounts of information are regularly saved, and users can look back at a system at a specified date in the past. This is known as 'an incremental backup'.
- If a fire burns down an office of computers and the backup drive is permanently plugged in, then it, too, will be lost. Using an off-site backup minimises the risk of losing data by making sure the drive or disks used are kept elsewhere, ideally in a secure location. This is called 'an off-site backup'.

> **Real world**
>
> There are manufacturers that claim to have created indestructible storage devices that can withstand fire, water, pressure and physical damage. These usually work by encasing the storage medium in a protective box.

> **Real world**
>
> Security concerns about the information we store has increased in recent years, especially as more and more personal data is being stored using **cloud computing** and therefore accessible via the internet. Data **encryption** scrambles computer files so that they can only be read with the correct encryption key.

Backup solutions

Depending on the needs of the user, there are a number of solutions available, ranging from practical to commercial options.

- **Manually copying files.** This is often the simplest solution and involves plugging in a USB hard disk and copying files to it on a regular basis.
- **Software backup.** There are numerous software solutions that will copy selected files to a backup drive at a selected time. This prevents people from forgetting to backup and can be set to happen when the computer is not used – late at night, for example.
- **Mirroring (often referred to as RAID).** Two or more compatible hard disks are linked in such a way that information is written to them both at the same time, creating clones of each other. If one drive fails, the other is still accessible.
- **Online or remote backup.** Rather than backing up files to a physical device, files are backed up via the internet to an online server. This is usually done via **third party software** installed on a computer. There are many businesses that offer this service, and price is based on the amount of storage required and the number of access features. Storing files online is a key element of **cloud computing**.

Language

Cloud computing is the term for accessing computer files, documents and programs remotely, either via a network or more commonly via the internet. This takes away the need for local storage devices and information can be accessed almost anywhere.

Activity 3

Research and discuss with your class the backup facilities built into Windows, Apple and **Linux** operating systems and compare the features they offer to third party solutions.

Review and revise

You should now be able to:
- understand the importance of regularly backing up data
- explain a variety of methods for carrying out backups.

SESSION 3.3 Banking facilities today

Background

Modern banking terminology

- **Electronic funds transfer (EFT).** This is used for paying by Chip and PIN or contactless payment (see Session 2.2) in shops and transferring money from one bank account to another, anywhere in the world. It may be a regular bill payment or payroll deposits. These can either be set up in person or electronically.

- **Automated teller machine (ATM).** Normally installed in public places, these installations have a direct communications link to a bank. They can release money and debit it from an account and can also manage some basic banking facilities. These include checking the balance or printing a mini-statement, paying bills or making money transfers. It is also possible to make cash and cheque deposits, usually by placing it in a specially provided envelope and sliding it into the ATM.

- **Credit and debit cards.** Used as an alternative to cash, this allows stores and organisations to debit money from an account for goods or services. Customers have a card and a PIN number. When the card is scanned and the PIN number entered correctly, it allows the store to contact the customer's bank. If the customer has sufficient funds, then the amount is deducted from their account and credited to the store. Information about magnetic stripe, Chip and PIN devices and contactless payments can be found in Session 2.2.

- **Cheques.** Rather than using cash, a cheque allows money to be withdrawn from one account and deposited in another. It contains the name and account details of the sender and the full name of the recipient. Being a paper-based system, it is often claimed to be the slowest way to transfer money as it needs to be checked and 'cleared' before money is transferred.

Real world

Many businesses are now introducing contactless payment systems that allow an individual to wave a debit/credit card or smart device over the reader that then automatically debits the users account. These are generally targeted at small value payments that would benefit from faster transactions such as queuing and paying for a coffee or snack. These systems use radio-frequency identification (RFID).

Modern communication methods and banking

It is becoming less and less essential to actually visit bank branches. Checking and changing balances, paying bills or applying for new accounts can all be done from home or from the office.

- **Telephone banking**. Done via either a conversation with a banking **call centre** or an automated system that responds using **voice recognition software** or telephone keypad choices.

- **Internet banking**. Account details are accessed through a **secure webpage** that provides direct access to a full range of account functions from setting up transfers to paying bills to applying for new products, overdrafts and updating personal details. Secure login and password details must be setup before use.

- **Mobile phone access**. Applications (or **apps**) are increasingly being produced that give direct access to a particular bank and account details, providing almost instant access to information wherever you are, without the need for a computer and browser.

Activity 1

Consider the following situations and describe the banking facilities that would be the most appropriate and why the different people might use them.

1   A university student living away from home.
2   An electronics store selling computers and mobile phones.
3   A retired couple who have moved to a remote rural house.

Advantages and disadvantages of modern electronic banking methods

Advantages	Disadvantages
• Instant access without having to visit a branch in person.	• **Identity theft** is a real concern as banks rarely see customers in person.
• Money can be transferred instantaneously to anywhere in the world.	• Mobile phone access requires a reliable data connection.
• Customers do not have to wait for monthly postal statements to check their balance and recent transactions.	• Users are constantly sent **spam** emails, asking them to confirm, and therefore, give away login details. This is called **phishing**.
• Banks can spot fraud activity more quickly by analysing patterns in your spending and online transactions.	• Those without internet access often miss out on the latest deals and interest rates.
• Additional functionality can be accessed online such as controlling overdraft levels, changing Chip and PIN codes or pay bills directly.	• Transactions using physical currency such as cash and cheques cannot be made.
• Customers with limited mobility can access full services remotely.	• An internet-based bank could potentially be closed at any time due to technical problems.

Activity 2

What do you think are the biggest security problems associated with the systems outlined in this session? Discuss your thoughts with your classmates.

Activity 3

Considering the storage devices and media described in the previous sessions, list the types of information that a bank would have to store on a daily basis. In small groups, discuss and decide on the most appropriate storage devices and media. Explain your choices.

Real world

Two-step verification is a system that requires two pieces of security data in order to access an online system, for example a password and an extra security code. This provides an extra level of protection should your password be lost or stolen and many **ecommerce** systems, including banks, require customers to use it.

Review and revise

You should now be able to:

● describe the various electronic methods and communication systems used in banking today
● explain the advantages and disadvantages of different methods in terms of use and purpose.

3 Theory review

What have you covered?

In these three theory sessions, you have:
- been introduced to the most common forms of storage devices and related media
- explored the most common uses for different storage devices and their capacities
- considered the most suitable application for different capacities of storage devices
- discovered the difference between main and internal memory and storage
- reviewed the advantages and disadvantages of different storage methods in terms of speed, access, use and cost
- come to understand the importance of backing up data regularly
- been introduced to a variety of methods for carrying out backups
- explored the various electronic methods and communication systems used in banking today
- reviewed the advantages and disadvantages of different methods in terms of use and purpose.

Some practice questions

1 Draw lines to connect the images on the left with the best example of its use on the right.

Fixed hard disk

Pen drive

Memory card

Magnetic tape

Storage device in a digital camera
Business wanting to take a weekly file backup
A student transferring a homework file to the school network
The main backing storage device in a desktop computer

See Session 3.1

2 For each of the devices below, indicate with a tick whether it is a magnetic, optical or solid state device.

	Magnetic	Optical	Solid state
Portable hard drive			
DVD			
RAM chip			
DVD RAM			
Tape			

See Session 3.1

3 Link the media type on the left with its most appropriate use on the right.

Hard disk drive
Magnetic tape
Flash memory
Pen drive
CD/DVD

Backup of files in a large commercial organisation
Storing images in a camera
Main storage in a desktop computer
Storage of film or music files
Temporary storage and transfer of files between computers

See Session 3.1

4 a A computer's internal memory consists of RAM and ROM. Each has different characteristics and uses. Fill in the missing words with either RAM or ROM:

_____ is non-volatile memory.

When we are using a computer, the program we are using and the data we type in will be held in _____.

The computer's basic input output system (BIOS) will be stored in _____.

When the computer is turned off the contents of _____ is lost.

b In the mid-1980s, personal computers had their operating system stored on ROM, so that as soon as you switched the computer on it was ready for use. Why do you think that today's desktop computers do not have the latest operating systems on ROM, but instead have it on the computer's hard disk?

See Session 3.2

5 Sergeiy runs a small business selling eBooks. Every week he runs a backup program.

a What is a backup?

b There are different types of backups, which depend on what exactly will be backed up. Sergeiy had a complete backup taken when he started this routine. Now his program just takes a copy of recently changed files. Give one advantage to Sergeiy of running a backup like this.

c Give *two* reasons why Sergeiy runs this program every week.

d Sergeiy receives an email from a company that offers a remote, or online, backup facility. The email tells him that for a yearly fee the company would hold copies of his files on their remote server. Sergeiy is not sure whether this backup service would be of use to him and asks for your advice. State the main reason that Sergeiy might want to make use of this service.

e State *one* reason that Sergeiy might choose not to use this service.

f How might Sergeiy still have the benefit of this type of backup, but without using a company like the one that contacted him?

See Session 3.2

6 a Identify *three* ways that a person can check his or her bank account balance without having to go to the bank itself.

b Many people are concerned about the increasing use of technology in personal banking. The biggest concerns are security of personal information and access to information. Describe *two* ways in which the bank makes sure that the personal details of customers are secure.

c How does the bank make sure that only authorised people access customer details?

See Session 3.3

Progress check

Aiming for good progress

- You are able to identify the main types of storage devices.
- You can determine which type of storage device might be used for a given application.
- You can distinguish between the different types of internal memory.
- You can describe the different types of backup methods.

Aiming for excellent progress

- You can describe the main types of storage devices.
- You can justify the choice of a particular storage device for a given application.
- You can identify the uses of RAM and ROM.
- You can justify a choice of backup method, depending on the user's requirements.
- You appreciate the concerns of bank customers regarding security of, and access to, personal details, and understand how the banking system addresses these concerns.

SESSION 3.4 Document preparation

Background

Working for an international bank called Abacus, you have been asked to produce a training document using suitable word processing software. This will inform the staff who are involved in backing up and storing data all about storage devices and media.

In this session, you will find out how to do the following:

- create a new document
- design a suitable page layout in keeping with the company house style
- save your work in a suitable format and location.

In the practical sessions throughout this unit you will reinforce and extend some document production skills.

Create a new document

In Session 1.7 you opened a document and imported data from existing files. In this unit you will create a new document. Shown below is a typical word processing package. Select **File > New** and you will get the following screen.

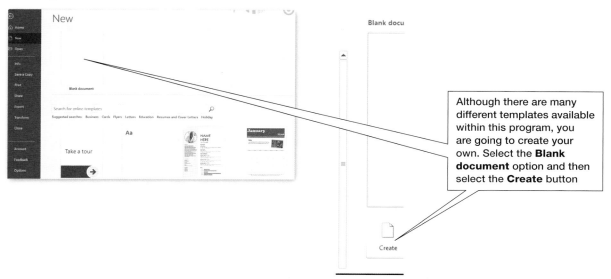

Although there are many different templates available within this program, you are going to create your own. Select the **Blank document** option and then select the **Create** button

Saving and file location

It is important that the file you have created has a suitable filename and location. This means that you can regularly save your work as you progress, and you will easily be able to find your work at a later date.

Activity 1

Set up a folder on your computer, and within it save a new blank document using suitable file and folder names.

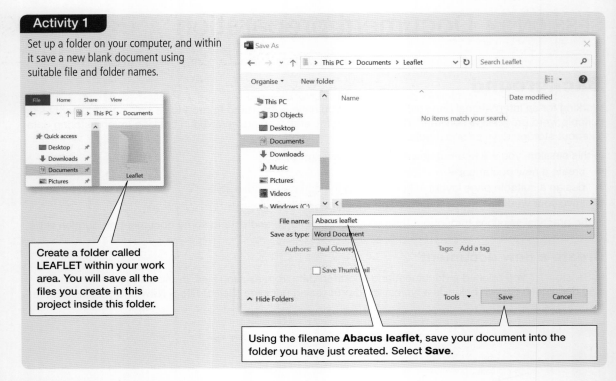

Create a folder called **LEAFLET** within your work area. You will save all the files you create in this project inside this folder.

Using the filename **Abacus leaflet**, save your document into the folder you have just created. Select **Save**.

Designing a suitable page layout

Before adding information, it is important to set the page layout to suit the type of document you intend to produce. You will change the following properties of a document:

- page size, margins and orientation
- headers and footers
- columns.

Page size and orientation

You can change the page size and orientation as follows:

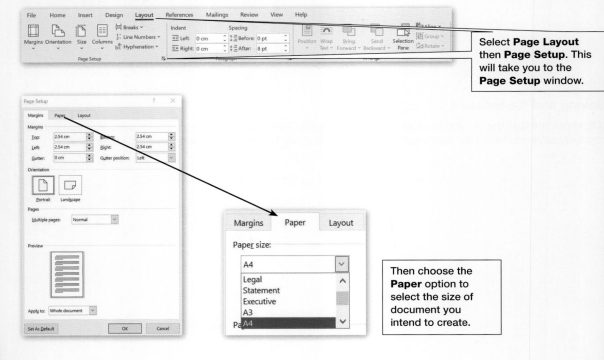

Select **Page Layout** then **Page Setup**. This will take you to the **Page Setup** window.

Then choose the **Paper** option to select the size of document you intend to create.

Activity 2

Using the Page Setup options, choose a suitable paper size for your document. This should be based on the size of paper and printer to which you have access.

Selecting the **Margins** option allows you to set the orientation of the document. The **Portrait** option will produce a tall, narrow document and the **Landscape** option will turn the page through 90 degrees to create a short, wider document.

The working area on any page is set using the **Margin** options. These settings adjust the space around the edge of every page in your documents.

Activity 3

Set suitable page orientation and margin settings for your document, bearing in mind the type of document you are creating and your printing facilities.

Headers and footers

Information added to the header (top) and footer (bottom) of any document will appear on every page of the document. They can be used to style a document and include the following types of information:

- titles, text and images
- page numbering
- file information
- current or document creation date.

Double clicking at the top of the page will open the header area. This is where a suitable document title can be added and formatted.

Alternatively select **Insert** from the ribbon and **Header** or **Footer**.

Standard formatting tools can be used to change the font, alignment and style.

Activity 4

Add a suitable title to your document using the header options and format it in the style of a modern banking business.

> **Tip**
>
> When creating documents that use columns, as in the task you have been set, the **Portrait** option is normally used.

> **Tip**
>
> Setting these options to zero will allow text and graphics to go right to the edge. However, most non-commercial printers cannot print to the very edge and so require the page to have a minimum margin. Documents are often cropped after printing so that printing appears to go to the very edge. Bear this in mind.

As headers are normally used for adding titles, additional information can be added to the footer as shown below.

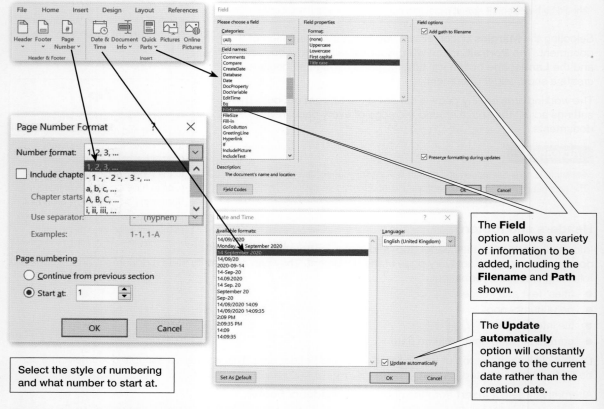

Select the style of numbering and what number to start at.

The **Field** option allows a variety of information to be added, including the **Filename** and **Path** shown.

The **Update automatically** option will constantly change to the current date rather than the creation date.

Text can be formatted using the formatting toolbar or by right clicking the text. The different fields can be spaced as shown by clicking the Tab button on your keyboard.

Author's name

Tab

Creation date

Page number

Filename

Activity 5

Using the Footer options shown, add the following to your document and style them accordingly: your name; the date; automatic page numbering; the filename and path.

Using columns

Columns, as you learnt in Session 1.8, are used to vertically divide a page before adding text, graphics and images. This is how newspapers and magazines are normally laid out.

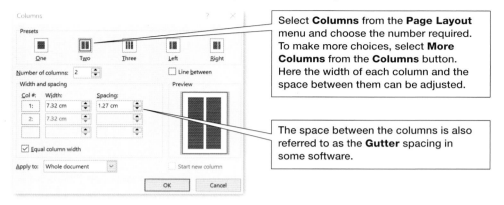

Select **Columns** from the **Page Layout** menu and choose the number required. To make more choices, select **More Columns** from the **Columns** button. Here the width of each column and the space between them can be adjusted.

The space between the columns is also referred to as the **Gutter** spacing in some software.

Activity 6

Add a suitable number of columns to your document, making sure you add sensible width and spacing values. Save your document.

Review and revise

You should now be able to:

- create a new document and save it with a suitable filename in a suitable location
- set the page size, margins and orientation of a document
- use the header and footer option to add useful information
- divide a document layout into columns.

Adding text and images to a document

Background

In this session you will build upon and discover the following skills:
- accurately adding and formatting text
- using tables
- inserting images into a document.

Adding and formatting text

Typing text straight into a word processed document is the simplest way to add information, and there are a variety of formatting tools to help you to present it in the most suitable way.

Text formatting

Below are a selection of fonts, styles and sizes.

Arial Size 12

Arial Size 10 in Bold

Times New Roman Size 14 Italic

Arial Black Underlined

~~Century Gothic Strikethrough Size 10~~

Impact Size 14 Highlighted

The **Font** window shown above can be found on the main menu or **Formatting toolbar**. The font, style and size of any selected font can be changed to suit the requirements of the document. **Bold** or underlined headings, for example, are a good way of highlighting important information. Additional font effects include superscript, adding very small letters above the line of text and subscript, small letters just below.

Text alignment

The text on the right has been added to a document with two columns. The four paragraphs are aligned to the left margin, the right margin, centrally and fully justified (which means the text is spaced to meet both the left and right edges of the text area).

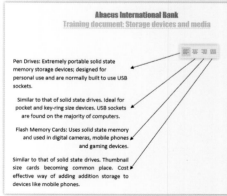

Create a new word processing document and type the name of the organisation in this unit – Abacus International Bank – six times on the page. Using different fonts and styles, create what you think are three modern headings and three more traditional ones. Share your ideas with a partner and discuss which would be most suitable for this type of business.

Bulleted and numbered lists

Bullet points or numbered lists are useful for displaying different points of information. They can be accessed from the main menu or by right clicking within a text area. Right clicking a bullet point or number will allow you to format it using the options shown.

Paragraph formatting

The space before and after paragraphs, line spacing, and tab settings can be edited to suit the style of document. The **Paragraph** dialogue box and settings can be found by selecting **Layout** from the ribbon bar.

The **Tab** settings can be changed allowing you to set how far the cursor moves when pressing the Tab key.

Additional positions can be added here.

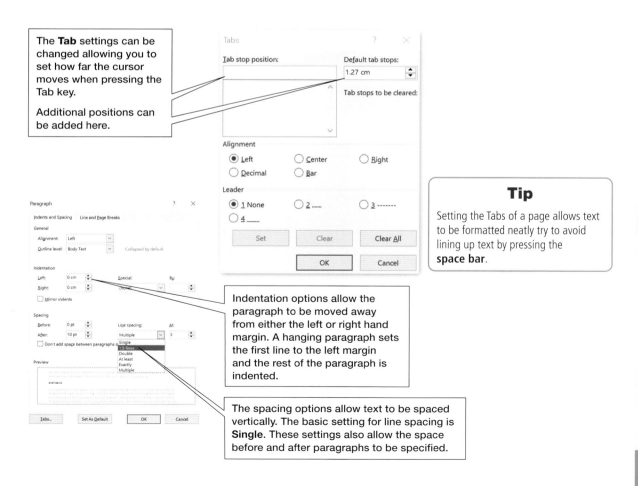

Indentation options allow the paragraph to be moved away from either the left or right hand margin. A hanging paragraph sets the first line to the left margin and the rest of the paragraph is indented.

The spacing options allow text to be spaced vertically. The basic setting for line spacing is **Single**. These settings also allow the space before and after paragraphs to be specified.

Tip

Setting the Tabs of a page allows text to be formatted neatly try to avoid lining up text by pressing the **space bar**.

The following window outlines the options that are open to you when formatting documents.

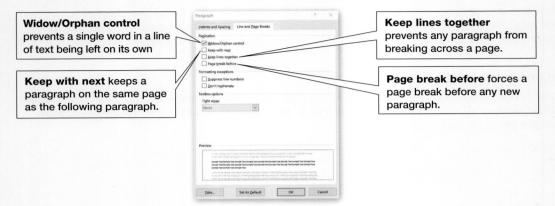

Widow/Orphan control prevents a single word in a line of text being left on its own

Keep with next keeps a paragraph on the same page as the following paragraph.

Keep lines together prevents any paragraph from breaking across a page.

Page break before forces a page break before any new paragraph.

Page, section and column breaks

At times, a break needs to be added to text before the actual end of the page or column. From the layout menu can be found the following options:

- Page break, where one page ends and another begins
- Section break, used to divide a document into sections
- Column break, where column text will stop and start again in the next column.

Using tables

Tables are used in word processed documents to present information in a structured way. They can hold text and/or images. The **Insert Table** dialogue box can be found by selecting **Insert > Table**.

How rows (horizontally) and columns (vertical) are set will depend on the amount of information that is to be added. The width can be set to fill the area where it is inserted, automatically, or a set width can be added.

Right clicking and selecting **Insert** within a cell allows extra rows and columns to be added. Similarly, selecting **Delete Cells** allows a row or column to be deleted.

The icon on the top left of a table is the handle to select and move it.

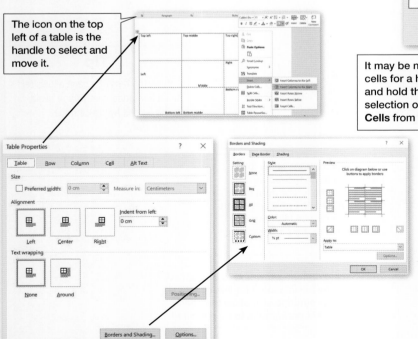

It may be necessary to merge two or more cells for a heading or title. To do this, click and hold the cursor in one cell and make a selection of other cells. Then select **Merge Cells** from the **Layout** menu.

Right click on the icon at the top left of the table to access the table properties. The border, fill and style of the table can now be edited.

Tip

The tools demonstrated for formatting text work exactly the same whether text is typed directly onto a page or it is pasted into a text box, table or shape.

Activity 2

Open the **Abacus leaflet** document you created in Session 3.4 and write a short introduction. Remember the requirements of the document – to provide training information on storage devices and media and their relative advantages and disadvantages for use. Format the text using the skills learned in this session.

Inserting images into a document

As already demonstrated in Units 1 and 2, images can be inserted into a document from many different sources. They may be stored on a CD-ROM of images, saved into a documents area on the computer or imported directly from a digital camera or scanner.

The process and skills for inserting an image into a document (as you covered in Session 1.9) is very similar to inserting an image into a presentation (Session 2.7). These two sessions also demonstrated how to edit and adjust images once they have been added, for example, text wrapping to combine text and images.

> **Tip**
>
> Many words that sound the same have two spellings; disc and disk for example. This will not be picked up by the spelling tool. A useful tool find a specific word and replace it is the **Find and Replace** tool.

Activity 3

Insert images of storage devices and media into your Abacus leaflet document after referring to the list of devices in Session 3.1. If you need a recap on internet searching and saving files from the internet, refer to Session 1.8. You need to consider the following when doing this.

- How many images can be placed in each column without overcrowding it?
- Each image will need space around it to enable you to add a title and text.
- Make sure there is no overlapping of information in the header or footer.

Make sure you keep saving your work as you progress through the project.

Hyperlinks and bookmarks

Hyperlinks are links from one file to another, this can be on the same computer or across the internet. When creating a leaflet a hyperlink can be used to add a link to a website for further reading. To add a Wikipedia page link to the text '**Uses solid state memory**', simply select the text, choose **Insert** and **Link** from the main ribbon and add a website address as shown.

> **Tip**
>
> Hyperlinks to an external file or website can be added to any object; text, images or graphic, in most office-based programs.

A bookmark is a saved location within a document. This can be useful in a document of more than one page, and links to a bookmark can be selected as destinations for a hyperlink. Simply select a word or object and select **Insert** and **Bookmark** from the main ribbon. Give the bookmark a name and then this can be selected from the hyperlink options window.

Bookmark	?	✕
Bookmark name:		
TheEnd		Add
		Delete
		Go To

The End

Authors Name

Activity 4

Using the information provided in this unit, and your own additional research, add the following to your leaflet:

- advantages and disadvantages of each type of storage device or media
- hyperlinks to useful research websites
- bookmarks to each section
- a short list of topics at the beginning of the leaflet to add bookmark links to.

Review and revise

You should now be able to:

- enter and edit text and images
- change the font, style and size of text to suit the style of document you are creating
- format text using alignment, line spacing and paragraph tools
- create, edit and complete tables
- position text and images within any document
- add internal bookmark locations and hyperlinks to external websites and files.

SESSION 3.6 Creating a simple data model and chart

Background

Working for Abacus International Bank, you have been asked to create a simple spreadsheet model and chart that can be used to calculate the available storage based on the number of devices and media available. The chart can also be imported into your training document.

In this session, you will find out how to do the following:

- use basic spreadsheet skills
- create a basic model using appropriate page layout, and using the header and footer
- add accurate data to create a simple chart
- print your work showing values and formulae
- import your chart into your training document
- save your work in a suitable format and location.

> **Tip**
>
> There is a reference chart on the digital download (in the Extra support folder) with an overview of spreadsheet features and functions.

Creating a new document

Below is a common spreadsheet package. Select **File > New** and you will get the following screen.

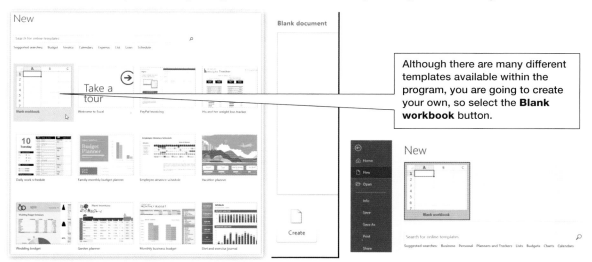

Although there are many different templates available within the program, you are going to create your own, so select the **Blank workbook** button.

Saving and file location

As already discussed in previous pages, it is important that all files you create have a suitable filename and location. This means that you can regularly save your work as you progress and you will easily be able to find your work at a later date.

Create a folder called SPREADSHEET MODEL within your document area. You will save all the files you create in this project inside this folder.

Data models: basic principles

Before creating your spreadsheet the following steps will guide you through the basics skills required.

Spreadsheets are made up of the following:
- Columns: go up and down.
- Rows: go across.
- Cells: are where the columns and rows cross.

We refer to cells by their column and row reference.

Where the cell in a spreadsheet is surrounded by a dark band it is known as the active cell. This means that anything you type in will go into that cell – because it is active.

The active cell in the spreadsheet image on the top right of this page is cell A1.

Activity 1

1 In which column are the dates of birth?
2 In what row can you find Billie Brown's data?
3 What is the cell reference for Hassan?
4 What is the cell reference of the active cell?

	A	B	C
1	Surname	Forename	Date of Birth
2	Elizabeth	Grace	14 June 1997
3	Brown	Billie	18 August 1997
4	Cheung	Charles	31 January 1997
5	Hassan	Hamal	03 April 1997
6	Eve	Isobel	04 November 1997
7	Wellcome	Wednesday	05 March 1997
8			

Tip

In spreadsheet software, simple mathematical symbols are represented by the following keyboard characters:

Equals: =

Add: +

Subtract: –

Multiply: *

Divide: /

In the cells

Cells can contain:
- a number
- a text label
- a formula or function.

The spreadsheet program will recognise the difference between numbers and text. It needs help to recognise a formula, though. To type in a formula you will need to begin with the = symbol.

Activity 2

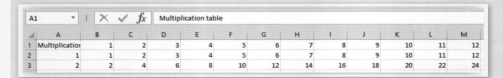

1 Open your spreadsheet program to begin a new sheet.
2 Type in the words **Multiplication Table** in cell A1.
3 Put the numbers 1 to 12 in cells B1 to M1.
4 In cell A2 put the number 1.
5 In cell A3 put the number 2.
6 Make cell B2 the active cell by clicking on it.
7 Type in this formula: =B1*A2.
8 Now complete the rest of the cells adding a formula to each.
9 If you have added the correct formulae it should look like the example below.

A1		fx	Multiplication table									
	A	B	C	D	E	F	G	H	I	J	K	L	M
1	Multiplicatio	1	2	3	4	5	6	7	8	9	10	11	12
2		1	1	2	3	4	5	6	7	8	9	10	11	12
3		2	2	4	6	8	10	12	14	16	18	20	22	24

Changing the width of a column

Cell A1 is not wide enough to show all the characters in the cell. This means that you have to make it wider in order to see everything.

Double click on the line between columns A and B.

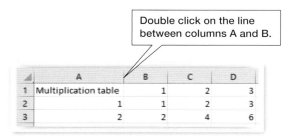

	A	B	C	D
1	Multiplication table	1	2	3
2		1	1	2	3
3		2	2	4	6

This makes sure that each cell is wide enough for the characters that need to be shown.

Activity 3

Save your work as **Multiplication Table – Your Initials – The Date**. Your filename should look similar to this: **Multiplication Table – ACJ – 13June21.xlsx**. Make sure you save this in your SPREADSHEET MODEL folder.

Page setup and using the header and footer

The following steps will show you how to change the page size, orientation and add information to the header and footer.

Select **Page Layout > Page Setup**.

Tip

Editing these settings is very similar in the majority of office-based software.

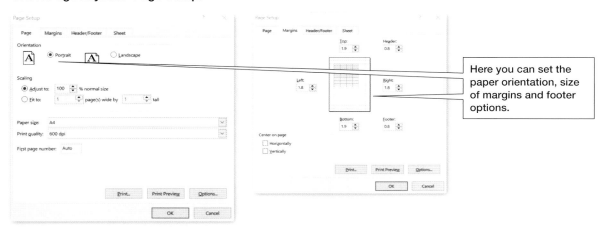

Here you can set the paper orientation, size of margins and footer options.

Inserting and deleting rows and columns

Occasionally, you might need to add or remove an additional row or column. This might be just to improve the layout or a column may have been missed with creating a table. The Insert and Delete cells options can be found on the main ribbon. Alternatively, right click on the column letter or row number where you wish to edit cells.

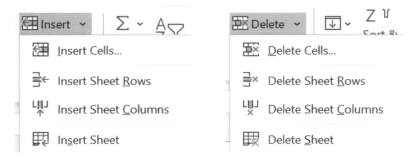

Merging cells

Depending on the layout of a table, it may be necessary to merge two or more cells together. The merged cells then behave as one single cell.

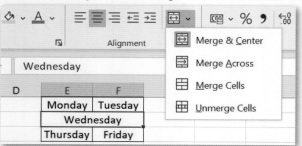

Selecting **Header/Footer** allows the header and footer to be customised with the following options:

- custom text
- page numbering
- inserting date and time
- filename and location
- inserting an image.

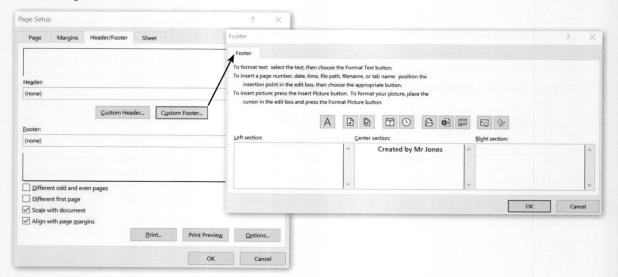

Activity 4

In the document you created in Activities 2 and 3, experiment with and add the following:
- Suitable page layout, orientation and margin settings for your document. Keep in mind the printing facilities which you have access to.
- Add the title **Multiplication Table** to the header, plus your name and any suitable additional information to the footer.

Creating a simple model and chart

The following steps will show you how to create a simple model and chart that represents the storage capacity of different devices and media you looked at in Session 3.1. This can then be inserted into your training document **Abacus leaflet** from Sessions 3.4 and 3.5.

A simple formula

=F2+F3+F4+F6+F7+F8+F10+F11+F12+F13

The program knows that it is a formula because you have inserted the = symbol at the beginning. But this is a long way round of inputting a formula.

Functions

Most spreadsheet programs have functions. These allow you to bypass writing out complicated formulae by using the cell references and mathematical operators.

The functions you need to know about are structured like this:

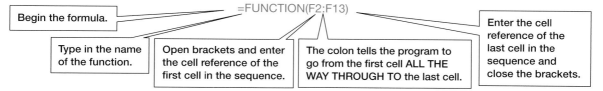

Begin the formula.

=FUNCTION(F2:F13)

Type in the name of the function.

Open brackets and enter the cell reference of the first cell in the sequence.

The colon tells the program to go from the first cell ALL THE WAY THROUGH TO the last cell.

Enter the cell reference of the last cell in the sequence and close the brackets.

For the following model you want to use the SUM function.

=SUM(F2:F13)

Using multiplication formulae and the SUM function, create a simple spreadsheet model as a table that calculates the total storage capacity based on the quantities of each device or media. The headings for columns and rows are provided in this table.

	A	B	C	D
1	**Storage Device / Media**	**Capacity (Gb)**	**Quantity**	**Total capacity (Gb)**
2	CD	0.7		
3	DVD	4.7		
4	DVD-RAM	4.7		
5	Blu-ray	25		
6	Pen Drive	64		
7	Flash Memory Cards	64		
8	Portable Drive	320		
9	Solid State Drive	1000		
10	Hard Drive	2000		
11	Magnetic Tape	500		
12	**Total**			

The chart function

Data within a spreadsheet model can be represented visually as a chart or graph.

A bar or column chart of some sort would be the most suitable way to represent this data.

Select only the data that is relevant (including headings as shown below) and then chose a chart from the **Insert** menu. The example shown is a 3D column chart.

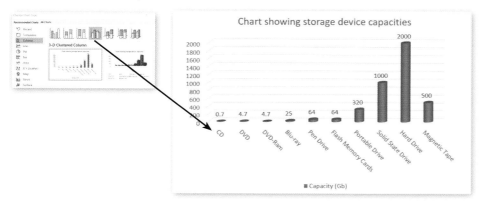

Customising graphs and charts

Once created, a chart can be customised to user requirements or to match the style of a larger document. The different components can also be selected to be formatted. The steps below demonstrate a selection of customisation.

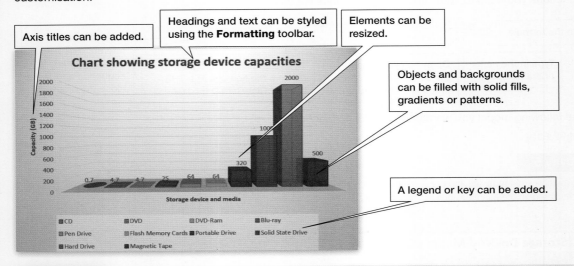

Axis titles can be added.

Headings and text can be styled using the **Formatting** toolbar.

Elements can be resized.

Objects and backgrounds can be filled with solid fills, gradients or patterns.

A legend or key can be added.

Activity 6

Using the model created in Activity 5, create a chart that represents the capacities of different storage devices, as requested by Abacus in the introduction to this unit.

Importing a chart into another program

Once created, a chart can be copied into another program by simply using the **Copy** and **Paste** command (or **Paste Special** for more options). **Paste Special** can be found from the main or **Edit** menu.

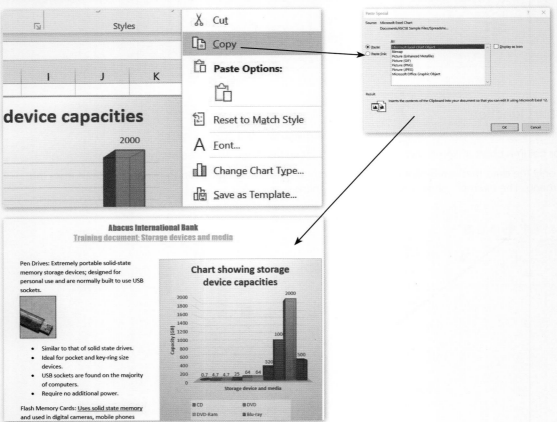

Activity 7

Add your chart to your training document. If you have used columns; keep the size within one column and make sure the chart has a title and brief description. Make sure that you save all your work afterwards.

Review and revise

You should now be able to:

- create a simple spreadsheet and save it with a suitable filename in a suitable location
- set the page size, margins and orientation of a spreadsheet
- use the header and footer to add useful information
- add accurate data to create a simple chart and insert it into a word processed document.

SESSION 3.7 Final document checks and presentation

Background

Your employer has asked you to carry out the following tasks before you move onto your next project:

- Print the storage devices and media training booklet as a full colour sample, ready for final checking before going to print.
- Your spreadsheet must be printed so that its layout, functions and formulae can be checked.
- Having already seen samples of your work and being impressed with the quality, your employer has asked you to produce an additional information leaflet.
- Exporting documents into alternative formats, depending on end-user requirements.

In this session, you will find information on the following:

- checking your completed documents for spelling mistakes and visual errors
- using test data to check that a spreadsheet model works correctly
- printing options for each of your documents, including numerical and formula printouts for your spreadsheet model.
- exporting documents into alternative formats, depending on end user requirements
- using compression tools to combine multiple files into one package, suitable for emailing to colleagues.

> ### Tip
>
> When using the automated spelling and grammar checks of any office-based software it's important to remember that these tools are not guaranteed to correct all mistakes and understand the grammatical variations of every language. They should be combined with visual proofreading and it is essential to ensure the correct language option has been chosen before using these tools.

Spelling and grammar checks

All office software packages have some sort of spelling and grammar checking facilities built in. The following steps will guide you through how to check your documents.

Word processing software

The **Spelling and Grammar** tool can either be found from the Review section of the main ribbon or by simply right clicking over the incorrectly spelt word.

> ### Tip
>
> Although the functionality hasn't changed, sometimes the tool name does. For example in the latest version of Microsoft Word, spelling and grammar functions are found within the **Editor** tool.

The grammar check works in exactly the same way.

Spreadsheet software

The process is the same here, although there is no grammar check, just spelling.

Use spelling and grammar tools to check the training guide and spreadsheet model you have created, correcting any mistakes that are identified.

Proofreading and visual checks

Software spelling and grammar checks can make mistakes, and you will miss obvious errors just by reading your work too often. Proofreading and visual checking is the process of letting someone else read and analyse your document – ideally someone who has had nothing to do with its creation and who may fit with its intended audience. The easiest way to do this is to pass out printed copies of your work to friends and colleagues and ask them to annotate it (make notes on the page), indicating any errors they find and making suggestions about its layout or content.

These checks prevent a poor experience for the eventual reader and can also allow any additional pagination to be carried out if required. This may include the following:

- Check for inconsistent line spacing that may be off-putting for the reader.
- Remove any blank pages or slides not being used.
- Remove widow/orphan elements.
- Look for inconsistent or incorrect styles being used within the same document.
- Where tables and lists have been used, ensure they don't cross from one page or column to another.
- Incorrect spelling, not picked up by software, names for example.
- The removal of inconsistent character spacing or sentence case.
- Two adjacent numbers could be reversed, or transposed, and this would not be picked up by a computer but could spoil a spreadsheet or telephone number.

> ### Language
>
> **Pagination** is the process of analysing the content of any document and making decisions on how it should be divided into separate pages, either electronically or printed. **Widows/Orphans** within this type of publication relate to content spilt across pages, such as the last sentence of a paragraph or a subheading sitting at the bottom of a page and its related content on the next. Although not grammatically incorrect, these can produce a poor experience for the reader.

Activity 2

Print a copy of your training guide. Swap with a classmate to look for any errors in content or layout. If possible, give a copy to a family member and ask them to check your work, too. Make changes to your document based on the feedback you receive.

Spreadsheet testing

Before passing on any spreadsheet model for others to use, it should be tested to make sure that the results it produces are accurate and that any errors are resolved. The simplest way to test the functions and formulae of a spreadsheet is to use sample data that can be easily confirmed. The following examples will guide you through testing formulae.

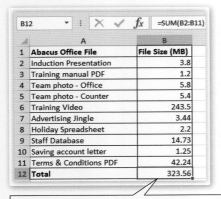

Calculating the total in the example shown is done by using the SUM function. It calculates the answer to be 323.56 MB, but without using a calculator this could be difficult to confirm.

By changing all the data to 5s and 10s, the answer can be easily confirmed:

5 + 5 + 5 + 5 + 5 + 10 + 10 + 10 + 10 + 10 = 75.

Please note that this example is slightly different from the one you created in the previous session.

Activity 3

Create a new simple spreadsheet model using data of your choosing that includes the SUM function. You can also try other functions that subtract, divide and multiply. See the Tip box on page 132 or the reference chart in the digital download (in the Extra support folder) for help with these functions. Carry out tests for each formula using sample data wherever possible. If any of your tests produce an error or an incorrect answer, examine that area with a friend to rectify the problem.

Tip

Most testing errors are the result of an incorrect cell reference or a simple typing mistake. Using basic sample data allows such errors to be found more quickly.

Printing options

When printing any piece of work, there are a number of options to consider:

- Should it be in colour or black and white?
- How many pages should be printed to a sheet?
- What elements need to be seen in the printed version?
- Does the printer setup match the computer's document layout?
- Does the document need collating?

The following steps will guide through the options available to you.

Word processing software

The following options are used in most office software packages. The following options are found by selecting **File > Print** or using a keyboard shortcut Ctrl + P.

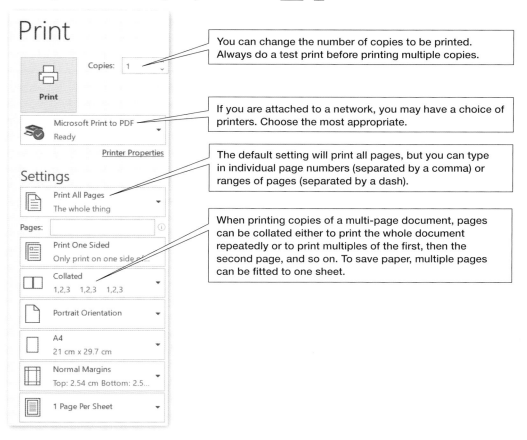

You can change the number of copies to be printed. Always do a test print before printing multiple copies.

If you are attached to a network, you may have a choice of printers. Choose the most appropriate.

The default setting will print all pages, but you can type in individual page numbers (separated by a comma) or ranges of pages (separated by a dash).

When printing copies of a multi-page document, pages can be collated either to print the whole document repeatedly or to print multiples of the first, then the second page, and so on. To save paper, multiple pages can be fitted to one sheet.

Spreadsheet software

Spreadsheet software uses the same general options as those above, but it also has additional options relating to which specific elements of the spreadsheet are printed.

From the **Print** window, users can select whether to print the page they are currently working on, the whole workbook (if the document uses multiple worksheets) or a specific area already selected.

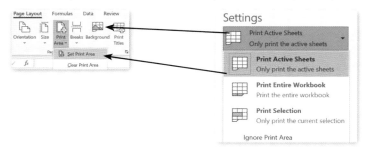

Additional options can be found in **Page Setup**. Refer to pages 122 to 125 for a reminder. Most are self-explanatory. However, the **Row and column headings** option is useful when printing spreadsheets in formula view.

Tip

At times you will want to switch between the datasheet view and the formula sheet view. The *Excel* keyboard shortcut is Ctrl + ` to toggle between the views. Or, select **Formulas** from the main menu and use the **Show Formulas** button.

Activity 4

Print a copy of the following documents produced for Abacus International Bank:
- The storage devices and media guide
- The storage space spreadsheet model in numeric view
- The storage space spreadsheet model in formula view, with gridlines, row and column headings and fitted to one page.

Keeping in mind the printing facilities which you have access to, choose the most relevant settings in regard to page layout, colour and quality. Once complete, make sure all your work is saved with a suitable filename and location.

Activity 5

Your employers are very happy with your work. They are impressed with the way you have combined text and images in the training document and they have asked you to create an additional document before you move on to your next project. They would like you to create an information sheet that outlines the basics of modern banking methods to students who will be visiting the bank hoping to work in the industry in the future. Refer to the information in Session 3.3 on the devices and methods used in banking, and create a leaflet that students can take away with them.

Exporting and compressing documents

Having now created three documents for your employer you have been asked to provide electronic versions that can be sent electronically anywhere in the world. Rather than sending individual files it makes sense to combine the documents into a single compressed format that not only saves file space but means only a single file needs to be either passed on electronically or emailed as an attachment.

To ensure maximum compatibility you have been asked to create portable document format (**PDF**) versions of the files just in case the office applications your colleagues use are slightly different to yours.

Creating a PDF version of your word-processed documents

From the **File** tab, select the **Export** option and **Create PDF/XPS**.

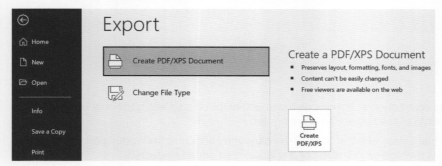

Creating a compressed package of multiple files

Using **File Explorer**, make sure all the files are together in one folder, select the folder and select **Share** and then **Zip**. This will create a single **compressed** file in the same location that contains all the files you need to share.

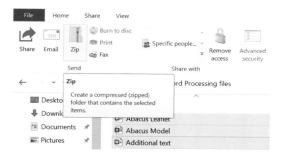

PRACTICAL

Real world

When compressing files and folders you may see examples using either ZIP or RAR file extensions. Both are compression file types with one key difference. ZIP compression is commonly used and built into operating systems, including Windows and Apple, whilst RAR is a proprietary file format that requires third-party software to use it.

To extract, or un-zip, files from a compressed folder

Using **File Explorer**, select the compressed folder, select the **Compressed Folder Tools** tab and select **Extract All**.

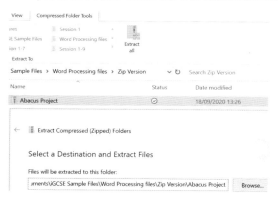

Real world

Creating compressed zip folders of multiple files is very useful but unfortunately it is also a favoured method of sending email attachments containing viruses, disguised as files the recipient has requested. It is important to always check and scan any suspicious email attachments and if in doubt, delete them.

Activity 6

Create a single compressed folder of all the files you have created for your employers including:
- the word-processed documents outlining storage devices and media, and modern banking methods
- the data model of device storage capacities
- PDF versions of all three files for easy viewing.

Review and revise

You should now be able to:
- check any document for spelling and grammar mistakes and correct them using software facilities and proofreading to identify any problems before a document is printed
- use sample test data to test a spreadsheet model and confirm that the functionality you have added works correctly
- use the most suitable printing options in word processing and spreadsheet software to meet the needs of the audience
- use compression tools to combine a selection of documents into one transferrable file that also reduces its overall file size.

3 Practical review

What have you covered?

In the three practical sessions about document production, you have:
- revised and extended your skills for working on documents covered in Unit 1
- entered and formatted text
- created, edited and completed tables
- imported and placed a chart that had been created with a spreadsheet
- checked documents for errors of spelling or grammar.

In the practical session using a spreadsheet, you have:
- created a new spreadsheet and saved it with a suitable filename in a suitable location
- set the page size, margins and orientation of a spreadsheet
- used the header and footer to add useful information
- added text and numerical data to a spreadsheet
- used the SUM function to add values across a range of cells
- created and edited charts to represent data visually
- formatted and styled all elements of a spreadsheet to meet users' needs and produce a professional looking model
- used sample test data to test a spreadsheet model and confirm that the functionality you have added works correctly.

Having created two types of practical document, you have:
- exported office-based documents as PDF documents to maximise their audience
- compressed and zipped a selection of files into one file, suitable for transmission.

Some practice questions

Miss Brown is organising a school trip to a music concert, which includes one of the set pieces for the Cambridge IGCSE Music syllabus that her students are studying.

A poster needs to be created to advertise this concert trip.

1 Using a suitable software package, load the file **ConcertPoster.txt**, which contains details for the trip that Miss Brown is organising.

2 Work out which lines of text are headings and which are details and apply suitable font, style, sizes, paragraph spacing and colours for them.

3 Search the internet to find the URL for the home page of the National Youth Orchestra. Add this URL to the poster in a suitable position.

4 Search the internet to find a picture of the inside of the Birmingham Symphony Hall, including the organ. Download and save this image.

5 Place the image saved at step 4 in the document so that it creates a banner across the top of the page. Resize and crop the image to achieve this, but make sure the aspect ratio is maintained.

6 Search the Cambridge Assessment International Education website (https://www.cambridgeinternational.org/) to find the URL of the page for the Cambridge IGCSE Music syllabus. Add this complete URL to the poster in a suitable position.

7 Save the poster in two different file formats, one in the native software it was created in and another as a PDF document.

8 Using a suitable software package, load the file **Coach.csv**. The spreadsheet shows the seating plan of the coach with two seats either side of the aisle (column C). A booked seat has the person's name in the cell. A "1" (one) in a cell means that the seat has not yet been booked.

9 In cell H5, use the SUM function to add up the values in cells A1 to E12. This will tell you how many seats are still not booked.

10 In cell H8, create a formula that uses the values in cells H2 and H5 to calculate the number of seats that have been booked.

11 Enter 4 into cell H11.

12 In cell H14, create a formula, which uses the values in cells H8 and H11 to calculate the amount of money collected (seats booked multiplied by the cost per seat).

13 In order for the trip to go ahead, Miss Brown has to have 34 people on the coach.

Type into cell H17: =IF(H8>33,"YES","NO")

After entering this, cell H17 should display "NO"

This is known as an 'If' statement, and you'll learn more about this in Unit 6. Alternatively you can look at a description on the spreadsheet features and functions reference chart on the digital download (in the Extra support folder).

14 Look carefully at the numerical values in the cells down column H.

Marianna Rodriguez wants to book seat D8. Enter **Rodriguez** into cell D8.

Check that the values in cells H5, H8 and H14 all change.

15 Enter 'White' into cell E12.

Cell H17 should now indicate 'YES'. If this does not happen, go back and check your formulae, starting with cell H17.

16 In the page header, enter: **Coach bookings for music concert**.

17 Use the text alignment buttons to centre all the data in the spreadsheet.

18 Adjust the margins and cell widths so that all the data in the cells is fully visible and so that the printout will fit onto one A4 sheet with portrait orientation.

19 Save the spreadsheet as **CoachBookings**.

20 Create a zip folder of the documents you have created for Mrs Brown so that you can easily email her all the files.

Progress check

Aiming for good progress

As well as the points listed under 'Aiming for good progress' in Unit 1, you can:

Word processing

- enter and format text
- create and complete tables
- check documents for errors of spelling or grammar
- print your work in a suitable size and orientation for the audience
- export files as PDF versions to maximise their viewing potential.

Spreadsheets

- create a new spreadsheet and save it with a suitable filename in a suitable location
- set the page size, margins and orientation of a spreadsheet
- use the header and footer to add useful information
- add text and numerical data to a spreadsheet and format it to suit the users' needs
- use the function SUM and create simple formulae within a spreadsheet
- create charts to represent data visually and import them into a word processed document
- use sample test data to test a spreadsheet model to confirm that the functionality you have added works correctly.

Managing your files and folders you can:

- use suitable file and folder names
- compress multiple files as a single zipped folder to help transfer files electronically.

Aiming for excellent progress

As well as the points listed under 'Aiming for excellent progress' in Unit 1, you can:

Word processing

- enter and format text
- create, edit and complete tables
- check documents for errors of spelling or grammar
- confidently export work in the most suitable electronic or printed format to meet the needs of the audience or target user.

Spreadsheets

- create a new spreadsheet and save it with a suitable filename in a suitable location
- set the page size, margins and orientation of a spreadsheet
- use the header and footer to add useful information
- confidently use the SUM function
- create charts to represent data visually, importing them into a word processed document
- format and style all elements of a spreadsheet to meet users' needs and produce a professional-looking model
- use sample test data to test a spreadsheet model to confirm that the functionality you have added works correctly.

Managing your files and folders you can:

- use appropriate file, folder and sub folder names
- compress and share electronically multiple files as a single zipped folder to meet the needs of the audience.

4 Networks and the effects of using them

Why this unit matters

Computer networks help us to organise our data and to access information much more efficiently than simply using stand-alone computers.

Junaid works for All Computer Supplies Inc. – the company for which you produced an information sheet in Unit 1 – and is responsible for setting up computer networks. There are many different types of networks, and even stand-alone computers will link to other computers when using the internet. Junaid has to deal with all sorts of enquiries about the networked systems that All Computer Supplies Inc. helps to put together.

Here are some of the enquiries that Junaid deals with:

I access the web all the time: playing games, using VoIP to call my friends and downloading music. I also love blogging and tweeting. It just happens through Wi-Fi and Bluetooth – but I don't know how it works and would like some ideas on how I can apply it to my business. (Interior designer)

I work in a shop and I know that when I scan an item at the till, all sorts of things happen. My till connects with the ordering department, the warehouse, payment and customer loyalty records. It seems as though I'm part of a really big network. Is that true? (Cashier attendant)

Our school has a large network. I don't know how it works but I overheard someone talking about LANs and WANs. I'm not sure what all that means. I'd like to know – after all, I am the head teacher! (Head teacher)

I'm setting up a network at home so that the whole family can use the same printer and access the internet at the same time. It will be so much easier for me to do online banking and make bookings for theatre and travel tickets. How does my network connect with the business networks when I book my tickets or make a payment? (Parent)

Your practical task

All Computer Supplies Inc. has decided that it would be helpful if the company developed a series of webpages to provide details about how networks operate in personal and business environments. The company has asked you to tackle this task.

What this unit covers

THEORY

Sessions

Theory review

PRACTICAL

Sessions

Practical review

By the end of the theory sessions you will be able to:

- describe the use of various devices used to set up computer networks
- describe the use of Wi-Fi and Bluetooth in networks
- define the terms LAN, WLAN and WAN, identify their characteristics and note any differences
- identify a variety of methods of communication over networks
- describe the advantages and disadvantages of the internet and intranets in business environments
- understand the advantages and disadvantages of accessing the internet using different types of computer
- understand and explain the need to use IDs and passwords
- understand and explain the need for confidentiality and data security on computer networks
- identify and explain the need for encryption and authentication techniques.

In the practical sessions you will develop and apply skills in:

- applying the theory of web development layers in your work
- website authoring and understanding the basics of HTML
- combining text, images and numeric data in your work
- using style sheets to improve the look of your work
- how to test and publish a website.

SESSION 4.1 An introduction to computer network hardware

Background

Computer networks allow devices to communicate with each other and share data and information. There are many different types of computer networks. In this session, we will look at the hardware needed for computer networks. You may recognise some of the technical terms associated with networks in this session from your home or classroom and you will learn how the hardware devices enable communication and the transfer of data.

> **Language**
>
> When data is transferred across a network it is broken down into small pieces called data packets. These packets are transmitted and then reassembled at the destination.

Hardware devices

Component	Description
Routers	A router is a device that connects two or more networks together by managing and directing the data packets transferred between them. It achieves this by: • analysing the source and destination to create the most efficient route to take • Searching for and building a database (or **routing table**) of nearby IP addresses in case alternate routes are needed • formatting, or translating, it to a similar **protocol**, so that it can be accessed by the receiving network. Routers can join very different networks together; one of the most common uses of a router is to connect a home or business network to the internet. Most modern routers can manage both wired and wireless devices simultaneously.
Hub or Switch	When connecting to the same network, computers, printers and storage devices are plugged into a hub or switch. A hub joins together computers in a network so that they can share files and an internet connection. It sends data packets to all computers on the network. A passive hub simply broadcasts or sends the signals. An active hub makes a signal stronger as it sends it on. Switches are able to look at a data packet, target the computer for which it is intended, and send it. This helps to speed up data transmission in a network.
Bridges	In large companies, it is sometimes necessary for workers in one area to access data from other areas. In a bank, for example, the loans and insurance departments might need to look at a customer's account details to check their account history. • A bridge allows different networks to communicate with each other. • In all connections with another network, the data packets that pass between the networks must be in the same format. • Because of this disadvantage, most modern networks use routers, not bridges.

Component	Description
Network Interface Card (NIC) 	A network interface card is a device that allows access to a network via either Ethernet cable or Wi-Fi. Whilst older computers required an NIC to be fitted, most modern computers will have both wired and wireless functionality built in.
Wireless technology	Wireless technology allows devices to be connected to a network without physical wires, instead using radio transmitters and receivers. Two common systems are Bluetooth and Wi-Fi, although both are designed to connect devices without wires; they are designed for slightly different purposes. **Bluetooth** technology is limited to a short range of around 10 metres and generally used to link and transfer data between smartphones, tablets and computer peripherals like the keyboard, mouse and printer. This ability to directly connect devices means Bluetooth has also become a common protocol that manufacturers licence and add to devices that would benefit from wireless audio connectivity via headphones or speakers. **Wi-Fi** technology has a much wider range, depending on conditions, up to 100 metres, It is able to transfer large amounts of information and used with larger computer networks and devices as described in the next session. This ability means Wi-Fi is often used to connect devices to the internet.

Similarities and differences between Bluetooth and Wi-Fi

Although providing a common wireless functionality, there are similarities and differences to consider:

- Range: Bluetooth is ideal for personal devices or devices within the same room but a stronger Wi-Fi signal is needed to transmit within the same building for example.
- Security: Bluetooth devices can be paired together, often with a pin number, but Wi-Fi is required to send securely transmit encrypted data.
- Strength: Bluetooth can transmit instructions between devices and high quality audio streams but Wi-Fi is required for larger network requirements such as video streaming or large data files.
- Power: Bluetooth devices use very little power, ideal when part of rechargeable portable devices. Wi-Fi requires a mains power supply and additional transmitting equipment to function.

Communicating across a network

When analysing the needs of a network, there are a number of elements to consider; from the transmission media, choice of devices to the user requirements.

Activity 1

Read the information in the hardware devices table. Give reasons why a chain of supermarkets would find a router more useful than a bridge.

Choosing transmission media

The choice of a wired or wireless network connection will depend on four factors:

1	The speed of data transmission required	Large computer networks are more likely to use cables because they allow a greater rate of data transfer.
2	The size of the computer network	Too many users on a wireless network can slow the speed of data transmission.
3	The distance that data will need to travel	Most NICs can only send and receive radio signals over relatively short distances.
4	The need for portability of devices	Laptop or tablet users might want access to the network as they move around. This might not be possible on a wired network, so a wireless network would be most suitable.

Evaluating network-connected devices

Users can now access networks and the internet using a variety of devices. Each of the following has advantages and disadvantages and end-users must consider which would be the best for them.

- Laptop computer
- Desktop computer
- Tablet computer
- Smart phone.

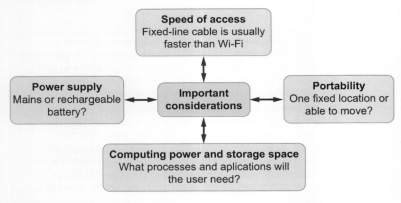

Speed of access
Fixed-line cable is usually faster than Wi-Fi

Power supply
Mains or rechargeable battery?

Important considerations

Portability
One fixed location or able to move?

Computing power and storage space
What processes and aplications will the user need?

There is also a choice in the type of cable that can be used:

Twisted pair (Ethernet) cable

This cabling usually has four pairs of copper wire. Each pair is twisted together.

The pairing and twisting reduces interference caused by other electrical cables.

Fibre optic cable

Fibre optic cables transmit data using light. Light signals are not affected by interference and this means fibre optic systems can transmit at a higher speed, and at a much longer range, than copper wire cables. However they are more expensive and generally only used in large scale infrastructure systems.

Cloud computing

Cloud computing allows data to be stored at a remote, internet connected, location. This means network users do not have to be in one location and therefore files, documents and programs can all be shared and accessed from all over the world.

Accessing data via cloud computing

Data is stored on a server in the same way as a traditional network (See Session 4.2) but rather than a local wireless or wired connection, an internet connection forms the link between devices.

Uses of cloud computing

Businesses are taking advantage of cloud computing services in the following ways:

- Sharing documents and files
- Staff can work remotely on files normally stored in an office
- Multiple users can work on the same document simultaneously.

Activity 2

1 A school has two ICT classrooms, one with fixed desktop computers and one with tablet computers. Explain the advantages and disadvantages of each during lessons requiring internet based activities.

2 A mining engineer is using a hand-held device to scan materials extracted from a test dig. She also needs to transmit the data to the laboratory that is up to 100 metres away. Explain why the system would communicate using radio waves and the devices that would be required.

Real world

Interference can disrupt the transmission of data packets. This may be high-voltage electrical cables running alongside network cables, or wireless signals clashing with devices using the same broadcast frequencies such as portable telephones.

Activity 3

An international bank needs to communicate with its branches in different countries. What advantages would the bank find in using fibre optic cables, rather than twisted pair cables or wireless transmission?

Real world

Undersea fibre optic cables cross our oceans, providing network connectivity and shared internet access across the globe.

In the home we use cloud computing to:
- stream music, video, television and educational services
- store our photos online so they can be shared
- share files between family members.

Advantages and disadvantages of cloud computing

Advantages:	Disadvantages:
<ul><li>Software can be remotely updated.</li><li>Team members can work remotely.</li><li>Remote backups can be made.</li><li>Services can be accessed by a range of smart devices.</li></ul>	<ul><li>Files and services cannot be accessed without an internet connection.</li><li>Potential security risks, files being accessed by external users.</li><li>Online storage space may be limited.</li><li>If the cloud server goes down, users cannot access files.</li></ul>

Review and revise

You should now be able to:
- describe the common network devices (routers, hubs, bridges and switches) and the use of Wi-Fi and Bluetooth in networks
- explain how network communications devices can be used in business organisations
- evaluate network and internet-enabled devices based on end-user requirements.

SESSION 4.2 Computer networks

Background

There are different kinds of networks designed to meet different needs. In this session, you will look at three main types of computer network and their advantages and disadvantages.

Internet Service Providers (ISPs) and setting up a home network

Both home and business users require computer hardware, browser software, local wiring infrastructure and an Internet Service Provider (**ISP**) to connect to the internet. Users will have their own hardware computer systems and browser software, and the availability of either traditional copper wires or fibre optic cabling will depend on their location. An ISP will provide a modem or router to allow users to connect their hardware to the internet through the available wires. The modem or router will connect to the ISP's own servers and, for a monthly or annual fee, users can access the internet through them.

Providing internet access to multiple home devices and allowing them to connect to one another also requires creating a small network. One of the most common ways is using a wireless router – an easy way to share information if all devices have wireless technology. Alternatively a small LAN (see below) can be set up. Most operating systems will automatically create a small home network; linking all devices to a network name and using a common **wireless key** between them.

Internet browser and email software

Browser software converts the data from the ISP and allows users to read and view online information in a form not unlike a presentation or desktop publishing document. Email software sends messages using the internet directly from one email address to another, displaying the message in plain text to the user.

Local Area Networks

Local Area Networks (LANs) consist of computers and peripheral devices such as printers, all connected. It is 'local' because it is spread over a small area. You might find a LAN in a workplace or a school. Each computer in a LAN can work as a stand-alone computer, with its own software, and can also use software stored on the network server. The server runs the network operating system and manages resources over the network. Computers on a LAN are known as clients and are usually connected to the server by cables.

Types of LANs

There are two main types of local area networks: the client-server network and the peer-to-peer network.

A client-server network needs a server that is linked to a number of computers. The server will be more powerful than the clients, with a faster processor, more RAM and more data storage. Large LANs could have more than one server to provide a more specific service to the clients on the network. There are three very common types.

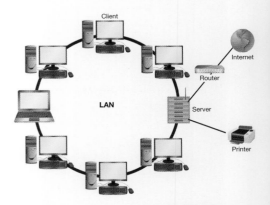

- File server: this stores all data files created and used by the organisation. Users access all files by sending commands to the file server.
- Database server: provides multiple user and computer access to a large, singular database server.
- Print server: on larger networks, a print server will manage all jobs sent to a network printer. This allows the computers on the network to work more efficiently.

In a peer-to-peer network, every computer can communicate directly with other computers on the network. Access speeds can fall dramatically if the network has more than 10 clients. They are more common in small businesses and within departments in large organisations.

Activity 1

Read the following statements and identify whether they are true or false descriptions of LANs:

1 LANs are made up of computers and peripherals that are connected.
2 Computers in a LAN can only communicate with the file server.
3 A client in a LAN cannot be connected to its own printer.
4 Servers are usually more powerful than the client computers in the LAN.
5 File servers store all the data files created and used on the LAN.

Advantages and disadvantages of LANs compared with stand-alone computers

Advantages	Disadvantages
Users can: • access their own files from any computer • share files and software • work together on the same document • communicate with each other by email or instant messaging.	The cost of setting up a LAN is much higher than just buying stand-alone computers, due to the cost of the server and its maintenance. The extra cabling can be expensive. It is also likely that attached peripherals will be larger and therefore more expensive.
It is often cheaper to buy a software licence for a number of machines than to buy software for each computer.	Viruses can spread more easily from one computer to another than using stand-alone computers.
Access rights can be controlled centrally. A user could log on to a personalised screen and have access to certain files but not to others.	Changes may be made to a document, but another user may end up working on an earlier version of the document, causing problems.
Users can share hardware devices. Larger, faster and more economical printers can be attached to the network rather than having smaller printers attached to each client. This also makes it easier for the organisation to monitor what and how much is being printed.	Passwords may not be secure, which could mean that restricted files are made available to users who are not supposed to have access to them. This could lead to data security problems across the whole network. If it happened on a stand-alone computer, only the data on that computer would be affected.
Computers can be maintained remotely. A technician will be able to log on to the server or to another client and reinstall software or reset passwords.	If the server breaks down, the whole network will stop working.

Activity 2

Look at the following statements. Which of them are advantages of a LAN and which are disadvantages?

a Data and software can be shared among many users.
b Viruses brought into one computer can be shared quickly across the network.
c Users can share printers and other peripherals.
d Software licences can be less expensive.
e Data can be corrupted because files are shared among multiple users.

Real world

In your school, teachers will have access to data files to which students will not have access. Students are likely to have their own work area that other students should not be able to access. All of these files will be accessible through a LAN with usernames and passwords, set by the administrator of the system, allowing teachers and student access to areas that are only relevant to them.

Wireless Local Area Networks (WLANs)

WLANs are different from LANs because they use a wireless link to connect computers to the network rather than connecting them by cable. There are five types of components that may be needed to make the wireless connection possible:

- wireless access points
- Network Interface Cards (NIC)
- signal boosters (amplifiers).
- wireless repeaters
- routers

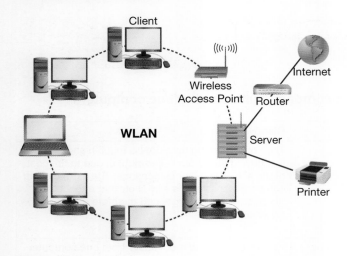

> ### Tip
>
> Routers are not essential for a WLAN. They are only needed if you want to connect a WLAN to the internet.

Wireless access points broadcast and receive signals from the NICs on the network. Routers allow several computers to access the internet through a wireless access point at the same time. This means that WLANs can be used in areas where a cabled system would not be practical, such as large warehouses and hotels. In schools there may be a need for several wireless access points, so that when you walk around with a laptop it will lock on to the most powerful signal. Although communications can be maintained over a distance of 100 metres or more, boosters are useful so that signals can be amplified. This means that a user will be able to work further away from an access point and will still be able to use the network. Wireless repeaters duplicate an access point with the same IP in a different location, increasing range.

Advantages and disadvantages of WLANs

Advantages	Disadvantages
Access to a WLAN is more flexible than access to a LAN. Users can work anywhere inside or even outside the building, as long as they are within range of a wireless access point.	WLANs are relatively slow. Other users, and sometimes other devices, could interfere with the network.
Because wireless access points are also installed in public areas – like libraries, cafes, hotels, trains – it means that people can still access the internet and email from anywhere.	Anyone with a compatible NIC could gain access to the WLAN. Network managers should ensure that access to the WLAN is not possible without the correct password.
	The distance across which computers can connect to the server is usually less than in a cabled network.

Activity 3

Sort the following list into three categories: WLANs, LANs and both WLAN and LAN.

a Users can work anywhere inside or even outside the building.

b Cabling can be expensive.

c Access rights can be controlled centrally.

d Users can share hardware devices.

e People can access the internet and their company emails from anywhere.

f You need a network interface card.

Wide Area Networks (WANs)

A wide area network, or WAN, connects local area networks to each other over a large geographical area. Each LAN connects to the WAN by means of a router or a broadband modem. The WAN could cover an area as small as a local district, or as large as a whole country, or even internationally. The internet itself is a WAN.

There are a number of different ways in which data can be transmitted across such a network, depending on the distance between one network and another:

- high-speed telephone lines
- fibre optic cables
- radio waves
- satellite links.

WANs are more likely to be used by large organisations that have branches in different countries and need to use all of these methods of transmitting data. Many WANs are developed specifically for large organisations. Others, like those set up by Internet Service Providers (ISPs), connect individuals to the internet. When you use the internet from home, you connect to a WAN managed by your ISP.

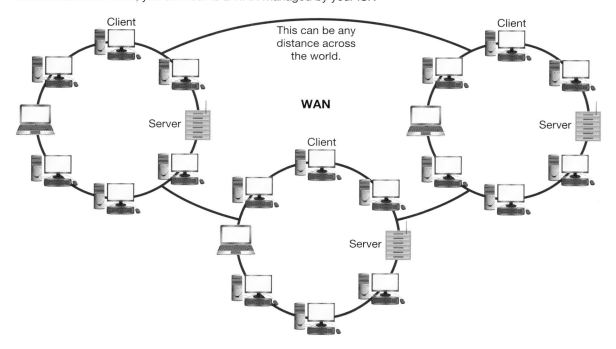

Advantages and disadvantages of WANs

Advantages	Disadvantages
Multinational organisations can share important data quickly.	If the telecommunication links fail, then communication across a WAN would not be possible. It would, however, be possible for LANs to operate in their home countries.
Transfer of data from one branch of an organisation to another is faster than by other methods.	Viruses are more commonly transmitted through a WAN than a LAN, and hackers are more likely to attack servers by accessing a WAN rather than a LAN.

Review and revise

You should now be able to:

- define the terms LAN, WLAN and WAN and the differences between them
- describe the characteristics of common network environments
- describe the advantages and disadvantages of different types of networks.

Activity 4

A bank has offices in Beijing, Hong Kong, Taipei, Islamabad, London, Washington and Dubai. Each office has its own LAN. Draw a diagram to show how each LAN is connected in a WAN. Refer to the diagram above to help you.

SESSION 4.3 The internet and intranets

Background

The internet is an **inter**national **net**work of computers that allows users to use email, browse the World Wide Web or to chat either by text or by voice.

Schools, banks and other organisations often restrict access to the internet, but want to provide internet-type resources and experiences to their users. They do this by setting up an intranet, best thought of as an **in**ternal **r**estricted **a**ccess **net**work.

The internet

Websites

Internet browsers accessing the World Wide Web allow us to visually access some of the information stored on the internet through websites. As of 2014 there are well over one billion websites, each containing any number of webpages.

Webpages	Websites
Documents that can be seen on a computer screen. May contain: • text • animations • images • video • sound.	Lots of webpages that are linked together by hyperlinks. Clicking on a hyperlink allows a user to navigate between webpages in the website. They also allow you to move to other websites.

Each webpage has a unique address. This address helps web browsers to find them. The address is known as the **U**niform **R**esource **L**ocator or **URL**. This is how a URL is made up:

https://www.harpercollins.co.uk/corporate/about-us/

Protocol	Host name	Domain name			File path	Filename
		Second level domain (SLD)	**Sub domain**	**Top level domain (TLD)**		
https://	www	.harpercollins	.co	.uk/	corporate/about-us/	

Activity 1

Look at the following web addresses. Break them down into their component parts. The first one is done for you.

• http://images.example.com
• http://www.examples.gov.za/example/page1
• http://examples.mycompany.org.in/example/page5

Protocol	Host name	Domain name			File path	Filename
		Second level domain (SLD)	**Sub domain**	**Top level domain (TLD)**		
http://	images	.example		.com		

Language

The World Wide Web is also referred to as www, or the web.

Tip

It is important that you know that the World Wide Web is part of the internet. You access the web by using a web browser like Mozilla Firefox, Google Chrome, Safari (Apple) or Microsoft Edge.

Real world

You can recognise hyperlinks easily. Hyperlinks are normally shown in blue underlined text and can link to a webpage, image or any other computer file. When the mouse pointer hovers over them, it will either change to a small hand or a box will appear providing a URL to click and follow.

Real world

You will notice the example given doesn't have a filename as part of the address. The way websites are structured, some will show a file and extension (such as index.html .htm or .php) and some will only display a file path.

Accessing the internet

Users access the internet through an Internet Service Provider (ISP). There is usually a fee for this service. Users are allocated login details when they sign up to an ISP, including a username and a password.

Each time a user logs in, the ISP can monitor how they are using the service. In many countries, ISPs are required to keep records of the webpages, websites and emails that users access and create.

There are three main methods of connecting to the internet:

Method of internet access	Equipment required	Advantages	Disadvantages
Dial-up	Dial-up modem	Usually very cheap. Only requires access to a telephone line.	Slowest connection – 56 kbps. Telephone line tied up while the modem is in use.
Fibre optic cable	Cable modem	Very fast, stable connection, does not tie up telephone line. Cable network supplier can also offer other Internet-based streaming services.	Often only available in cities and towns.
Broadband (Digital Subscriber Line – DSL)	ADSL modem	Fast connection. Always on – does not tie up the telephone line. Uses traditional copper-wire infrastructure.	Heavy users can find download and upload limits to be too restrictive. Areas with multiple subscribers will suffer from lower download speeds.
Mobile broadband (via dongle or tethering)	Mobile phone with mobile data access	Mobile access, available anywhere a mobile data signal is available.	Can be very expensive Mobile download speeds can be slower Not suitable for multiple devices

The internet and networks

Networks often have many users. In order for multiple users on a network to access the same internet connection, a **proxy server** is used. A proxy server acts as a gateway between network users and the internet by submitting all the internet requests for those users and then returning to them the results of their requests and the information received. You can see in the diagram below that users access the internet through the proxy server.

The proxy server:

● submits just one request for all the users to the router
● can also store copies of webpages for easy access
● restricts access to some users
● checks the source or destination of a data packet and allows or refuses access.

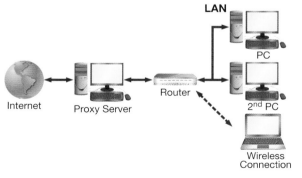

<aside>
Language

Proxy means 'stands in for' – so a proxy server stands in for all the users.
</aside>

<aside>
Real world

In some organisations, like schools, there are restrictions on the webpages students are allowed to see.
</aside>

Access to the internet is often managed by a **firewall** to protect users from hackers. A firewall is software that prevents unauthorised communication to or from the network, usually placed between the internal network and an external network, like the internet. A firewall restricts access to identified computers by noting and blocking specific **IP addresses** or blocking certain types of internet traffic.

Intranets

Large organisations with lots of electronic material, that needs to be accessed by staff, often use an intranet. In the same way as the internet, an intranet allows users to access web-based material, share files and send email but all communication and data transfer is confined to the local network. Data can be shared also using a WAN if required (see page 161) but data cannot be allowed to freely travel online onto the internet as it may be confidential.

(see page 161)

Activity 2

Many schools have an intranet. Describe what a school intranet can be used for by teachers and students.

Advantages of intranets	Disadvantages of intranets
Data is relevant to the user.	Limited resources when compared with the internet.
Data has been checked and validated by the organisation.	Limited range of views offered.
Smaller size makes communication and searching for information faster. The structure will also be relevant to the organisation, so it will be easier for users to understand.	There is limited access to/by customers and other organisations.
Intranets ensure that all the material is more likely to be safe and appropriate.	Expensive to set up and maintain: technicians need to be trained to manage the intranet and staff need to be trained to upload material.

Extranets

A controlled private network, an extranet is designed to let only authorised external users access parts of an internal network. This external access is normally via an internet connection and requires a secure login. An example might be allowing a designer brought in by a company to work on a project to access files and folders specific to that project.

Internet	Intranet	Extranet
The internet is an international network.	Intranets are internal to companies or organisations.	• Extranets are private internal networks with limited external access via the internet.
The internet provides open access to many areas of interest.	Intranets provide information that is relevant to the company or organisation.	• Extranets provide limited information of relevance to specific external users.
The internet is open to all users with an ISP user account. It can be accessed from anywhere.	Intranets can block access to the internet altogether, or provide limited access. This makes it much more difficult for hackers to access the data stored on the file server. Data is stored locally on an intranet, which makes it more secure.	• External users can only access the information allowed by the network administrator.
The internet is difficult to make secure because of its size and because there are so many access points.	Intranets often have user-level access, so users can only access relevant areas.	• Access is strictly limited and password protected.

Review and revise

You should now be able to:
- define the terms 'internet', 'intranet', 'extranet' and 'web browser'
- describe proxy servers
- recognise and explain the structure of a web address or URL
- explain the difference between the internet and an intranet
- describe how organisations make use of the internet
- explain why organisations use intranets and extranets.

Computer networks in business environments (1)

Background

In this session you will look at how networks are used in school management systems, computer aided learning and booking systems.

School management systems

Excelsior Academy has two LAN networks that together form the basis of their School Management System (SMS). Each with specific roles and user access levels. One network records learner registration, attendance and administration, the second is a teaching and learning network with a focus on learning in the classroom. Both networks are part of an intranet and connected to a print server and the head teacher and network administrators have access to the whole SMS.

Administration and management network

With a focus on learner registration and attendance, only administration staff and teachers have access, students are not permitted to access this system.

The key modules of this network are:

- School library
- Human resources
- Site management
- Finance
- Assessment, student progress, data registration and attendance
- Student admissions
- Staff administration
- School communications and reporting to parents.

Teachers can access class registers to record attendance at the beginning of each day, as well as attendance at each lesson. Teachers can also enter assessment data from classwork and examinations. The head teacher can access the data that teachers have entered to see how well the school and its students are doing.

> ### Language
>
> The human resources department within any organisation is responsible for all staff related issues, including hiring, training and the use of external contractors.

> ### Language
>
> Learner registration is essential in all schools. It links student details with the courses they are studying and the exams they are taking.

> **Activity 1**
>
> With the assistance of your teacher, write a list of all the modules that make up your school network.
>
> How does it compare with the list given in this session and what differences are there?

Teaching and learning network

All classrooms are attached to the teaching and learning network, to which students and teachers have access. This network has a focus on computer aided learning and providing support for students to work independently both within and outside of the classroom. The network is broken down into individual subjects and extra-curricular activities.

This network is also designed as an extranet, allowing students to access learning material, using a username and password, outside of the classroom. This might be for specified home learning or exam revision or for unexpected occasions when students cannot access the school building.

The key modules of this network are:

- Lesson by lesson teacher presentations
- Student workbooks and exercises
- Links to useful revision websites
- Links to multimedia material; videos, podcasts and animations
- Overall learning plans for the school year

> **Activity 2**
>
> Why do you think students are not usually permitted to access all areas within the school management system and what measures should be put in place to control access?

Online booking systems

We all now take for granted the ability to book tickets online for a future event. This removes the need for long phone calls to a booking office or turning up without a ticket to be disappointed when the event is sold out. The example shown follows the sequence for booking a cinema ticket but it could equally apply to booking concert or sporting event tickets or even booking holiday or flight tickets.

Customers log on to the cinema booking website and follow these steps:

Customer	Cinema booking system
Chooses cinema they want to visit	Cinemas appear as a drop-down list to make selection easier.
Selects the date they want to visit	Finds opening times and titles of films available on that date.
Chooses the film	Film titles appear as a drop-down list to make selection easier.
Chooses the time of the screening	Database is searched to see if there are seats available.
Decides where they want to sit	Seat choice offered. Seats are temporarily reserved until customer pays, which means that no one else can choose those seats. If the customer decides not to book them, the seats become available again.
Enters personal details to confirm the booking	Checks to see whether or not the customer is a returning customer or a new customer. For a returning customer their details will be used for the booking. New customers will have to enter their details.
Selects payment method and makes the payment	Checks the payment card details and authorises payment details with customer's bank.
	Seats confirmed as booked – now no one else can book them.
	Details of booking are shown on-screen. Customer is given a reference number.
Prints email as proof of purchase	An email is sent to the customer as a record of the transaction.
Goes to the cinema and uses payment card to collect the tickets.	Checks details of payment card against transactions. If there is a match and tickets are not yet printed, then the tickets will be printed. If there is no match, the customer would need to see someone at the cinema with their proof of purchase or reference number.

Booking system advantages:
- Individual seats and showings can be booked.
- Payment can be made online.
- You don't have to visit the cinema or theatre to book.
- Returning customers can have their details and preferences saved.
- Knowing advanced numbers means cinemas and theatres can plan ahead.
- Customers can shop across the world, looking for the best deal.

Booking system disadvantages:
- Events and showings can become booked up very quickly.
- Not having internet access can mean you miss out.
- Some people prefer to book in person.
- An internet or system failure during booking can result in duplicate, cancelled or doubled bookings.
- Fake booking systems can be created by criminals, taking payment for events that don't exist.

Tip

Booking systems are also used for transport and accommodation. Booking flights, trains or buses can be more complicated because the customer may have more choices to make.

Review and revise

You should now be able to:
- describe how networks are used in schools to support administration and student learning
- define examples of online booking systems
- describe the advantages and disadvantages of online booking systems.

Activity 3

1   What is the advantage of the cinema having a WAN?

2   Mr Lewis wants to book a room in the Excellent Hotel in Hong Kong for two nights. He wants a double, non-smoking room, with a harbour view. There will be two people in the room. He wants breakfast in the morning. Use the cinema booking system as an example and describe the booking process.

SESSION 4.5 Computer networks in business environments (2)

Background

In this session, you will look in more detail at networks in banking, medicine and expert systems.

Banking

ICT is an important feature of the banking industry. Banks receive and send money by **electronic funds transfer** (EFT). When an employee receives his or her salary, or when you make a payment at a supermarket checkout, funds are moved from one account to another.

As banks have branches throughout a country, and may have international branches, they will have a WAN that utilises real-time processing.

A bank branch will have its own LAN, where ATMs (automated teller machines – see Sessions 2.2 and 3.3), terminals at each counter and office computers will all connect with the fileserver. Each LAN will connect to the WAN, so that people can get access to banking from ATMs wherever they are.

Electronic funds transfer

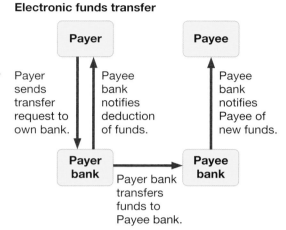

Customer	Network operation
Inserts card into ATM.	Details read from magnetic stripe or embedded chip; contact is made with WAN fileserver; customer offered choice of language if appropriate.
Enters PIN by using the keypad.	Card checked; is it valid (does the card number exist, has it been stolen or is the expiry date passed?) PIN checked; is it correct?
Chooses from these options: • Get money • Change PIN • Mobile phone services • See balance. Decides to withdraw money, with or without a receipt.	System offers choice of cash amounts. There may be a message about the cash available 'Only multiples of $20 …'.
Selects an amount or types in their own choice.	Customer account file is accessed; is there enough money in the account? Are they asking for more than their daily limit? If there is not enough money in the account, or the customer is going beyond their daily limit, other options will be given 'You have $50 available …'.
Takes back the card.	Transaction completes (money is dispensed or denied); customer account is updated.
Takes money (and receipt if requested).	Receipt is printed if requested.

Banks also have their own intranets (distributed across their WAN) so that staff can communicate with one another and so that products and services can be explained and demonstrated to customers when they visit the branch.

Advantages of banking systems	Disadvantages of banking systems
Money can be accessed from anywhere in the world where there are ATM machines.	Banks aren't familiar with local customers, increasing the chance of fraud.
Balances and transactions can be done remotely using the internet and mobile phones.	Fraud can be carried out electronically from anywhere.

(continued)

(continued)

Session 4.5 Computer networks in business environments (2)

161

Advantages of banking systems	Disadvantages of banking systems
Money can be moved between accounts quickly.	Those without access or computer systems can miss out on facilities and special offers.
Payroll dates can be set to benefit the employer and employee.	High street branches are often no longer required, affecting local communities.
Accounts can be monitored to look for suspicious activity.	Computer problems and power 'black-outs' prevent customer access.

Medicine

Dr Hallan works at a medical centre with four other doctors. They have a receptionist, who deals with entering details of each patient's appointment into the computer, and a pharmacy where patients can pick up their medicines. When seeing a patient, the doctors use their computers to access the file server and download the patient's file. Afterwards, they make changes to the file and save it again.

If medicines are prescribed, the doctors send an order to the pharmacist, who checks the stock on the computer and gets the order ready. If another appointment is needed, the doctor lets the receptionist know. The network allows the doctors access to a hospital network so that patients can be referred to specialists for hospital treatment if necessary.

Activity 1

What kind of network and processing would you recommend for Dr Hallan's medical centre? How would they connect with the hospital network?

Patient Records

It is essential that accurate patient records are kept within medical systems. The unique data linked to every patient may be accessed by a doctor from multiple locations. When making a diagnosis or prescribing medicine, the doctors or facility involved should have access to the following:

- Name, age and current address
- Local doctor and medical facility
- Any diagnosed health conditions
- Current treatments or medicines being taken
- Any allergies or known reactions to medicines
- Recent test, x-rays scan results
- Important lifestyle information
- Recorded medical appointments or hospital admissions.

Pharmacy Records

The pharmacy stores drugs, treatments and medical supplies that are prescribed to specific patients by the doctors working in the medical facility. Many of the items it stores are controlled and potentially dangerous and it is essential that accurate records are kept. These records may include the following:

- Quantity levels of specific stock items
- Prescription records, linking doctors to the patient and medicine prescribed.
- Any important stock dates, 'use before' for example.
- Notes on how specific items should be stored, 'refrigerated' for example.
- Known risks and side effects of specific items
- Associated costs of each item
- Re-order levels and suppliers for each item.

Activity 2

Consider the different staff working at the medical centre. Write a list of staff roles and for each assign which areas of the network they should be able to access.

Activity 3

Explain some of the security concerns linked to storing patient medical records on a network with online connectivity.

Expert systems

Expert systems collect knowledge from experts and make it available for others working in a particular field. People in the same field ask questions (doctors might be asked 'how do you treat a particular illness successfully?'), the answers are put into the expert system (knowledge base) to be used by others (doctors, for example). Expert systems use the combined knowledge of many experts rather than relying on one individual. In order to work the system has to be carefully designed.

Simple expert systems are made up of at least five different elements:

- The **user interface** is an input and output system, allowing a non-expert user to ask their query (question) of the expert system and receive a response.
- **Inference engines** act like a search engine, following the rules base to try to get answers from the knowledge base, using a form of reasoning.
- A **knowledge base** is a database of agreed relevant facts that can be checked, stored and retrieved.
- The **rules base** is made up of 'inference rules' that the inference engine can use to apply reason and make a decision. For example, IF the country is in the United Kingdom AND its name begins with W, THEN it must be Wales.
- An **explanation system** explains to the user of the expert system the reasoning behind the results they have been given.

Examples of expert systems

- A mineral prospecting system will use a knowledge base of rock formations and geological characteristics to help predict the likelihood of specific minerals in a particular location.
- Car engine fault diagnosis recommendations can be made on known faults, the parts involved, and the systems displayed by the vehicle.
- Medical diagnosis systems will use the combined medical knowledge of experts, linking symptoms, medical supply availability and historical data to suggest treatment strategies.
- Chess and strategy game systems will consider all the potential player moves and their resulting actions.
- Financial planning systems can be built upon historical data, the amount being invested and the success rates of individual products.
- Route scheduling for delivery vehicles can consider the traffic levels on particular routes at different times, the nature of the product being delivered and real-time delays due to road works or accidents.
- Plant and animal identification systems can be built on analysing a sample, testing against biological rules and using comparison and elimination to make an identification.

Setting up an expert system

Expert systems rely on an accurate and extensive knowledge base. Experts contribute to the knowledge – they help to define what is needed to create a knowledge base.

The experts would define the knowledge base and develop the inference engine, making sure that the questions that people are likely to ask can be answered. They also need to test the system. Expert systems learn from the answers. Each answer adds rules to the rules base and adds new facts to the knowledge base. It is important that the user interface is designed so that users can ask the questions they need.

Advantages of expert systems	Disadvantages of expert systems
Answers are always consistent.	Decisions are based on what the experts have provided - there is no 'common sense' to fall back on if a question is misunderstood.
Questions cannot be ignored. All questions are answered.	Mistakes in the knowledge base can lead to incorrect decisions.
Expert systems reduce the amount of time it takes to solve a problem.	It takes a lot of time and money to set up an expert system.
Expert systems do not need a highly-qualified workforce. A patient can be guided through a medical expert system without a doctor. This could be useful in areas where doctors are not available.	Operators need to have high levels of training in the use of the expert system so that they are able to 'ask the right questions' and guide users to the answers they need.

Activity 4

A car mechanic uses an expert system to check the performance of an automobile. The expert system identifies that the exhaust gases from the engine fail to meet new standards for emissions. The car needs a new part to be fitted. The mechanic uses a computer to get information about the work done on the car and about the part. Information is sent to other departments for action.

Identify which tasks will be done by the mechanic and which will be done by the service department's receptionist or by the finance department.

Task	Mechanic	Service Reception	Finance
Identify other work that has been done on the car – has this been a problem before?			
Check that the part is in stock.			
Find the price of the part.			
Inform Finance how many hours the job will take.			
Calculate the price of the job (parts + (hours × hourly rate)).			
Contact customer to inform them of the required work and how much it will cost them.			
Book the car in for the work.			

Real world

In a medical expert system, doctors are asked to contribute all they know about symptoms and conditions so that effective diagnoses can be made.

Real world

An expert system linked to a computer network would be helpful to a car mechanic, who would be able to access the server for data about the car, and to check with the parts department if replacement parts are needed. The system would also connect with the finance department to work out the bill for servicing the car.

Real world

A doctor would also apply their own experience and expertise when considering the results from the system.

Review and revise

You should now be able to:
- use the terms LAN, WLAN and WAN in a number of contexts
- describe the advantages and disadvantages of:
    - banking systems
    - weather systems
    - library systems
    - expert systems.

SESSION 4.6 How does ICT help business and personal communication?

Background

In this session, you will learn how ICT and computer networks support and improve business communication.

Methods of electronic communication

Email

The most common method of communication in a business context is email.

All email applications allow users to:

Send	Receive
Create messages	Open and read messages
Choose recipients – either from an address book of regular contacts or by typing the email address in	Download, save and read attachments
Attach files	Identify the sender of the message and save their address in their regular contacts address book
Send messages	Save and organise their emails in folders.

> **Tip**
>
> Remember that both the receiver and sender of an email need access to email software but that they can use different types of email software.

> **Tip**
>
> Some email addresses have a country code as well. For example: .uk (United Kingdom) and .sa (Saudi Arabia)

Setting up an email account

Email addresses come in two parts: the name of the user and the location of the account on the internet. ISPs will offer users an email account and give them an email address, which will look something like this:
mrchangis@home.net

Username or User ID	@	Location element	Domain type
mrchangis	@	home	.net

Most businesses will have an email address linked to their website domain name, therefore the location element of the email will show the name of the company. Personal email is available from many free email services that can be accessed on the web or from a mobile device. You can fill out an online form to get an account and an email address. You can access mail by entering your email address (or username) and password.

SMS text messaging

SMS (Short Message Service) is a text-based messaging system designed for the mobile phone networks around the world. Limited to around 160 characters, SMS messages can be sent, and the service provider will keep trying to send the message until the recipient turns on their device. SMS messages use the mobile or cell phone network, but many people now use IM (Instant Messages). IM allows two or more people to exchange messages over the internet. Messages are transferred instantly. This type of communication is known as real-time communication and is often built into social networking applications.

> **Real world**
>
> If people need to make decisions about a project quickly, IM can be a much more efficient way to communicate with others than sending many individual emails and waiting for responses. The system is very similar to texting on a mobile phone.

Video conferencing

Text-based messaging systems have their disadvantages. However well written, it is hard to tell how someone is feeling and easy to misinterpret a message. Video conferencing uses cameras and a screen to allow users to see and talk to each other in a more personal way. Although possible in the past using traditional broadcasting systems, video conferencing is now commonly an internet-based system based on streaming live video and audio between users. Businesses are more likely to use specialist video conferencing software that will allow them to communicate securely with several people at the same time. Despite the initial investment required, time and money is saved as because people do not have to travel long distances to attend meetings.

Audio conferencing

Telephone calls have always been an essential business communication tool. Audio conferencing allows multiple users to join a single conversation from any telephone, or internet accessible, location in the world. Conference calls can be arranged using traditional analogue telephone lines but in recent years the use of internet telephony and voice over internet protocol (VoIP) is increasingly popular. Using VoIP systems extends the range of conversations to any location with internet access that is often much cheaper than international land-line calls and multiple-user calls are handled with software rather than expensive fixed-line hardware.

Web conferencing

Web conferencing uses internet technology to allow multiple users from any internet enabled location to meet in a virtual conference room. Users can then share any electronic content with the others in the meeting; from text, images and presentations to live voice or video streams. As internet connectivity becomes more commonplace, as does the availability of smart devices, the lines between web, video and audio-conferencing are blurring.

Conference technology

Modern video conference technology relies on a stable, high speed internet connection to stream high quality video and audio. A slow, stuttering connection will make live interaction quite difficult.

Audio conferencing using VoIP will function with a slower connection and the nature of the web conference will dictate the requirements, especially if large documents are being shared.

All three require a modern computer, connected to a router with a high-speed connection with the ability to install conference applications. Any computer without an inbuilt webcam or microphone will require additional peripherals. Many smartphones and tablets are also now able to access online conferences, allowing users to connect remotely using a mobile internet connection.

Language

Video conferencing is sometimes known as electronic conferencing. Audio conferencing can also be termed as teleconferencing, or telecon.

Real world

You may be familiar with Skype, Zoom, Facetime, Google Meet or Microsoft Teams, these are examples of how we can use a video conferencing application to communicate cheaply with friends and business colleagues all over the world.

Real world

The audio and visual quality of video conferencing depends on the speed of the internet connection. A fast broadband connection with a large bandwidth will allow for a clear smooth transmission. Attempting video conferencing over a slower connection or using mobile phone networks often results in stuttering sound and video.

Activity 1

1   Make a list of five freely available webmail providers for your region. How are their email addresses structured and how does it compare to an email address from your school?

2   Both email and facsimile (fax) machines can send a copy of a document from one location to another. Which one would be the most appropriate in the following situations and why?

   a   Sending legal documents with a signature.

   b   Sending engineering drawings from an architect to a customer.

   c   Sending photos of a new baby to family members.

Activity 2

Make a comparative list of the advantages and disadvantages of the methods below in a business environment.

Method	Advantages	Disadvantages
Email		
Instant messaging		
Video conferencing		
Audio conferencing		
Web conferencing		
Facsimile transmission		

Blogs

Blogs (a shortened version of the term weblog) are personal or business online journals that are frequently updated. Normally free to set up and run, blogs offer a great opportunity to present ideas, articles and links to other websites. All content is presented in chronological order so that the most recent entry is always shown first; meaning readers can quickly see if the site is being updated. A blog without frequent updates will not attract regular readers. Readers can then be allowed to comment on the entries made, creating an interactive service similar to a forum.

Real world

As blog entries can be sent from any internet enabled location or mobile phone they have become very popular with celebrities, journalists and political readers as they can quickly put messages out to younger audiences. They are also used as a more interactive extension of established web sites.

Wikis

A wiki is a collaborative website that allow groups of users to build an online database on a specific topic, or range of topics. Any member of the wiki can add and edit content. The popularity of wiki sites depends on how reliable or extensive the information they present is. As with any user-generated content, questions about the validity and reliability of wikis will be asked and unlike a blog, changes or additions to the wiki do not appear in the order they were made, making it difficult to know when content has been changed.

Real world

Current examples of very large and influential wiki sites are Wikipedia (an online encyclopaedia) or Wikileaks (a political information site).

Tweets

Twitter is a popular communication application in which users communicate with one another using messages called tweets that work in much the same way as a blog. Posts generally answer the question, 'What are you doing?' and users can either respond to it or post their own message. Tweets can be published using a computer or a mobile phone but limited to 140 characters or less, so users have to choose their words wisely. Twitter users have usernames in Tweets in this format: @johnsmith. Tweets on the same topic can use a hash tag: a key word starting with a hash symbol (#), for example, #CambridgeIGCSE. Tweet readers are known as followers or 'tweeps'.

Language

A Tweet is sometimes referred to as a 'micro-blog'.

Social networking

Social networking sites offer a way for people to communicate online in a very open and accessible way. Unlike group email, social networking sites allow users to choose to participate or not. With membership in billions, popular social networks include Facebook, QZone, Google+ and more professionally focused sites like LinkedIn.

Each social network focuses on making the experience of social networking relevant and enjoyable for their users. Users sign up to the network and describe themselves, including information such as their age, gender, likes and dislikes. This is called their 'profile'.

Real world

Many dating sites are social networking sites that put people with similar interests and backgrounds in touch with each other. In Facebook, making a 'friend' gives you access to other people or groups that you could make friends with.

Session 4.6 How does ICT help business and personal communication?

167

Businesses find social networking sites useful in other ways: they are a great place for advertising products and services that are likely to appeal to the target group for the social network. Some employers may investigate a job applicant's 'profile' to see if the applicant is 'the sort of person they want to employ'. Embarrassing photographs or inappropriate comments may change someone's opinion of you. Some social networking sites have settings to ensure that certain areas of the site are limited to 'friends' only but it is often up to the user the ensure the right settings are in place. Dangers linked to eSafety are discussed in more detail in Unit 8.

Mobile telephones

Mobile telephones work by linking to a signal from a radio communication mast. For a constant signal, a mobile phone needs to be within 10 kilometres of a mast (or base station), and your mobile phone will constantly search for the strongest signal. When you make a call, the signal is received by the mast and sent to the mast nearest the phone whose number you are calling. Mobile phones have become an essential connectivity tool in business.

Mobile communication

Originally designed for voice and text based systems, modern smartphones can connect to the internet via mobile data networks or Wi-Fi hotspots. Services now provide two networks, the standard mobile phone network and an internet data service network. This increased connectivity adds the following functionality to mobile devices:

- Mobile website browsing and email
- VoIP (see below)
- Face to face video calls using the smartphone camera and screen
- Mobile multiplayer gaming.

Voice over Internet Protocol (VoIP)

Voice over Internet Protocol (VoIP) uses an internet connection to make the telephone calls through a computer with VoIP software. As most broadband users have a fixed price for their internet connection, this makes the call essentially free, other than the standard internet costs.

Users of VoIP on their computer can either use the built-in microphone and speakers usually found in most modern computers or an external headset with microphone for greater clarity.

There are some disadvantages with VoIP. Sound quality can be poor, which is not so much of a problem for personal calls, but it can be for important business calls. VoIP can also be targeted with the same security concerns as other internet communication such as identity and service theft, viruses and malware.

Activity 3

Describe the social networking sites that you have used. Explain why you might choose one social networking site over another, highlighting the advantages and disadvantages of the networking sites you choose. What features would you like to see in your ideal social networking site?

Real world

Call centres sometimes use VoIP. Many call centres consist of a very large room where operators deal with phone calls. Some use operators who work from home. The calls are received from anywhere in the world to the main call centre and are redirected through VoIP to the operators working from any office or even home. This reduces the cost of the telephone service, so that companies using this system save a lot of money.

Activity 4

List three advantages and three disadvantages for businesses using VoIP or internet telephony.

Review and revise

You should now be able to:

- identify a variety of methods of communication using ICT, including: fax; the internet; email; electronic conferencing; mobile phones; internet telephony services; blogs; wikis and social networking websites
- explain some of the advantages that companies can get from using a variety of communication techniques.

SESSION 4.7 Keeping computer network data confidential and secure

Background

In this session, you are going to review network security and the confidentiality and security of data. More information specifically focussed on personal security and online systems can be found in Session 8.2.

Securing the network

Within any large organisation, and even your own school, different people have different access rights to certain information depending on their position within it. For example, you have access to your own area of the school network but you shouldn't be able to access a friend's account or records of student test results. The person that manages the computer network at school, setting access rights for different users, is often referred to as the **network administrator** and this is the same for any large network.

User IDs

A user ID, or username, is a short collection of letters or numbers. It should be easily remembered by the user and is sometimes based around their real name. The network administrator, who allocates each user a network user ID (or username), manages access to areas of the network. Each time a user logs in, the network system software begins by checking that the ID exists – if it does, then it will check to see what hardware and software the user can use and what files and resources are available to the user.

Activity 1

Look at your school user ID. Talk about it with a partner. Are your IDs similar? If they are, what rules do you think the network administrator put in place to create them?

Passwords

Most computer systems will not allow you to log on with only a user ID, as this is not very secure. To increase security, users are asked to create a password that has to be entered when prompted. Very often, as you type in a password, it will be hidden from view, often replaced by a display of symbols such as *******.

Linked to a user ID, passwords prevent unauthorised access and are an essential part of any network or online account access. From email accounts to social networks, streaming services and online shopping, we have to manage so many passwords and it is essential we follow the rules:

- Passwords should be at least eight characters long.
- Use a mix of upper and lowercase characters.
- Include special characters (#, _ and % for example).
- Don't use real dictionary words as these can be guessed.
- Avoid including personal information that can be found out: family members, important dates, the names of pets or telephone numbers.
- Regularly change any password and never use it for more than one system.
- If you struggle to remember multiple passwords, use a password manager.

A strong password follows these rules, a weak password does not.

> **Real world**
>
> Operating systems, computer networks and online accounts will often ask you to change your password. Regularly changing a password is a good practice as it prevents it being guessed or calculated by those wishing to unlawfully access your data.

Activity 2

Passwords are so important as networks with multiple users often have private and confidential data.
- Why is it never a good idea to write down your password?
- What helps to make a password secure?
- Give examples of secure and insecure (strong and weak) passwords (make sure they are not ones you currently use).

Keeping your data confidential

Think about supermarket loyalty cards, created to offer discounts and special offers based on our shopping habits. The loyalty card will have details of the holder's name, age, address, gender, shopping habits and other personal data and is often used at the same time as a payment card in store. These two sets of data should be confidential and a link between them should not be made. There are rules to prevent this but there are examples of individuals and organisations passing on or even selling our personal data.

One of the ways in which user ID and passwords are unlawfully acquired is through **spyware**. Spyware is a computer program, usually attached as a zip file for an email or disguised alternative file installed without the knowledge of the user, that logs, records and transmits records of the activities of the user and the personal data their computers hold to an external location. Anti-spyware continuously scans a computer system for such programs, notifies the user and tries to remove it.

Data protection acts

Governments have had to act to ensure the increasing amount of data kept on networks is correctly handled. This has led to data protection acts being created all over the world and the majority follow the same principles. The examples below are typical of data protection legislation:

- Data should be used fairly, lawfully and transparently.
- Data must be obtained and used only for specified purposes.
- Data shall be adequate, relevant and not excessive.
- Data should be accurate and kept up to date.
- Data should not be kept for longer than necessary.
- Data must be kept safe and secure.
- Those organisations working with our data are accountable for all data protection and must produce evidence of their compliance.

Activity 3

1. You have just bought a new smartphone from a store where you have a loyalty card. What problems might occur if the store does not keep your personal details secure?
2. Banks and finance departments are supposed to keep financial transactions confidential. What might happen if this was not the case?
3. Investigate the data protection law in the country you live, how does it compare to the example given?

You can protect your access to the internet, email accounts and important networks with a user ID and a password but you can also apply these rules at home. A home computer login, family photos or a piece of important homework can also be protected by adding a password.

Encrypting data

In many organisations, data is **encrypted** to protect it further. Banks and government departments, for example, insist that data is encrypted so that if an unauthorised user gets access to the data, they are unable to read it.

Encryption converts data using a public encryption key into a meaningless form that cannot be read if intercepted. It can only be decrypted using the private key, or cypher, generated by the owner. The encrypted text and the private key are never transmitted together.

Real world

Spyware, a form of malware, can install itself onto your computer in a number of ways.

- You may receive an email that you download as an attachment or follow a link to a website.
- Sharing files by USB, email or the internet is an easy way for infected files to be passed on.

Real world

Look at the requirements that a government department has set out for its workers:

- Laptops must use a system where data can be encrypted.
- You must not use your own personal ICT equipment for work tasks.
- Only government supplied pen drives can be used for transferring data and must be encrypted to a certain standard.
- All paper data must be kept locked away while in your possession.
- All paper data must be shredded when no longer required.

Real world

When you pay for goods using a payment card, permission to access to your account may now be granted by a Personal Identification Number (PIN), a thumb print or a facial scan.

Language

Encryption encodes the data into unreadable code. Decryption decodes the code back into readable data.

Activity 4

Identify three advantages and three disadvantages of encryption.

Authentication techniques

Having user IDs in combination with passwords is an example of an authentication technique. Authentication techniques are used to identify users to a computer-based system or network. Each technique provides a range of methods for proving your identity, and the higher the security requirement; the more techniques may be used. There are three factors that can be used in authentication:

	Factor	Example
1	Something that you know	<ul><li>a Personal Identification Number (PIN)</li><li>username ID</li><li>a password or phrase</li><li>a challenge response (you must provide the correct answer to a particular question).</li></ul>
2	Something that belongs to you	These items are normally provided by the organisation providing secure access:<ul><li>a personal card with a magnetic stripe or smart card with an embedded chip.</li><li>a security wrist band</li><li>a physical or electronic token or key</li><li>a smart phone</li><li>personal identification, such as a passport or driving licence.</li></ul>
3	Something unique about you	This may be biometric data from the following unique features:<ul><li>the face, the unique pattern formed by our common facial features</li><li>a scan of either the retina or iris part of our eye</li><li>a recording of the pattern formed by either a thumb or finger print</li><li>the shape of our hand and the pattern formed by fingers and thumb</li><li>a recording and analysis of an individual's voice print.</li></ul>Other sources such as your own DNA can be used but such a test would be time consuming and expensive.

Real world

Many schools have introduced cash-less payment systems. Funds can be added to the account at home and students can pay for lunch or other services in school by using something that is unique to them, like a thumbprint or a magnetic stripe card.

Real world

It is possible in some airports to fast-track through passport control by registering to use your biometric data. A scanner scans face or eye, verifies that you are who you say you are and allows you to pass through.

Review and revise

You should now be able to:

- explain why it is important to keep data secure and confidential
- describe the processes and practices that businesses employ to ensure that data is held securely and confidentially
- give examples of data security in finance, schools, banking and in the retail industry.

4 Theory review

What have you covered?

In these seven theory sessions, you have:
- identified common network devices such as routers, modems, hubs, bridges, switches and proxy servers
- discovered how network communications, including wired, Wi-Fi and Bluetooth devices can be used in business organisations
- been introduced to LAN, WLAN and WAN and the differences between them
- considered the characteristics of common network environments
- considered how businesses use networks in their everyday operations and the different devices we can use to connect to them
- identified a variety of methods of communication used by businesses
- considered the benefits that companies can get from using a variety of communication techniques
- been introduced to the terms internet, intranet, web browser and ISP, web address and URL
- discovered the difference between the internet and an intranet
- considered how and why organisations make use of the internet and intranets
- considered the importance of keeping data secure and the methods that businesses employ to ensure its security and confidentiality.

Some practice questions

1 Connect a term on the left with the most appropriate example on the right:

LAN	A network across a university campus
WAN	A network used to connect offices of a car hire company across the country
WLAN	A network operating within company headquarters

See Session 4.2

2 Use the terms in the list to complete the paragraph below, which describes a school network.

client-server	network card	bridge	file server	WLAN
network cable	router			

To connect a computer to a (___), your computer needs a (_____ ____) so that you can plug in the (_____ ____). Your school computers will be connected through a (_____) to a (_____ ____). This kind of network is known as a (_____ ____) network. It is possible that although the student and administration networks might be separate, a (_____) will allow data to be passed between the two.

See Session 4.1

3 State whether each of these statements is true or false.

		True	False
a	The internet can only connect computers within a small geographical area.		
b	An intranet will only be accessed by users within a single network.		
c	A WLAN requires users to be connected with a fibre optic cable.		
d	An email address is needed before a user can access information on the internet.		
e	A WAN could be considered as a network of networks.		
f	Modems can only connect to the internet via fibre optic cable		

See Session 4.2

4 Explain the difference between the internet and an intranet. If your school has an intranet, what does the school use it for and explain how an organisation like a hospital might use one.

See Session 4.6

5 In order to keep data secure, an organisation will often use *encryption* methods when transferring data. *Usernames* or *IDs* and *strong passwords* may also be required in order to make sure that only authorised users have access to data. It is also common for a company to use a network *firewall* in order to further restrict access.

Explain the terms in italics.

See Session 4.7

6 Pete is a veterinary surgeon. He also runs a rescue centre where pet parrots, which have been abandoned by their owners, can be taken in and cared for. The rescue centre and animal hospital are built alongside his house. He has an office in his house and another in the rescue centre where his assistant works. All the files about the animals are held on a data server in the house. Pete wants to create a network so that he can access the data on his laptop as he moves around the buildings. His assistant also needs to be able to access the same data as she monitors the birds in the animal hospital.

a What kind of network does Pete need?

b List the hardware requirements of the system that Pete will need.

c Pete wants access to the internet. Explain why he needs an ISP. He has been offered the choice between ADSL and a cable modem.

d Discuss the advantage and disadvantages of the connection types that Pete has and suggest which would be the better option for him.

e Pete has been given the email address: pete@parrotsanctuary.co.uk

Explain what the different parts of this address represent.

See Sessions 4.2, 4.5 and 4.6

Progress check

Aiming for good progress

- You are able to identify all the hardware components required to create a network.
- You understand the differences between various network types.
- You can describe the different ways in which organisations can communicate and share information.
- You understand the ways in which users can connect to the internet and the hardware and software they need to achieve this.
- You recognise that within the workings of a network, security and confidentiality of data are vital.

Aiming for excellent progress

- You can identify all hardware and components that are necessary to create a network.
- You can describe the differences between the ways in which various networks operate.
- You can identify and evaluate the different ways in which organisations communicate with each other and how they share information.
- You can describe and evaluate the ways in which the internet is made available to users, including the hardware and software required.
- You can explain the necessity for keeping data secure and confidential, and you can offer suggestions about how this can be achieved.

Background

Before starting work on the All Computer Supplies Inc. website, it is important to become familiar with how websites are designed and created today and the different options that are available.

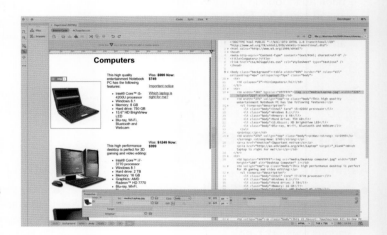

Writing a page using HTML and CSS

HTML (Hyper Text Markup Language) is a programming language for creating web pages. It allows a designer to specify content, colours and formatting through a text-based script. All early websites were created using this language and it is still the basis of websites today. It requires no specialist software to define a page other than a basic text editor, and the coding knowledge to create it. Once written, HTML the web page can then be displayed using a web browser.

CSS (Cascading Style Sheets) describes how the content within an HTML file is displayed. A CSS is also a markup language and sets a series of rules, or styles, that can be attached to one or more HTML pages. This means a single CSS style can control the style of a number of web pages.

Web design or WYSIWYG software

As many more people became interested in web design, software packages were developed to remove the need to learn and program HTML from scratch. Commercial software packages like Adobe Dreamweaver use a WYSIWYG (what you see is what you get) interface, allowing the user to visually create a website but with access to the scripting language being generated behind it. Commercial software can be expensive but there are open source alternatives such as BlueGriffon.

Website content management system

Creating a website, whether using HTML or specific software, requires the site to then be uploaded to a hosting server for viewing on the internet. An online CMS (content management system) allows a user to log into a platform that hosts template-based websites and develop it as their own. This may include changing colours, fonts, images and menu systems to meet the user's own house-style requirements. Such systems are very popular for those with little web design skills who would like a professional looking website online in a short space of time, and plan to make regular changes to their site. There is a cost involved for most commercial systems, and users are limited to how much the look of the page can be changed.

Real world

Many people now use blogs as a simple, user friendly, alternative to web design software to create an online presence. Blogs are usually free to set up, very customisable, and offer many of the advantages of an online CMS. A popular example of this is Wordpress.

Activity 1

Search for examples of web design software, or CMS platforms, either commercial or open source, and compare the features they offer.

Web design development layers

In order to create an effective website it is important to become familiar with the three **web development layers**. Considering these layers throughout the design, development and maintenance of a site can save time and repetitive work.

Content layer	Presentation layer	Behaviour layer
Sometimes referred to as the structure layer, this refers to the HTML framework of a page. This will include the visual layout, placement of text and images and hyperlinks used to navigate both within the page and to external pages.	The presentation layer defines the format of a page through styling elements and how it will appear to the user. This maintains visual consistency across browsers and platforms. The layer is defined through cascading style sheets (CSS) that can be applied to one or multiple pages.	Real-time interactive or dynamic content on a site that provides users with something to do is often generated using JavaScript and this is the behaviour layer. This may include image galleries, forms, the setting of multimedia element sizes or adding a live clock, video or music track.

Activity 2

Choose one page from three popular websites and for each, analyse and describe the key elements that make up the content, presentation and behaviour layers.

Review and revise

You should now be able to:
- identify and describe alternative methods of designing websites
- identify and describe the three web development layers
- understand the function of the content, presentation and behaviour layer.

SESSION 4.9 Using HTML to create and edit webpages

Background

The World Wide Web allows access to millions of websites, with more added every minute of every day. Stored on web servers that are interconnected via the internet, each website is made up of one or more **websites** which are linked together by hyperlinks. Webpages are created using a language called **HTML**, which stands for **H**yper **T**ext **M**ark-up **L**anguage that instructs a computer to display visual data in a user-friendly format. All webpages were originally written in HTML but web authoring software that combines visual design tools and HTML coding are becoming more popular. These programs store their pages in HTML format, but developers do not necessarily need to know the HTML language to develop effective websites.

Junaid at All Computer Supplies Inc. has asked you to create webpages by following the steps in these sessions.

Beginning to create a webpage using HTML

Use a text editor to create your first page. Open a text editing program such as *Microsoft Notepad* and type in the lines of code shown here:

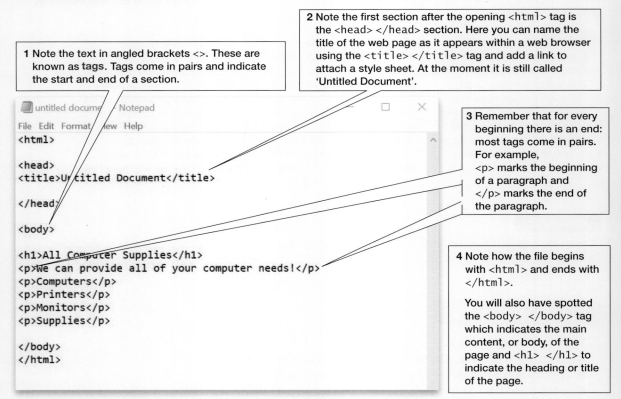

1 Note the text in angled brackets <>. These are known as **tags**. Tags come in pairs and indicate the start and end of a section.

2 Note the first section after the opening <html> tag is the <head> </head> section. Here you can name the title of the web page as it appears within a web browser using the <title> </title> tag and add a link to attach a style sheet. At the moment it is still called 'Untitled Document'.

3 Remember that for every beginning there is an end: most tags come in pairs. For example, <p> marks the beginning of a paragraph and </p> marks the end of the paragraph.

4 Note how the file begins with <html> and ends with </html>.

You will also have spotted the <body> </body> tag which indicates the main content, or body, of the page and <h1> </h1> to indicate the heading or title of the page.

```
untitled docume    Notepad                             □   ×
File Edit Format View Help
<html>

<head>
<title>Untitled Document</title>

</head>

<body>

<h1>All Computer Supplies</h1>
<p>We can provide all of your computer needs!</p>
<p>Computers</p>
<p>Printers</p>
<p>Monitors</p>
<p>Supplies</p>

</body>
</html>
```

Tags

Tags are used to mark up, or describe, a webpage. A web browser such as Internet Explorer or Firefox uses tags to interpret what the page looks like. Webpages use HTML to mark up the page.

HTML elements and nesting

Everything contained in the opening and closing tag is known as the **HTML element**. HTML elements can have other elements contained within them. This is known as **nesting**. In this example the <body> </body> element is nested within the <html> </html> element.

Then save the file as **index.html.** Make sure that you save the file in your work area with the .html extension. Now open it in a browser.

You have created your first webpage! Note:

- The use of the file extension **(.html)** is crucial as the browser will not see the file as a webpage without it.
- Sometimes the file extension is shortened to .htm – either is fine!

In the Microsoft Edge browser, the webpage that you have created looks like this:

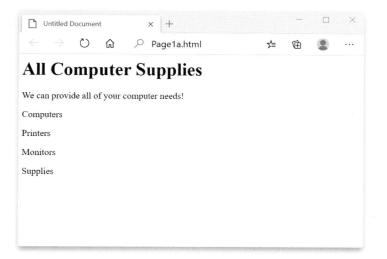

As you can see, the browser does not display the tags but interprets them to show the page:

- The browser knows that it has some HTML to display because it is contained by `<html>` `</html>` elements.
- The main content to show is within `<body>` `</body>`.
- The heading at the top is in big letters as the HTML indicated it is a first level heading: `<h1>` `</h1>`.
- The remaining text is in separate paragraphs, as indicated by `<p>` `</p>`.

Tip

To display an HTML file as a webpage, either drag the file into a browser window or double-click it to open your default browser.

To edit an HTML file, either open within a text editor or right click and select open then text editor.

Real world

Popular web browsers at the moment include:

Google Chrome
Microsoft Edge
Mozilla Firefox
Opera
Apple Safari

Tip

The home or start page of any website is normally saved with the name **index.html**. Web servers look for this filename when opening a web address.

Structuring the content

Junaid recognises that this webpage needs a better layout. He decides it would be better if you could list the products he has in his shop. You change the webpage by editing your .txt file.

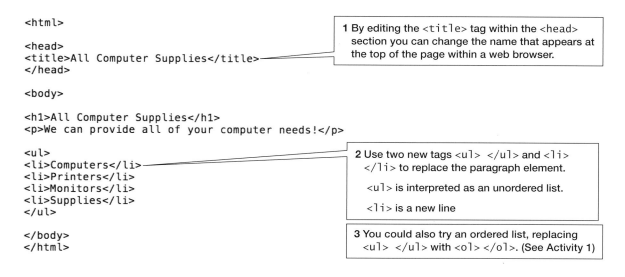

```
<html>

<head>
<title>All Computer Supplies</title>
</head>

<body>

<h1>All Computer Supplies</h1>
<p>We can provide all of your computer needs!</p>

<ul>
<li>Computers</li>
<li>Printers</li>
<li>Monitors</li>
<li>Supplies</li>
</ul>

</body>
</html>
```

1 By editing the `<title>` tag within the `<head>` section you can change the name that appears at the top of the page within a web browser.

2 Use two new tags `<ul>` `</ul>` and `<li>` `</li>` to replace the paragraph element.

`<ul>` is interpreted as an unordered list.

`<li>` is a new line

3 You could also try an ordered list, replacing `<ul>` `</ul>` with `<ol>` `</ol>`. (See Activity 1)

Activity 1

1 Save and preview your file in a browser. Write down any differences you see between the first version of the webpage you created. What does an unordered list look like on a webpage?

2 Change your HTML coding to replace the unordered list with an ordered list. Save your file and preview, how do the lists differ?

Changing the look of a webpage

Junaid and you both realise that this webpage does not look very attractive. You decide to change the appearance of the page.

```
<html>

<head>
<title>All Computer Supplies</title>
</head>

<body>

<h1>All Computer Supplies</h1>
<p>We can provide <b>all</b> of <i>your</i> computer needs!</p>

<ul>
<li>Computers</li>
<li>Printers</li>
<li>Monitors</li>
<li>Supplies</li>
</ul>

</body>
</html>
```

Tip

Once a file is saved as a **.html** file, it will always open within a web browser. To open the file for editing, either open within a text editor directly or right click and select **Open with** and select a text editor such as **Notepad**.

1 You can place new tags around all and your. What do you think these look like on a webpage?

2 There are other tags you could use.

For example, you could try `<strong>` and `<em>`.

Other common tags include `<sup>` for superscript and `<sub>` for subscript text.

Activity 2

● Insert the tags **<b> </b>** and **<i> </i>**. You should find that **<b> </b>** makes text appear **bold** and that **<i> </i>** makes text appear in *italics*.

● Experiment with other tags such as **<strong>**, **<em>**, **<sup>** and **<sub>** in your file. Remember that HTML elements have a start and an end. Don't forget to save your file as .txt and .html. Remember also that you will need to save and refresh the view in your browser to see the changes.

Using attributes to change the look of a webpage: Colour

There are other things that you can format on the webpage by using HTML. Junaid asks you to add some colour to the page and then to change some of the formatting.

```
<html>

<head>
<title>All Computer Supplies</title>
</head>

<body>

<h1>All Computer Supplies</h1>
<p>We can provide <strong>all</strong> of <em>your</em> computer needs!</p>

<ul>
<li style="color:red">Computers</li>
<li style="color:green">Printers</li>
<li style="color:blue">Monitors</li>
<li style="color:olive">Supplies</li>
</ul>

</body>
</html>
```

1 Look carefully at how colour is added to the page, using style within the tag. Style is an attribute of the HTML element.

Note:

● The spelling of color (US spelling)

● The use of quotation marks. Used to define attributes in HTML. These should be at the beginning and end of an attribute, such as a size or a colour.

● The use of spaces. Attributes are separated by spaces or line breaks.

Activity 3

Try adding other colours to your page. Choose from the list of 17 standard colours. You must be careful to type the code correctly.

2 There are 17 standard colours, which all browsers can interpret correctly: aqua, black, fuchsia, blue, grey, green, lime, maroon, navy, olive, purple, red, silver, teal, white and yellow.

Using attributes to change the look of a webpage: Formatting

Junaid suggests you change some of the other formatting to help improve the page.

```html
<html>

<head>
<title>All Computer Supplies</title>
</head>

<body style=background-color:yellow>

<h1 style="font-family:arial;text-align:center">All Computer Supplies</h1>

<p style=font-family:verdana;font-size:large">We can provide <strong>all</strong> of <em>your</em> computer needs!</p>

<ul>
<li style="color:red">Computers</li>
<li style="color:green">Printers</li>
<li style="color:blue">Monitors</li>
<li style="color:olive">Supplies</li>
</ul>

</body>
</html>
```

> Note how there are different values with the style attribute in <body> <h1> and <p>.

> The style attribute can have a range of different values and can be added to an HTML tag to define the content with it. The most common ones are:
> - font-family, which indicates the font to be used
> - font-size, which indicates the size of the font
> - text-align, which indicates whether the text is aligned to the left, centre (center) or right
> - font-style, which indicates normal or italic
> - font-weight, which indicates bold or normal
> - background-color, which indicates the colour of the background
> - color, which indicates the colour of the text.

Previewed in Chrome, the page would look like this.

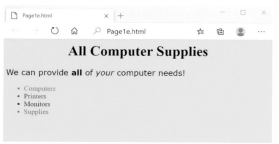

Real world

All web design colours are based on the RGB model, mixing together Red, Green and Blue. Up to 16 777 216 possible colour combinations are available using three pairs of two digit hexadecimal references in the format of #RRGGBB.

Activity 4

1   Type the changes into your file. Save and review in a browser.
2   Experiment with different values of the style attribute and see what happens. For example, try and replace the standard named colour references with their hexadecimal equivalents. Remember, you need to save the file and refresh it in the browser to see the results.
3   Print the HTML code of your last page and highlight it in different colours on the printout:
    a   the opening and closing body tags
    b   the opening and closing tags of paragraphs
    c   the opening and closing lines of a list
    d   the attribute of the heading <h1>
    e   the value of the attribute for <h1>.
4   Answer the following questions:
    a   How does a browser know that a file is a webpage?
    b   How many standard named colours are there and how many hexadecimal references can be used?
    c   How can you tell if an HTML file contains a 'nest'?
    d   What are:
        i   HTML elements?
        ii attributes?

Adding a table to a webpage

Using tables is a good way to organise information. Junaid would like the three different office locations adding to the page you have made and has suggested using a table. There are no drawing tools when using HTML but the following tags allows you to specify the structure and size of the table.

```
<html>

<head>
<title>All Computer Supplies</title>

</head>

<body style=background-color:yellow>
<h1 style="font-family:arial;text-align:center">All Computer Supplies</h1>
<p style=font-family:verdana;font-size:large">We can provide <strong>all</strong> of <em>your</em> computer needs!</p>

<ul>
<li style="color:red">Computers</li>
<li style="color:green">Printers</li>
<li style="color:blue">Monitors</li>
<li style="color:olive">Supplies</li>
</ul>

<table>
  <tr>
    <td>Main Office</td>
    <td>Technical Office 1</td>
    <td>Technical Office 2</td>
  </tr>
  <tr>
    <td>High Street</td>
    <td>Unit 3 Industrial Park</td>
    <td>Unit 7 Industrial Park</td>
  </tr>
</table>

</body>
</html>
```

1 The table is defined using the `<table>` `<table/>` tags.

2 Each row is defined by the `<tr>` tag and each cell within the table is defined with the `<td>` tag.

As you can see, this table will have two rows and three columns.

The page will now look like this. 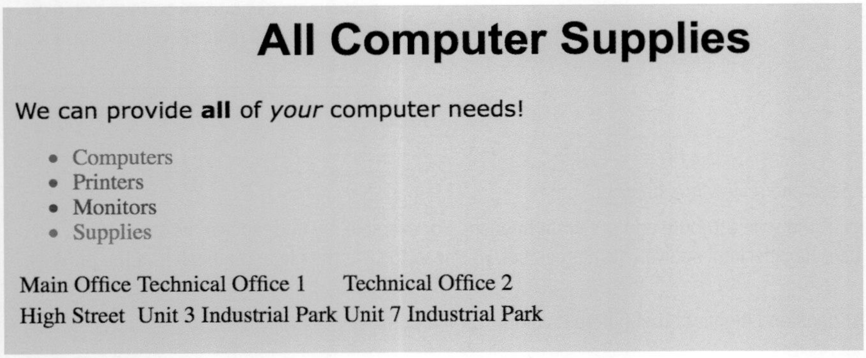

All Computer Supplies

We can provide **all** of *your* computer needs!

- Computers
- Printers
- Monitors
- Supplies

Main Office Technical Office 1   Technical Office 2
High Street Unit 3 Industrial Park Unit 7 Industrial Park

Formatting a table in HTML

Once previewed, it is clear that the blocks of text in the table are quite close together. Using additional attributes, it is possible to adjust widths, add styling and allow a single cell to span more than one column.

```
<html>

<head>
<title>All Computer Supplies</title>
<style>
table, th, td {
    border: 1px solid black;
    border-collapse: collapse;
    text-align: left;
}
</style>
</head>

<body style=background-color:yellow>
<h1 style="font-family:arial;text-align:center">All Computer Supplies</h1>
<p style=font-family:verdana;font-size:large>We can provide <strong>all</strong> of <em>your</em> computer needs!</p>

<ul>
<li style="color:red">Computers</li>
<li style="color:green">Printers</li>
<li style="color:blue">Monitors</li>
<li style="color:olive">Supplies</li>
</ul>

<table style="width:100%">
  <tr>
    <th>Main Office</th>
    <th colspan="2">Technical Support Offices</th>
  </tr>
  <tr>
    <td>High Street</td>
    <td>Unit 3 Industrial Park</td>
    <td>Unit 7 Industrial Park</td>
  </tr>
</table>

</body>
</html>
```

1 Look carefully at how a single black border and left alignment has been added by adding a page style to the page in the <head> section.

2 Note how the width of the table can be defined by adding an in-line style to the <table> tag. This can be set as a percentage or in pixels.

3 By replacing the <tr> tag with <th> it now becomes a table heading.

4 If a heading applies to more than one column then one heading can be made to span multiple cells using the colspan function.

The page will now look like this.

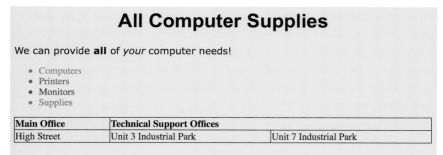

Inserting an image in HTML

Junaid would like his new logo inserting at the top of the page. He has provided you with an image file and has specified it should be no wider than 100 pixels, whilst still maintaining the aspect ratio.

```
</head>

<body style=background-color:yellow>

<img src="acs-logo.jpg" alt="ACS Business Logo" width="100">
```

1 Insert the <img src> tag before the main heading to add the logo. Note the additional attributes:

- The file name of the image is located in the same location as the webpage, otherwise the file path should also be included.

- The alt attribute provides an alternative text or description for the image, used if a user requires a screen reader.

- The width attribute specifies the width in pixels. The height can also be specified but if only the width is set the image ratio is automatically maintained.

This logo should now appear at the top of the screen.

Inserting metatags

Metadata is data about data, metatags are additional blocks of background information about a web page that are used by search engines and web browsers but don't actually appear on screen when browsing.

Metatags are inserted into the <head> section of a page and generally include the following:

● description: a short description of the site and its contents.
● keywords: important words that are analysed by search engines to help search for relevant sites.
● author: simply the name of the website author.
● viewport: tells the browser the zoom level that should be used when the site is first opened on different devices.

Adding metatags the home page of the ACS website might look like the following:

```
<head>
<title>All Computer Supplies</title>
<link rel="stylesheet" href="css/acsupplies.css">

<head>
  <meta name="description" content="Great value computer supplier">
  <meta name="keywords" content="laptops, desktop computers, printers, supplies">
  <meta name="author" content="ACS">
  <meta name="viewport" content="width=device-width, initial-scale=1.0">
</head>
```

Activity 5

1. Add a table to your web page similar to the example shown.

2. Experiment with the style options and column widths.

3. Add suitable metatags to your page, including relevant keywords and your name as author.

Review and revise

You should now be able to:
● set up a simple webpage using HTML
● recognise and use tags to change the appearance of a webpage
● recognise and use attributes to change the appearance of a webpage
● understand when HTML commands are nested
● use metatags to define aspects of a webpage.

SESSION 4.10 Creating and using cascading style sheets

Background

The presentation layer of the web design development process defines the look of a webpage through the creation of **CSS (cascading style sheets)** that can be applied to one or any number of webpages. If you are creating a single webpage, then the styles; fonts, colours and backgrounds can be set within the website authoring software for that page but CSS becomes really useful if you plan to create more than one page.

Consider a mini shopping website of three pages; an external CSS file can define how each one of them looks. Fonts, colours and background images can be set within the style sheet meaning changing this one file changes all the files it is linked to. Imagine how useful this could be with a website of ten or fifty pages and the task of maintaining consistency and a particular **house style**.

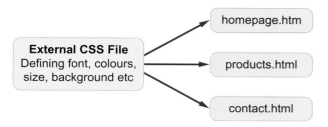

> **Tip**
>
> Try to avoid moving files within a website using the file explorer of your operating system as this can break the links between relative files. Always save and modify locations within your web authoring software.

In this session you will create a CSS file to define the presentation of the page you created and also apply it to pages you create in the following session.

Organisation and relative file paths

When creating any website, the organisation and location of your files is really important. Websites work most efficiently when created with relative file paths. This means the links between the files you create, HTML files, images, sounds and style sheets, are all relative to each other. By creating a folder structure for your website before you start, files will all have a set location and relative links will be easy to maintain.

Activity 1

Create a folder in your document area called **website** and within that folder create two **sub-folders** called **CSS** and **media**.

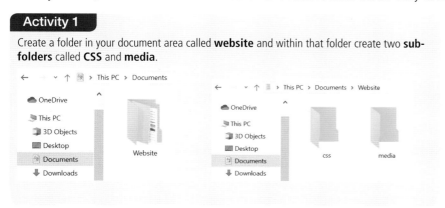

The difference between attached style sheets and in-line style attributes

In this session you are going to create an external CSS style sheet that will be attached to more than one page within your website. This allows the rules created within the style sheet to impact upon multiple pages, saving time and coding.

Alternatively, you will have already used in-line style attributes to style elements of your web pages. The key difference of in-line styles are that they affect every element of the page with the same style attribute. For example, the table styling created in Session 4.9 will affect every table in the page if more were added. In-line styling is useful for single web pages and creating HTML emails.

The difference between a style and a class

Within the language of CSS styling can be applied in different ways. A style attribute can be applied to a specific element within the same line, often referred to as in-line styling.

A style can be attached to an id attribute of an HTML element, this means only one unique element will be affected. The # symbol is used to identify an HTML id element.

A class can be applied to multiple elements in the same page with the same class selector. A period (.) is used to identify a CSS class element.

> **Tip**
>
> Like .html files, .css files can also be opened and edited in *Notepad* or any other basic text editor.

Activity 2

In order to attach a style sheet to one or more web pages we need to remove the in-line styling added so far.

Edit your index.html file so it matches the new version below.

```
<html>

<head>
<title>All Computer Supplies</title>

<link rel="stylesheet" href="css/acsupplies.css">
</head>

<img src="media/acs-logo.jpg" alt="ACS Business Logo" width="100">

<h1>All Computer Supplies</h1>
<p>We can provide <strong>all</strong> of <em>your</em> computer needs!</p>

<ul>
<li>Computers</li>
<li>Printers</li>
<li>Monitors</li>
<li>Supplies</li>
</ul>

<table>
    <tr>
      <th>Main Office</th>
      <th colspan="2">Technical Support Offices</th>
    </tr>
    <tr>
      <td>High Street</td>
      <td>Unit 3 Industrial Park</td>
      <td>Unit 7 Industrial Park</td>
    </tr>
</table>

</body>
</html>
```

Creating a new CSS file

Junaid would like the background of the webpage to be yellow and all the text to be in an Arial font. Creating a new style sheet for a website allows total control of these styles can be added to and edited at any time.

Look carefully at the code and you will recognise many common features. The element (body) is described by the values contained within the curly brackets { }. The names of the values are the same as those you met in the previous session for the style attribute. What is different is the way the colour is described. Rather than yellow, which you used before, it now says #FF0.

A CSS file can be created in the same way as a html file using any text editor. Once written, the file should be saved with the .css extension.

```
body {
        font-family: Arial, Helvetica, sans-serif;
        font-size: 12px;
        font-style: italic;
        background: #FF0;
}
table, th, td{
        width: 50%; text-align: center;
        border: 1px solid #000;
        padding: 0 px; border-spacing: 0px
}
```

> The main text will use the Arial font family, be white, 12 pixels high and in italics. The background of the page will be yellow.

> Any table will be 50% of the screen width with a solid black border with no padding or spacing.
>
> Including the th and td tags means the styling will be applied to the heading and data rows of any table.

Attaching a new CSS file to an existing page

To add a CSS file to a webpage, simply add the following line between the <head>   </head> tags:

`<link rel="stylesheet" href="css/acsupplies.css">`

The href should point to the relative location of the .css file to the .html file.

> **Tip**
>
> **CSS Comments**
> Sometimes it is handy to add notes to explain your code at a later date. A CSS comment starts with /* and ends with */ and is ignored by web browsers.

Activity 3

1 Create a new blank CSS file, save it as acsupplies.css into the css folder of your website folder.

2 Add body and table styles similar to the ones shown that will suit Junaid's requirements.

3 Attach your style sheet to index.html

Headers, paragraphs and lists

Website design conventions allow for many common elements to be specified: the headers, paragraph and list options are three that can be either set within your website authoring software or set using a CSS rule. There are six heading tags **<h1>   </h1>** through to **<h6>   </h6>** with h1 recognised as the most important and h6 the least. The tags for paragraphs and lists were outlined in session 4.9.

> **Tip**
>
> Try to avoid clashing header tags and CSS rules as all the rules you apply may not appear. Decide which is the most efficient to use for your site.

The example below shows how to add a rule by hand to the CSS script and these headings can be used instead of specifying additional styles to a title or subtitle.

```
h1 {
        font-family: Arial, Helvetica, sans-serif;
        text-align: center;
        font-size: 36px;
        font-weight: bold
        color: #000;
}
```

Activity 4

1 Open up the **index.html** and its associated CSS file, **acsupplies.css** and edit the CSS coding to add the **h1** header rule as shown. Then apply this rule to the title.

2 Junaid has decided against using italics in the main text, remove the italics reference from the body section of the CSS file.

3 The text within the table is a little large, add a font-size of 10px to the table section of the CSS file.

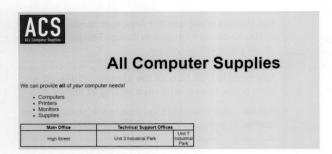

All Computer Supplies

We can provide **all** of *your* computer needs!

- Computers
- Printers
- Monitors
- Supplies

Main Office	Technical Support Offices	
High Street	Unit 3 Industrial Park	Unit 7 Industrial Park

Style sheet hierarchy and in-line styles

CSS styles can be applied to a HTML document either internally or externally but having multiple instances of styling means sometimes rules can clash and it is important to consider which element will take precedence over others. Although there can be issues relating to browser inconsistencies that are often out of web designers hands, the general consensus is that the order of application is as follows:

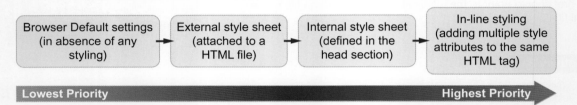

Browser Default settings (in absence of any styling) → External style sheet (attached to a HTML file) → Internal style sheet (defined in the head section) → In-line styling (adding multiple style attributes to the same HTML tag)

Lowest Priority ——————————————————→ **Highest Priority**

This however is a very general rule; the more specific a rule is, and its placement within the HTML is also a factor. For example if an external style sheet is placed after an internal one in the HTML coding, the external one will have priority.

Review and revise

You should now be able to:

- understand the difference between internal and external HTML styling
- understand the reasons why web developers use cascading style sheets
- describe the different elements that can be defined by style sheets
- create and apply external style sheets (CSS) to a webpage
- explain in general terms the order in which styling is applied to a webpage when viewed through a browser.

SESSION 4.11 Using HTML to add website content

Background

You are now going to build on skills and improve the look of your web pages by using tables to organise the layout and structure. You will also learn how to add additional content including images, video, sound and links to other web pages and emails.

Using tables to organise webpages

Junaid needs to add four extra pages to the website in addition to the **index** page. He has asked you to put together these pages and each should link to the external style sheet created in the previous session.

2. Computers		
Laptop image	Details	Price
Desktop image	Details	Price
All-in-one image	Details	Price

4. Monitors		
19" image	Details	Price
23" image	Details	Price
25" image	Details	Price

3. Printers		
All-in-one image	Details	Price
B + W Laser image	Details	Price
Colour Laser image	Details	Price

5. Consumables		
A4 paper image	Details	Price
B + W ink image	Details	Price
Colour ink image	Details	Price

Each page has:
- a table with three columns and four rows, the top row is merged
- a title in the top row
- three product images
- three sets of product details
- a discounted and original price for each item.

So let's make a start with page 2. Open an empty text file and in the same way as you created the index.html page in Session 4.9, add a table to match the structure shown above.

Take a look at the example below, it follows the layout as described above with a 3 x 4 table with a merged header cell. Notice the structure of the table and the use of bullet points and placement of images.

```
<html>

<head>
<title>All Computer Supplies</title>

<link rel="stylesheet" href="css/acsupplies2.css">

</head>

<body>
<table>
  <tr>
    <td colspan="3"><h1>Computers</h1></td></tr>
  <tr>
    <td><img src="media/laptop.jpg" width="200" height="200" alt="Laptop"></td>
    <td>This high quality entertainment laptop has the following features:</p>
      <ul>
        <li>Processor Type</li>
        <li>Operating System</li>
        <li>Memory</li>
        <li>Hard drive</li>
        <li>Monitor</li>
        <li>Extras</li>
      </ul></td>
    <td>Original and sale price</td>
  </tr>
  <tr>
    <td><img src="media/desktop.jpg" width="200" height="200" alt="Desktop computer"></td>
    <td>This high performance desktop is perfect for 3D gaming and video editing:</p>
      <ul>
        <li>Processor Type</li>
        <li>Operating System</li>
        <li>Memory</li>
        <li>Hard drive</li>
        <li>Monitor</li>
        <li>Extras</li>
      </ul></td>
    <td>Original and sale price</td>
  </tr>
  <tr>
    <td><img src="media/all-one-computer.jpg" width="200" height="200" alt="All in one"></td>
    <td>This touchscreen All-in-One PC is space-saving and powerful enough for any home office.</p>
      <ul>
        <li>Processor Type</li>
        <li>Operating System</li>
        <li>Memory</li>
        <li>Hard drive</li>
        <li>Monitor</li>
        <li>Extras</li>
      </ul></td>
    <td>Original and sale price</td>
  </tr>
</table>

</body>
</html>
```

> **Tip**
>
> When you are creating your own version of this site, try and use a similar file structure and file names, the more confident you become, the more you can experiment.

Activity 1

1   Using the example in this session as a starting point, create pages 2, 3, 4 and 5.

2   Replace the sample text with computer specifications taken from computer shopping websites but you do not need to add images yet.

3   Notice the reference to the CSS style sheet has changed to acsupplies2.css. Edit and resave your original CSS file with following changes to the table section.

```
table, th, td{
        table-layout: auto; width: 600px;
        text-align: left;
        font-size: 10px;
        border: 1px solid #000;
        padding: 0 px; border-spacing: 0px
}
```

Image sizes in webpages

When you browse any webpage with images, the images will not display properly until your computer has downloaded a copy of them. This means your browsing speed is often affected by the file size of images within a webpage and how fast your connection can download them. Digital images are measured in pixels and whereas the physical size and pixel resolution are considered when printing, only the pixel size is important in web design. A standard computer screen has a size of 1024 x 768 and upwards, and images should be scaled with this in mind.

Manipulating an image

Ideally, images for use in websites should be formatted so that their size matches the available space within a webpage. There are a number of software packages available that can perform image manipulation and a variety of image file types that can be used in web design. The following steps will guide you through using an **open source** software package called *Gimp*.

Image editing terminology

The following terms are often used in image editing.

Term	Description
Resizing	Changing the size of an image without editing its resolution; this normally relates to printed work and not internet images.
Resampling	Changing the pixel height and width of an image; relevant to internet use, as sizes are measured in pixels.
Rotation	Changing the visual angle of an image by rotating either clockwise or anti-clockwise around its centre point.
Reflection	Creating a mirror image of an image by reflecting it about its vertical or horizontal axis.
Colour depth	Refers to the number of colours that can be stored for a particular image. It is measured in bits and this relates to the number of computer memory bits that can be used to store colour information. ● 2-bit allows four colours ● 4-bit allows 16 colours ● 8-bit allows 256 colours ● 16-bit allows 65 536 colours ● 24-bit allows 16 777 216 colours.
Image resolution	Normally measured in pixels per inch (ppi). The higher the value the greater the detail. Screen resolution is normally 72 or 96ppi, while 300ppi is recommended for professional printing.
Aspect ratio	The ratio between the height and width of an image. By maintaining or fixing an aspect ratio an image will look the same and not stretched when resized or resampled.

Tip

It is common practice in HTML coding, and email addresses, to use lowercase with creating filenames. It is also important to avoid including spaces in webpage names.

Real world

Inserting alternate text for an image is really important for businesses. It allows those with partial sight access to image descriptions, and it helps businesses get their sites noticed as the image descriptions are read through by popular internet search engines.

Real world

As lower cost high resolution monitors become more commonplace, the screen resolution of webpages is obviously increasing. A full HD screen for example has a resolution of 1920 x 1080. However with more smartphones and tablets displaying webpages, pages are having to be developed that can adapt to a range of different sizes. This is often referred to as adaptive or responsive web design.

Tip

Whilst reducing the resolution and/or the colour depth of an image will reduce its file size, it will reduce the quality of the image and this cannot be restore once saved.

Resizing an image

The following high-quality image needs resampling in order to fit into the cell of a table that is 200 by 200 pixels.

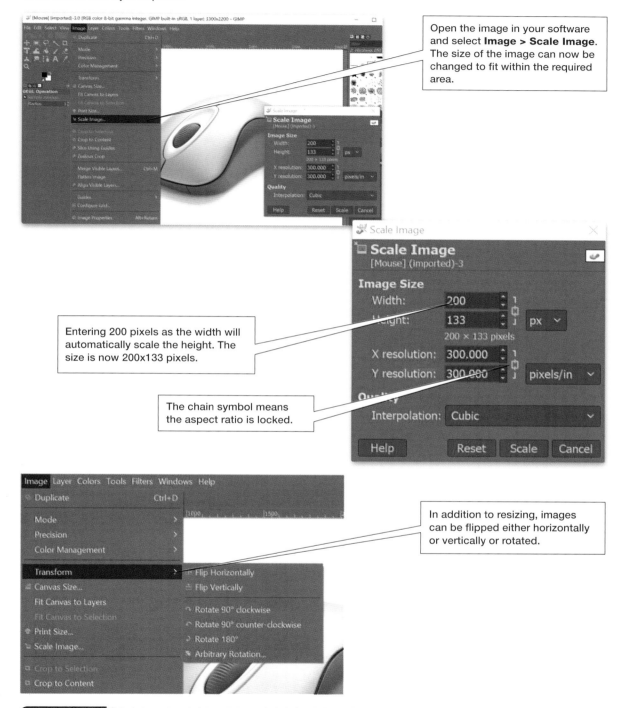

Open the image in your software and select **Image > Scale Image**. The size of the image can now be changed to fit within the required area.

Entering 200 pixels as the width will automatically scale the height. The size is now 200x133 pixels.

The chain symbol means the aspect ratio is locked.

In addition to resizing, images can be flipped either horizontally or vertically or rotated.

Activity 2

Find a suitable image from the internet of a desktop computer. Resample the image to the following approximate size: 200 pixels wide by 200 pixels high.

Changing the colour depth

The standard colour depth for internet images is 256 colours or 8-bit. This can be adjusted and the lower the colour depth the smaller the file size. It should be noted though that lowering the colour depth will result in loss of image quality.

Experiment with the colour depth of your image from Activity 2. At what colour depth does the quality of the image become unusable?

Saving in different file types

Most image editing packages will have their own software specific file extension for saving. When saving files for internet use, you will be required to export your image in a web-friendly format. Below are the most common.

Image file type	Description
JPEG (.jpg)	(Joint Photographic Experts Group) Designed for flat, rectangular images. Lots of compression options and the quality of the image can be selected when saved.
GIF (.gif)	(Graphics Interchange Format) Limited to 8-bit, this file is often used for diagrams or cartoon-style images. Also used in animation. Images can also have transparent areas.
PNG (.png)	(Portable Network Graphics) Similar to a GIF file but can support 16 million colours and therefore higher-quality images.
BMP (.bmp)	(Windows Bitmap) Uncompressed images created in the Microsoft Windows operating system. File sizes are often too large for internet use.

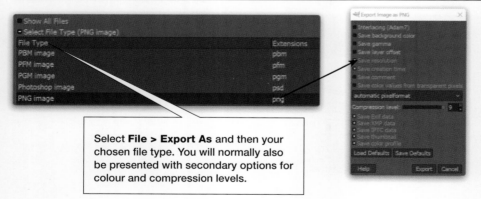

Select **File > Export As** and then your chosen file type. You will normally also be presented with secondary options for colour and compression levels.

Experiment with image files by resaving the original image file you found from the internet in Activity 2 into the four file types listed. Discuss with a partner the differences, if any, between the saved files. Use the image you resampled in addition to or instead of one of the images in your website.

Tip

Compression allows smaller file sizes to be created but this reduces the quality.

Activity 5

You are going to add suitable images to your web pages. Refer back to Junaid's outline at the beginning of the session.

1   Using either the images supplied, or ones of your own, add images to the media folder.

2   If necessary, resize images, adjust the colour depth and export to a suitable web format.

Below is an example of how Page 2 might look.

> **Tip**
>
> Refer back to Session 4.9 if you need a reminder about adding an image using HTML.
>
> The process of adding an animated GIF is done in exactly the same way.

Computers

		This high quality entertainment laptop has the following features: • Processor Type • Operating System • Memory • Hard drive • Monitor • Extras	Original and sale price
		This high performance desktop is perfect for 3D gaming and video editing: • Processor Type • Operating System • Memory • Hard drive • Monitor • Extras	Original and sale price
		This touchscreen All-in-One PC is space-saving and powerful enough for any home office.	

Inserting sound and video

Websites often use sound, video or animated images to enhance their website. Junaid has asked you to experiment with adding some multimedia content to the home page, index.html.

Modern HTML tags allow an audio file to be simply added to a web page, along with a controller.

The example below shows a simple sound effect being added to the index.html page. You will see it has been added below the table, just below the closing </body> tag.

```
<audio controls>
        <source src="media/chime.mp3" type="audio/mpeg">
</audio>

</body>
```

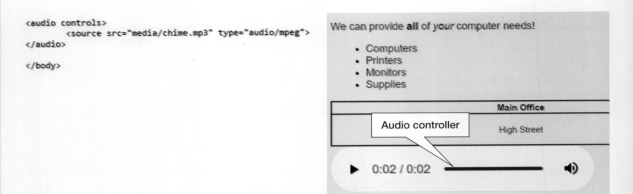

Video can be added in a similar way, along with a controller. It is also important to consider the size of the video and how you wish to see it on screen.

The example below shows a video being added to the index.html page. You will see it has been added below the table, just below the closing </body> tag. In addition, a <br> has been used to add a line break between the sound and video.

```
<br>

<video width="320" height="240" controls>
        <source src="media/harddrive.mp4" type="video/mp4">
</video>

</body>
```

> ### Tip
>
> MP3 and WAV files are popular sound file choices and MP4 files are most commonly used for video when adding to webpages.

> ### Real world
>
> Rather than take up file space within their own websites, many web designers now prefer to **embed** content from other sites. Videos, music, games, animation, maps and utilities can be added to a site with only a few lines of code. Popular sites like **YouTube** and **Vimeo** offer **embed** codes that can be added to your HTML code.

Activity 6

Using the provided examples, or ones of your own, add a sound or audio clip onto the index. html homepage. Remember to add the files to your media folder and ensure they are accessible for the viewer. Remember to preview the page within a browser to check the playback.

Activity 7

Use the internet to try and find some additional files that could be added. However it's important to justify any files you add, thinking of the aim of the the web site and its target audience.

Inserting hyperlinks

Now you need to link all the pages together. Open **index.html**.

A hyperlink is a link from one file or document to another and within web design this can be to another page within the same document, an external document or directly to a document.

Take a look at the bullet points on your index page. Each of these can be turned into a link to that page.

Locate the term **Computers** in the HTML of the index page and add the following code:

```
<ul>
<li><a href="page2.html">Computers</a></li>
<li>Printers</li>
<li>Monitors</li>
<li>Supplies</li>
</ul>
```

This is the page reference we wish to link to.

This is text the will be shown on screen to represent the link.

Save and preview the page and the link should look like the example below, underlined and blue to represent a hyperlink. The mouse should also turn to a hand icon or display the link when hovered over it.

We can provide **all** of *your* computer needs!

- Computers
- Printers
- Monitors
- Supplies

Using and inserting bookmarks

Creating a **bookmark** is the process of saving a particular website title and URL address in order to revisit it. Modern website browsers have this functionality and will create a bookmark and add it to a list of saved addresses you can access at any time.

This process isn't limited to home pages, it can be used to link to any particular page within a website and also to a specific location within a single page, especially useful if a content rich page is very long.

Consider a product long listing page within the All Computer Supplies website that contains lists of laptop, desktop and tablet computers. Users may wish to jump down to the tablet section. At the point in the page where the tablet computers start, you could add the following lines to the HTML.

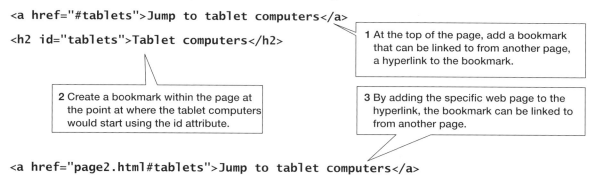

```
<a href="#tablets">Jump to tablet computers</a>

<h2 id="tablets">Tablet computers</h2>
```

1 At the top of the page, add a bookmark that can be linked to from another page, a hyperlink to the bookmark.

2 Create a bookmark within the page at the point at where the tablet computers would start using the id attribute.

3 By adding the specific web page to the hyperlink, the bookmark can be linked to from another page.

```
<a href="page2.html#tablets">Jump to tablet computers</a>
```

Relative and absolute file paths

A relative file path gives a directory listing in relation to the file it is being linked to. For example **index.html** and **page2.html** are in the same folder so the link would be simply **page2.html**.

If we consider the photo of a laptop in page2.html then the relative link of that image from page2.html would be as follows:

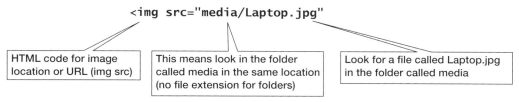

```
<img src="media/Laptop.jpg"
```

HTML code for image location or URL (img src)

This means look in the folder called media in the same location (no file extension for folders)

Look for a file called Laptop.jpg in the folder called media

An absolute (full or root) file path provides a complete directory listing for the location of a file when creating links. For example the absolute file path of the same image would be:

```
<img src="C:/Users/Public/Documents/Website/mediamedia/laptop.jpg"
```

This goes right back to the main computer C: drive

It is therefore more efficient to use a relative file path when considering website design. As you will see in the next session, only the folder containing the website would be uploaded to an online server if the site went online therefore any absolute references relating to C: drives would not work correctly.

> **Real world**
>
> Although not a problem when developing websites on a **local** computer, file paths online are generally **case sensitive**, so it is good web design practice to use **lower-case** for all folders and filenames when creating any web projects.

Activity 8

1 Add hyperlinks from the other products on the index page to their respective page.
2 Create an additional link from each page back to the home page.

Creating an external link

An external link works in exactly the same way as an internal link but takes the user to an online webpage rather than a local one.

You have decided to add some background information to each of the products to help buyers make a decision. The Wikipedia (http://en.wikipedia.org/wiki/Laptop) page on laptops provides useful information so you are going to add it as a link beneath the discounted price listing. You've also decided to have the link to an external site open in a new window rather than the existing one. The example below links directly to the Wikipedia page on laptops:

```
<a href="https://en.wikipedia.org/wiki/Laptop" target="_blank">Which laptop is right for me?</a>
```

Notice the **_blank** reference, this tells the browser to open in a new window.

Choosing a hyperlink target

When linking from one webpage to another the default option is to simply open in the same page. The Target option provides the following alternatives:

Target Option	Description
_blank	Opens the linked file or webpage in a new browser window
_parent	Opens the linked file or webpage the parent frame or parent window if frames are used. Note: Frames are not commonly used now in web design as they can cause browser problems, especially with mobile devices.
_self	Opens the linked file or webpage in the same window or tab. This is the default option.
_top	Opens the linked file or webpage in a new full window, removing any frames. Again frames are not used in modern web design.

Adding an email link

Junaid would like you to add an email link to the home page of your website. He would like the site to say: **Contact ACS via email** and when users click the address that it opens a new email message to junaidacs@ allcomputersupplies.com in their default email program. Adding the following line to the home page (index. html) will open the users default mail program.

```
<a href="mailto:junaidacs@allcomputersupplies.com">Contact ACS via email</a>
```

Printing web pages

There are occasions when content needs to be printed from a website. Most internet browsers contain following printing options:

● Printer selection: Either a connected printer or a virtual print to PDF option, creating a print friendly PDF document can can be viewed or printed at a later date.

- Scale: the ability to scale the page to fit as required on the printed page, useful for larger websites
- Pages per sheet: Useful for condensing long pages that may span two pages onto one
- Headers and footers: This will normally add the current date and the title of the web page at the top and the full web address at the bottom
- Background graphics: Often it is the text that the essential information to be printed, this options removes background images.

Rather than print out the website as it is viewed on screen, it is possible to view and print the HTML code behind the page. This option is normally called **View page source**, this will show a code version of the page that can be printed using the same printing options.

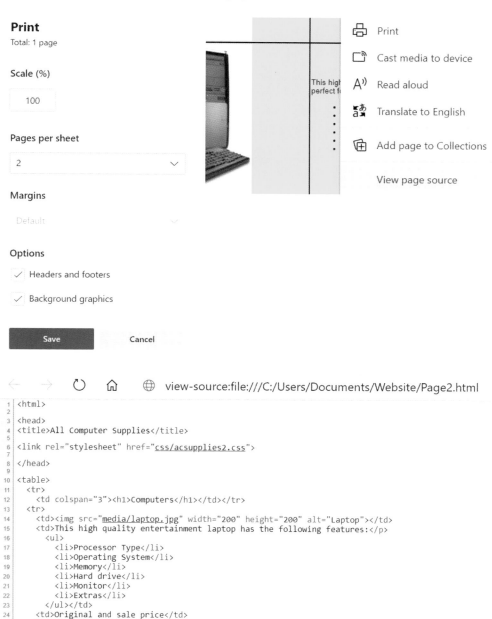

1   Add background information using external hyperlinks to all of your webpages.

2   For each of Pages 2, 3, 4 and 5, add an extra row of three cells to the bottom.

3   Browse the source files for the image **homebutton.jpg**.

4   Insert the image in the centre of the bottom middle cell of each page. This icon represents the homepage (**Page1a**) and needs linking to that page.

5   Add a hyperlink to the homepage icon for each of Pages 2, 3, 4 and 5.

6   Add the email link shown to the home page of your site.

7   Rename the first page of your website to index.html. You will have to check and change some of your hyperlinks accordingly.

Using <div> tags in page design

This tag is used to define a specific area, or division, within a web page. Within that area, CSS can be used to style content. Content is placed between the <div> and </div> tags.

Refer back to Session 4.10 on cascading style sheets if you need to.

The following example shows a basic div tag, adding a style to the bullet points on the home page:

```
<div style="color:blue";>
    <ul>
        <li>Computers</li>
        <li>Printers</li>
        <li>Monitors</li>
        <li>Supplies</li>
    </ul>
</div>
```

We can provide **all** of *your* computer needs!

- Computers
- Printers
- Monitors
- Supplies

A class attribute can also be applied to a <div> tag. The example below shows a style called .table defined within <style> tags in the header and then wrapped around the table:

```
<head>

<style>
.table {
        background-color: red;
        color: yellow;
        border: 2px solid black;
}
</style>

</head>


<div>
<table class="table">
  <tr>
    <th>Main Office</th>
    <th colspan="2">Technical Support Offices</th>
  </tr>
  <tr>
    <td>High Street</td>
    <td>Unit 3 Industrial Park</td>
    <td>Unit 7 Industrial Park</td>
  </tr>
</table>
</div>
```

Tip

<div> styles defines in the header can be linked to multiple areas within the same page.

1   Experiment with adding a style and class based **<div>** tag, using the examples shown, to one or more of your pages.

2   Besides tables, what other areas of a large website would benefit from the use of **<div>** tags? Discuss with a peer.

We can provide **all** of *your* computer needs!

- Computers
- Printers
- Monitors
- Supplies

Main Office	Technical Support Offices	
High Street	Unit 3 Industrial Park	Unit 7 Industrial Park

Review and revise

You should now be able to:

- create additional web pages and attach style sheets to them
- use and format tables to organise a webpage
- insert and organise images, sound and video
- resample, resize and format images suitably for internet use
- add internal and external hyperlinks to webpages
- understand the difference between relative and absolute file paths
- use bookmarks within a document and link to them
- insert email links to webpages.
- print web pages in normal and HTML view
- use <div> tags to specify the style of content.

4 Practical review

What have you covered?

In these four practical sessions, you have:
- seen how a webpage is structured in HTML
- practised the use and effect of a wide variety of `<tags>`
- investigated the creation and use of cascading style sheets
- created style sheets and seen how to attach them to a webpage or webpages
- investigated the creation of tables as a way to help organise webpage content
- added tables to a web page and formatted them
- practised adding content (text, images and multimedia content) to your webpage and applying styles
- discovered how to create internal and external hyperlinks

Some practice questions

You are going to create a website for Colin, who owns a shop that sells and buys coins and banknotes.

1 Create a new folder called COLINCB in your personal folder.

2 Copy the relevant source files from the digital download into your folder.

3 Edit the style sheet **CCBShop.css**.
- Change the background colour so that it has no blue element.
- Change the font size of `<h1>` to be 24px.
- Save the style sheet with the name **CCBShopB.css** in your COLINCB folder.

4 Using a suitable text editor, create a new webpage called **CCBShop.html**.

Create a structure that will look like this, using a table:

	A	
	C	
	D	E
B	F	G
	H	I
	J	

5 Attach the style sheet **CCBShopB.css** to this webpage.

6 Set the table width to 95% of the width of the window.

7 Set cell spacing and cell padding for the table to 4 pixels.

8 Using the contents of the file **CCBText.txt**:
- place the text: Welcome to Colin's Coin & Banknote Shop into cell A as style `<h1>`
- place the text: Visit these recommended … Banknote Dealers into cell B and format this as:
    - Visit these recommended sites – as style `<h2>`
    - The International Banknote Society (IBNS) – as style `<h2>`
    - Professional Coin Grading Service – as style `<h2>`
    - Numismatists Directory – as style `<h2>`
    - Rare Coin Dealers – as style `<h2>`
    - Banknote Dealers – as style `<h2>`
- place the text: Colin's Coin Shop is one of the north of England's … area of the dealership into cell C as style `<p>`
- place the text: Treasury Notes … 1949–1962 into cell H with each of the five lines as style `<li>`
- place the text: Hammered coins … 1658–date into cell I with each of the lines as style `<li>`.

9 In cell D, enter the text Banknotes as style `<h2>`.

10 In cell E, enter the text Coins as style `<h2>`.

11 Using the internet, search for an image of an old bank note. Save it as **banknote.jpg** and insert it into cell F. Set the width to 300 pixels and maintain its aspect ratio.

12 Again using the internet, find an image of an old coin. Save it as **coin1.jpg** and insert it into cell G.
Set the width to 150 pixels and maintain its aspect ratio.

13 Add the following text in style <p> to cell J at the bottom of the table: last edited by (your name).

14 Search the internet to find the URL of the home page of the International Banknote Society. Create a hyperlink from the text: The International Banknote Society (IBNS) in cell B

with this URL, so that the IBNS home page opens in a new window called **_ibns**.

15 Create a hyperlink from the image in cell G to open the file CCBCoins.html in a new window called **_CCBcoins**.

16 Save the page **CCBShop.html**.

17 Using a suitable software package, open the webpage **CCBCoins.html**.

18 Attach the style sheet **CCBShopB.css** that you saved at step 3.

19 Replace the text Heading here with the text Hammered and Milled Coins as style <h2>.

20 Replace the text Colin Derbyshire, 01/03/2015 with your name and today's date.

21 Save and print your work if required.

Progress check

Aiming for good progress

- Given an outline, you can successfully create a webpage's structure with a table.
- You are able to attach a style sheet to a webpage.
- You are able to add content (text, images or multimedia elements) to the webpage.
- You can apply styles to text.
- You can create a hyperlink to another webpage or website.
- Link directly to an email address from a webpage.
- You can use a range of HTML tags.
- You know how to print web pages.

Aiming for excellent progress

- Given an outline, you can successfully create a webpage with a table.
- You can create and edit a style sheet as required and attach a style sheet to a webpage.
- You are able to add content to a webpage and, when inserting images, either crop or resize them as required.
- You can add styles to text and use heading and paragraph options.
- You can link directly to an email address from a webpage.
- You are able to control the appearance and content of a table cell using alignment, merged cells, cell spacing and cell padding.
- You can create hyperlinks to other webpages using relative file paths and control how they appear.
- You can create and use bookmarks within the same document.
- You are confident in using a range of tags, including <div>, to style content.
- You are able print web pages in both browser an HTML view.

5 The effects of using ICT

Why this unit matters

ICT continues to change our lives. As more and more technologies are brought into an organisation, its workforce has to change. Jobs that in the past could only be done in the workplace can now be done at home, or on the move. We can shop and manage our finances online, and while these are useful aspects of ICT, they can pose problems. For example, online transactions require us to enter our personal and financial details, which raise security issues.

New ICT solutions also carry legal, ethical, moral and cultural considerations. And, of course, wherever we use computer technology, we need to consider potential health issues.

I have a very young family and both my wife and I have full time jobs. Isn't technology supposed to be improving our quality of life? We don't see it. What's happened to our work/lifestyle balance?

More and more of the employees at my company are working on computers these days, so I have been asked to draw up a health policy. What issues should I consider?

Are lots of jobs disappearing because of computers, or is working in and with ICT helping to create new job opportunities?

Your practical task

You have been asked to help with four projects, each for a very different situation.

You will revise some of the skills learnt in Unit 3 and you will develop new skills to create spreadsheet models, analyse data and prepare charts and graphs. The four projects are:
- looking at income and payments for a Summer Fair at Excelsior Academy
- helping Shilpa to solve a puzzle
- enabling Mr Singh to analyse his students' geography examination results
- creating an analysis of stock held by Señor Ibanez for his tapas bar.

What this unit covers

THEORY

Sessions

Theory review

PRACTICAL

Sessions

Practical review

By the end of the theory sessions you will be able to:

- describe the effects of ICT on employment
- describe the effects of ICT on patterns of work
- explain what is meant by software copyright
- describe the effects of microprocessor-controlled devices in the home
- describe the potential health problems related to ICT equipment
- demonstrate an understanding of the impact of ICT in terms of modelling applications.

In your practical work you will develop and apply skills in:

- developing and amending a spreadsheet model
- entering and amending text, numerical data, functions and formulae with 100 per cent accuracy
- testing a spreadsheet model to ensure that it works
- creating functions and formulae to analyse data in a spreadsheet
- sorting, searching and selecting data
- producing graphs or charts from the spreadsheet model.

The use of microprocessor-controlled devices in transport systems and manufacturing

Background

Microprocessor-based devices are becoming integrated into our society and infrastructure. From the way we move from place to place to how our products are manufactured, smart technology plays a major part, and as more and more systems become automated, smart technology is also being allowed to make decisions.

This session will explore the effect of increased use of microprocessor-controlled systems in our transport systems and the use of robotics in manufacture and production line control.

This session will explore the effect that ICT has had, and continues to have, on the workplace and our role in it.

Warehousing: Robots store, move and collect items.

Autonomous vehicles: Controlling themselves and monitored by external traffic systems.

Manufacturing: Robots assemble and paint cars.

Data security: Knowing where we are at all times.

Transport

As our methods of transportation have increased and developed over the decades, so have the levels of microprocessor technology. Computer systems are intertwined with modern combustion engines and as electronic motors are being used more and more the gap between these systems is disappearing.

Control and monitoring

Electronic engine management and cruise control have long been part of modern automotive vehicles. These systems, and many others, help maintain the vehicle on a long journey where once the driver would need to monitor how the vehicle was running and make adjustments as required. From checking fuel and supply levels to maintaining a constant safe speed based on other near-by vehicles, this applies to just about any form of transport from cars, trains, motorbikes, electric-bikes, buses to aeroplanes, ships and planes.

Technology used in the control and monitoring of transport might include:

● Global positioning systems to monitor a location, speed and direction
● Standard and infra-red cameras used to observe and record vehicles surroundings
● Sensors that monitor sound, movement and the position of objects
● Actuators that control physical movement, steering for example
● Communication systems, transmitting and receiving data commands or telemetry.

Security of data

As discussed later in this Unit and in Unit 8, we are allowing the increased use of smart automation to monitor, and in the case of transport even directly control, our daily lives. We need to be aware of the amount of personal data being recorded and potentially shared using these systems. The following are examples of transport data that may be recorded in a typical person's day:

● The choice, route and cost of a bus or train to school or employment
● The route and time taken by a car to a place of work
● The details of every person on a boat or plane anywhere in the world
● The exact speed and location of an electric car at any time.

Activity 1

Choose three forms of transport and for each list how computers are used to:

● Drive or pilot them
● Monitor their position and destination.

Transport safety

One of the major reasons for introducing computer technology into transportation systems is to improve safety. A microprocessor can respond to a command in a fraction of a second, but it must also be able to know when to make a decision. Examples of transport safety might include:

● Speed limitation
● Airbags and inflation aids
● Obstacle and collision warning sensors
● Adaptive lighting and headlights
● Seat-belt reminders
● Cruise control and brake assistance.

Real world

Many jobs are a direct result of emerging technology and did not exist even a few years ago. Not many people leaving college in the mid-2000s would have imagined a job programming autonomous vehicles or security policies for booking a taxi via smartphone.

Activity 2

Consider the following types of transport and suggest a microprocessor-controlled safety system.

Transport	Safety system
Car	
Motorbike	
Electric bike	
Aeroplane	
Train	
Bus	

Real world

Someone buying a mass-production car will appreciate the exact safety standards and specification they expect but someone buying an expensive custom sports car will often expect elements to be hand-made and checked with the naked eye.

Manufacture and Production Control

One of the largest introductions of computer-controlled systems is in manufacturing and production lines. Robotic arms produce popular cars and household appliances twenty-four hours a day, seven days a week and many of our favourite foods and drinks at some points go through an automated production line, checking quality and hygiene. Examples might include:

- Mass production of common electronic items where each must look and function exactly the same
- Drink bottles are steam-cleaned, filled and sealed to meet food safety standards
- Robots position and weld car parts together without the need to protect their eyes or worry about high temperature working conditions
- Product packaging can be folded, checked and sealed hundreds of times an hour.

Activity 3

Choose three products you or your family own and investigate how they are produced and the technologies involved. Are there still any human-led aspects to its production?

Humans versus computer control

As long as computers systems have existed, people have been concerned about humans being replaced in the tasks we carry out. From autonomous vehicles to automated manufacturing, there a many advantages and disadvantages to these systems that may relate to:

- The cost of implementation
- The replacement of manual labour
- Safety concerns
- Placing our safety in the hands of a computer
- Employment levels
- The new skills needed to program and use these systems.

Activity 4

Take a look at the scenarios below and complete the table, adding potential advantages and disadvantages of each system. Consider the following elements, discussed in this session:

- Technology
- Privacy
- Safety
- Practicality

Scenario	Advantages	Disadvantages
Going to a restaurant with friends in an automated car.		
Making payments on a bus using a smartphone or smartwatch.		
The production of high-end sports cars.		
An animal running out into busy traffic.		

Review and revise

You should now be able to:

- Describe the effects of microprocessor systems in monitoring and controlling transport
- Consider the data security, safety and the development of autonomous vehicles on our lives
- Consider the advantages and disadvantages of computer-control over human-control systems.

SESSION 5.2 The impact of satellite systems

Background

Consider a time before satellites, our exact location on the planet could be confirmed in a number of ways: through a visual analysis of our surroundings and comparison to an existing map or by noting the position of the sun, moon and stars. The introduction of world-wide satellite systems now means our exact position and altitude can be provided electronically and when taken at multiple times, can provide our direction and speed.

This session will consider some of the many uses of this technology and its impact on our world.

Global Positioning Systems (GPS)

Orbiting the earth at a height of around 20 200 km, at least twenty-four satellites (in equally spaced orbital planes) pass over our heads twice a day. Each satellite transmits a radio signal that all GPS-compatible devices can access and by comparing the signal from four or more satellites the device can calculate its exact position and height in relation to them. Devices that now include the ability to listen to these GPS signals include:

- Desktop and laptop computers
- Smartphones and smart watches
- In-car navigation systems
- Portable mapping equipment
- Digital cameras and camcorders
- Personal fitness devices.

Activity 1

Consider your household, how many devices can you think of that use GPS data in some way?

Geographic Information Systems (GIS)

While GPS data will provide an exact location, a Geographic Information System will provide additional information relevant to that location. Multiple sources of data, or layers, can be selected, combined or isolated to answer a specific query about a location. Examples of data that might be included in a GIS are:

- Population statistics
- Geographical boundaries or borders
- Building development or structures
- Water, rainfall and weather-related statistics
- Environmental data
- Government and military installations
- Agricultural and soil mapping
- Geo-political data.

Satellite navigation

One of the most popular early uses of GPS was the ability, through hand-held devices and then in-car systems, to navigate from one location to another. Rather than plotting a journey beforehand using a map, directions could be followed 'live' via on-screen graphical directions or listening to voice prompts. The core functionality of any navigation systems is based on the following:

- knowing the start and finish of a journey
- the exact position, speed and direction at any point
- geographical and road mapping data
- the ability to calculate the most efficient route.

Activity 2

There are multiple satellite systems orbiting the earth, and many more proposed. Research some of the systems and what are some of the dangers of having multiple systems?

Real world

Putting one's faith in the ability to plot the most efficient route across a town or city has led to many drivers being stranded on inaccessible roads, private driveways and even going the wrong way in a one-way system!

Satellite communication systems

In addition to transmitting data to support GPS technology, satellite communications have changed the way we can consume media and communicate. Radio waves can be transmitted around the world using a combination of satellites and ground-based transmitters to bounce signals across large distances. This technology forms the basis of the following systems:

- Live radio and television signals can be broadcast across continents
- Sat-phones can make a direct call from any location on the planet to another without land-based signal towers.

Advantages and disadvantages of satellite-based systems

Advantages	Disadvantages
• The GPS system theoretically allows anyone to access their exact location at any time at no cost.	• Users can be given a false sense of security, relying on GPS data for directions.
• Emergency rescue services can use GPS data to find those in need of assistance.	• Connection to GPS can be lost under trees or inside buildings.
• Systems can provide a time of arrival and the location of useful stops for fuel or food.	• Connecting to fewer than four satellites can provide inaccurate data.
• Concerts and important events can be broadcast simultaneously around the world.	• Satellite phones are very expensive to own and run.
• Proposed building developments can use GIS to prevent costly mistakes.	• Unless updated, maps and service data can quickly become outdated.
	• Many are concerned about the number of satellites above our planet and the potential for collisions.

Review and revise

You should now be able to:

- Describe the characteristics of GPS and GIS
- Explain how GPS and GIS can be used in navigation and communication
- Describe the advantages and disadvantages of GPS and GIS.

SESSION 5.3 Health issues

Background

Using computers can raise a number of health issues. Many countries have regulations that support and encourage the safe use of computer systems. These regulations often include advice about the causes of potential health risks and methods of prevention. During this session you will look at the common problems and injuries associated with poor ICT working conditions and how they can be reduced or eliminated.

Health issues

Sometimes working with computers can impact on our health. Problems can develop with our neck and back, eyes, wrists and thumbs and fingers. For each problem, there are preventative measures to take for reducing or eliminating the problem.

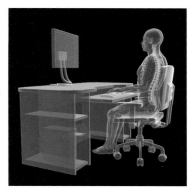

This diagram shows Neville, sitting at his computer. If he sits and works like this for long stretches, he may damage his health seriously in the parts of the body indicated.

Bad posture causes aches and pains in the back and neck. Staring at the monitor for long periods causes eyestrain and headaches. Many young people have reported thumb problems because of heavy and repetitive texting on their mobile phones. This is an example of repetitive strain injury (**RSI**) – the result of performing the same action over and over again.

Activity 1

1. Find out what the term **ergonomics** means. How could **ergonomic design** help to reduce some of the stresses and strains that Neville is experiencing?

2. RSI affects arms, elbows and wrists in particular. Find out what upper limb disorders are. Make notes on the causes of carpal tunnel syndrome and cubital tunnel syndrome.

3. Complete the right-hand column of this table by adding as many solutions as you can discover to prevent each problem:

Problem	Method of prevention
Neck ache	
Backache	
Eye strain	
Headaches	
Aching wrists and fingers	

> ### Tip
>
> Some methods you may not have considered relate to improving the devices that Neville is using. For example, using a touch screen or voice recognition software for his word processor. When gaming, an ergonomic joypad or movement sensor can minimise the impact of RSI.

Minimising the risks to health

The devices that we use while sitting at our desks do not have a health risk label on them because they are not dangerous – it is often our poor use of them that does the damage. Usually this is because we simply do not even contemplate that we are potentially harming ourselves.

- **Mouse or trackpad**: If you have a desktop computer, where on the desk is your mouse? Is it placed at a comfortable distance, or are you stretching or cramped? Are your wrists and/or forearms supported as you use it?

- **Screen**: What kind of screen do you have? A older CRT screen will have a very shiny surface and light will glare from it. Do you have an anti-glare screen? Is the screen tilted properly for good vision? Is it a comfortable distance away from your eyes?

- **Printer**: Printers should be positioned in a well ventilated area and can also cause vibration when running.
- **Keyboard**: Consider the same questions to that of mice and trackpads, ensure both arms are comfortable and the keyboard is usable for long periods of time. Should an ergonomic keyboard be considered?

Activity 2

Create a poster which looks similar to the picture of Neville, but shows all the devices listed above. Make the poster informative, indicating the problems that can arise when devices are used incorrectly or posture is not good. Also highlight the correct way to use devices and how to try and maintain good posture. Make the poster big enough to be displayed at various places around your school where computers are regularly used such as the IT lab or library.

Review and revise

You should now be able to:
- review and describe health issues connected with the use of computers at home and in the workplace
- identify possible solutions to health issues.

SESSION 5.4 Commercial and ethical considerations

Background

In this session you will look in some detail at how the development of ICT has changed the nature of how we shop and do our banking. In Sessions 2.3 and 3.3 you learned about some aspects of shopping and banking, particularly in relation to buying tickets or using ATMs. It is important to remember that in spite of the growth of ICT, some people still may not have (or want) access to the advantages of online shopping and banking. Yet, as more people take advantage of shopping and banking from home, fewer store outlets or banking facilities may be needed. This could affect people with no access to online goods and services. If their local bank or shop closes, they may have to travel further to find an outlet; as more shops and banks close, many towns and villages will lose even more shopping outlets.

Internet shopping

Many stores already have websites that allow you to shop online. This allows them to trade their wares outside the physical boundaries of their stores and warehousing, and outside normal trading hours.

After you have completed Activity 1, your list should highlight the variety of goods that are available online. In fact, these days, many commercial activities only take place online. For each category in your list you will be able to find traders who only sell goods and services through their website as well as people who run their own businesses from home using webpages as their shop front.

Many businesses have an online store to supplement their physical store. The trend seems to be that once stores develop an online presence there is the temptation to concentrate only on this aspect of the business.

Having an online presence has advantages and disadvantages for the store owner:

Activity 1

Here are three types of goods and services that can be purchased online.

1   Housing

2   Food

3   Furniture

Add **seven** more items to this list.

Advantages	Disadvantages
• Potentially, there is access to a much wider customer base than having stores. • No need to rent or buy stores, thus saving these costs. • The business does not need to be based in a populated or expensive area. • Fewer staff are needed in order to sell the products; the focus is on warehousing and delivery rather than on shop staff.	• The potential difficulties in getting customers' attention that the business is online and available, for example, marketing and appearing in relevant internet searches. • A physical store can create and maintain an atmosphere that an online site can only attempt to achieve through its design.

Many people shop online a lot – from the weekly grocery shop and birthday presents to clothes, household electronics and garden furniture. Other people, even though they have internet access, simply do not want to buy online. Why do some people shop online so happily and others do not? What are the advantages? What are the disadvantages?

Activity 2

Draw up a table with two columns, headed: Advantages; Disadvantages.

Under **each** heading list at least **three** points to illustrate why people choose, or don't choose to shop online.

Point of sale (POS) systems

Many stores make use of POS systems, which track purchases that have been made (and the customer's details). This enables stores to manage their stock control and payment functions directly from the till (or point of sale). POS systems connect the activity at the checkout to the stock control system. As items are purchased, the system deducts a unit from the quantity recorded as being in stock. If the stock level drops below a predetermined level a message is sent to the reordering system, to build up an order with the product's supplier. See Session 7.2 for a diagram explaining the process step-by-step. The system helps to ensure that the level of stock never reaches a critically low level, and that the store never carries too much stock.

Electronic funds transfer point of sale (EFTPOS)

POS systems can be extended to allow purchases to be paid for by debit or credit card. The store will have a Chip and PIN or contactless reader (pictured, see Session 2.1) connected to the POS system. The cost of the purchase is displayed in the reader as well as on the checkout screen:

1   The customer inserts a bank card into the Chip and PIN reader, or very near if it has contactless capabilities or they are using a smartphone device.

2   The card is checked for the expiry date and to see if it is valid (not stolen).

3   The store's computer contacts the customer's bank.

4   The customer authorises the amount to be deducted by entering the card's PIN number or follows the authorisation sequence of their card or smart device.

5   The bank's system matches the account details to the account details and a check of the balance/credit is carried out to see if the customer has available funds.

6   If available funds are present, money is deducted from the customer's account and added to the supermarket's account.

7   The EFTPOS system will print a receipt and the customer can retrieve the card or payment device.

Some people are worried about the security of online payments, which can discourage them from using the internet to shop. However, the vast majority of online transactions go through secure servers – recognised by the symbol of a padlock and the use of **https** to show that the system is secure.

> ### Real world
>
> Recent improvements in the EFTPOS process have seen the majority of credit and debit cards include the ability to make contactless purchasing using Near Field Communication (NFC). The card is simply held near the reader and doesn't require a PIN entry. Payment levels are generally set at a low level to prevent fraud.

> ### Real world
>
> The NFC technology used in contactless payments is now being introduced to smartphones and smartwatches. The account details of the chosen payment card are entered and stored on the device, allowing it to be used to make payments. Different devices have different authorisation methods from thumb print or facial scans to entering a PIN into the device.

Activity 3

Common facilities used by banking customers are: opening accounts, paying in money or making withdrawals, transferring money between accounts or to other account holders, paying bills, organising loans and mortgages, planning investments and booking appointments with an account manager.

1   From the banking facilities mentioned above, decide which would need face to face contact with someone in the bank itself and which could be done online.

    Banks are reducing the number of branches, so online banking is providing vital services for customers who find that physically getting to a branch is difficult.

2   Imagine that you are a bank customer who is living in an area where your bank is planning to close the only nearby branch. Draft a letter of complaint, stating three reasons why you are unhappy and think that the branch should reconsider its decision to close.

3   Imagine that you are the manager of the bank that has decided to close the branch. The customer's letter of complaint has been passed on to you. Draft your reply, explaining three reasons why the bank feels it has good reason to close the branch.

Moral and ethical considerations of ICT

There is a moral and ethical dimension to consider when access to ICT is raised. For each advantage of the use of ICT there are concerns about its impact on the way we live. If access to ICT and to the internet is a 'right' then we need to consider how the advantages and disadvantages associated with widespread use of ICT might impact on our lives.

In the sections above you have considered the way in which online activities such as shopping and banking can be carried out 24 hours a day, 365 days a year. This immediate and constant access to information does have its advantages, as you have seen, but it also presents issues with no easily resolved answers – problems that we need to deal with as individuals.

Do the advantages of ICT outweigh the disadvantages? Are the advantages of ICT felt by all people in the same way?

Consider these particular statements suggesting advantages of ICT:

- People are more connected and can share information or conduct business 24/7.
- Creating a website for a small business means it can be run from home and not a shop on the high street.
- Increased productivity can lead to economic growth.
- As we experience more and more online or telephone voting systems, ICT may bring about changes to the way we conduct our politics, perhaps making us feel that we can engage more easily with politics.
- The communication advantages of ICT means that companies can open offices where labour costs are cheaper.
- Improved robotics means that products previously made by hand can now be made by computer-controlled machinery.
- Monitoring by closed-circuit television (CCTV) can lead to reductions in crime; it can deter criminals simply by being there; it can also enable face recognition in large crowds.

Should internet use be controlled or policed?

At the moment the internet has no international body that controls the way it operates, to ensure that it meets certain standards of performance.

There are advantages and disadvantages in laying down standards for the internet.

A controlled internet would:

- prevent illegal material from being posted on websites, which would make it easier to find and prosecute people who did
- help to guarantee the accuracy of information posted on the internet
- help to protect vulnerable groups and young people by restricting access and content.

However:

- much of the material that can be accessed on the internet is already available in other forms
- an international organisation would be expensive to run. It may mean that free access to the internet is removed entirely, with people having to pay for content
- it would be extremely difficult to get participating countries to agree to a common set of standards, so cultural, political and religious differences could prevent international agreement

Tip

It is important to remember that with all moral and ethical concerns in ICT there are aspects that will differ depending on circumstances and beliefs. Bear in mind that advantages are often balanced by disadvantages, and vice versa.

Activity 4

In small groups, take each statement and explore:

- What advantages arise from the statement?
- Does this advantage favour just one section of society?
- Could anyone not feel the advantage?
- What could be done to make the advantage felt by everyone?

Activity 5

At your school, internet access may be restricted by filters or other software. You may have issues with this and with having to ask your ICT team to unblock various sites or allow certain activities. Your parents may monitor your activities on the internet, so you might have to negotiate with them about what you can and cannot do on the internet.

In groups, discuss the advantages and disadvantages of having an international governing body to control internet access. How would they agree on the guidelines? How would these 'rules' be changed? Who would change them?

Real world

Illegal material could include documents or images that are racist, explicit or designed to promote illegal activity.

- many countries have laws about freedom of information and a policed internet would go against those laws
- material that is illegal is already covered by law and so policing the internet would mean that there would be two laws for one problem.

Review and revise

You should now be able to:

- describe the social impact of ICT
- describe the impact of ICT on shopping and banking
- discuss moral and ethical considerations including the arguments for and against the need to police the internet.

SESSION 5.5 The need for copyright

Background

The growth of ICT over the last 20 years has led to more and more software, music, films, books and other materials being available for downloading. Many of these materials have **copyright** attached to them. Copyright means that the owners of the material have the right to own, sell, distribute or give away copies of the material as they wish. Some materials are available free of charge. In this case, the owners or developers of the materials are allowing that resource to be freely distributed.

If material is copied or downloaded without permission then the person making the copy is, in most countries, breaking the law.

Software copyright

Software is protected by copyright laws, which protects software manufacturers because it gives them the right to all the profit from selling the software. This means that it is illegal to make a copy of software that you own and then sell it or give it away.

Software can be obtained on a physical format, such as CD or DVD or via internet download. Proprietary software is owned by the individual or company who created it and copyright law means that it cannot be:
- copied and given away without permission from the owner
- used on a network unless a licence has been bought
- included in other software and passed off as an original without the permission of the copyright holders
- rented out without permission.

Illegally downloaded or copied software can cause viruses to be loaded onto a computer system. A computer will be better protected if all of the software that is installed on it is done so with the permission of the copyright owner because it means that the software is:
- genuine
- more likely to come from a trusted source
- less likely to be infected by a computer virus.

As a user, you can check that new software has come from the copyright owner by looking for:
- a product key – a unique sequence of letters and numbers that is typed in when new software is installed, which can be checked to see if it is valid
- a security label on the package.

Language

Copyright refers to laws that govern the use of the work of a creator, such as an artist or author. This includes the right to copy, distribute, alter and display creative, literary and other types of work. Unless otherwise stated in a contract, the author or creator of a work owns the copyright.

Real world

The entertainment industry has been badly affected by illegal downloads (also referred to as online piracy). By bypassing official streaming and download services, the original creators are receiving no payment for their work and this then reduces the amount of original content being created.

Real world

Internet **streaming** services such as Spotify, Apple and Amazon provide access to music, TV and films through paid subscription that ensures copyright is followed and the original creators are compensated. The ease of these services has reduced the amount of material illegally downloaded.

Zaphira has just bought a new laptop from All Computer Supplies. She knows that an operating system has been installed on the computer but it doesn't include any word processing, spreadsheet, database or presentation software. Junaid at All Computer Supplies has told her that he can obtain all the software she needs from a well-known company. A friend of Zaphira's has emailed her to say that she can copy his software for free.

Prepare the reply that Zaphira should send to her friend. Include:
- the reason why she should not accept her friend's offer of a copy of the software
- an explanation to her friend of how he should check that the software he has is genuine.

Preventing software copyright being broken

The 2018 release of the game Shadow of the Tomb Raider cost over $135 million to develop, market and release. This costs more than many Hollywood blockbusters. This is a huge investment and the games makers want to ensure that the copies of the game that find their way onto games consoles have been legitimately bought. The same is true of giant companies like Microsoft and its products, just as much as the programmers in small companies. Time, money and effort have been invested and the sales of their products are what keeps the company going.

So how do companies prevent copyright being broken?
- Education: ensuring computer users of all ages are aware of the problems caused by copyright theft.
- Use of serial or activation keys: a new product will often include a key that must be entered on the device being used. This can then be linked to a particular device, preventing copying.
- Subscription services: software, games and entertainment are now being made available through low-cost subscription. Have quick, legal access to a range of products is removing the need for many to look for illegal sources. However, many of these services will remove your access once your subscription ends.
- Internet connectivity: Many software packages, and games, now require a permanent online connection to function. This means there is clear, recorded link between the user and software creator that is difficult to fake or duplicate, preventing sharing and copying.
- Download only: offering software via download, rather than physical product, means it is virtually impossible to sell on or give away the product.

There are organisations around the world that promote the legal use of software. One example in the UK the Federation Against Software Theft, or FAST.

Legal protection

In the UK, The Copyright, Designs and Patents Act (which was last amended in 2014) covers copyright issues.

Open source software: Downloads

Zaphira may decide that she doesn't want to purchase any software. She knows she can download software legally if it is **open source**. Open source software is created to be shared openly online at no cost, with no limits on how it can be edited, copied or distributed.

A good example of open source software are the many versions of *Open Office*, which you might be using a version of at your school. When you download open source software you may still need to

register your use of it. This is because the developers like to know who is using the software, and may want to alert you to updates or other changes that have been made. It is important to make sure when downloading such software that you are confident of downloading from a reliable source.

Activity 3

1   Now search for **Open Office download**. You may have over 6 billion results. Usually, the top of the list will show the *Open Office* organisation's website. Go to the home page and examine its contents to find out what you can about the software and who is promoting it.

2   Go back to your search results. Look at the webpage of another site that offers the download.

   a   Is it offering the same version as **www.openoffice.org**?

   b   Does it even seem to be the same software?

   c   If you wanted to download the software, which site would you choose? Why?

3   Zaphira has decided to download *Open Office* to her computer. Prepare an email to explain to her from which source she should download the software and why.

Review and revise

You should now be able to:

● explain what is meant by *software copyright*
● describe how to check that software is copyrighted
● describe how software companies are combating software piracy.

SESSION 5.6 ICT applications: Modelling

Background

In this session, you will learn how computer modelling can be used to support and predict events from personal finance to climate change.

Computer modelling

In ICT, a model is a mathematical representation of a real system in order to analyse how it behaves and importantly, how it might behave in the future. Computer modelling can be used to support and predict events from personal finance to climate change.

Examples of computer modelling

Personal finance

Being able to model our own finances is essential as we move to online shopping and banking systems, work from home or on the move and travel the world more than ever before. Examples might include:

- A model of household expenses, including wages and household bills. This can then be modelled to include potential wages increases, moving home or additions to the family.

Bridge and building design

The design of bridges and buildings needs to be more than simply the physical dimensions and materials. Safety is of upmost importance, they also need to consider usage, the environment and how the materials will react over time. Examples of the modelling that might take place to predict outcomes include:

- What might happen to the building or bridge in response to an earthquake or severe weather? The modelling of actual earthquakes is also a goal of scientists in order to predict them.
- How might the materials used degrade after years of use?
- How much impact will the weight of people, traffic and daily use have on the design?

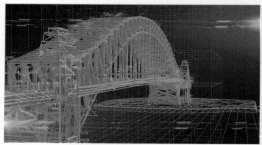

Flood water management

Flood damage happens all over the world, some from extreme weather, some from the way we develop and farm our natural landscape. Examples of modelling might include:

- Can levels of rainfall over specific areas be predicted?
- How will the type of landscape, from grass to concrete, impact on the flow of water?
- What will be the financial impact of planned developments?

Traffic management

The number of vehicles in a certain area has an impact on road design, housing developments, pollution and access to those on foot. Modelling the flow and levels of traffic, and trying to predict how it will change in the future can help with the following?

- How will the changing number of vehicles now, and in the future impact on pollution?
- How will traffic change as more electric and autonomous cars/vehicles appear on our roads?
- Testing out new potential traffic management road layouts and signage.

Weather forecasting

Predicting the weather has become part of our daily lives, making travelling decisions and even what to wear, based on weather modelling systems. More important uses of weather modelling include the potential size and direction of storms, the strength of the sun and how climate change is altering weather patterns. Accurate weather modelling can help with the following:

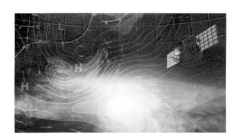

- How might the strength and direction of a hurricane change during its course? Which areas of land and sea will it cross?
- How might rainfall and sunshine levels change in areas of farming and what impact might climate change make?
- Planning ahead for large outdoor events and the choice of facilities they should offer.

Advantages of computer models

- Various scenarios can be tried out in advance.
- Time scale. It is often faster to carry out a simulation than the real thing.
- Preventing waste. Building a model is cheaper for testing purposes, such as modelling a supermarket's queuing pattern (see Unit 7) before installing several new checkouts (which may not all be needed).

Limitations of computer models

- The mathematical formulae and data used for models must be accurate. If not, then the model may be faulty and the outcome incorrect and potentially very misleading, if for instance testing the likely effects of an exchange or taxation rate.
- They can be expensive to set up and run, often requiring specialist software.
- Those using models to predict events must be aware of their limitations.

Activity 1

1   Explain why modelling has been useful for calculating climate change.
2   Modelling would allow builders and engineers to test the stress levels of a new road bridge. Where are the stress levels? How much stress can be safely borne? What are the advantages of this in terms of:
    a   Time scale?
    b   Preventing waste?
    c   Safety?

Activity 2

Take a look at the system of weather forecasting where you live and see if you can find out about the following:

1   How far ahead to look in respect to predicting the daily weather?
2   What key pieces of information do they focus on?
3   Do you think they are accurate?

Modelling in the wider world

In the wider world, models can become very complex requiring huge amounts of data from a very wide variety of sources – as you can imagine from the question about climate change in Activity 1. Large retail organisations will build models to help predict growth patterns across their business, sector by sector (food, clothing, online sales, store sales, and so on), to predict profit and market share. These models are extremely complex and take into account thousands of variables, including historical data as well as current data.

The government, Bank of England and other financial institutions have models of the economy. If the government is thinking of changing tax allowances or the VAT percentage, they need a model to enable them to gauge the long term consequences that this will have, not just in terms of tax revenue but also the effect on employment and household income.

Three limitations of using models are noted above, but you should now have a clear understanding that a model cannot recreate the system it is modelling with completely accuracy – variables that were not included nor considered (a violent storm that requires your parents to spend money making repairs to the roof of the house, a retail store not predicting that the exchange rate between the US dollar and the euro might suddenly change) limit its reliability. The outcomes of models should only be used as the best possible estimate of performance.

Review and revise

You should now be able to:
- describe the use of computer modelling to mimic real events
- describe how a model can help with the planning of a range of world-wide issues.

Microprocessor-controlled devices in the home

Background

Microprocessor-controlled devices have not only had an impact on our workplaces – they have also impacted our homes and are continuing to do so. Consider the following introductions of new technology: the XBOX in 2002, the iPhone and Kindle in 2007 and the iPad in 2010. These devices, and others, are now commonplace and seem like they have always been with us. In this session you will look at the impact that ICT is having on our home life – the gadgets and appliances that we use. These two images show how simply watching television has changed over the years.

Microprocessors in the home

It is not just about computers and access to an internet connection: many of our household devices each have a microprocessor, and the development of 'smart household goods' has become a reality.

The effect of microprocessors in the home on our lifestyles

Embedding a microprocessor into a device allows that device to be programmed to function in different ways, to enhance its original purpose. A television, originally designed to receive television signals via an arial, now often can connect to the internet. This allows applications to be installed; from streaming services to games and social networking. Similarly, the modern smart phone is not just for talking to someone, it is a small computer, video and music player, camera, and so on.

When considering the advantages and disadvantages of improvements in technology the question to think about is – what impact do they have on our lifestyle?

Think of a modern kitchen and make a list of the devices containing microprocessors.

Labour-saving devices such as washing machines and dishwashers might feature on your list but what about the refrigerator or oven? Other devices are used for entertainment; perhaps you also have a television, a music player or a radio? All these items contain a microprocessor, which controls their function in some way.

Positive effects on our lifestyles might include:

- Many things no longer need to be done manually.
- You do not necessarily need to be in the home when food is cooking or clothes are being washed.
- This allows for more time for other things (work, leisure) at times that are convenient for us.

While microprocessor-controlled devices do offer a number of advantages there are arguments against their use, especially an over-reliance on them. For example:

- People can become lazy because the machines do so much.
- They raise expectations and instead of being seen as an extra appliance in the home some people expect to have them.

Activity 1

Labour-saving devices typically found in the kitchen, such as washing machines, dishwashers or microwave ovens have had an impact on the amount of time we spend on tasks in the home. In small groups, discuss what advantages these devices have on family life, remembering not only time saved but also possible health issues. Try to think of four different advantages they offer.

Real world

'Smart' fridges analyse food constituents, which can lead to a healthier lifestyle.

- Some people become preoccupied with owning and upgrading expensive devices.
- When devices are left on standby, electricity is wasted.
- Some people may find new devices difficult to manage or operate.

Activity 2

Consider the following household appliances and decide what advantages they bring to family life (the first one has been done for you):

Appliance	Advantage to family life
Heating or air-conditioning system	Makes home life more comfortable by regulating the temperature in the rooms.
Satellite television	
Dishwasher	
Home computer and internet	
Burglar alarm	

Using microprocessors to control applications in the home

To control an application, the computer takes data from sensors; reviews that data against data stored in memory and follows a set pattern of responses.

A central heating system is an example of a **control application**. Following the way systems were represented as diagrams in Session 2.3, we could show the central heating system like this:

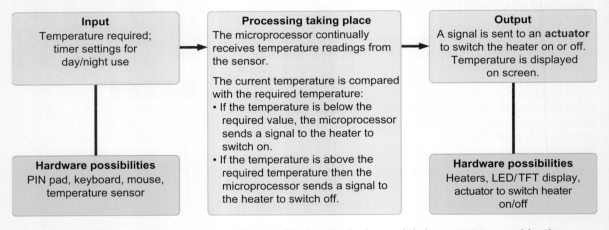

Input
Temperature required; timer settings for day/night use

Hardware possibilities
PIN pad, keyboard, mouse, temperature sensor

Processing taking place
The microprocessor continually receives temperature readings from the sensor.

The current temperature is compared with the required temperature:
- If the temperature is below the required value, the microprocessor sends a signal to the heater to switch on.
- If the temperature is above the required temperature then the microprocessor sends a signal to the heater to switch off.

Output
A signal is sent to an **actuator** to switch the heater on or off. Temperature is displayed on screen.

Hardware possibilities
Heaters, LED/TFT display, actuator to switch heater on/off

When looking at how microprocessors control applications in the home, it is important to consider the processing that is taking place. The microprocessor is constantly receiving a signal and comparing the preset value (in a heating system this would be the required temperature) with the readings that are coming in. Depending on the results of the comparison, some predetermined action is taken (heater switched on or off).

Data from sensors such as temperature is analogue data – it is a physical variable, varying continuously. It needs to be converted by an analogue to digital convertor (**ADC**) into a digital signal for the microprocessor to process it (remember that a microprocessor is a digital device). The digital signal from the microprocessor must be converted back to an analogue signal by a digital to an analogue convertor (DAC) in order to control the actuator. See Session 2.1 for more information on analogue and digital data.

Activity 3

Other commonly discussed control applications might involve: burglar alarms; water temperature control in an aquarium; control of soil moisture in a greenhouse.
- Draw a diagram for each of these, like the one for a central heating system on the previous page.
- Explain the processing that is taking place using the key phrases in the Tip box.

Leisure time

In our homes, the way we spend our leisure time has radically changed over the last few years. Traditional broadcast television and radio, games and music have expanded to include a vast array of streaming services, computer and console-based gaming, electronic toys and relaxation aids. Microprocessors allow users to simply ask for any song, film or television show to be streamed via internet services installed on smart devices. With the vast increase in choice comes concerns about spending leisure time with purely electronic devices and those without a stable internet connection aren't able to access all services.

Physical fitness

Exercising around the home, either using equipment or simply a mat has always been a popular alternative to outdoor activity or a gym membership. Microprocessor controlled devices combined with smart connectivity now impact on almost every possible activity. From smart watches monitoring our heart-rate to internet connected treadmills and exercise bikes, to console games using sensors to track our position and body movements. Many of these systems are inspiring people to take more exercise in the home and adding fun elements but many are concerned that some of these activities are limiting our experiences, focussing on the data generated and shared and distracting from actually spending time outdoors.

Security of data

As smart devices are appearing in almost every room in our home, schools and workplaces, wearable technology tracks our movements and smartphones are permanently carried, many are asking about the vast amounts of data we produce. Many of these smart devices need to analyse our choices, habits and even voices to provide the functionality we enjoy.

What users aren't always aware of is the amount of data we share with the device manufacturers and software owners. It is important to check the terms and conditions and privacy settings in smart devices, in the same way you would check social network settings, are set at a level you are comfortable with.

Social Interaction

The ability to use video call services with family members across the world has its obvious advantages, as does the ability for parents to quickly chat with children, and even check their location. The increased use of devices for social interaction has raised as many concerns as it has benefits. Choosing to communicate purely electronically means some are missing out on face to face interaction, and the anonymity of many of these platforms raises social and ethical questions. Many of these issues are discussed further in Unit 8.

The price of connectivity

Access to computer technology and the internet is not consistent around the world, and isn't consistent within many countries. This means the many benefits that access to microprocessor-controlled devices and smart technology offers aren't available to others. This divide may be linked to geography, cultural tradition or affordability but as many services move away from the physical to the virtual, this divide will increase.

Review and revise

You should now be able to:

- outline the advantages and disadvantages of using microprocessor-controlled devices in the home
- describe the function of control and monitoring applications in the home
- explain the positive and negative effects of these devices in our homes.

5 Theory review

What have you covered?

In these seven theory sessions you have looked at:
- the way in which the introduction of ICT impacts on employment
- how the use of new ICT technologies is changing employment patterns
- health issues connected with the use of computers
- the moral and ethical issues related to ICT
- the issue of software copyright and considered the need for copyright protection
- the use of modelling applications to mimic real systems and help with planning
- how new technology is being used in the home.

Some practice questions

1 Pooja is applying for a job as a computer programmer. The job specification mentions that this is an ideal position for someone who wishes to work flexi-time and flexi-place. This is Pooja's first job after university. She comes to see you to ask what these terms mean.

Explain to Pooja the significance of flexible working and the advantages that the two specified working conditions could have for her.

2 Myriam and Omar work in a library. The managers of the library have been investigating the possible introduction of new self-service style checkouts for the borrowing and returning of books and other media. They are both worried that they may lose their jobs?

Why might Myriam and Omar be worried?

The library managers understand Myriam and Omar's fears and have tried to reassure them that their jobs are safe. In a presentation given by managers to the library staff, the phrase 'retraining' was used a lot. Omar asked whether they actually meant '**deskilling**'.

What do these terms mean? What is the difference between them?

See Session 5.1

3 You have been on the lookout for a cheap version of the new episodes of your favourite massive multi-player online game. One of your school friends tells you that he has bought one at the Saturday market for a really great price.

Without even seeing the packaging you are convinced that he must have been sold a counterfeit copy (an illegal copy).

Explain to your friend about copyright law and what he should look for on the packaging which should indicate whether the purchase really was a good buy or not.

See Session 5.5

4 Why would you create a financial model using a spreadsheet?

What are the advantages of building a model compared to carefully recording details as they happen?

See Session 5.6

5 For each health problem in the left-hand column, suggest a method of prevention.

Problem	Method of prevention
You have backache.	
Your eyes are tired.	
You have pain in your wrists.	

See Session 5.3

6 A clothing company plans to use robots in their warehouses to collect products. Each robot will locate the shelf where the product is, pick one up and then find its way back to a human operator, who will pack the product to be sent to the purchaser.

a Describe the advantages and disadvantages of this method for the company.

b Describe two ways in which work for employees will change.

See Session 5.1

7 A clothing company has decided to close its city store and become an online business. Discuss the advantages and disadvantages for the company's customers of online shopping.

See Session 5.4

8 An adventure holiday company has launched a new website. Current and future customers can open a chat box to chat to other travellers, upload videos of previous holidays, post comments about holidays, or ask for other adventurers' advice.

a Describe one advantage that this interactive website offers to the company.

b Describe one advantage that this interactive website offers to travellers.

The company has considered including a facility for transferring funds from the traveller's bank account to the company's bank account. The traveller's money could then be accessed by the holiday representatives to pay for visas or additional transport costs while travelling.

c What concerns might the travellers have about this system?

d What can the holiday company do to reassure their customers?

See Session 5.4

Progress check

Aiming for good progress

- You understand the impact that the introduction of ICT can have in employment.
- You understand how the employment of new technologies can offer a change in employees working patterns.
- You understand the need for copyright law and software copyright.
- You can discuss health issues connected with ICT and possible solutions and you can state the effects of ICT on various aspects of society.
- You understand the need for modelling applications to mimic real systems.

Aiming for excellent progress

- You can discuss the impact that the introduction of ICT can have in employment.
- You can appreciate how the employment of new technologies can offer a change in employees working patterns.
- You understand the need for copyright law and can justify the necessity for software copyright.
- You can offer advice and possible solutions on health issues connected with ICT, and discuss social, moral and ethical issues relating to ICT.
- You can describe the use of modelling applications to mimic real systems and help with planning.
- You understand how new technology is being employed in the home.

SESSION 5.8 Data analysis: Spreadsheet modelling skills

Background

In Unit 3 you were introduced to spreadsheets, which are often used to create mathematical models. A model enables you to put different data into the system and look at the impact of that data on the decisions that are made. It is possible to develop mathematical models that do not use computer programs such as spreadsheets, but there are advantages in using them to create models:

- Changes can be made easily.
- Calculations are carried out automatically.
- Results of well developed and tested models are accurate.
- The results can be seen very quickly.

In this session you will have the opportunity to revise and improve the skills that you have developed so far. You will also apply some new techniques to generate an effective model.

The summer fair

Excelsior Academy has decided to hold a summer fair with games, entertainment and refreshments. The fair will need staffing while costs and income also need to be carefully planned. The academy has asked you to create a data model for the fair.

Using your spreadsheet software, open **SummerFair.csv**, which can be found on the digital download, and save it as a spreadsheet. Adjust the column widths so that all the data labels are fully visible.

Your model looks like this and has two main sections.

1 Money in (INCOME)

2 Money out (PAYMENTS)

	A	B	C	D	E	F
1			Estimated number of visitors	350		
2						
3	INCOME	Cost	No. bought per person	Money in		
4	Entrance fee	1.5	1			
5	Hot drinks	0.5	1			
6	Cold drinks	0.45	1			
7	Cakes	0.3	1			
8	Hot food	1	1			
9	Rides	0.75	4			
10	Games	0.4	3			
11	Raffle	0.5	2			
12	Plants	1.5	2			
13	Tombola	0.5	2			
14				Total INCOME		
15	PAYMENTS			Money out		
16	PA system/music			650		
17	Support staff			150		
18	Stock of tea/coffee/milk/sugar			43		
19	Cakes			60		
20	Ingredients for hot food			180		
21	Hire of rides			500		

> **Tip**
>
> Every time you open a .csv file you need to save it as a spreadsheet with whichever software you are using.

> **Activity 1**
>
> 1 Format cells A1 to E1 with a fill colour Black, and a font colour White.
>
> 2 Format cells A3 to E3 and cells A15 to E15 in the same way.
>
> 3 Make sure the font of all cells formatted in rows 1, 3 and 15 are sans-serif, size 11 point, bold.

Introducing functionality

1 Cell D4 will represent the income from selling entrance tickets. This is the entrance fee cost (B4) multiplied by how many each person buys (C4) multiplied by the number of people expected to attend (D1). Into D4 type: =B4*C4*$D$1. Replicate this function in cells D5 to D13. (Can you remember why D1 is written as an absolute reference, $D$1?)

2 Cell D14 needs to contain a function that adds up all the income values in cells D4 to D13. Into D14 type: =SUM(D4:D13)

3 Cell D27 needs to contain a function that adds up all the payments in cells D16 to D26. Into D27 type: =SUM(D16:D26)

4 Cell D29 will calculate the profit (or loss) made at the fair. This is the total income (D14) minus the total payments (D27). Into D29 type: =D14-D27

Formatting for currency

Cells B4 to B13, D4 to D14, D16 to D27 and D29 all represent amounts of money, so they should be formatted for a currency. You can choose from a wide range, selecting the symbol and number of decimal places to display.

Select the cells and either right click and choose **Format cells**, or you may have an icon on a toolbar for currency.

1 Format the money cells to be a currency of your choice. For the rest of the steps in this session we have used dollars ($).

2 Add a footer to the spreadsheet, to include the filename and your own name.

3 Save the spreadsheet as **SummerFair**. (Note: You may either need to choose the format, for example, Excel Workbook, or you may need to follow the instructions that appear when you do this.)

Activity 2

The model shows you that if 350 people attend the fair then the school will make a profit of $2049.50. What will happen if the number of visitors (D1) changes? Test the model and write in the second row of the following table, the profit/loss that will be made if the following numbers of visitors attend:

Visitors	100	150	250	300	400
Profit/Loss					

Break-even is a term used to describe the situation where the profit/loss is equal (or as near as possible) to zero.

This spreadsheet needs to be tested to make sure that it works properly. In Session 3.7 the idea of testing was introduced. You would not want to pass the spreadsheet over to one of the organisers and have them come back to you after the event saying the spreadsheet was inaccurate.

Validation

One way to increase the accuracy of data entry is to provide validation routines.

The cost of each item for sale (as well as the Entrance Fee) must be a value greater than 0 (or $0.00), and looking at the data in the spreadsheet already, should be $2 or less. A validation routine can be set up so that if someone enters a value that is not within this range an error message will be displayed. This will ensure that all the values in column B are acceptable. Of course, this is not guaranteeing that the value is absolutely correct, just that it is acceptable – and useable.

Click on cell B4 (the cost of the Entrance Fee). Look for a button connected to 'Data' which indicates that validation can be attached to the cell. It may look something like this:

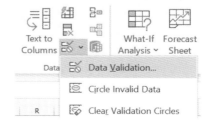

Tip

Absolute references are copied unchanged from one cell to another. Relative references are adjusted according to column or row movement when they are copied from one cell to another.

Real world

From mathematics you should recall the rules of **BIDMAS**. This stands for **B**rackets (), **I**ndices^, **D**ivision /, **M**ultiplication *, **A**ddition +, **S**ubtraction -. This indicates the order that arithmetic operators are carried out. Remember to place operations that must be done first in brackets. Square brackets [] and braces {} are never used.

After clicking on the Data Validation option you get the chance to enter the values you are restricting data entry to, and the text for the error message that will be displayed. Enter these choices and click 'OK'.

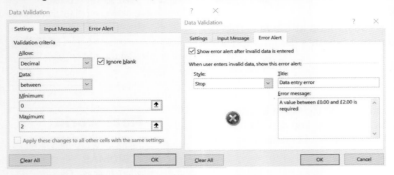

Language

Validation is a software check that ensures that the data that has been entered can be used by the system. It is a check to see that the data entered lies within specified limits or fits a particular format.

You need to repeat this routine all the way down column B.

Now click on a cell in column B and enter either a negative value or a value greater than 2. The error message will be displayed.

Save the spreadsheet.

In order to test the spreadsheet properly, a testing plan is required. This plan outlines the values (the test data) that will be entered into the spreadsheet, the outcome that is expected and that which actually occurs. The most useful way to record this is in a table.

Three types of data are used: normal, extreme and abnormal.

For the Summer Fair spreadsheet, the table for the testing plan may start to look like this:

A value between £0.00 and £2.00 is required

Retry   Cancel   Help

Language

Test data should be a mix of these three types:

Normal data: the usual, expected data that the system will have to process

Extreme data: unusual, but acceptable data that could occur and should be processed

Abnormal data: unacceptable data that should be rejected.

Cells	Acceptable range/ Calculation	Test data	Data value to test/Test to make	Expected outcome	Actual outcome	Test okay?
Cost	0.00 – 2.00	Normal	1.50	1.50		
		Extreme	0.00	0.00		
		Abnormal	3.00	Error message		
		Abnormal	−1.50	Error message		

For D14 the needed check is that the SUM function work correctly. The easiest way is to put another SUM function in B14 adding up the cost of each of the items in column B and setting the number bought of each item to 1. Put 100 into cell D1. The test is then whether D14 matches 100 x B14.

D14	Calculation (in B14 enter: =SUM(B4:B13))	Normal	Cells C4 to C13 all set to 1	100 times the value in B14 ($790)		

Activity 3

How might you test the contents of cells D4 to D13?

Create a test row in the table for cells D27 and D29.

Now carry out the tests you have decided upon and see if the expected outcome matches the actual outcome, fill in the empty cells of your table.

If any of these tests were not okay you need to go back and revise the formulae you placed in cells D4, D27 and D29

Remove the extra formulae placed in, for example, B14 that you used to carry out the test. Restore the values of cells C4 to C13 and D1.

Save the spreadsheet.

Activity 4

You need to use the spreadsheet to get some idea of the way changes to some of the figures may affect the overall profit. Into cell D1, type **350** again, so that the spreadsheet indicates the original profit of $2049.50. (After you have completed each of the following five tests, restore the model back to this position.)

1 If 400 people attend and each person buys two hot drinks, how much profit will be made?

2 Change hot drinks back to 1 per person. The support staff charge three times the current rate, and the insurance is $650. Will there be a profit if only 150 people attend? If not, how many visitors are needed to make a profit?

3 Return to the original settings (insurance $750 and support staff $150). If you want a profit of $2500 and only 350 visitors attend, how much should you charge for the entrance fee?

4 Change the entrance fee back to $1.50. If you charge $0.50 for the cakes and $0.75 for the hot food, how many visitors will you need to break even?

5 Change the prices for cakes and hot food back to $0.30 and $1.00. You want to make a profit of $4000. How many visitors will you need if each person buys six rides and four raffle tickets?

More about absolute referencing

You have been able to see in the Summer Fair model how useful an absolute cell reference can be. All the formulae in cells D4 to D13 refer to cell D1. Without using the $ symbols in the formulae you would not have been able to replicate the formulae easily. There is another way to set a cell reference. It can be done by *naming* cells.

Naming a cell

Select cell D1. At the top left of the screen in the reference box you will see D1 displayed (this indicates the active cell – the cell you are at).

Click this box, type **Visitors** and press the Enter key.

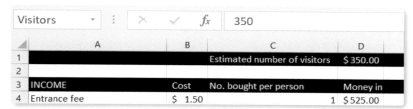

Select another cell on the sheet. That cell reference should appear in the reference box. Now click back on D1. Instead of D1 you should see **Visitors**.

Now change the formula in cell D4. Type: =B4*C4*Visitors. Replicate this formula into cells D4 to D13. The model will still display exactly the same values throughout. Nothing has changed in the view of the user, but this method makes the functionality of a spreadsheet much easier to read by anyone who may be developing it.

Activity 5

1 Name cell D14: **Income**

2 Name cell D27: **Expenditure**

3 Change the formula in D29 to reflect the changes you have made to cells D14 and D27.

4 Save the spreadsheet as version 2 of your original.

Producing printouts: Print areas and gridlines

At times you will have to manage the layout of the printed spreadsheet. You may only want to print a certain part, or sometimes you will have trouble fitting a large spreadsheet onto one page.

You may want to give the person who is organising the fair a list of the income and expense categories that you are using. In this case, you need to ask only for cells A3 to A26 to be printed. Highlight cells A3 to A26 and then find an icon (or item in a list) for **Set Print Area**. You might have something like this:

Click on **Set Print Area**. When you print the spreadsheet only the selected cells will be printed. Clicking on **Clear Print Area** will remove any print area setting you have made.

Sometimes a large printout will not easily fit onto one page and you may spend a long time adjusting cell widths and viewing the print preview. However, the spreadsheet software has a function that will automatically adjust the page layout so that it does fit onto one page.

Find the page layout options and look for the option to have the printing fit a page. You may find an option like this:

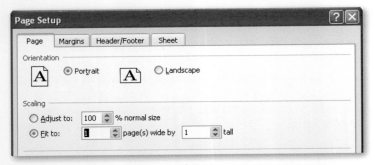

Select **Fit to**, and the page orientation you require.

Another useful option is to print the gridlines (and maybe the row/column headers). In the panel above you could click on the tab **Sheet** to view the options shown on the right.

Print
- ☐ Gridlines
- ☐ Black and white
- ☐ Draft quality
- ☐ Row and column headings

Review and revise

You should now be able to:

- create a layout for a spreadsheet model
- enter text, numerical data, formulae and functions into the model
- edit by replicating and formatting for currency values
- name a cell and reference it by name rather than by the cell reference
- add validation rules and message alerts to cells
- devise a testing plan and create a range of test data which tests the model
- adjust page settings so that a spreadsheet fits onto a single page.

Activity 6

Print two copies of the model you have developed:

- ones showing the values
- one showing the formulae.

On each printout adjust the settings so that the spreadsheet fits the page and shows gridlines and column/row headings. Save the spreadsheet.

Developing your spreadsheet modelling skills

Background

Spreadsheets can be used to model many different kinds of problems. If it is possible to create a mathematical or logical formula, or to find a suitable function, then a model can be created. In this session you will be introduced to a number of different functions that can be used to help solve problems.

> ### Language
>
> A **function** is a pre-defined routine for a calculation (SUM, for example). A **formula** is an expression that you create to carry out a particular calculation (=B4*C4*$D$1).

Problem solving with spreadsheet models

Shilpa is a great fan of difficult puzzles that are printed in her local newspaper every week. One week she sees this problem:

If MIRZA is 67 and PALTROW is 105 who is the biggest movie star in this table?

MIRZA	RAMBHA	THOMPSON	HUNTER	SHETTY	SARANDON	MCDORMAND
HUNT	PALTROW	TANDON	ROBERTS	BERRY	KULKARNI	THERON
LOHAN	MUKHERJEE	SHERAWAT	MIRREN	TAYLOR	KELLY	WITHERSPOON

It took Shilpa some time to figure it out, but finally she realised that MIRZA was 67 because M is the 13th letter in the alphabet, and A is the first letter. So, if you add together the values of all the letters in the name, you get 67.

She decided to model a solution to the problem, and was able to get the answer quite quickly. In doing so she developed these new modelling skills and techniques:

- Name a range of cells and use that name in a formula.
- Use the VLOOKUP function.
- Use an IF function.
- Use the MAX function to find the highest value.
- Use the MIN function to find the lowest value.
- Use the AVERAGE function to calculate the mean value.
- Use the COUNT function.

> ### Real world
>
> Your spreadsheet software, for example *Open Office*, may use the function AVG instead of AVERAGE.

Open **MovieStars.csv**, from the digital download, and save it using your spreadsheet software.

Each cell only contains one letter so all the columns can be narrow. The top right-hand corner of the spreadsheet looks like this:

In Session 5.8 you named a cell. This allowed you to use that name instead of the cell reference whenever you used it in a formula or function, making them more understandable. You are now going to name a range of cells.

1 Highlight cells A1 to B26.

2 In the reference box type: **Alphabet**.

This tells the spreadsheet program that each cell in the range A1 to B26 is in the data table called Alphabet.

The VLOOKUP function

You now want the model to look at each letter of the movie star names and allocate the correct number to the letter. For example, in D1 the letter is M, so a function needs to look down the data table we have named Alphabet and return the number 13.

The VLOOKUP function will do this. There is also an HLOOKUP function, which will be explained in the next session. VLOOKUP is used because the data is arranged in a vertical table – our data (letters of the alphabet and their number) are listed in vertical columns.

The function syntax is =VLOOKUP(what to find, where to look, what to return)

The three parts in this example will be:

1 What to find: D1.

2 Where to look: Alphabet.

3 What to return: the value in the second column.

Into cell D2, type =VLOOKUP(D1,Alphabet,2)

The value 13 appears as a result of this function being carried out – exactly what you want.

The longest name in the list is WITHERSPOON, which extends to column N, so replicate this function across row 2, from D2 to N2.

> **Tip**
>
> HLOOKUP and VLOOKUP are very useful functions and work in similar ways. The choice of which to use will depend on how the data is arranged – a vertical table or a horizontal table.

	A	B	C	D	E	F
1	A	1		M	I	R
2	B	2		=VLOOKUP(D1,Alphabet,2)	=VLOOKUP(E1,Alphabet,2)	=VLOOKUP(F1,Alphabet,2)
3	C	3		R	A	M

A strange result happens now. Columns E, F, G and H all have values in them (9, 18, 26 and 1) but columns I to N all have #### or #N/A displayed. The #### symbols mean that the column is not wide enough to display the result, so if you stretch the column you will see #N/A. This indicates an error. The mistake is that in these cells (I2 to N2) VLOOKUP is looking for a blank space in Alphabet and there isn't one, so it cannot return a value.

The easiest way to resolve this problem is to add something to the function that will test to see if the cell contains a blank space. When there is a blank space, simply do nothing; when there is a letter, find it in Alphabet as you want. To eliminate the problem add the IF function.

The IF function

This function is very easy to understand and to use.

The syntax is =IF(what is being tested, what to do if true, what to do if false)

The three parts in this example will be:

1 What is being tested: cell=blank space?

2 What to do if true: print a blank.

3 What to do if false: use the VLOOKUP function.

In cell D2 type =IF(D1="","",VLOOKUP(D1,Alphabet,2))

> **Tip**
>
> Be careful with quotation marks. Make sure you use the double open and close quotation.

Replicate this across to cell N2. This time you get the same values in columns D to H, but blank spaces in columns I to N.

The function you have just typed is an example of what is known as a **nested function**, because there is one function (VLOOKUP) inside another (IF).

Activity 1

1 Copy the functions that are in cells D2 to N2 and paste them into the rows under the other names in the list. This will give number values for all the letters of each of the 21 movie star names, with no #N/A appearing anywhere.

2 Refer back to Session 5.8 and remind yourself of how the SUM function works.

● In cell P2, type a SUM function that adds together the values in cells D2 to N2.

● Copy the function in P2 and paste it into P4, P6, P8, and so on, down to P42.

Who has the highest value for their name? Who has the lowest value?

MAX, MIN, AVERAGE functions

Shilpa wants to find out what the biggest movie star value is. She could look down column P and find the largest number. She could also use an appropriate function.

- Highlight cells P1 through to P42. Name this range: **Values**
- In cell R1 type: **MAX**
- In cell R2 type: **MIN**
- In cell R3 type: **AVERAGE**

Activity 2

1 Use your software to investigate the functions that will find or calculate the maximum, minimum and average values across a range of cells.

- In cell S1, type a function to find the maximum value in the range named Values.
- In cell S2, type a function to find the minimum value in the range named Values.
- In cell S3, type a function to calculate the average value in the range named Values.

The top few rows of your completed spreadsheet will look like this:

⊿	A	B	C	D	E	F	G	H	I	J	K	L	M	N	O	P	Q	R	S
1	A	1		M	I	R	Z	A										Max	162
2	B	2		13	9	18	26	1								57		Min	43
3	C	3		R	A	M	B	H	A									Average	86

Add a footer to the spreadsheet to include the filename and your own name. Save the spreadsheet with the name **MovieStars**.

2 Print a copy of your spreadsheet so that it:

- shows the values, making sure that all the labels are visible
- prints the gridlines and column/row headers
- prints the spreadsheet to fit a single page in portrait orientation.

The COUNT function

Having added so much to the puzzle Shilpa decides to add just one more feature: the number of letters in each movie star's name. To work this out Shilpa can use the COUNT function. The syntax is really easy:

=COUNT(What range of cells to count if there are any numbers in them)

You want to count cells that have numbers, so you will count across the rows that have the alphabet numbers in them, not the rows containing the actors' names.

To count how many letters there are in MIRZA, type into cell U2:
=COUNT(D2:N2)

This should display 5. Replicate this function down column U for the other cells for each actor and then save the spreadsheet.

> **Tip**
>
> Be aware that COUNT counts all the cells **that contain numbers**. It does **not** count **how many cells have something in them**. To count the cells that have something in them (are not blank) use the **countA** function.

Printing restricted views of the spreadsheet

1 Change the view of your spreadsheet to show the formulae (see Tip box). Make sure that the functions are fully visible. They are very long, so the columns will need to be stretched.

2 Set the print area to cover only cells A1 to C42 and print to fit on a single sheet again, with gridlines and row and column headings.

3 Undo the print area by going back to the icon or menu where you set it and choose: **Clear Print Area**.

4 Return the view of the spreadsheet back to displaying values and not formulae.

> **Tip**
>
> At times you will want to switch between the datasheet view and the formula sheet view. The *Excel* keyboard shortcut is Ctrl + ` to toggle between the views. Or, select **Formulas** from the main menu and use the **Show Formulas** button.

It would be a good idea if you could print only columns A, B, C, D, P, Q, R, S and U. This will give you the alphabet list and numbers, the first use of the nested function, and the results: MAX, MIN and AVERAGE.

To do this you need to hide the columns that you do not want to print. A hidden column has a width of zero pixels. Adjust the width of column E to zero pixels. In effect it is hidden – you cannot see it now and would not see it if the spreadsheet was printed. Pull the width of column E back to the size it was.

Look for an icon or menu item that allows you to adjust the column width or hide/unhide columns. You may find something like the image on the right

For either of these you will be highlighting columns and then selecting **Hide** (**Unhide**) or setting a width of zero. Practise Hide and Unhide until you are confident of the method.

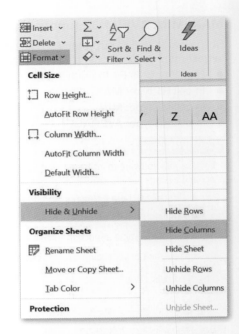

Activity 3

1 Hide columns E to O.

2 Switch the spreadsheet view to show formulae.

3 Adjust the visible column widths so that the functions can be seen fully.

4 Print the spreadsheet with gridlines, column/row headings and to fit on a single portrait sheet.

5 After printing, switch back to viewing the values and unhide columns E to O.

The top of the printout should look like this:

	A	B	C	D	P	Q	R	S	T	U
1	A	1	M				Max	=MAX(Values)		
2	B	2	=IF(D1="","",VLOOKUP(D1,Alphabet,2))	=SUM(D2:N2)		Min	=MIN(Values)		=COUNT(D2:N2)
3	C	3	R				Average	=AVERAGE(Values)		
4	D	4	=IF(D3="","",VLOOKUP(D3,Alphabet,2))	=SUM(D4:N4)					=COUNT(D4:N4)
5	E	5	T							
6	F	6	=IF(D5="","",VLOOKUP(D5,Alphabet,2))	=SUM(D6:N6)					=COUNT(D6:N6)
7	G	7	H							
8	H	8	=IF(D7="","",VLOOKUP(D7,Alphabet,2))	=SUM(D8:N8)					=COUNT(D8:N8)
9	I	9	S							
10	J	10	=IF(D9="","",VLOOKUP(D9,Alphabet,2))	=SUM(D10:N10)					=COUNT(D10:N10)
11	K	11	S							
12	L	12	=IF(D11="","",VLOOKUP(D11,Alphabet,2))	=SUM(D12:N12)					=COUNT(D12:N12)

Review and revise

You should now be able to:

- create a layout for a spreadsheet model
- successfully use the IF, COUNT, MAX, MIN and AVERAGE functions
- enter simple and nested functions into a spreadsheet model
- replicate formulae and functions in a workbook
- print a spreadsheet showing formulae or values
- print a spreadsheet, having set a print area
- hide and unhide columns for printing purposes.

SESSION 5.10 Analysing spreadsheet data and preparing graphs

Background

You have learned how spreadsheet models can be used to simulate complex situations and that they can be used to analyse events using mathematical formulae and functions. So far, the output of your work has been limited to numerical data, text labels and the outcomes of calculations. However, spreadsheets can also be used to create graphs and charts of the numerical and text-based data. This session will explain how the spreadsheet model can be developed so that data can be analysed and how a pie chart can be prepared and used to illustrate the data.

The teacher's mark book

You have already used the IF function to:

- test a condition (Did a cell contain a blank space?)
- carry out one task if the answer to that test was true
- do another task if the answer was false.

IF also helps us to define how data can be calculated, changed, or formatted if certain conditions are met.

Mr Singh teaches Geography at Excelsior Academy. He wants to be able to use a spreadsheet model to show the marks (1–100) and the grades (A star, A, B, C, D, E, F and Fail) for each student in his class.

A conditional function

In a simple model of Mr Singh's mark book a **conditional function** would look like this:

$$=IF(mark>70,"PASS","FAIL")$$

With this function the cell will display PASS if the mark is greater than 70, and FAIL if it is less than, or equal to, 70. In Mr Singh's mark book there are seven conditions to test, so multiple conditions must be met. They could be built into a **nested IF** statement.

Nested IF statement

As an example, if you had to achieve a mark of 40 for Pass, 60 for Credit and 80 for Merit, with anything else being a Fail grade, you could produce an IF statement like this:

$$=IF(mark>79,"Merit",IF(mark>59,"Credit",IF(mark>39,"Pass",Fail)))$$

Can you follow the elements of this statement?

If the mark is greater (>) than 79, then it's a "**Merit**", if not, then test again. Is it greater than 59? If so, then it's a **Credit**, if not, test again. Is it greater than 39? If yes, then it's a **Pass**, if not, it's a **Fail**.

Look at this example mark book.

The marking system is based on the rules that you can see in columns A and B. If a mark falls between 80 and 90, then Grade A is awarded. In this example you should be able to see that Aidan's mark falls between 60 and 70 and is therefore a Grade C.

	A	B	C	D	E	F	G
1	Mark	Grade	StudentID	Forename	Surname	Assignment 1	Assignment Grade
2	90	A*	1001	Aidan	Aronvitch	65	C
3	80	A	1002	Bella	Bold	29	Fail
4	70	B	1003	Charlie	Chan	59	D
5	60	C	1004	Delia	Downey	73	B
6	50	D	1005	Eema	Erikson	80	A
7	40	E	1006	Fiona	Fowler	92	A*
8	30	F	1007	Gok	Kwan	49	E
9	0	Fail	1008	Hakeem	Khan	73	B
10			1009	Ishmael	Azam	64	C
11			1010	Junior	Jones	90	A*
12			1011	Khalid	Khan	67	C
13			1012	Leonie	Lawson	73	B
14			1013	Michael	Moore	72	B
15			1014	Natalia	Norson	71	B
16			1015	Ophelia	O'Reilly	70	B
17			1016	Peter	Piper	25	Fail

Dealing with seven conditions of an IF statement

The formula to place the assignment grade (column G on page 233) becomes complicated because it is dealing with seven conditions.

It takes each condition in turn and checks to see if the condition is true. If it is, then the value is output. If not, then the next condition is tested. This continues until each condition has been tested. If none of the seven are true then the final outcome of Fail is output to the cell.

The nested IF function in cell G2 looks like this:

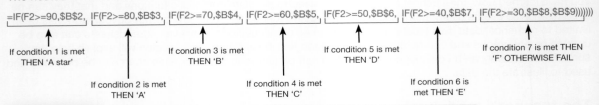

=IF(F2>=90,$B$2, IF(F2>=80,$B$3, IF(F2>=70,$B$4, IF(F2>=60,$B$5, IF(F2>=50,$B$6, IF(F2>=40,$B$7, IF(F2>=30,$B$8,$B$9)))))))

If condition 1 is met THEN 'A star'

If condition 2 is met THEN 'A'

If condition 3 is met THEN 'B'

If condition 4 is met THEN 'C'

If condition 5 is met THEN 'D'

If condition 6 is met THEN 'E'

If condition 7 is met THEN 'F' OTHERWISE FAIL

Activity 1

- Open **MarkBook.csv** from the digital download and save it in your spreadsheet program as **MarkBook**.
- Make the columns wide enough to display cell contents correctly.
- Insert a footer on the spreadsheet to include the filename and your own name.
- Now insert the nested IF function from the bottom of page 233 into cell G2 and replicate it through to G27.

Does your spreadsheet display the same results as those in the image on the previous page?

This is a difficult task, as it involves creating the nested function and typing it into each cell, and then testing it to make sure that it works correctly for any data value in the column.

VLOOKUP

Another problem with this nested IF approach would arise if the grade boundaries changed. You would have to go back into the nested IF and change the values. But, as you have the grade boundaries in columns A and B, why not make use of those?

In the last session, the function VLOOKUP was introduced. Remember that the criterion for its use was whether data was in a vertical table – which is the situation here.

1 Revise the syntax for VLOOKUP in Session 5.9 on page 230.

2 Into cell G2, type: =VLOOKUP(F2,$A$2:$B$9,2)

3 There appears to be a problem. The grade for Aidan should be C, not Fail. This highlights a commonly (and easily) made mistake. The values in a VLOOKUP table need to be in **ascending** order.

4 Rewrite the table A2 to B9 so that 90 and A star are at the bottom, and 0 and Fail are at the top (use 0 and not <30).

5 The grade in G2 should now be C.

6 Replicate the function in G2 into the cells G3 to G27. The grades displayed now should still match those you had before (and in the image on the previous page).

7 Save the spreadsheet to your work area.

Tip

This will display the same grade boundaries as the example mark book pictured above.

Using VLOOKUP has created a far easier solution than a very long, and complex, nested IF.

HLOOKUP

Session 5.9 mentioned HLOOKUP. Look at Mr Singh's mark book again. In the digital download find **MarkBookH.csv** and open it with your spreadsheet software.

Adjust the columns so that all data labels are fully visible. The first rows should look like this:

	A	B	C	D	E	F	G	H	I	J	K	L	M	N	O
1	Student ID	Forename	Surname	Assignment 1	Assignment Grade		Mark	0	30	40	50	60	70	80	90
2	1001	Aidan	Aronvitch	65			Grade	Fail	F	E	D	C	B	A	A*
3	1002	Bella	Bold	29											

The syntax of the HLOOKUP functions matches that of VLOOKUP. Look for a value's (D2) position in the top row of a table (H1 to O2) and return the content of the cell in the chosen row (2).

1　To get the correct grade in E2, type: =HLOOKUP(D2,$H$1:$O$2,2)

2　Replicate this function down column E so that all the students have grades.

Text wrapping and row height

The labels in row 1 are much longer than the contents in the columns below. This is especially true of columns D and E. Maybe "Assignment" and "Grade" would be better on separate lines in the cell. This is known as text wrapping. However, when the columns are reduced, the text in the right of the cells is not displayed; the words do not automatically fall to a new line:

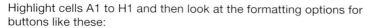

	A	B	C	D	E	F
1	Student ID	Forename	Surname	Assignment 1	Assignment Grade	

"Assignment Grade" is fully visible, but only because cell F1 has no contents.

Highlight cells A1 to H1 and then look at the formatting options for buttons like these:

Alignment

Wrap Text

Merge & Center

Use a combination of the Wrap Text button and the alignment buttons to centre the text vertically and centrally.

Just as you can alter the width of a column, it is possible to adjust the depth of a row.

You may have something looking like this:

Click and drag here to resize the row

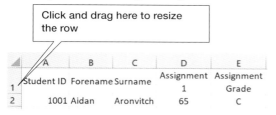

	A	B	C	D	E
1	Student ID	Forename	Surname	Assignment 1	Assignment Grade
2	1001	Aidan	Aronvitch	65	C

Activity 2

1　Use the formatting tools so that the cells in **MarkBookH** look like this:

	A	B	C	D	E	F	G	H	I	J	K	L	M	N	O
1	Student ID	Forename	Surname	Assignment 1	Assignment Grade		Mark	0	30	40	50	60	70	80	90
2	1001	Aidan	Aronvitch	65	C		Grade	Fail	F	E	D	C	B	A	A*
3	1002	Bella	Bold	29	Fail										
4	1003	Charlie	Chan	59	D										

2　Save the spreadsheet.

Conditional formatting

Mr Singh is keen to have an indication of whether the grades are a good pass or not. He defines a good pass as a grade C – a mark of 60 per cent or more. It is possible to highlight cells depending on a condition that the cell's content fulfils. In this case it would be possible to have all the cells in column D have a certain background and text colour when the score, column D, is > 59 per cent, and another background and text colour combination if the score is < 60 per cent.

Highlight cells D2 to D27.

Look for the conditional formatting buttons that may look like these and find the condition "Greater than".

When you select this you can select the value that is to be used as the comparison, and what format the colour scheme should be.

Click 'OK' for this to take effect. You should see that all the cells with a score or 60 per cent or more are shaded in. With the cells again highlighted, go through the same routine, but select the condition "Less than" and indicate that all cells with a value of less than 60 be another contrasting colour scheme. If the colour combinations offered are not ones you like, then you can customize.

Your top part of the spreadsheet should now look something like this:

	A	B	C	D	E
1	Student ID	Forename	Surname	Assignment 1	Assignment Grade
2	1001	Aidan	Aronvitch	65	C
3	1002	Bella	Bold	29	Fail
4	1003	Charlie	Chan	59	D
5	1004	Delia	Downey	73	
6	1005	Eema	Erikson	80	

Analysing the data

Mr Singh wants to use the mark book to help him analyse the marks and grades that his students are achieving, not just to record them. In your work area, find the spreadsheet **MarkBook** that you had saved and reopen it with your spreadsheet software.

Activity 3

Previously you have used MAX, MIN, AVERAGE and named a range of cells.

1 Name the range D2:D27: **Marks**

2 Name the range E2:E27: **Grades**

3 Name the second tab in the workbook: **Analysis**

4 Click on the **Analysis** tab to open that worksheet. It is here that you are going to start providing the analysis of the student scores.

5 Create this layout:

6 In cell B3, type: =MAX(Marks)

7 In cell B4, type the function to return the lowest score.

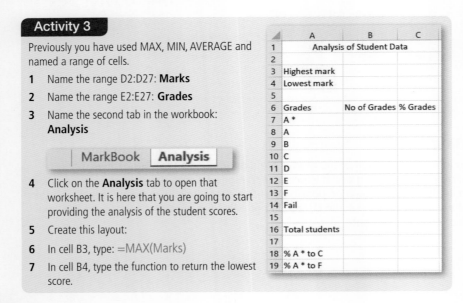

COUNTIF

A very useful function that can be used to help Mr Singh in his analysis is COUNTIF, which counts all the values in a specified range that match a particular criterion.

The syntax is: =COUNTIF(where to look, what to look for)

In cell B7, you need the number of students who have achieved Grade A star. In cell B7, type: =COUNTIF(Grades,"A star")

B7 should display 4.

The labels in column A might change (maybe a score of less than 30 has grade "G" assigned to it). This would mean adjusting the functions that had "Fail" as the criterion and changing them all to "G".

A better way of writing the function in B7 would be: =COUNTIF(Grades,A7)

1 Change the function in B7 and replicate it in cells B8 to B14.

2 In cell B16, type a function to add together all the numbers in B7 to B14.

In cell C7 you need a formula to calculate the percentage of students in the group that achieved that grade. Type into C7: =B7/$B$16

This displays 0.15385, not a percentage. All cells where you want to see a percentage displayed, need to be formatted as percentage and with no decimal places.

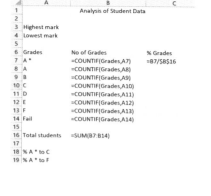

Activity 4

1 Format cells C7 to C14 and B18 and B19 as percentage with no decimal places. You should see 15% in C7.

2 Replicate the formula in C7 into cells C8 to C14.

3 Work out a formula to place in cell B18 which will add up the values in cells B7 to B10 and then divide by the total number of students (B16). (77%)

4 Work out a formula to place in cell B19 which will add up the values in cells B7 to B13 and then divide by the total number of students (B16). (92%)

5 Make sure that your name and the filename are in the footer of the spreadsheet.

6 Print two copies of the spreadsheet, values and formulae, making sure that the cell contents are always fully visible.

7 Save the spreadsheet.

Preparing graphs and charts

Graphs and charts are useful tools in helping users to analyse data quickly. They present numerical data visually. It is important to understand which type of bar or chart is best suited to represent the data you are analysing.

- Pie charts are used to compare parts of a whole. You could use a pie chart to graph the percentage of grades.
- Bar charts (with vertical columns) are used to compare differences. You could use a column chart to show how each student in the group performed.
- Line graphs are used to plot trends over time.

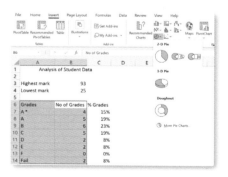

To finish this session you are going to prepare a pie chart from your **MarkBook** spreadsheet. You will save this so that it could be used in a word processed document or a presentation – a skill covered in Unit 3. You are taking data from the **Analysis** sheet of your spreadsheet, so make sure that this is the active sheet.

A pie chart

Mr Singh wants a pie chart that shows the distribution of grades across the whole group of students.

Highlight cells **A6:B14** and select **Insert**, which allows you to select charts and graphs. From the range of charts, look for **Insert > 2-D Pie**.

This gives you a pie chart of the data, but you need to change the title to represent the chart more accurately:

- Right click on the title.
- Select Edit Text from the menu.
- Change the title to: **Assignment 1 Grades**.

Activity 5

Right clicking on any of the elements of the pie chart (sectors, legend, labels) and the surrounding area will allow you to make selections about how that element is displayed. Experiment with the chart's display and see if you can make the finished chart look like this:

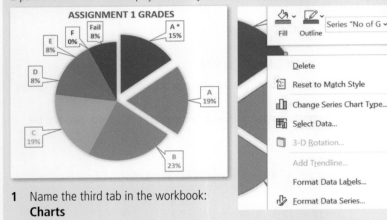

1 Name the third tab in the workbook:
   Charts
2 Cut and paste the pie chart from the sheet **Analysis** and paste it into the sheet **Charts**.
3 Save the spreadsheet. The chart will be saved in the **Charts** worksheet.

Tip

If you are printing to a black and white printer, consider changing the colours so that the pie chart segments are distinct from one another – by using darker to lighter shades of grey, or patterns. This will help the segments stand out. In edit mode, segments can also be pulled away from the main chart as shown, to highlight a particular value.

Tip

Remember that pie charts are used for one set of data at a time.

Review and revise

You should now be able to:

- replicate formulae, functions and formatting in a workbook
- recognise that there are times when one function might be able to be used as a more efficient solution than another
- successfully use the HLOOKUP, COUNTIF functions
- format cells to display percentages
- create, label and format the layout of a pie chart.

SESSION 5.11 Importing additional data and further work with graphs

Background

In Session 5.10, Mr Singh had a mark book with an analysis sheet. This sheet represented data from only one assignment. Over time more assignments will be taken by students and Mr Singh will need to build those results into the spreadsheet model. This session will develop Mr Singh's spreadsheet model by importing some summary data from a text file, and you will continue your analysis of that data by searching and sorting the data. Other charting options will be explored as the data that becomes available is also more varied.

Inserting additional data into a spreadsheet

Open the spreadsheet **MarkBook,** as you last saved it in the previous session.

You are going to insert additional data into the spreadsheet model to represent the development of data over time, to analyse the data further, and to produce more informative charts and graphs. The summary data you will insert is held in text file **NewGeographySummaries.txt**, which is in the digital download.

Make **MarkBook** the active sheet and F1 the active cell.

From the main menu, look for the Data menu and an option to import from a text or CSV file. When a dialogue box opens to import the file, find and import **NewGeographySummaries.txt**.

You will be guided through the import procedure in a similar way to that seen in Session 6.5 when importing data to a database. The first step is to confirm that the text values are separated by a tab (**Delimited**). Click **Next**. When asked, select the **Load to** or **import** menu to import to the data to an existing worksheet in into cell F1.

NewGeographySummaries.txt

File Origin		Delimiter	
1252: Western European (Windows) ▼		Comma ▼	

Assignment 2	Assignment 3	_1	Assignment 4	_2
67	68		72	
32	46		61	
57	63		71	
72	75		78	
81	84		85	
93	93		94	
52	56		60	
76	81		83	
65	69		72	
92	93		94	

You should find that three columns of data with empty columns for Assignment Grades, have been inserted into your spreadsheet – the scores for three further assignments.

Activity 1

To begin the analysis of this data you need to:

1 Put appropriate headings in G1, I1 and K1.
2 Copy the formulae from column E to the appropriate cells in columns G1, I1 and K1.
3 Name cells G2:G27: **Grades2** (note that there is no space)
4 Name cells I2:I27: **Grades3**
5 Name cells K2:K27: **Grades4**
6 Save the spreadsheet.

> ### Tip
>
> Depending on the software you are using, the table may need converting from a table to normal cells before naming cells. In Excel this is done with the **Convert to Range** function.

Activity 2

Select the sheet **Analysis** as the active sheet. Amend it so that it analyses the data you have just inserted into the **MarkBook** worksheet. Use the formulae and functions already there to help you with this task. Most can be copied and pasted, but check that they reference the correct cells. Once completed, your results should look like this:

	A	B	C	D	E	F	G	H	I
1	Analysis of Student Data								
2									
3	Highest mark	93							
4	Lowest mark	25							
5									
6	Grades	No of Grades	% Grades	No of Grades	% Grades	No of Grades	% Grades	No of Grades	% Grades
7	A *	4	15%	3	12%	4	15%	4	15%
8	A	5	19%	5	19%	4	15%	5	19%
9	B	6	23%	7	27%	8	31%	13	50%
10	C	5	19%	5	19%	6	23%	3	12%
11	D	2	8%	3	12%	1	4%	1	4%
12	E	2	8%	1	4%	3	12%	0	0%
13	F	0	0%	2	8%	0	0%	0	0%
14	Fail	2	8%	0	0%	0	0%	0	0%
15									
16	Total students	26		26		26		26	
17									
18	% A * to C	77%		77%		85%		96%	
19	% A * to F	92%		100%		100%		100%	

Save the spreadsheet.

Check the footer and then print the **Analysis** worksheet showing both values and formulae. For the formulae printout:

- Ensure that all labels and formulae are fully visible.
- Print with an orientation of landscape.
- Print gridlines and row/column headers.
- Print to fit **one** page.

Bar charts – (Column chart)

You are going to create a bar chart that displays the surname and marks for Assignments 1 and 2. This data is in the **MarkBook** worksheet. The surname provides the data labels for the chart.

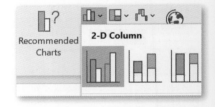

1 Select cells C1 to C27. Hold down the CTRL key and select cells D1 to D27, and cells F1 to F27. When you release the CTRL key the data in columns E, F and H are highlighted. This method allows you to select data for charts, which does not appear in adjacent cells.

2 Select **Insert**, which allows you to select charts and graphs. From the range of charts, select a **2-D Column** chart.

Click on the chart to select it. The charting tools menu will be displayed.

3 Select a chart layout with a title and give the chart the title: **Assignment Grades – Geography**

4 Cut and paste the chart into the Charts worksheet so that you now have two charts there.

5 Save the spreadsheet.

6 The information in the new chart is not that easy to read. Click and drag the frame of the chart to enlarge it. Do this on a corner so that the aspect ratio is maintained.

Tip

Cells that are next to each other are referred to as being **contiguous**. Cells that are not adjacent are known as **non-contiguous**.

Activity 3

The format of the chart needs to be changed. As you did in the last session, experiment with the various elements of the chart, and introduce as a minimum:

- an *x* axis title of: **Students in Mr Singh's class**
- a *y* axis title of: **Percentage achieved**
- Add minor gridlines instead of having just a gridline at every 10 per cent mark.
- Adjust the minimum and maximum y axis values so that the y axis starts at 20 per cent, rather than zero.

When completed, the chart might look like this:

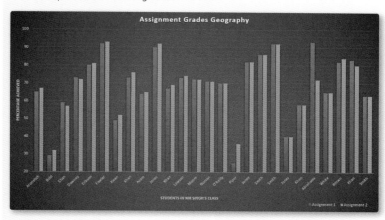

Save the spreadsheet.

> **Tip**
>
> To adjust the y axis, select the chart and look for the **Chart Area** option in the **Format** menu.

Activity 4

Using the same **Markbook** data, create a column chart for Assignment 3 that displays Assignment 4 data as a secondary axis.

1. Use the surname data and percentage results from Assignment 3 and 4.
2. Insert a **Custom Combo Chart** from the chart list.
3. Experiment with the options shown, displaying Assignment 4 data as a secondary line over Assignment 3 data.

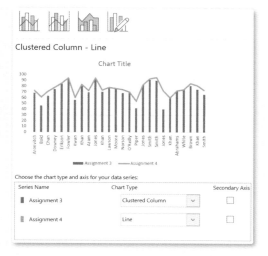

Sorting data

You can use sorting to restructure the data. This allows you to reorder the data, and to select and group the data according to your needs.

1   Go back to the **MarkBook** worksheet and select cells A1 to K27.

2   Click on **Data** at the top of the screen, and then select **Sort** so that the Sort dialogue box is displayed. Notice that when this is displayed, row 1 is deselected. This is because the sort assumes that this first row contains headings – which it does. See that there is a check box in the dialogue box to indicate this.

3   Use the drop-down menu to:
   ● Sort by – Assignment 1
   ● Sort on – Values
   ● Order – Largest to smallest.

> **Tip**
>
> When selecting data to sort, make sure to select the whole table, including headings. Otherwise the data sorted might lose its link with other parts of the table.

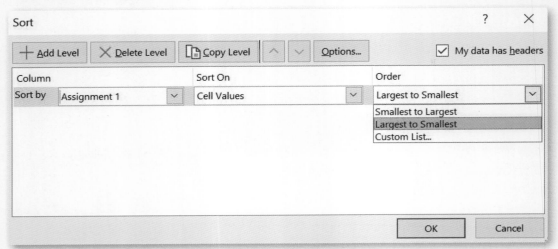

Mr Singh would also like to display the average score for each student.

4   **Insert** a new column after the surname, between column D and E.

5   Add the heading Average and in cell D2 add: =AVERAGE(E2,G2,I2,K2). Violet should now receive an average of 77.25.

Mr Singh is interested in displaying only a whole number score.

6   Format the Average column to have no decimal places displayed. This will cause the value in the cell to be rounded to the nearest whole number.

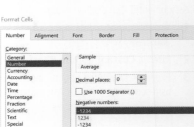

Repeat the sort again, but this time select cells C1 to N27 and use the drop-down menus in the Sort dialogue box to:

● Sort by: Average Score (or the label you used)

● Sort on: Values

● Order: Largest to smallest

Click **OK** and you will see that Fiona is at the top of the list with an average score of 93 per cent.

Some other students have the same average score, such as Junior and Stefan (92 per cent) and Ophelia and Khalid (70 per cent). It might be useful to have these students sorted by how they have done in the last two assignments (Assignments 3 and 4), since the data is about improvement and not averages. The sort order needs changing so that the first sort item is Assignment 4. If there are any duplicates here then Assignment 3 is used, giving you a sort of Assignment 3 within Assignment 4. Select the whole table again and open the Sort dialogue box.

1   Add a second level by clicking **Add level**.

2   Select the drop-down options as shown.

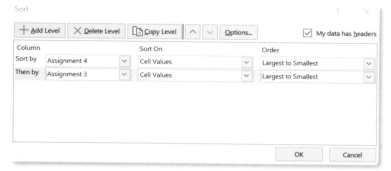

You would refer to the sort as being Assignment 4 within average score. Click **OK**.

With a large number of students, a useful addition to this model is to be able to quickly search for a student.

The XLOOKUP function allows the user to look up an item in one column and return the value from another in the same row.

Take a look at the example shown, it breaks down as follows:

P4 - The cell where a first name is entered

B2:B27 - The cell range of first names

D2:D27 - The cell range of average scores

The result will then be returned in cell P5.

	N	O	P
3			
4		Name	Delia
5		Average	=XLOOKUP(P4,B2:B27,D2:D27)

Activity 5

Mr Singh wants a copy of the spreadsheet that he can easily refer to at a Parent/Teacher meeting.

1   Sort the spreadsheet so that the student details in C1 to N27 are sorted by forename within surname (To check, look at the Khan family, for example).

2   Print a data values copy of the worksheet with:
   ● a page orientation of landscape
   ● gridlines and row/column headings
   ● printed to fit one page.

Save the spreadsheet.

Review and revise

You should now be able to:
● import data into a spreadsheet from another data source
● create formulae that use data values from within another sheet in the spreadsheet
● create a bar chart using non-contiguous data
● create, label and format the layout of a bar chart
● sort the data into various orders using different field types and with multiple criteria.

Data analysis: Referencing an external file and searching the data

Background

During the previous sessions in this unit you have been introduced to a number of analysis tools that are available in a spreadsheet. You have created models that represent solutions to a number of different situations. In this session you will be importing some information into a model and then developing that model to provide some summary analysis of the data that has been provided. You will also be introduced to some search techniques as well as refining some of the statistical skills you have already been using.

Señor Ibanez runs a small tapas bar. He holds a wide range of stock and has all the items he stores, together with details of his food suppliers, in a stock book. This is partially computerised. Gradually, he has been typing the product details that he has in the store into a program on his computer. You have been asked to complete his stock book and add some statistical analysis.

Named ranges and references to external data

You will be using two files from the digital download: **IbanezTapas. csv** and **SupplierCodes.csv**. Open **SupplierCodes.csv** using your spreadsheet software.

Column A has a list of three letter codes and column B has the name of the supplier for each code. Highlight cells A1 to B7 and name the range **Suppliers**. Save this as a spreadsheet file **SupplierCodes**.

Open **IbanezTapas.csv** using your spreadsheet software. Adjust the column widths so that all the headings and data labels are fully visible.

In cell B2 you are going to create a function that looks up the Supplier Code (cell A2) in the spreadsheet **SupplierCodes** and returns the supplier's name.

The data in **SupplierCodes** is a vertical table so you will use the VLOOKUP function. You are looking for the value in cell A2, in the range Suppliers, and need the supplier name from the second column.

There are two ways of achieving this and you will use both:

1   Into B2 type: =VLOOKUP(A2,SupplierCodes.xlsx!Suppliers,2)

   SupplierCodes.xlsx is a reference to the external file where the data can be found. Check the extension of the spreadsheet software you are using – it may not be .xls.

   Suppliers is the named range in that external file.

2   Into B3 type: =VLOOKUP(A3,

   Now, without pressing the Enter key, switch to **SupplierCodes** and highlight cells A1 to B7. As you are highlighting the cells notice that the function is automatically being completed for you.

   Complete the function by typing: ,2) and pressing the Enter key.

   The result is a function that achieves the same result as the one in B2, but this way you do not need to remember the exact syntax of the second element of the function.

	A	B
1	AFS	Ace Food Supplies
2	DFE	Danny's Food Emporium
3	EFI	English Food Imports
4	LIF	Lucio's Italian Foodstuff
5	SFS	Spanish Foodstuffs
6	SJS	Spanish Garden Supplies
7	SSF	Southern Spanish Fisheries

Real world

If you are not using Excel, your spreadsheet software may not support making a reference to a named range in an external file.

This is easily solved by copying the data in the external file into a new worksheet in your existing file, called **SupplierCodes**, and naming the range A1:B7 **Suppliers**

The function in cell B2 would then be:

=VLOOKUP(A2,SupplierCodes!Suppliers,2)

The only difference is that the reference to the external file (.xls) is removed.

	A	B
1	Supplier Codes	Supplier Names
2	AFS	=VLOOKUP(A2,SupplierCodes.xlsx!Suppliers,2)
3	DFE	=VLOOKUP(A3,SupplierCodes.xlsx!Suppliers,2)
4	EFI	=VLOOKUP(A4,SupplierCodes.xlsx!Suppliers,2)
5	LIF	=VLOOKUP(A5,SupplierCodes.xlsx!Suppliers,2)
6	SFS	=VLOOKUP(A6,SupplierCodes.xlsx!Suppliers,2)
7	SJS	=VLOOKUP(A7,SupplierCodes.xlsx!Suppliers,2)
8	SSF	=VLOOKUP(A8,SupplierCodes.xlsx!Suppliers,2)

Replicate the function in B3 into cells B4 to B8. The top left of **IbanezTapas** will look like this:

Activity 1

1   Name the range H16 to H55 as **SupplierCode**.

2   Format cells A16 to A55 as number with no decimal places.

3   Format cells G16 to G55 as number with 2 decimal places.

4   Format cells E16 to E55 to be number with a comma separator (or decimal point depending on local settings) for 000s and no decimal places.

5   Cell D2 needs a function which counts up how many products have the same supplier code (column H) that can be found in cell A2.

6   Replicate the function in cell D2 into cells D3 to D8.

7   Add a function into cell D9 that adds up the values in cells D2 to D8.

8   Save the spreadsheet.

	A	B
1	Supplier	Supplier Names
2	AFS	Ace Food Supplies
3	DFE	Danny's Food Emporium
4	EFI	English Food Imports
5	LIF	Lucio's Italian Foodstuff
6	SFS	Spanish Foodstuffs
7	SJS	Spanish Garden Supplies
8	SSF	Southern Spanish Fisheries

SUMIF function

In cells E2 to E8 you need a function that will add up all the daily quantities for each supplier. So far you know that Ace Food Supplies provide four of Señor Ibanez's products, but he needs to buy a quantity of each of them. The function in E2 will tell you how many total products Señor Ibanez will buy.

The syntax of the function is:

=SUMIF(where to look for something, what you are looking for, what to add to the total)

In this case, these three parts are:

●   Where to look for something: the range SupplierCode

●   What you are looking for: A2

●   What to add to the total: the daily quantity

Type into E2: =SUMIF(SupplierCode,A2,$I$16:$I$55)

This results in the value 31 being displayed, which is true. Check down the list – the four different articles from AFS need 10, 1, 10 and 10 to be bought. Replicate this function into cells E3 to E8. The seven totals are: 31, 21, 17, 4, 57, 0 and 45. Save the spreadsheet.

	A	B	C	D	E
1	Supplier Codes	Su		Prc	Daily Articles
2	AFS	=\			=SUMIF(SupplierCode,A2,$I$16:$I$55)
3	DFE	=\			=SUMIF(SupplierCode,A3,$I$16:$I$55)
4	EFI	=\			=SUMIF(SupplierCode,A4,$I$16:$I$55)
5	LIF	=\			=SUMIF(SupplierCode,A5,$I$16:$I$55)
6	SFS	=\			=SUMIF(SupplierCode,A6,$I$16:$I$55)
7	SJS	=\			=SUMIF(SupplierCode,A7,$I$16:$I$55)
8	SSF	=\			=SUMIF(SupplierCode,A8,$I$16:$I$55)

Activity 2

1   In cell J16 type a formula that calculates the daily cost of the product: its price multiplied by the daily quantity. Replicate this function into cells J17 to J55.

2   Format the cells J16 to J55 to be number with 2 decimal places.

3   Cell K16 requires a formula that calculates the daily weight of the product, which is its weight multiplied by the daily quantity. Replicate this function into cells K17 to K55.

4   Format the cells K16 to K55 to be number with a comma separator (or decimal point depending on local settings) for 000s and no decimal places.

5   Save the spreadsheet.

Cell F2 needs a function that adds up the daily cost of the products from the different suppliers. It will be a SUMIF function and will have similar elements to the one in cell E2. This time the three parts are:

●   Where to look for something: the range SupplierCode

●   What you are looking for: A2

●   What to add to the total: the range of costs J16 to J55

Into cell F2 type: =SUMIF(SupplierCode,A2,$J$16:$J$55)

You should get 54.49. Replicate this function into cells F3 to F8, and format cells F2 to F8 as being a number with two decimal places. Replicate the totalling function in cell D9 to E9 and F9. Save the spreadsheet.

Move to the bottom of the spreadsheet and find the set of headings starting in row 57. Cell D58 needs a function that will add up all the daily quantities of food that come in a packet – Pkt. Again you will use SUMIF. Type into cell D58: =SUMIF($D$16:$D$55,"Pkt",$I$16:$I$55)

Can you identify the three elements used this time? You should get 43.

Activity 3

1 Replicate the function in cell D58 into cells D59 to D61. You will then need to change the second element in each of these replicated formulae. Can you see why, and what it should be changed to in each case?

2 Create another SUMIF to go in E58. This one will add up all the daily weights of foods that come in each of the four packages.

3 Replicate the function in E58 to cells E59 to E61, again making the required change to the second element.

4 Format cells E58 to E61 to be numbered with a comma separator (or decimal point depending on local settings) for 000s and no decimal places.

5 Place your name in the left of the footer and the date in the right of the footer.

6 Save the spreadsheet.

7 Hide rows 11 to 55.

8 Print a copy of the spreadsheet:
  - showing values
  - with an orientation of landscape
  - showing gridlines, row/column headers
  - to fit on one page.

9 Print another copy of the spreadsheet:
  - showing the formulae and functions
  - making sure that all labels and function/formulae are fully visible
  - with an orientation of landscape
  - showing gridlines, row/column headers
  - to fit on one page.

	A	B	C	D	E	F
1	Supplier Codes	Supplier Names		Products Supplied	Daily Articles	Daily Cost ($)
2	AFS	Ace Food Supplies		4	31	54.49
3	DFE	Danny's Food Emporium		6	21	42.42
4	EFI	English Food Imports		8	17	27.25
5	LIF	Lucio's Italian Foodstuff		1	4	7.00
6	SFS	Spanish Foodstuffs		15	57	82.10
7	SJS	Spanish Garden Supplies		0	0	0.00
8	SSF	Southern Spanish Fisheries		6	45	69.85
9			Totals	40	175	283.11
10						
57			Packaging	Daily Quantity	Daily Weight	
58			Packets	43	10,320 g	
59			Tins	58	12,435 g	
60			Jars	13	8,445 g	
61			Boxes	4	1,200 g	

When complete, the top and bottom of your spreadsheet will have these values:

Searching the data

You will see when you begin working with databases in Unit 6 that data can be searched for specific values so that only a selection of information is presented. The same ideas apply to data in a spreadsheet. This section will demonstrate the different ways data can be searched using filters.

Tip

A filter is a tool used to search through data, selecting that which matches particular criteria.

Use will be made of your final spreadsheet solution for Señor Ibanez, as saved in the middle of Activity 3 above, so unhide rows 11 to 55, if you haven't already.

Highlight cells A15 to L15, the headings from the details section of the spreadsheet.

Find in the toolbar of your spreadsheet an icon or item in a drop-down menu that allows you to **Filter**. When you click or select this option you will notice that next to each heading that is highlighted in row 15 there is now a little drop-down arrow.

15	Product ID	Producer	Description	Pkt/Tin/Jar/Box/E	Weight
16	5010000000000	Ben's Original	Express Golden Vegetable Rice	Pkt	250 g
17	8410000000000	Orlando	Tomate Frito	Tin	800 g
18	8480000000000	Alteza	Pate al Oporto	Jar	110 g

Searching for a particular producer – Alteza

Click on the little arrow in the Producer header. A drop-down dialogue box like the one on the right will be shown.

Initially, all the different Producers may be listed. If so, then click on the **Select All** check box to deselect all the Producers and then click on **Alteza** so that it is the only selection in the list. Click **OK**.

The spreadsheet will search through all the products, selecting only those where the Producer is Alteza. The results are displayed – there are seven Alteza products.

Notice also that the filter arrow in the header now has a picture of a small funnel indicating that this is the filtered data item. Click on the funnel next to the filter arrow in the header. The drop-down dialogue box appears again. Select the option **Clear Filter From "Producer"**. This removes the filter and restores the full list of products.

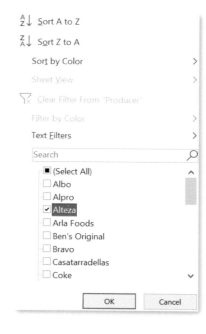

Searching for particular numerical values – greater than $1.00

Select Price as the filter and then click on **Number Filters** in the dialogue box. Choose **Greater Than…** from the available list.

Another dialogue box appears where you can set the value (or values) that you want to select by. Type **1.00** in the box beside the option **is greater than** and click **OK**.

You should have 29 products returned. Clear the filter on Price.

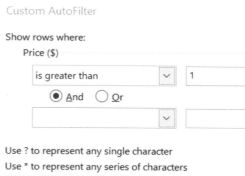

Finding similar text in different products

Select the Description header for the filter.

Choose **Text Filters > Contains** to display the Custom AutoFilter and copy these settings. Type the words **Zumo** and **Squash**.

Four products are shown. Clear the filter.

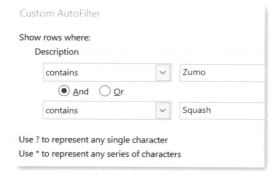

Combinations of filter elements

How can you find which products weigh 250 g or less and come in either a packet or box?

Two selections are needed.

- Weight less than or equal to 250 g.
- Pkt/Tin/Jar/Box/Btl selected as either Pkt or Box.

Wildcards

There are times where we might not know one or more of the characters in a search. For example you might want to search for a first name but not be sure if it is spelled Tony or Toni, however you are confident about the first three letters. **Wildcard** symbols can be used in searches in place of characters that you either do not know or want to ignore. An asterisk (*) is used to represent one or more characters, and a question mark (?) represents a single character.

Señor Ibanez wanted to know which products came from Southern Spanish Fisheries or from Lucio's Italian Foodstuffs.

You could apply a filter on Supplier which selected only products with SSF or LIF. To use wildcards for this example choose **Text Filters > Contains** from the filter on Supplier, to display the Custom AutoFilter. Type **??F**, which is asking for any two characters followed by **F**. When you click **OK** you will get seven results. What result would *?F?* offer?

Wildcards can also be used for database searches, which is discussed further in Session 6.4.

Activity 5

Create filters to select these products and record how many products are returned. Check your answers by going through the whole list of products and asking yourself the same question.

1 Which products come in a bottle or jar?

2 Which Alteza products come in a tin?

3 What products come in one-litre bottles?

4 How many Spanish Foodstuffs packets weigh less than or equal to 250 g?

5 How many products are made in Spain (hint: barcode begins with 84)?

6 Which UK products (barcode starts with 50) come in packets?

7 How many products have *Tomato* or *Tomate* in their description?

8 How many products that have a daily quantity of five or more, cost more than $1 each?

Scaling printed output

In Session 5.8 you were introduced to printing certain areas of a spreadsheet and being able to choose that the sheet was scaled to fit onto a single page. At times this is not practical because there would be too much and the print size would be too small to read comfortably.

If you were to print out Señor Ibanez's spreadsheet it would cover four pages of A4 set at landscape.

In this case it is preferable you choose that, for example the page be scaled to a lesser extent even to ask for scaling horizontally only – you might ask that the printout be no more than one page wide.

Open up the same menu or panel where printing options (or page setup) are displayed that you used when asking for printing to fit one page.

Page Setup

Page	Margins	Header/Footer	Sheet

Orientation

○ Portrait   ● Landscape

Scaling

○ Adjust to: 80 % normal size

● Fit to: 1 page(s) wide by 2 tall

Set the options as in the image above, fitted to a single page wide and two tall (long). This is a more useful and manageable printout. Use the 'Print preview' options and change the settings a little so that you can see the various effects that this scaling can have.

Save and close the spreadsheet.

Review and revise

You should now be able to:

- reference data in spreadsheets that is within another data source
- use a full range of analysis functions
- search data in a spreadsheet using filters with single, multiple criteria and wildcards.

5 Practical review

What have you covered?

In these five practical sessions for using spreadsheets you have:

- revised the skills introduced in Unit 3
- created a layout for a spreadsheet model
- entered text, numerical data, formulae and functions into the model
- created simple and nested functions and formulae, including using data values from within another sheet in the workbook
- named cells and referenced them in functions and formulae
- edited by copying, pasting and formatting (for currency and percentage)
- imported data from another data source into a spreadsheet
- replicated formulae, functions and formatting in a workbook
- used hide and unhide for columns and rows
- printed a spreadsheet showing formulae or values, adjusted page settings and print areas
- created, labelled and extracted segments from a pie chart
- tested the data model
- sorted data in the spreadsheet with single and multiple criteria
- searched data with single and multiple criteria, and wildcards.

Some practice questions

You are going to create a spreadsheet for a travel company who are monitoring the flights from Leeds Bradford International Airport. The spreadsheet contains details of the first flight each day to various UK and Irish airports. The relevant files can be found in the digital download.

1 Using a suitable software package, load the file **AirportCodes.csv**.

2 Create a range called **UKCodes**, which contains only cells A2 to B14.

3 Using a suitable software package, load the file **LBIADesinations.csv**.

4 In cell A2, use a LOOKUP function to show the names of the 13 UK and Irish airports served by LBIA. Use the Code column for the LOOKUP value and the named range **UKCodes** in file **AirportCodes.csv** for the array.

5 Replicate the function in cell A2 into cells A3 to A14 so that the airport name is shown for each of the codes.

6 In cell D2, use a function to count the number of flights that depart from this airport on a weekday where the value under the Depart Code column (cells B20 to B80) matches the content of cell B2. The function must include both absolute and relative referencing and must not use a named range.

7 In cell E2, use a function to count the number of flights that depart from this airport on a weekend where the value under the Depart Code column (cells B81 to B95) matches the content of cell B2. The function must include both absolute and relative referencing and must not use a named range.

8 Replicate the functions created in steps 6 and 7 into cells D14 to E14 to calculate the flight departures for each of the other 12 airports.

9 In cell F2 use a formula to return one of these three outcomes:
  - If the sum of D2 and E2 equals 7, display the message **Daily**.
  - If E2 equals 0, display **No weekend**, otherwise display **Selected days**.

10 Replicate the formula in cell F2 into cells F3 to F14.

11 In cell L2 create a formula that uses the number of seats in the aircraft and its number of flights to display the total seats available with those flights.

12 Replicate the formula in L2 into the cells L3 to L8.

13 In cells K9 and L9 use a function to display the total number of flights and available seats.

14 In cell J11 create a formula that uses the values displayed in cells K9 and L9 to calculate and display the average number of seats per flight.

15 Format cell J11 so that it displays the average with no decimal places.

16 Insert a new row to become row 1.

17 Merge the cells A1 to L1.

18 Into cell A1 type: **Earliest Departures From LBIA**.

19 Format the text in cell A1 to be a font that is sans-serif, size 20 point.

20 Save the spreadsheet.

21 Using the data in cells H2 to H9 and cells K2 to K9, create a pie chart with the label **Aircraft Used**.

22 Format the pie chart so that:
- all the sectors are extracted
- each sector shows the aircraft name and the percentage of flights.

23 Save the chart so that it can be inserted into a presentation at a later stage.

24 Set the print area to be cells A1 to L15.

25 Switch to view the spreadsheet formulae and make any adjustments to margins and cell widths so that all the formulae are visible and the selected print area will fit onto two landscape pages.

Progress check

Aiming for good progress

- You can create a layout for a spreadsheet model.
- You can enter text, numerical data, formulae and functions into the model.
- You can create simple functions and formulae.
- You can edit by copying, pasting and formatting (for currency and percentage).
- You can import data from another data source into a spreadsheet.
- You can replicate formulae, functions and formatting.
- You can print a spreadsheet showing formulae or values, adjusting page settings and print areas.
- You can create and label a pie chart.
- You can test the data model.
- You can sort data in the spreadsheet with single criteria.

Aiming for excellent progress

- You can create a layout for a spreadsheet model.
- You can enter text, numerical data, formulae and functions into the model.
- You can create simple and nested functions and formulae, including using data values from within another sheet.
- You can name cells and reference them in functions and formulae.
- You can edit by copying, pasting and formatting (for currency and percentage).
- You can import data from another data source into a spreadsheet.
- You can replicate formulae, functions and formatting.
- You can hide and unhide columns and rows.
- You can print a spreadsheet showing formulae or values, adjusted page settings and print areas.
- You can create, label and extract segments from a pie chart.
- You can test the data model.
- You can sort data in the spreadsheet with single and multiple criteria.
- You can search data with single and multiple criteria, and wildcards.

6 Data types and databases

Why this unit matters

There is data all around us all the time. This data is stored in countless places. Once data is collected and stored it can be analysed, edited, searched, updated, collated, merged and reported. In other words, it can be manipulated in many ways.

You have already seen how data is collected (Unit 2) and how it is stored (Unit 3). In this unit you will look at how you can make the data useful. Data by itself, in the form of long strings of letters, numbers and symbols, is useless. It needs to have some structure and meaning attached to it. Only then does it become useful. Only then does it become information.

Your practical task

Miss Brown, the head of music at Pinetree School, has distributed a questionnaire to her students, asking for details such as:

- the instruments that they have
- whether these instruments belong to the school or to the student
- the number of lessons they have each week.

I need to know how many, and which students all my music teachers teach in a week. (Miss Brown – head of music)

I need to know which students (and their instruments) I will be teaching next week. (Music teacher)

I need to know how much money we will be getting each week from students, and how much money we need to pay the music teachers. (Accountant)

All 45 music students returned their questionnaires. They have been completed by both boys and girls, students of all ages and players of lots of different instruments. Miss Brown is keen to see all of this data placed in a database that can be added to and edited. Such a database would be an excellent source of information.

Imagine that you are a student at Pinetree School and that Miss Brown, knowing you are an ICT expert, has asked you to create this database. The database needs to fulfil all of Miss Brown's requirements and be flexible enough to allow for expansion and future development.

What this unit covers

THEORY

Sessions

Theory review

PRACTICAL

Sessions

Practical review

By the end of the theory sessions you will be able to:

- describe what is meant by the terms file, record, field and key field
- describe different database structures such as flat files and relational tables, including the use of relationships, primary keys and foreign keys
- identify different data types – logical/Boolean, alphanumeric/text, numeric (real and integer) and date
- select appropriate data types for a given set of data – logical/Boolean, alphanumeric/text, numeric and date
- describe the data processing required in a library.

In the practical sessions you will develop and apply skills in:

- defining and creating appropriate database record structures
- entering and amending data in a database
- using arithmetic operations or numeric functions to perform calculations
- sorting data and searching to select subsets of data
- producing reports to display fields and other data for a user
- combining text, images, database extracts and graphs and charts
- saving and printing documents, data and objects
- creating data entry forms.

Background

You all have collections of data: school folders, telephone contact lists, music playlists and so on. How you store and use data is important because you want to be able to add, delete and search data easily. You also expect the data to be in some sort of order. In this session, you will discover how data is stored, how it is structured and how you refer to parts of the data collection.

Files, records and fields

Miss Brown has given you a folder of 45 questionnaires from all her music students. How can you describe this collection of data?

A file is a collection of related structured data. Related means that all the data is concerned with the same purpose or theme (in this case, music students). Structured means that you are storing the same variety of detail about each item (student) in the file.

In ICT terminology:

- The set of questionnaires completed by the students is a **file**.
- Each questionnaire (the details from a single student) is called a **record**.
- Each separate detail on a questionnaire (such as the student's name) is a **field**.
- Each record has the same set of fields – the same **record structure**.

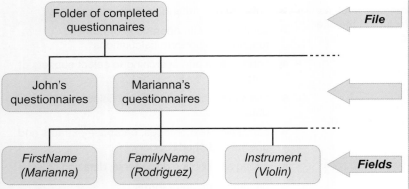

This breakdown of file, record and field is true for any collection of data. For example, a car salesman has a file that contains details about all the cars he is selling or has sold. Details about one car make up one record. Each record will have the same set of details (fields) for each car: make, model, colour, engine size and so on.

> **Activity 1**
>
> Create a record structure for the music students' personal details questionnaires by listing all those details (fields) that might be on a questionnaire.

Tip

A **file extension** is a label (usually three letters) added to the end of a file name, which identifies the kind of data in the file. This means that the applications program knows how to load and interpret the data. Common extensions you will be familiar with are:

.CSV (comma separated variable) files are used to transfer data between applications. Each field of data is separated by a comma. The data is plain text without formatting.

.RTF (rich text format) A kind of text file where any formatting (such as colour, bold, cell shading) is preserved. It is a universal format, so it can be read by nearly all word processors.

.TXT A 'plain' text file. This data only includes characters in standard **ASCII** code. No formatting is included. This is the most common means of transferring data between application packages.

A **file** can contain many **records**.

A **record** can contain many **fields**.

A **field** can contain letters, numbers, symbols (*more about this in section 6.3*)

Real world

Data is structured with rows for records and columns for each field, a two dimensional table. Partly for these reasons, data is referred to as being stored in a table. Throughout this unit, 'table' will be used to refer to a collection of data.

Key fields

At some stage records in a file need to be sorted, searched or merged. When searching through the records there may be times when there is more than one possible 'answer'. For example, the file for the cars might have more than one Ford Fiesta. How can you be sure that you retrieve information about the correct car? This is a vital, or key requirement. In fact, a car does have a unique identifier – the registration (licence) plate. No two cars have the same registration plate. This needs to be included as a field within the records, and because of its special use it is called the **key field**.

ISBN numbers for books, telephone numbers, passport numbers and bank account numbers are all unique and could be used as key fields for records.

Sometimes there is no obvious key field. Did you notice that no field in the music student file could actually be a key field? It could be that there is no unique identifier for each student. What about your school? Sometimes schools issue a 'student ID' or 'registration' number.

If you do not have such a field in your database, you need to create one. For example, you would start with the questionnaire at the top of the file and mark it as Student 1, the next as Student 2, and so on all the way down to Student 45. Sometimes, key fields might be designed to contain additional information. For example, M1, M2, F1, F2 might be male and female students 1 and 2.

Activity 2

For the music students, a friend suggested using data 09M1, 10F2 (Year nine, male student one and Year 10, female student two) within the key field. Explain why this might not be a good idea.

Activity 3

If you have not been able to identify a unique identifier for your record structure, create a key field of your own to add to the music student record structure.

Flat file or relational database?

A **flat file database** is a collection of data held in a single table, meaning data can only be viewed in a limited way. In a **relational database** data may be held in a number of tables where links (or relationships) are created to connect the data in different tables to each other.

If the car salesperson needs a letter sent to customers, advising of an approaching yearly inspection for the car they purchased, it is not so easy. Somehow the customer needs to be linked to the car.

The car salesperson actually has two files: **Cars** and **Customers**. Both files contain a field called CustomerID. In the **Customers** file, this is the key field. If a car has not been sold, the field CustomerID in its record in **Cars** is empty. When the car has been sold, the CustomerID field contains a value which is the same as the key field of the file **Customers**.

> **Tip**
>
> A primary key field within a database must contain unique entries, a barcode for example. This can be used as a key field to create a relationship to a second database. This field in the second database is then known as the foreign key.

Primary and foreign keys

Doesn't this give a record structure for **Cars** with two key fields? No. In **Cars**, the key field is Registration – referred to as the **primary key**. The CustomerID field is referred to as a **foreign key**. It is this foreign key that links the two files and creates the relationship between them.

Primary Key					Foreign Key	
Registration	Make	Model	Colour	Engine size	Customer ID	Date sold
AB12CDE	Ford	Fiesta	Red	1600	34527	12/01/2009

1 record from **Cars**

Primary Key							
Customer ID	Title	First	Family	Address1	Address2	Address3	Contact
34527	Mr	John	Smith	Riverside Cottage	Estuary Road	Seaford	01234–771254

1 record from **Customers**

In ICT terminology:

- The music student file is a flat file database. All the details needed are contained in that single file – there is no relationship with any other files.
- There is a relationship between the two car sales files, so they represent a relational database. In a number of versions of database software, the files are referred to as tables.

This ability to extract details from various small related tables/files is what makes a relational database so useful (and powerful).

Relationships

When two tables are joined together a relationship is created between them, as between Cars and Customers. There are different types of relationship depending on the kind of connection made.

The relationship between the Customers and Cars tables is a one-to-many relationship (the order of the table names matches the 'one' and 'many') – the record key is the primary key in one table and a foreign key in another. The CustomerID will appear only once in the Customer table, but may appear many times in the Car table – this is possible if the customer has, over a period of years for example, bought a number of cars from the car salesroom. There is one arrowhead at the one end of the connecting line and double arrowheads at the many end of the line.

A one-to-one relationship is also possible (with a single arrowhead at each end of the connecting line). This would indicate that for each primary key in one table there can only be one match in the other table. However, this is not a common relationship type. It is sometimes used to break a table with records of many fields into two or more, smaller tables. For every record in one table there must be a corresponding record in the second table.

> **Tip**
>
> Your database software will also allow a many-to-many relationship to be created. This is a complex type of relationship, often requiring a new table and two one-to-many relationships to put into effect.

Veterinary Practice

Vets keep files with details of all the animals that they treat. The primary key is the animal's passport number (if there is one) or else an ID that the vet creates. Each record contains an ID for the animal's owner (a foreign key). The vet has a second file which contains address and contact details for each owner (their ID is the primary key). These two files have a relationship because of the owner ID.

Activity 4

Create a diagram (like the one on the previous page) of the animal and owner files, indicating the primary keys, foreign key and relationship type.

Review and revise

You should now be able to:

- describe the structure of a file and use the terminology to link to real-life data collections
- understand the difference between flat file and relational databases
- understand the purpose and importance of relationships, primary key and foreign key
- create suitable record structures for given situations
- understand the relationships that can be created between tables.

SESSION 6.2 Data-handling situations

Background

Now that you have discovered what a database is, you can look at two commercial situations. Insurance companies and retailers rely heavily on database software to promote products, contact customers with special offers, or send customers information. This session investigates how companies use databases in more complex situations.

Insurance

Noura's parents recently received a reminder from their insurance company. The cover for the family car is due for renewal soon. Her parents look at a rival company's website to see if they can reduce the amount of money they will need to spend.

First, they have to enter the details of their car: make, model, year, engine size. After that there are questions about their use of the car, what distance they drive each year, their address and other details. The website starts its calculation based on a number of factors, including:

- the 'insurance group' of the car
- the 'CO_2 emissions' of the car
- how long they have been driving
- the area in which they live
- any extra cover required such as windscreen replacement and breakdown cover.

At the end, the website lists all the components of the cover and how much Noura's parents would pay. There is a lot of database activity going on here.

Noura's parents then go onto their current insurance company's website. First they have to log in. They use their email address and the password provided by the company.

Having logged in, they enter their car registration number. On the screen they see all aspects of the insurance cover they have. Alongside details of the car, their address and details of the extra cover they have, such as windscreen damage is shown. Some services they pay for are provided by another company, so there is also another customer number in their record, which identifies them to this other company called ServicePlus.

Just within this simple description, you can see that there is a relational database at work, with at least three tables: car details, customer details and additional services. Each table will have not only a primary key but also foreign keys.

> **Activity 1**
>
> Will the insurance company website be using a flat file or relational database? Give reasons for your answer.

> **Activity 2**
>
> Using as an example the diagram of the car and customer tables in Session 6.1 on page 262, draw a representation of these three tables (car details, customer details and additional services). Use a different colour to show the primary and foreign keys, together with the relationships that these keys provide.

The data processing requirements of a library

A library has quite complex data processing needs. Let us look at a simple system which might be used by a small library. There is a need to keep, as a minimum, three sets of data focussing on the books in the library, the library members and the books currently borrowed:

Books: Details of all the books in the library. The ISBN number is the unique identifier and so is the primary key for the file. There is a field which indicates whether the book is available 'Y', or already lent out 'N'.

Members: Details of all the members of the library. A 'MemberID' is created to provide a unique primary key. The member is allowed three books out at any one time. A book which has been borrowed has its ISBN number placed in one of the three available fields. This is a foreign key in the record and creates a relationship between the member and the book that has been borrowed.

Borrowed: This file is constantly having records added to (a book has been borrowed) and deleted from (a book has been returned). The record contains the book's ISBN (primary key), the MemberID (foreign key) and the date due for return.

Primary Key

ISBN	Title	Author	Classification	Hard/Soft cover	Pages	Available
978034087046	Beginner's Russian	Rachel Farmer	Languages	Soft	246	N

Primary Key / **Foreign Key**

Member ID	First	Family	Address	Contact	ISBN1	ISBN2	ISBN3
AB1234	Colin	Stobart	Estuary Cottage	01234-123456	978034087046		

Primary Key / **Foreign Key**

ISBN	Member ID	Date Return
978034087046	AB1234	30/08/2014

Relationships

There are three relationships here. Members to Books, Borrowed to Members, and Borrowed to Books.

All are a one-to-many (one arrow-double arrow) relationship. One member may have many books (in our case a maximum of three). The other two relationships at first glance might seem more suited to be one-to-one (one arrow at each end) because, for example, the ISBN can only point to a specific record. There cannot be any duplication in either the Books or Borrowed files (there is only one copy and it can only be borrowed by one person at a time). However, as mentioned in Session 6.1, for one-to-one relationships to be effective there need to be the same number of corresponding records in each table, which is obviously not the case, as Borrowed only records the books that are currently borrowed by members. So although you know that an ISBN can only appear once in both Books and Borrowed, and the same for MemberID in Members and Borrowed, the relationships are identified as one-to-many.

Borrowing a book

When a library member brings a book to the librarian, the ISBN needs to be entered to start the borrowing process. The member's ID also needs entering. As you have read in Session 2.2 there are a number of ways that this data can be entered.

Once the system has identified the book and the member, there are a couple of checks that need to be carried out. First of all the record for the book needs to be retrieved. It should have an availability of 'Y', if not then there is an error – the book should be with another member. The librarian will have to follow some library/system process to deal with this. If the book record is correct then the member's record needs checking.

Once the book and members records are checked okay, a new record is created and added to the Borrowed file. This contains the ISBN, the

Activity 3

This system allows for the library to only have one copy of each book. Why is this?

Describe at least three different methods of data entry for the ISBN and member's ID. Identify the hardware used together with the advantages of each method. What method is used in your school/local library?

Activity 4

Why do you think the MemberID in the Borrowed file is a foreign key and not the primary key?

Describe the steps taken when a book is returned. What data is added/deleted from the three files?

MemberID and the date the book should be returned. At the same time the book's record has its availability switched to 'N', and the book's ISBN is placed in an available ISBN field in the member's record.

Overdue books

On a regular basis the librarian will need to generate a list of overdue books indicating which members have them. The starting point for this process will be to look at the Borrowed file. The file will be searched for records where DateReturn <today's date, meaning that the book is now overdue. For each of the records returned from this search, the ISBN will lead to the book that needs returning and the MemberID leads to the member who currently has that book. A message/letter can then be sent to the member using the address or contact details, indicating the book's title and author, along with the date that the book was due for return.

Review and revise

You should now be able to:

- describe the data needs of an organisation in terms of tables and relationships
- create a 'map' of these tables and relationships, linked by record keys.

SESSION 6.3 Data types

Background

So far you have looked at what data needs to be stored by an organisation in order to achieve specific purposes. You have also considered how that data might be collected together in terms of tables, records and fields. But how does the database know what type of data it is using? In this session, you will look at the different data types and see why it is important to specify a data type for each field in the record structure.

Why are data types important?

The music questionnaires contain a lot of information. Each questionnaire provides data for one record, and in Session 5.1 you created a record structure for this. You created field names, and identified or created a unique data item, which can be used as a key field. You can see immediately that a student's name is text, but the number of lessons the student has is a number.

It is important that the database knows what type of data it is using, for two main reasons. Firstly, data such as numbers is stored differently to text. Secondly, as a result of being stored differently, this determines what operations can be carried out on it. You would not be able to perform arithmetic with text fields, for example.

Numbers need to be stored in such a way that arithmetic can be performed efficiently. Dates need to be stored so that they can be referenced in order and have comparisons made between them. Some data is simply a 'yes' or 'no' type.

Before creating a database, it is vital that you have considered the fields in the record structure and given each one its correct data type.

> ### Real world
>
> You might have included a field: age, in your record structure from the questionnaires. This is not practical, because it would need to be updated every year, for every student. It makes more sense to have a date of birth (DoB) instead. As well as telling us exactly when someone was born, you can ask the database software to calculate their age by comparing the DoB with today's date.

What data types are there? When do we use them?

Use this type ...	When the data is ...
Text/**alphanumeric**	Text. There may be a limit to how long the data is – often 255 characters.
Number	Any number type. It will be possible to specify how many decimal places to use. A number with no decimal places is called an **integer**. A number that has decimal places is called a **real number**. Also used to represent percentages.
Date/Time	A date. Formats can vary.
Currency	For example, $, € or £.
Boolean/logical	Only two alternatives: yes/no, on/off, true/false.
OLE (Object Linked and Embedded)	A graph, video, clip, picture, sound file

> ### Language
>
> An integer is a whole number, one that has no decimal or fractional part, such as 8, 219 or −7.
>
> A real number is one that does have a decimal part, such as 8.9, 0.005, or −7.65.

These are the most common data types that you will be using in the practical sessions. Each type can also have different settings. For example, a number could be set to have a fixed number of decimal places, or it could be an integer.

Open up your database software program and use the help facility to discover:

1 whether percentage is a setting for a numeric field or a separate data type in itself

2 what formats a date can take; try and think what problems arise when transferring data that contains dates between different databases

3 what currency settings are available to you.

Work your way through the music students record structure and:

● Make sure you have meaningful field names.

● Choose a data type for each field; be prepared to justify your selection.

● Consider if you could include any OLE data type fields in the student record. Justify your decision.

Assigning types to fields

In Session 6.1, Activity 3, you completed the record structure for the music student flat file database by adding a key field. Here are some fields you may have included in your record structure:

Field name	Example data	Data type	Comment
StudentID	M12	Text	
FamilyName	Al-Saleh	Text	Letters and special characters, less than 255 characters
DoB	12/05/98	Date/Time	Short date for dd/mm/yyyy
LessonWeek	4	Number	Can use integer setting
CostWeek	$12.00	Currency	
Orchestra	Y	Boolean	Only two possible values – yes or no

Alongside each is the data type that would be most suitable, with, if necessary, a comment. Do you agree? Are your date settings dd/mm/yyyy or mm/dd/yyyy?

It is important that field names are meaningful. When someone looks at a record structure, they need to know what the field contains. It is more sensible to have FirstName and FamilyName than name1, name2; and better to have Cell or Home rather than just Telephone.

You now have a full and complete record structure for the music students flat file database.

Real world

An OLE data type allows you to combine information from different applications into a database: text from a word processor; data or graphs from a spreadsheet; images; sound files; video clips. The difference between embedding and linking is this: if you have a graph from a spreadsheet in your database that was linked, whenever you updated the data in your spreadsheet that new data would be reflected in the graph in the database, but if the graph was embedded it would not be updated because when you embed an object the original data is saved in the database as well.

You should now be able to:

● describe why data types are important

● describe the range of types that are available for use

● choose sensible and meaningful field names

● select an appropriate data type for each field in a record structure.

Searching and querying

Background

You have now reached the stage where you have a complete record structure for a flat file database. This structure includes field names and field types. Before you move on to the practical sessions, where additional tables and relationships will be introduced, this last theory session will explore:

- basic operations to carry out on the database such as sorting and searching
- the ways in which sorting and searching are carried out: queries and search criteria.

Sorting

To **sort** a data set is to rearrange it – to put it into a different order. This is something you do constantly. You often put things in alphabetical order automatically, such as a phone contact list, or an online music playlist.

When you look at a folder of files on a computer, they may be displayed in order of filename. The list could be displayed in other orders, though: by date created, by size or by type, for example. When you ask for the list to be rearranged, you expect all of the files to remain in the list and just be shuffled around. Sometimes you may ask for more than one sorting order to be applied at the same time. For example, you will want song titles to be sorted within the artist names on your music player.

Here are eight records from the database created by the car salesperson you met in Session 6.1.

Registration	Make	Model	Colour	Built	Price $	Kilometres driven
ALZ 128	Ford	Fiesta	Red	1999	2100	85 284
AHG 243	Opel	Corsa	Silver	1999	1800	105 585
JFA 857	Ford	Mondeo	Grey	2005	4250	74 728
BZE 439	Ford	Fiesta	Red	2000	2000	100 031
CCA 876	Seat	Malaga	Red	2001	2200	63 516
DZH 236	Fiat	Punto	Blue	2003	2450	51 750
AVN 192	Opel	Corsa	Black	1999	1750	115 658
ABD 439	Fiat	Panda	White	1998	1000	65 432

If the records are sorted into ascending order of registration, the registration, make and model of the car which would be at the top of the new list would be: ABD 439, Fiat Panda. What if the records are to be sorted by descending order of kilometres driven within alphabetical order of make? The eight registrations in their new order would be: ABD 439, DZH 236, BZE 439, ALZ 128, JFA 857, AVN 192, AHG 243, CCA 876.

Searching

When you **search**, you expect to see only a selection of records from the original list. This is called a **subset**. For example, you might have hundreds of files in a folder and you might want to display only those created in the past week. When you issue the search command, the list will be reduced – you just see those files that match your search request.

To search a database is to locate records that fit your search criteria. In database terminology this involves creating a **filter**.

Activity 1

Write out the records as they would appear after using this sort order – to check and to see how the records are now listed.

Criteria and operators

The conditions used to define a sort or a search (alphabetical, by date, sizes, by file type, etc.) are called **criteria**. When sorting records, the data set is rearranged according to our criteria. When searching, the criteria concerns the actual content of fields, such as born after 2000 – one **criterion**, or all males in Year 10 – two criteria.

Searches can be made quite complex and precise by using operators and logical conditions:

<	less than
>	greater than
=	equal to
<>	not equal to
<=	less than or equal to
>=	greater than or equal to
AND	both conditions are met
OR	either condition is met
NOT	a condition is not met
LIKE	to find values within a field

DateOfBirth > 2000 will return all records where the date of birth is later than the year 2000.

Gender = "M" AND YearGroup = "10" will return the records of all males in Year 10.

These examples are written in a 'query language', a type of structured sentence, using field names, operators and conditions.

Wildcards

As well as operators and logical conditions, there are two more search tools. These are called **wildcards**, used to search through text fields. An asterisk (*) is used to represent one or more characters in a string of text, and a question mark (?) represents a single character. For example:

- searching a library database and not sure if the author's name is White or Whyte? Search for Surname Like "Wh?te"
- searching a transport database with Model Like "*ship" will return all warships – battleships, airships, steamships and so on.

Activity 2

Using the car records on the previous page, list the registrations of the cars which:

- are Fords built in 2000
- are red cars with less than 100 000 km (kilometres)
- have less than 80 000 km or were built after 2002
- are any make except Ford
- are Opels or Fiats that cost less than $2000.

Review and revise

You should now be able to:
- understand the difference between sorting and searching
- understand the use of search criteria – operators and logical conditions
- express a search in 'query language' statements
- see how wildcards can be used to identify records.

Activity 3

Write the 'query language' statements, which would achieve each of the required searches.

6 Theory review

What have you covered?

In these four theory sessions, you have:
- discovered how a collection of data can be structured and the associated terminology
- practised creating record structures, including identifying key fields – primary and foreign
- considered the differences between flat file and relational databases
- investigated what data types are available in your database software and selected appropriate types for fields
- compared the processes of sorting and searching data sets
- been introduced to operations, logical conditions and wildcards.

Some practice questions

1 Put these terms in order of size, with the smallest first:

file   field   record

See Session 6.1

2 Link each term with a description. One has been done for you.

Foreign key	A data item, which uniquely identifies a record in a table
Relationship	A link between two tables
Key field	A data type, indicating a whole number
Flat file database	A data item, which points to another record in a related table
Integer	A single collection of data

See Session 6.2

3 A database is created about the mobile phones of a group of students. Complete each sentence with one term from the list:

key field   integer   text   OLE
Boolean   currency   date/time.

The name of the phone will be assigned a data type of _____.

The phone Number could be used as a _____.

The price would be given a data type of _____.

Payment is either by 'Contract' or 'Pay-as-you-go'. This could be a _____ data type.

A photo of the mobile phone's owner is assigned a data type of _____.

See Session 6.3

4 A doctor has a file that stores details of the appointments for her patients.

a Give one reason why she might want to sort the file.

b Give one reason for searching this file.

See Session 6.4

5 a A bookshop has a relational database. One table in the database is **Books**. What likely item of data in the record's structure could be used as the key field?

Another table is **Customers**, which holds information for the bookshop membership scheme. A key field was created and a MemberID given to each customer.

The bookshop owner is going to create a relationship between these two tables.

b Suggest two reasons why the bookshop owner might want to link these tables.

c What kind of relationship will this be?

d Using the terms primary key and foreign key, describe how relationships for these two tables would be created.

See Sessions 6.1 and 6.2

6 Here is a section of a database about student music lessons:

AdNo	First Name	Family Name	TG	DoB	Gender	Instrument
199603	Paul	Tomlinson	10SMS	01/10/96	M	Trombone
199617	Daniel	Jones	10SMS	12/11/96	M	Tuba
199504	Colin	Boyes	11MEB	08/10/95	M	Drums
199903	Kirsty	Tomlinson	07CKD	09/11/99	F	Guitar
199502	Julie	Firth	11MEB	12/11/95	F	Cello
199604	Sara	Tomkins	10SMS	08/12/96	F	Guitar
199505	Kim	Walters	11MEB	10/09/95	F	Guitar
199302	Megan	McConnel	13CPS	12/04/94	F	Flute
199804	Paul	Cornwall	08BRJ	12/09/98	M	Clarinet
199609	Lizzie	Poulsen	10SMS	10/08/97	F	Cornet

a How many records are there in this section?

b How many fields are there in each record?

c Which field would be most suitable for the key field?

d What type of data is held in the Gender field?

e These records are going to be sorted into ascending order of DoB. Who will be at the top of the list?

f Who is at the bottom?

g These records are searched to find the guitar players in TG 10SMS or 11MEB. What are the AdNos of the students who meet these criteria?

h The search: Family = "Tom*" AND Instrument = "Guitar" is applied. What are the AdNos of the students who meet these criteria?

See Sessions 6.1, 6.2, 6.3, 6.4 and 6.5

Progress check

Aiming for good progress

- You are confident with the terminology in this unit. Most key words are to do with concepts rather than physical objects – you will not see a photograph of someone holding a data type or an office worker using a foreign key. Focus on the key terms as highlighted in **blue** and which are described in the glossary.

- You can state the differences between a flat file and a relational database.

- You can sort and search data set with given criteria.

- You can choose an appropriate data type for fields.

- You can perform a search with a given wildcard criteria.

- You will have been able to answer questions 1, 2, 3, 4 and 6 correctly.

Aiming for excellent progress

- You can confidently use the terminology in this unit to describe the concepts, not just be able to identify them.

- You can compare and contrast the differences between a flat file and a relational database.

- You can describe the need for a particular relationship to be created between database tables.

- You fully understand the use of operators and logical conditions in order to sort and search a data set.

- You can choose the appropriate data types for fields, justifying your selection.

- You can create a wildcard search using multiple criteria.

- You will have been able to answer all the questions successfully. Question 5 in the Theory Review will have allowed you to link some of the different aspects of this unit.

SESSION 6.5 Creating a database

Background

Creating databases can be achieved in a number of different ways:
- Create a record structure and then add in your own data record by record.
- Create a record structure and then import data from another source. This data may be in another format which needs converting as it is imported.
- Import the record structure and data from another source.

Creating a database can be done very easily and in several ways. Sometimes you need to create a database from scratch; you only have a record structure to work with, and no data. Sometimes there will be data available in another format, which needs converting and importing into the database. In this session you will create databases for the above situations using data stored on the digital download. You will also create some reports from the records in your new database.

Creating a new record structure in a blank database

Open your database software and select the option to create a new database; this might be under a menu as **New database**. This database will be empty, containing no tables, queries or reports. You may be asked to give the database a name, call it **MusicStudents**.

You need the design view for a table – the view that lets you see the field names and their data types. If you are asked to give the table a name, call it **StudentDetail**.

The very first task is to create the record structure. This involves choosing field names and allocating a data type for each field. The field names and data types you are going to use are these:

Field name	Data type	
AdNo	Number	Admission number – key field
FirstName	Text	
FamilyName	Text	
TG	Text	Tutor Group: year group + tutor's initials
DoB	Date/Time	Short date: dd/mm/yyyy
Gender	Text	
Instrument	Text	
Own	Yes/No	
SerialNo	Text	
Orchestra	Yes/No	
Teacher	Text	
LessonWeek	Number	Set to zero decimal places
CostWeek	Currency	Set to two decimal places
Notes	Text	

Enter the field names and their data types. Connected to each field is its data type. Select the required type from the list. You will also have to give some extra information for dates, currency and Yes/No data types:

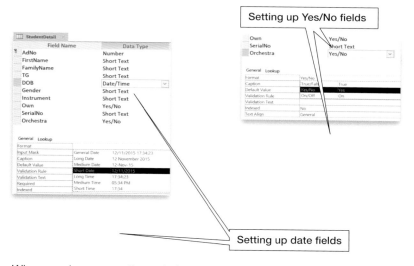

When you have gone through the entire field list, you will have a record structure like this:

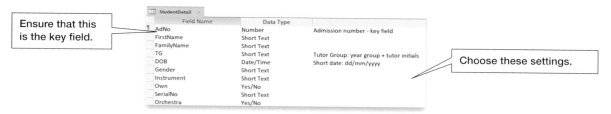

Close this view and, if necessary, save the table in your work area. You may need to delete a key field called, for example, ID, that your database software inserts for you.

Importing data into a table

You are now going to import some data into the database. The file **MusicDepartmentA.csv**, from the digital download, contains the details of 45 music students, each with details corresponding to the record structure.

Select the option for importing data. This will be under a drop-down menu for **File**, **Data** or **External Data**. The type of file (.csv) you are importing is a text file. Locate the file and choose for the data to be loaded into an existing table – **StudentDetail**. When prompted by your software, reply that the file is delimited with a comma.

The database software will take the details from the .csv file and create a record for each row. When this has completed you may be prompted to open the table where you should see the following records at the top, and that there are now 45 records in the table.

> ### Tip
> csv files are explained in Session 5.10.

StudentDetail ×					
AdNo ▾	FirstName ▾	FamilyName ▾	TG ▾	DOB ▾	Gender
199301	Bill	Atkinson	13CPS	07/11/1993	M
199302	Megan	McConnel	13CPS	12/04/1994	F
199401	Lucy	Potter	12MAH	10/12/1994	F
199402	Amir	Al-Tamani	12MAH	06/09/1994	M
199403	Alice	Derbyshire	12MAH	11/06/1995	F
199501	Mashood	Othman	11MEB	09/05/1996	M
199502	Julie	Firth	11MEB	12/11/1995	F
199503	Monica	Jimenez	11MEB	03/07/1996	F
199504	Colin	Boyes	11MEB	08/10/1995	M
199505	Kim	Walters	11MEB	10/09/1995	F

Activity 1

1 Spend a couple of minutes browsing through these records and becoming familiar with the details that have been loaded for each student. Notice that some fields can be left blank.

2 Look at the field AdNo. What do you think this field indicates about the student?

Editing: adding, changing, deleting

Three students have just started to have music lessons. They have filled in the questionnaires, so you are going to add their details to the **StudentDetail** table.

Field name	New music students		
AdNo	199702	199703	199618
FirstName	Harriet	Jon	Phil
FamilyName	Williams	Cornish	Bains
TG	09KIR	09KIR	10SMS
DoB	02/04/98	11/10/97	09/10/96
Gender	F	M	M
Instrument	Flute	Violin	Piano
Own	N	N	N
SerialNo	FLWAZX2	VIFWG3M	
Orchestra	Y	Y	N
Teacher	Mrs M Potts	Miss N Boyd	Miss P Bird
LessonWeek	1	1	1
CostWeek	8	8	8
Notes			

Your record count should now be 48.

Activity 2

Miss Brown comes to you with a note, which tells you about some students whose details need changing, as shown on the right.

Make these changes to the table records. Your record count should now be 47.

Close and, if necessary, save the table with these changes.

> Kim Walters now has her own guitar (no need for serial number)
>
> Cathy Davis now having 2 lessons a week - cost is $15 (2nd lesson half price)
>
> Kirsty Tomlinson has left the school

Real world

Adding an OLE data type may not be the only option to add 'external' data such as an image. *MSOffice 2007* onwards has a data type of 'Attachment' for example. Your software may have something similar. The difference between an OLE and an 'attachment' type is that the image, as an OLE, would become part of the database, whereas if it were 'attached' it would remain on the server as a separate file. This will have significant impact as far as the database's file size is concerned.

Activity 3

By only looking at the records on the screen, examine the database and find answers to these questions:

a How many students play the piano?

b How many students does Mr A Atkinson teach?

c How many boys take music lessons?

d How many students in Y10 play the violin?

e How many students in Y10 play the guitar (including electric)?

f How many music lessons a week does Miss N Boyd teach?

Some of these questions are fairly easy to answer, others a little more difficult. Imagine how difficult they would be to answer if there were not just 47 records but 470 – the number of students in a medium sized school, perhaps.

Importing data without creating a structure first

It is not always necessary to create a record structure before importing data. Sometimes the data source will have the field names as part of the data. For example, a .csv file might have been originally created as a spreadsheet, and the field names are actually the column headings in the spreadsheet.

	A	B	C	D	E	F	G	H	I
1	RegID	First	Family	TutorGroup	DoB	Gender	Instrument	Own	SerialNo
2	199301	Bill	Atkinson	13CPS	07/11/1993	M	Violin	Y	
3	199603	Paul	Tomlinson	10SMS	01/10/1996	M	Trombone	N	TR6I2CIGKU
4	199617	David	Jones	10SMS	12/11/1996	M	Tuba	N	TU0ETELK
5	199504	Colin	Boyes	11MEB	08/10/1995	M	Drums	N	

The difference in the process of creating a database from this file is minimal.

Create a new, empty database called **MusicStudentsB**. This time, instead of creating a record structure, go straight to the option of importing data from the file **MusicDepartmentB.csv** on the digital download. Import this data to create a new table. Again, indicate that the incoming data is delimited with a comma.

Now you will see an option like this:

Tick the option that takes the first row of the data source to contain field names.

The top row of the imported data is shaded to indicate that these will be used as field names and not taken as data.

At some stage towards the beginning of the import process, you will be able to set field data types to match your structure.

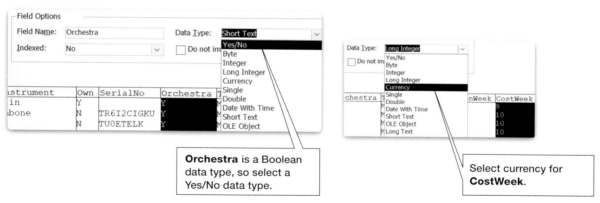

Orchestra is a Boolean data type, so select a Yes/No data type.

Select currency for **CostWeek**.

The rest of the process is the same.

After the process is finished, your software will probably have given the new table the same name as the original .csv file (**MusicDepartmentB**), so you might want to rename it. It is also a good idea to have a look at the record structure in design view, to ensure that each field has the settings that are needed.

This is a typical way of creating a table in a database. One advantage is that the person who has created the data source file has already considered the field names. This means that you do not have to do so (you may not be familiar with the data), and it also ensures that the field names are spelt as the person creating the data source wanted.

Activity 4

Find the file **MusicDepartmentC.csv** on the digital download. Create a new, blank database called **MusicDepartment** and import this file into a table without creating record structure. Rename the table **PupilDetail**. Open the table and see what the field names are in this copy of the data – some have been changed.

Close any database you might have open, except the original one, **MusicStudents**. For the remainder of this session and all the following sessions, **MusicStudents** is the database that you will be using.

Adding validation

Validation is a method of checking that the data that has been entered into a system can successfully be used by the programs processing the data. This is explained in detail in Unit 7, but it is useful to illustrate how this can be achieved in your database software – making sure that the database can process the data you are entering.

The field Gender can be set to hold a single character; M (Male), F (Female) or I (Identifies in another way). The field only requires one character and yet when you set a field as text it allows you a maximum of 255 characters. It would be useful to change the settings so that only one character is accepted (in validation terms this is a length check).

Open the table **StudentDetail** in design view again and click on the field name Gender.

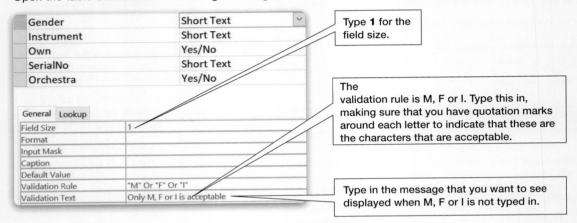

Type **1** for the field size.

The validation rule is M, F or I. Type this in, making sure that you have quotation marks around each letter to indicate that these are the characters that are acceptable.

Type in the message that you want to see displayed when M, F or I is not typed in.

Close the design view and go back to the datasheet view. Re-save the design, as you have just changed the design of the structure.

In the first record, change the Gender to something other than M, F or I. Then click on another field. Your message will be displayed, as by clicking on another field, you are asking the database to accept the new data. You cannot move away from this field until an accepted letter is entered.

Choosing only allowable field values

It is obviously very important that data entry is accurate. If not, it might not be possible to produce full and accurate lists and reports. A good example in the music database is the field for tutor group (TG). There are only specific values to expect, and if someone typing in the data made a mistake, then any list you made, such as a search by TG, would have that student missing.

You can get the database to accept only a certain range of values by displaying them, and giving the person typing in the data a list from which to choose. You will do this to the TG field.

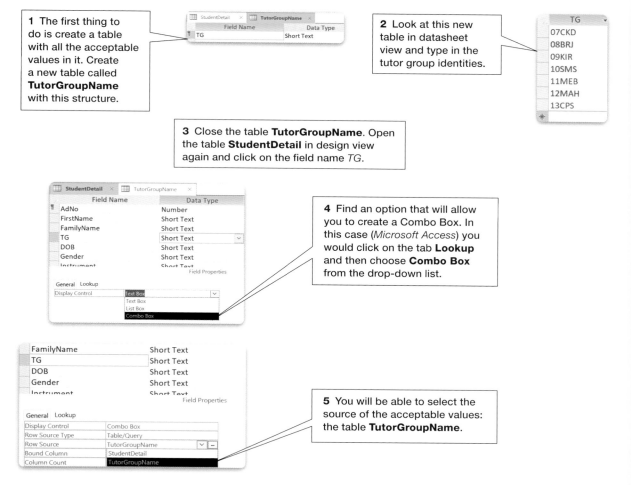

1 The first thing to do is create a table with all the acceptable values in it. Create a new table called **TutorGroupName** with this structure.

2 Look at this new table in datasheet view and type in the tutor group identities.

3 Close the table **TutorGroupName**. Open the table **StudentDetail** in design view again and click on the field name *TG*.

4 Find an option that will allow you to create a Combo Box. In this case (*Microsoft Access*) you would click on the tab **Lookup** and then choose **Combo Box** from the drop-down list.

5 You will be able to select the source of the acceptable values: the table **TutorGroupName**.

Close and save the record structure. Open the table **StudentDetail** in datasheet view, click on someone's TG and you will get a drop-down box and can only choose a tutor group from the list that is presented. This ensures that the person entering data visually checks the data entry (verification) and you can be sure that the database can use the data correctly (validated).

Review and revise

You should now be able to:

- create a record structure, selecting appropriate data types and the record key
- import data from an external source into that record structure.

SESSION 6.6 Creating relationships

Background

You now have a flat file database, **MusicDepartment**, which has 47 records and with two validation routines added. If you do not have this, return to and complete Session 6.5. This database is quite serviceable and much can be done with it. In Session 6.1 the idea of relationships between tables was introduced and illustrated in Session 6.2. You are now going to add some more tables to the database and create relationships between them.

Additional tables

You are going to create two more tables: **Instrument** and **Teacher**. On the digital download you will find **Instrument.csv** and **Teacher.csv**. Import these .csv files to create two new tables within the **MusicDepartment** database. In each case the first row contains headings and the data is delimited with a comma; SerialNo and Teacher are key fields. Case in **Instrument** is a 'yes/no' data type. The database now actually has four tables – remember that TutorGroupName is also a table, even though you used it to simply list the different groups. It does not form a part of any relationship.

The first few rows of each of these new tables should look like this:

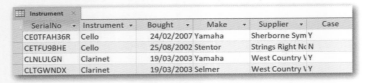

| Instrument | | | | | |
SerialNo	Instrument	Bought	Make	Supplier	Case
CE0TFAH36R	Cello	24/02/2007	Yamaha	Sherborne Sym	Y
CETFU9BHE	Cello	25/08/2002	Stentor	Strings Right Nc	N
CLNLULGN	Clarinet	19/03/2003	Yamaha	West Country \	Y
CLTGWNDX	Clarinet	19/03/2003	Selmer	West Country \	Y

| Teacher | | | | |
Teacher	Address1	Address2	Phone	email
Miss N Boyd	24 The Blackbir	Lillington	314876	n.boyd@pinetr
Miss P Bird	76 Bridge Road	Yetminster	315001	p.bird@pinetre
Mr A Atkinson	54 Back Lane	Yetminster	315716	a.atkinson@pir
Mr B Gibson	1 Short Street	Lillington	314142	b.gibson@pine

Activity 1

There are some new details that need adding to these tables.

A new music teacher has been appointed:

Teacher	Address1	Address2	Phone	email
Miss E Bryson	18 The Wharf	Longburton	313610	e.bryson@pintree.sch.uk

A new instrument has been bought:

SerialNo	Instrument	Bought	Make	Supplier	Case
HA6HGTK9	Harp	04/01/2010	Clarsach	Chaucer's Harps	N

A new student has taken up music and she has yet to make a decision on which instrument to learn:

AdNo	FirstName	Family Name	TG	DoB	Gender
199704	Reeta	Kapoor	09KIR	04/06/1998	F

When you have added these details you should have 48 students, 35 instruments and eight teachers.

You are going to create relationships between the three tables of data to match this schema:

	Primary Key				
	SerialNo	**Instrument**	**Bought**	...	**Case**
	COMSECVQK	Cornet	09/11/2008	...	Y

1 record from **Instrument** →

Primary Key					Foreign Key		Foreign Key		
AdNo	**First Name**	**Family Name**	**TG**	...	**SerialNo**	...	**Teacher**	...	**Notes**
199609	Lizzie	Poulsen	10SMS	...	COMSECVQK	...	Mr A Atkinson	...	

1 record from **StudentDetail** →

	Primary Key			
	Teacher	**Address1**	...	**email**
	Mr A Atkinson	54 Back Lane	...	a.atkinson@pinetree.sch.uk

1 record from **Teacher** →

The relationship Instrument-to-Student is one-to-many even though there is only one instrument with that serial number which is used by one particular student. This is because there is not a corresponding record in **StudentDetail** for each one in **Instrument** – some instruments have not been issued to students.

The relationship Teacher-to-Student is one-to-many because a teacher could be coaching many students.

Creating relationships between the tables

The first step is to see all three tables together so that the relationships can be created between them.

Look for an option that allows you to view and create relationships.

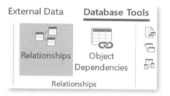

> ### Real world
>
> The following instructions and screenshots are taken from *MS Access*, but you will find very similar layouts in your software. The completed relationship 'map' should look exactly the same, although the steps to achieve it may differ slightly.

This should open up a blank canvas where you are going to display the tables and connect them together. Here you can see that the software is asking which tables need to be displayed – so the three tables (StudentDetail, Instrument, Teacher) need adding to the layout.

Now you can see the field list for each table with the three key fields marked. To create a relationship between StudentDetail and Teacher you need to click (and keep the button pressed down) on the **Teacher** field in **StudentDetail** and drag the pointer across to the **Teacher** field in **Teacher**. Release the mouse button. A dialogue box is displayed asking what kind of relationship is needed.

The suggestion is one-to-many which is what you anticipate, click on 'Create', and a connection is made between the fields. Notice that you do not get a visual indication of the type of connection – such as the arrowheads in the diagram.

The same steps need to be taken to connect the field **SerialNo** in **StudentDetail** and the field **SerialNo** in **Instrument.** This is a one-to-many relationship.

The competed layout now looks like this:

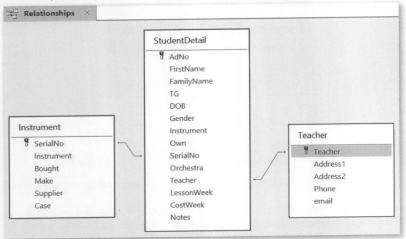

Close the layout page. You should be asked whether you want to save the layout or not. Answer 'Yes'.

Notice that there is nothing in the list of database objects (so far there are four tables) to show that you have done this, so do not panic, thinking that it has not been saved or recognised.

How can you tell that the data in the tables has been linked?

The reason for creating the relationships was to make connections between the data in the tables so you need to know that this has happened.

Open the table **Teacher** and you will see a + symbol is added to each record.

This indicates that this record has other information connected to it. This is a similar symbol used in some filing systems. If you click on the symbol the row is 'expanded', and all information connected to the record through relationships is displayed.

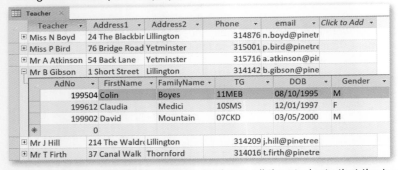

Expanding any of the Teacher records shows all the students that the teacher teaches.

You should find the same happens within the table **Instrument** linking instruments to students. If you expand an instrument's record and there are no student details, it simply means that the instrument is not issued to a student.

You will not find this in the **StudentDetail** table. The one-to-many relationships have the many end at **instrument** and **Teacher** – there are many records connected at that end of the relationship and that is why those tables have records that can be expanded.

Activity 2

You find a post-it note from Miss Brown which asks you to make some changes to the details in the database, as shown:

Reeta Kapoor will take up the harp, with two lessons a week – cost is $15 (second lesson half price), she isn't joining the orchestra, teacher Miss E Bryson.

Mashood Othman has changed from cello to flute, taking instrument FLE3BZK, lessons and costs stay the same, but the teacher is now Mrs M Potts.

Keiko Yamoto has left the school.

Paul Tomlinson now has his own trombone.

Kate Appleby has come out of the orchestra.

Make these changes to the various tables as needed remembering that changing the detail for a student might need more than one field changing.

Check your changes have had the effect you expect by expanding teacher and instrument records.

Review and revise

You should now be able to:

● build relationships between tables
● test relationships connect tables in the correct way.

Activity 3

Miss Brown is considering having the address and contact details of the instrument suppliers included. There are two possibilities: add these details as new fields in the table **Instrument**; create another table called **Supplier** and create a relationship between **Instrument** and **Supplier**. Which solution would you choose? Justify your answer.

Activity 4

Miss Brown decides that a new table **Supplier** should be introduced. On paper create a record structure in the same style as that on page 288. Decide on field names and data types. What will be the record key? What two fields in **Supplier** and **Instrument** will be linked? What type of relationship will you create?

SESSION 6.7 Creating a data entry form

Background

You now have a relational database with three data tables connected by two, one-to-many relationships. Activity 1 of the previous session required you to create a new record for each table – a typical data entry task. In most cases you would not expect users to enter data straight into the table; there should be a data entry form. That is what you are going to create in this session.

A data entry form

A very simple data entry form is illustrated in Session 7.2 (The system life cycle: Design and development) where data capture is being explained for a supermarket warehouse. In Miss Brown's case, forms are needed for entering details of new students, new teachers and new instruments. You are going to create a data entry form for entering details of new students.

Open the database **MusicStudents** as updated in the previous session. Locate the place where you can create **Form**. Look for something like the screen on the right.

Select the option that allows you to create a form using the form wizard. This is the best way to create a form until you have a better understanding of how forms and the various parts of them are put together.

There are a few steps:

● Choose the table **StudentDetail**.
● Ask for all the fields to be on the form.
● Choose a layout by column.
● If asked for a title: **View student details**.
● Name the form **ViewStudent**.

The form will be displayed and should look something like the screen on the right:

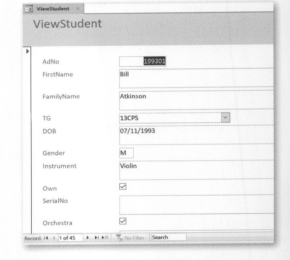

Improving the data entry form

This form is a perfectly workable data entry form but it lacks clarity and it lacks any visual clues as to its purpose. Good form design should also try to eliminate data entry errors. There are two fields on here which will validate and only allow certain values: Gender and Tutor Group.

It would be good to ensure that the music teacher's name and instrument serial numbers are completely accurate because these are primary keys and if they are incorrect on this form then they will not connect to the teacher and instrument tables. This is an important point. If 'Mr B Whizz' was entered as someone's teacher it would be saved, but there is no 'Mr B Whizz' in the table **Teacher** meaning that any query, filter or report that used the content and relationships connected to the **Teacher** table would not include the student. You must always ensure that the teacher is in the **Teacher** table before adding a new student; if not, add the teacher details first. The same applies to instrument serial number entered in the new student's record that did not exist.

You are going to introduce **drop-down lists** and **option buttons** onto the form.

In *MS Access* a **combo box** will produce a list of possible choices for a **drop-down list**. They look and work in exactly the same way as the Tutor Group drop-down list you created in Session 6.5. These will be used to select the instrument teacher and the instrument serial number when the instrument belongs to the school. **Option buttons** are sometimes known as radio buttons: clickable 'dots' that can be used to select one out of a number of choices. These will be used to indicate whether an instrument belongs to the student of the school.

Drop-down lists

Return the form to its design view. Combo boxes are a type of control.

Look for a panel or selection of controls which may look similar to this.

Identify and select the combo box/drop-down list and then draw one somewhere on the form (it will be tidied up later).

Two things happen: A label and a text box are placed on the form; a control
wizard will open.

Follow/Select these steps:

- The values that appear in the list come from the **Teacher** table.
- From the list of available tables select **Teacher**.
- The field that you want in the drop-down list is Teacher.
- Sorted values make selection easier for the user so ask that Teacher is sorted into ascending order.
- The teacher that the user selects needs to be stored in the Teacher field, so make this selection.
- Name the drop down list **Teacher**.

Go back to form view to see the form displayed with data again.

Notice that you have two fields showing Miss N Boyd. Click the new drop-down list and choose another teacher. That selection is immediately displayed in the original Teacher field. This tells you that the drop down list is working as expected. You can go back to the form design view and delete the original Teacher field leaving the drop down list as the means of selecting a teacher for a student.

Option buttons

Return the form to its design view. Option buttons are another type of control. Option buttons can be used alone like the check box (another control) already used for Own and Orchestra. In this case you are going to use two, one for 'own' instrument and one for 'school' instrument. You do not select 'Option button' from the control panel and place two separate ones on the form. You need to select 'Option group' and draw one on the form. This is because the option buttons are going to be used in combination, connected to the same field.

The wizard requires you to name each of the radio buttons in the group. Name them 'Own' and 'School' and then assume that school will be the default setting.

Originally the record structure was set up with field Own set as a Yes/No data type. This means that 'School' needs setting to 0 (meaning 'No', the student has not got a school instrument) and 'Own' needs setting to -1 (meaning 'Yes', the instrument belongs to the student.)

Chose to store the value in the Own field. For now accept the default button design settings and name the option group Own.

PRACTICAL

Tip

Controls are elements of a form or report which you can use to enter, edit or display data. See also Session 6.9 for use of a 'text box' control.

Tip

Wizard dialogue boxes appear because the option to use them has been selected (perhaps by default). If they do not appear you need to find an option such as 'Use control wizards' or an icon like this to turn them on.

Activity 1

A drop-down list also needs creating for the serial number of an instrument. Work through the steps you have just taken to create the Teacher drop-down list, but this time working with the table **Instrument** and the field SerialNo.

What label do you want for each option?

Label Names
Own
School
*

Real world

The values that the database stores to internally represent Yes/No, or True/false, are -1 for Yes and 0 for No.

What value do you want to assign to each option?

Label Names	Values
Own	-1
School	0

Go back to Form view to see the data properly.

Click on the new option buttons to see that the original check box for Own changes as you select 'Own' or 'School'. You can now go back to the design view and delete the original Own check box.

Layout

The form as it appears at the moment is not particularly attractive. There is nothing to indicate the form's purpose and the labels for each field need to be changed to be more informative. It might also be more useful to try and group related fields together. Managing the space (sometimes referred to as **white space**) around various fields may also help the user to see the connection between fields. These ideas will allow the form to be filled in quickly and accurately.

In the design view, click on a text box or its label and use the familiar font tools to change the appearance of the displayed text and data. You can freely change the text in a label, but do not change the text in the text box as this is the field name that connects to the text box.

Activity 2

Use the font tools to change the appearance of the labels and textboxes. Change the text in the labels to be more meaningful. Move some of the fields around (you can move the label and the text box independently of each other) making good use of the space to let the user see the various fields that are related.

Another control is a label. Find this in the selection of controls. You can use this to add a heading, some instructions or a hint/tip on the form, again using the font tools to manage appearance.

The top of the form might look like this:

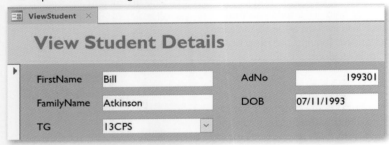

Close the form and save with the name **ViewStudent**.

Activity 3

Add some labels to provide a heading and some instructions, such as that there has to be an Admission Number (AdNo) entered, or that date of birth is in the format DD/MM/YYYY.

Tip

As with all forms designed for multiple users, remember to choose fonts and colours that are clear and easy to read on screen.

Adding a new student

To add a new student open the form **ViewStudent**. The form opens and shows you the details of the first student in the table.

Look at the bottom of the form. The record navigation bar indicates which record you are viewing and allows you to step though them. The button on the far right is for adding a new record, and when clicked will present a blank record.

Activity 4

Miss Brown passes a note to you about another student who has expressed interest in music lessons. As yet she has not selected an instrument. The details are:

AdNo	FirstName	Family Name	TG	DoB	Gender
199705	Tiffany	Lu	09KIR	08/08/1998	F

Using the form **View student** add Tiffany to the database. When you have added her details close the form and view the table **StudentDetail** to check that she has been added correctly – you should have 48 student records in the database.

Close the database. If prompted to save, then click 'Yes'.

Review and revise

You should now be able to:

- create a data entry form for a particular table
- navigate records of a table through the form
- add new records to a table through the form.

SESSION 6.8 Filters, queries and creating reports

Background

The **MusicStudents** now has quite a complex structure and a number of objects (four tables, one form). For this, and all the remaining practical sessions of this unit, you will continue to use and develop further **MusicStudents**.

In this session you will look at sorting and saving the data and displaying the results in a report.

Filters and queries

At the start of this unit you read that any collection of data needs to be analysed. In Session 6.4 you were introduced to sorting and searching, criteria and operators.

There are three points to remember:
- A **filter** is used to select certain records using criteria applied to fields in a record (a subset of the records).
- A **query** is a filter that you have previously saved so that you can easily access the subset of records again.
- Generally a filter will return all fields in a record, but within a query it will be possible to select which fields are displayed.

Sorting the records in the table

In this activity you need to produce a report of students sorted by surname within tutor group (TG). This will be achieved by selecting an alphabetical A to Z sort, identified by an icon similar to the one on the right.

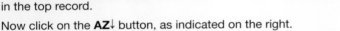

Open the table **StudentDetail** and click on the FamilyName of the person in the top record.

Now click on the **AZ↓** button, as indicated on the right.

The records in the table are now sorted into alphabetical order of FamilyName. You should have Rana Al-Bader and Amir Al-Timani at the top of the table, with Sarah Wilson and Harriet Williams at the bottom. But Amir Al-Timani might not be before Khalel Al-Timani. Check also the Boyes children and the Derbyshire girls. Are they in the correct order?

Usually you would expect students to be sorted by FirstName within FamilyName. Click in the FirstName of the person in the top record and then sort by the **AZ↓** button again. The sort has not put the FirstNames in order within the FamilyName. It has sorted the whole set of records into FirstName order – which is really what should have been expected.

You might see that just using the table view and applying sorts one at a time causes problems. You need to use an 'advanced' sort, where you can make multiple requests at the same time. This should make things much easier.

Applying multiple sorting criteria

In the tab or menu where you selected the **AZ↓** sort you should have an option to select an advanced filter/sort.

With Ahmed selected in the top record, click on this option and you will be presented with something like the example on the right.

Ask that the TG, FamilyName and FirstName all be sorted alphabetically. The order in which you ask these must be TG first. Your selection will look like the example at the top of the next page.

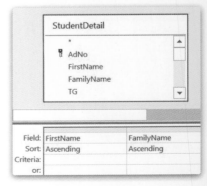

Field:	TG		FamilyName		FamilyName	
Sort:	Ascending		Ascending		Ascending	
Criteria:						
or:						

In the place where you found the **Advanced Filter/Sort** button, there should also be one that will **Toggle** or apply the filter criteria. Select to toggle between the design and the records with this applied to them.

Tutor grouping is obvious, but to check this has worked correctly, find the Poulsen twins in Year 10; Lizzie should appear before Tom. And the sort has arranged and displayed all the records, not just a subset.

Now imagine you want to see all the details of one tutor group: 10SMS. Select the **Advanced Filter/Sort** button again and then add "10SMS" to the sort criteria:

Field:	TG	∨	FamilyName		FamilyName	
Sort:	Ascending		Ascending		Ascending	
Criteria:	"10SMS"					
or:						

Click on **Toggle** again and you will see that the list of records has been reduced to show only the students in 10SMS (see the table below).

Notice that the order has been preserved; Lizzie Poulsen is before Tom Poulsen.

What has happened now is that you have changed the sort into a filter. Remember, a filter displays a subset (all students in 10SMS) of the record set. You are going to save this filter. This creates a query, so look for the **Save as query** option in the tab or menu near where you found the **AZ↓** button. Save this query as **FirstFamilyTG**.

AdNo	▾	FirstName	▾	FamilyName	▾↿	TG	▿▽	DOB	▾	Gender
199611		Khalel		Al-Tamani		10SMS		07/02/1997		M
199614		Kate		Appleby		10SMS		08/07/1997		F
199615		Ivan		Boraskyi		10SMS		03/04/1997		M
199610		Hannah		Derbyshire		10SMS		10/05/1997		F
199601		John		Hillman		10SMS		12/03/1997		M
199605		Matthew		Johnson		10SMS		09/09/1996		M
199617		David		Jones		10SMS		12/11/1996		M
199612		Claudia		Medici		10SMS		12/01/1997		F
199613		Robyn		Naylor		10SMS		09/12/1996		F
199602		Sophie		Potter		10SMS		11/04/1997		F
199609		Lizzie		Poulsen		10SMS		10/08/1997		F
199608		Tom		Poulsen		10SMS		10/08/1997		M
199606		Luke		Thompson		10SMS		12/12/1996		M
199604		Sara		Tomkins		10SMS		08/12/1996		F

Activity 1

Using the table **StudentDetail**, create an advanced filter which:

- has records sorted into descending order of TG within ascending order of Instrument
- selects only girls.

When you click on **Toggle**, you should have 25 records. Save the filter as a query called **GirlInstrument**.

Creating a report with sorted data

You are going to create a report where all the fields of all the records in the table are displayed. This will be as a result of a filter being applied, which means that the records can be sorted into one order. The key order of this set of records is AdNo (the student Admission Number).

Open the reporting element of your database. If you have a report wizard, it is best that you use that facility until you have a better understanding of how reports are generated and the parts of them.

There are a few steps:

- Choose the table **StudentDetail** as the source of data.
- Ask for all the fields to be displayed in the report.
- Choose to have the records ordered by ascending AdNo.
- Choose the title **All students by Admission Number**.
- Set page orientation to landscape.

Other choices, such as style or page layout, are there for you to decide.

Once you have worked your way through all options, you will be able to see a preview of the report. When you are asked about saving the report, give it the name **StudentsByAdNo**.

The first part of the completed report should look something like this:

All Students by Admission Number

AdNo	FirstName	FamilyName	TG	DOB	Gender	Instrument
199301	Bill	Atkinson	13CPS	07/11/1993	M	Violin
199302	Megan	McConnel	13CPS	12/04/1994	F	Flute
199401	Lucy	Potter	12MAH	10/12/1994	F	Violin
199402	Amir	Al-Tamani	12MAH	06/09/1994	M	Trumpet
199403	Alice	Derbyshire	12MAH	11/06/1995	F	Clarinet
199501	Mashood	Othman	11MEB	09/05/1996	M	Cello

Activity 2

Miss Brown has been asked to provide a report which:

- shows full details of all students
- has a heading – **Music students by date of birth**
- has all students sorted in ascending order of **DoB**
- has a page orientation of landscape.

Using the table **StudentDetail**, create this report for Miss Brown.

Creating a report using a query

You already have a query saved as **FirstFamilyTG**, which will list all the students in the tutor group 10SMS. This is going to be attached to a report instead of the table being attached to the report. This means that the records in the report will be selected by the query.

Open the reporting element of your database again, and start the report wizard. The steps this time match those from the last example:

1 Choose the data source: the query **FirstFamilyTG**.
2 Ask for all the fields (except TG) to be displayed in the report.
3 You do not need to choose an order because the query already contains this information.

Tip

Familiarise yourself with producing reports with either a landscape or portrait orientation. The default setting is usually 'portrait'.

Language

To attach a query or a table to a report means that query or table will be the data source for the report. Attaching a table will result in all the records being in the report. In the case of a query, the records for the report will be selected by the query.

Other choices, such as style or page layout, are there for you to decide.

Give the report the title **Students in tutor group 10 SMS**. Once you have worked your way through all options, you will be able to see a preview of the report. When you are asked about saving the report, give it the name **StudentsIn10SMS**.

The top of the report will look like this:

AdNo	FirstName	FamilyName	TG	DOB
199601	John	Hillman	10SMS	12/03/1997
199602	Sophie	Potter	10SMS	11/04/1997
199603	Paul	Tomlinson	10SMS	01/10/1996

Students in tutor group 10 SMS

Activity 3

Create a new report that shows the level of interest in music among the girls of the school. The report:
- uses the saved query **GirlInstrument**
- has an orientation of landscape
- has the title **Girl Instrumentalists**.

Save the report as **GirlInstrument**.

Sort or query for a report?

The report based on a sort:
- can be produced entirely through the report wizard
- needs the table to be attached as the data source
- shows all fields for all records.

A report based on a query:
- needs the query to be created and saved
- needs the query to be attached as the data source
- will display a selection of fields for a subset of the records.

Review and revise

You should now be able to:
- appreciate the difference between a filter and a query
- use a filter and save it as a query
- create a report based on a simple sort or a saved query.

SESSION 6.9 Reports and run-time calculations

Background

In the previous session you looked at creating simple reports. These were based on either a sort or a query. This session starts by investigating the layout of a report. You will discover how to include calculations in a report as well as practising your query-building skills.

Report elements

This diagram shows the different elements of a report.

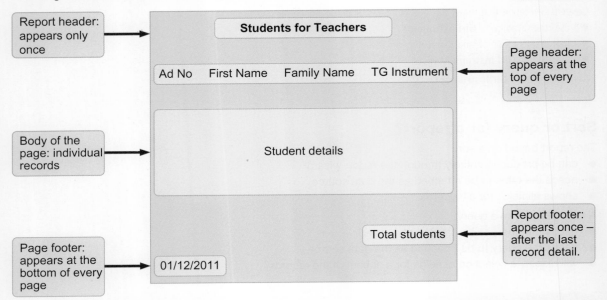

It is important to remember that some elements will appear on every page, but some will appear only once – at the start and end of the report.

Open the report **StudentsByAdNo**, saved in the previous session. It will have opened as a preview. Look for a tab or menu that is related to different views of the report and select **Design View** (or you might have to click on a small icon of a ruler and pencil, see Session 6.5).

You should see something like the example on the right.

In this session, you will be working in the design view of a report, placing new elements in the page and report footers, as well as in the detail section.

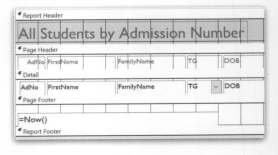

Take a few moments to identify the different headers and footers that are available and identify where each element that was displayed in the preview of the report can be found. Close the report. You do not need to re-save it because you have not changed anything.

Building a query

A query can be used to display only certain fields of data from a record. You are going to create a report of all the orchestra members again, but this time it will only display certain pieces of information for each student.

You only need to display the students' AdNo, FirstName, FamilyName, TG and Instrument. The records need to be sorted according to FirstName within FamilyName.

Open the **MusicStudents database**. Find the option that will allow you to build a query in design view. This may be located in the same place as your reporting options, or on a menu or tab dealing with database objects. It may look like the icon highlighted on the right.

The first question that will be asked of you is which table is to be attached to the query. Add the table **StudentDetail**.

Now set up the fields to sort/examine like this:

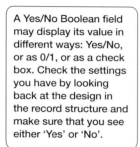

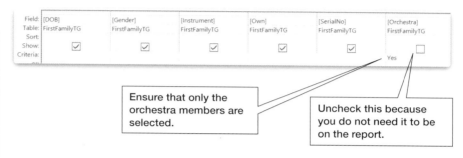

A Yes/No Boolean field may display its value in different ways: Yes/No, or as 0/1, or as a check box. Check the settings you have by looking back at the design in the record structure and make sure that you see either 'Yes' or 'No'.

Ensure that only the orchestra members are selected.

Uncheck this because you do not need it to be on the report.

Save the query as **FirstFamilyOrchestra**.

Open up a new report using the report wizard. Ask for the query **FirstFamilyOrchestra** to be attached to it and select all the fields to be displayed in the report.

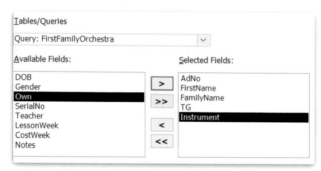

There is no need to select an order for the report, because the query contains this information. Give it the title **Orchestra members**.

Preview the report. It should look something like this:

Save the report with the same name as the query: **FirstFamilyOrchestra**.

Run-time created fields

There are other features of 'analysis' besides searching or sorting that need to be considered. You can ask that the report includes elements that are calculated at run-time. As the report is being produced, calculations are being made with the data being displayed.

For example, in this report you could count the students in each tutor group, or the total of all students, or count the boys/girls in each tutor group. These are called **run-time calculations**. Your database software will provide some functions such as: count, sum, average, maximum, or minimum. You can also create calculations of your own using addition, subtraction, multiplication, and division.

At the start of this session you looked at the layout of a report. These run-time calculations can be placed in headers, footers and the detail.

Adding a run-time element to a report

You are going to add in a run-time calculated field which totals up the number of students in the orchestra. This calculation will come after the last record to be displayed, so it needs to be placed in the report footer.

Use your database's Help facility to discover the **syntax** of the count function. It may look like this: =COUNT([FieldName]).

For FieldName you can use any field, because you are just counting how many records there are. You are not concerned with the content of the field. You will use: =COUNT([AdNo]), because every student has an AdNo.

Open the report **FirstFamilyOrchestra** in design view. Look for a panel or selection of controls, which might look similar to the example on the right.

You will be using text boxes and labels, so make sure you can find and identify them.

Select a text box and draw one in the report footer. You will get two boxes. One will have 'Text10' or something similar in it; the other will probably have 'Unbound'.

The 'Unbound' box is where you will type: =COUNT([AdNo]). Type it in now. The other box is the label or heading for the data item that is going to be displayed, so type in **Students in the orchestra** …. It should look like the image at the top of the next page.

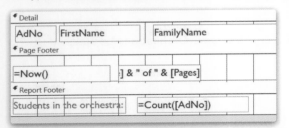

Change the view of the report to preview and you should see at the end:

199301	Bill	Atkinson	13CPS	Violin
199302	Megan	McConnel	13CPS	Flute
Students in the orchestra:	35			

Save the report as as **OrchestraCount**.

Activity 1

Find the syntax in your database software of the sum function. Add **LessonWeek** to the query **FirstFamilyOrchestra**. Save the query as **OrchestraLessons**.

Create a new report that:
- uses the query **OrchestraLessons**
- has a portrait orientation
- has the title **Total Orchestra Lessons**
- at the end of the report has the run-time calculation that totals (SUM) the number of music lessons (LessonWeek).

Activity 2

You are going to create another report using the table **StudentDetail**. The report is to list all the students of Miss N Boyd.
- For each student, only show the fields: AdNo, FirstName, FamilyName, TG, Instrument, LessonWeek.
- Students will be listed in alphabetical order of first name within family name.
- At the end of the report, there will be a run-time created field with a function to total the number of lessons per week that Miss N Boyd's students have. The function will be =SUM([LessonWeek]).
- The report will have a portrait orientation.
- The report will have the heading **Weekly lessons taught by Miss N Boyd**.

Other run-time functions

As well as the other functions mentioned above, it is possible to create your own calculation in a field. If you wanted to work out the cost per lesson for students, how would you do that? You would want the cost per week to be divided by the number of lessons per week:

$$=[CostWeek] / [LessonWeek]$$

This would need to be typed into a text box, just as you did for the COUNT and SUM functions. This is a calculation that needs to be created for every student in the list, and so will be placed in the detail section of the report layout. It will need to be formatted as currency and have two decimal places.

Tip

Formatting a field, such as setting decimal places, can be achieved by right clicking on the field and selecting **Properties** from the menu that is displayed.

Creating a report with a user-created run-time calculation

You are going to produce a report using the calculation for average lesson cost.

First, a query needs to be created that will return the AdNo, FamilyName, FirstName, TG, Instrument, LessonWeek of all students where CostWeek > 0. This is because there are some students who are on a music scholarship and they do not pay for lessons. The order of the records is to be FirstName within FamilyName within descending TG.

Open a query with **StudentDetail** attached to it and select these fields and settings:

Field:	[TG]	[AdNo]	[FamilyName]	[FirstName]	[Instrument]	[CostWeek]	[LessonWeek]
Table:	StudentDetail	StudentDetail	StudentDetail	StudentDetail	StudentDetail	StudentDetail	StudentDetail
Sort:	Descending		Ascending	Ascending			
Show:	☑	☑	☑	☑	☑	☑	☑
Criteria:						>0	
or:							

Save the query as **AverageCostLesson**.

Open the reporting wizard and attach this query to the report. Ask for all the fields except LessonWeek and CostWeek to be displayed. You need these two fields in the query so that they can be used in the calculation, even though you do not need to display them. Preview the report to check that you have the students in the right order.

Switch to the report design view. You are now going to add the run-time field into the detail section of the report. Select a text box and place one at the end of the row of student details:

Page Header

| TG | | AdNo | FamilyName | | FirstName | | Instrument | | Cost/Lesson | | | |

Detail

| TG | ∨ | AdNo | FamilyName | | FirstName | | Instrument | | =[CostWeek]/[LessonWeek] | | |

New label

Your calculation goes in here

'Text13:' is deleted because you do not want the label here. The formula created above replaces 'Unbound' in the other box. Select a 'Label' from the control options and add it into the 'Page Header' section.

TG	AdNo	FamilyName	FirstName	Instrument	Cost/Lesson
07CKD	199902	Mountain	David	Drums	£8.00
07CKD	199901	Rodriguez	Marianna	Violin	£10.00
07CKD	199903	Tomlinson	Kirsty	Guitar	£8.00

In this new label, type **Cost/lesson** and format it to the same colour and font scheme of the other headings.

Before you preview the report there is one more task. The field with the calculation in it needs to be formatted to currency and two decimal

Format	Data	Event	Other	All	
Name				Text13	
Label Name					
Control Source				=[CostWeek]/[LessonWeek]	
Format				Currency	⌄
Decimal Places				2	

places. Right click over the field and look at the field properties, where you will be able to choose and set this format.

Once you have done these things, switch to preview the report. The top part might look like this:

Save the report as **CostPerLesson**.

Dates and page numbers in the page footer

Open the **CostPerLesson** report again, but this time in design view. Look at the page footer. Your software will probably place today's date and an automatic page number in there. You may see =NOW(). This is a function that returns the current date. These fields are placed there because they are very common items that people like to see at the bottom of a report. You do not have to keep them in there. You might prefer to see your name there instead.

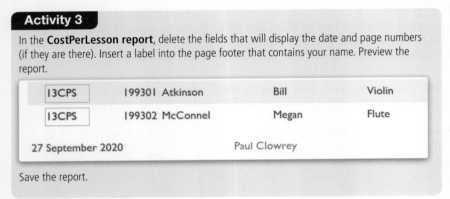

Activity 3

In the **CostPerLesson report**, delete the fields that will display the date and page numbers (if they are there). Insert a label into the page footer that contains your name. Preview the report.

13CPS	199301	Atkinson	Bill	Violin
13CPS	199302	McConnel	Megan	Flute

27 September 2020   Paul Clowrey

Save the report.

Review and revise

You should now be able to:

- identify all sections of a report and understand their roles
- use a query to select a subset of the data set
- use built-in functions that will count, sum
- create a run-time calculation
- set fields to have currency and number data types, with decimal places
- make use of the report and page footers for titles and author identity
- add a query to a report.

SESSION 6.10 Complex queries and wildcards

Background

In the practical sessions so far you have sorted data, displaying all the records in a new order. You have also displayed a selection of records by using a query. One report, listing the orchestra members, had a selection criterion of Orchestra = "Yes". In this session, you are going to look at using a query to select records using multiple search criteria.

Creating a query

Miss Boyd teaches many other students, not just the ones at your school. She has one student who has recently given up playing the violin. This student has asked Miss Boyd to see if any other violin students would like to buy her violin.

You need to create a query, making sure that it selects only the records you are interested in.

Open the database **MusicStudents**. Locate the place where a query can be created. Look for something like these:

Select the option that allows you to create a query by design. The first question you will be asked is about what table is to be connected to the query. Select, or add, the table **StudentDetail**.

You now need to identify the fields that are to be displayed and the criteria that are going to be used to select the right students. In order to identify the right students for Miss Boyd, the fields you need to see are the student's FirstName and FamilyName and their tutor group, TG. For the purposes of selecting the right students you also need the fields Instrument and Own.

To select the right students, the criteria will be Instrument = "Violin" and Own = "N". You do not need to see the Instrument and Own fields displayed in the report.

The query with selections and settings will look something like this:

Ask for the query to be run. To do this, find somewhere around the window you are working in, or within a menu headed **Query**, an icon indicating **Run Query**. It might look like this.

You should see four students' names listed: Cathy Davis, Marianna Rodriguez, Andrew Green and Jon Cornish. Save the query with the name **NoViolin**.

This query can be used to illustrate the difference between a logical AND and an OR condition (see Session 6.4, Criteria and Operators). You have Instrument = "Violin" and Own = "N" on the same criteria row, meaning that both criteria need to be true in a single record for the record to be returned – the logical AND condition.

Remove Own = "N" from the criteria row and place it in the next row underneath, the 'Or' row. Run the query. You now get 34 records returned. This is because a record is returned if the Instrument = "Violin" OR if Own = "N". There are eight violinists and a total of 30 who have no instrument of their own (but our four violinists with no instrument are listed once, not twice, hence 34 records and not 38!).

Close the query but do not save it, as it has the OR condition.

Activity 1

Create a query with the table **StudentDetail** that selects all the students taught by Miss Boyd and who have their own instruments. You should have five students who fit these criteria.

Mixing AND and OR

Mr Atkinson and Mr Hill both give lessons on a Monday. Next week, there is a holiday on Monday. Miss Brown, the head of music, needs to be able to get a message to the students of Mr Atkinson and Mr Hill.

This will be an OR search: Teacher = "Mr A Atkinson" OR Teacher = "Mr J Hill"

Miss Brown will also need the students' TG field so that she knows where to find them during morning registration. It would also be good for the list to be in TG order and to see Instrument.

Open a new query in design view with the table **StudentDetail** added. Create the criteria and conditions like this:

Field:	TG	FamilyName	FirstName	Teacher	Instrument
Table:	StudentDetail	StudentDetail	StudentDetail	StudentDetail	StudentDetail
Sort:					
Show:	☑	☑	☑	☑	☑
Criteria:				"Mr A Atkinson"	
or:				"Mr J Hill"	

Run the query. You should get 17 students, with Jane Boyes of 08BRJ at the top and Amir Al-Timani of 12MAH at the bottom.

Miss Brown has to improve the search because she realises that some students only have one lesson each week. For these students, a letter will need to be sent to their parents, explaining that for this week, their child will have no lesson.

The query needs to be modified. You need to add an AND condition. LessonWeek = "1". This extra criterion needs to be added to each of the conditions you have already, because the whole search criteria becomes: (Teacher = "Mr A Atkinson" AND LessonWeek = "1") OR (Teacher = "Mr J Hill" AND LessonWeek = "1")

Field:	TG	FamilyName	FirstName	Teacher	Instrument	LessonWeek
Table:	StudentDetail	StudentDetail	StudentDetail	StudentDetail	StudentDetail	StudentDetail
Sort:						
Show:	☑	☑	☑	☑	☑	☑
Criteria:				"Mr A Atkinson"		1
or:				"Mr J Hill"		1

If you run the query now, you will get 14 students. Save the query as **AtkinsonHill**.

A logical NOT condition

A NOT condition is used when searching for records that do NOT have a particular criterion. If you wanted to return all the students who did not have their own instruments, you might ask Own = "No". It would be a strange thing to do, but you could also ask Own = NOT "Yes".

Open a new query and add the table **StudentDetail**. Show the fields FirstName, FamilyName and Instrument when the criterion is Own = "No".

Field:	FirstName	FamilyName	Instrument	Own
Table:	StudentDetail	StudentDetail	StudentDetail	StudentDetail
Sort:				
Show:	☑	☑	☑	☑
Criteria:				No
or:				

Run the query. You should get 30 students.

Go back to the query design. Now change the criterion for Own so that it is "<>Yes" instead of "No". You have to use "<>" (which means not equal to) instead of "NOT". Run the query. You should get the same 30 students.

Save the query as **NoInstrument**.

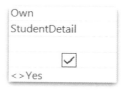

Activity 2

A more likely query could be that Miss Brown is organising a music concert, but students in examination years (Years 11 and 13) are not allowed to take part as it interferes with their revision programme. Here, the query will need to return all students except those where TG is 11MEB or 13CPS.

Create this query and run it. You should get 32 students.

Save the query as **NoExamination**.

Using wildcards

Session 6.4 introduced the idea of a wildcard. This is a symbol (? or *), introduced into a search criterion in place of characters that you either do not know or want to ignore. ? stands for a single letter, while * stands for multiple letters.

Two simple examples.

First, Mrs Brown needs to know who plays a tuba, a trumpet or a trombone. You could set up a query with three OR conditions: Instrument = "Tuba" OR Instrument = "Trumpet" OR Instrument = "Trombone".

Alternatively, you could say Instrument = "T*". The syntax for the criterion will be similar to this one:

Field:	AdNo	TG	FamilyName	FirstName	Instrument
Table:	StudentDetail	StudentDetail	StudentDetail	StudentDetail	StudentDetail
Sort:					
Show:	☑	☑	☑	☑	☑
Criteria:					Like "T*"
or:					

Create this query using **StudentDetail** and run it. You should get seven students' names.

Secondly, a list is needed of all music students who have a birthday in November. Remember, you have set the date to have a data type of 'short date' – dd/mm/yyyy. This means a wildcard search for DoB as: '??/11/????'. The syntax would be: Like '??/11/????'.

Create this query and run it. Again, you should get seven students.

Activity 3

- In order to try and promote more music lessons, Miss Brown wants to talk to all students who have only one lesson a week (**LessonWeek = 1**). Of these, the only students whom she will not contact are those whose TG field contains 11MEB or 13CPS.
- Create and save a query that will select these students.
- The list should show: AdNo, FirstName, FamilyName, TG, Instrument.
- Attach the query to a report.
- The list should be ordered: FirstName within FamilyName within descending TG.
- Add a run-time calculated field at the end of the report that counts the number of students in the list.
- The report is to have the heading **Students who have one lesson a week**.
- The page footer is to display your name on the left.

Using the table relationships to create a query for a report

Miss Brown needs a report to send to the school accountant which details the amount of money each teacher is generating for the school. For each teacher (Teacher, Street, Town, Email) a list is required showing each student (AdNo, FirstName, FamilyName, TG, Instrument, LessonsWeek, CostWeek > 0). For each teacher the sum of their student CostWeek is needed, together with a sum of all the student's CostWeek.

Open a new query in design view and this time ask for two tables: **StudentDetail** and **Teacher**, to be used.

Add the required fields to the query.

Field:	AdNo	TG	FamilyName	FirstName	Instrument
Table:	StudentDetail	StudentDetail	StudentDetail	StudentDetail	StudentDetail
Sort:		Ascending	Ascending	Ascending	
Show:	☑	☑	☑	☑	☑
Criteria:					
or:					

LessonWeek	CostWeek	Teacher	Address1	Address2	email
StudentDetail	StudentDetail	Teacher	Teacher	Teacher	Teacher
		Ascending			
☑	☑	☑	☑	☑	☑
	>0				

Save the query **StudentsForTeachers**.

If you view the results of the query you will see 46 records displayed. There are 48 students in the database but two students (Alice Derbyshire and Amir Al-Timani) have a scholarship and so do not pay for lessons, and Tiffany Lu has yet to decide on an instrument.

Close, and if necessary save the query.

Open the report wizard and attach this new query to the report asking for all the fields to be attached and view according to the Teacher field.

Preview the report. It will probably look quite messy and complicated but it does contain the necessary information drawn from the two tables.

The information in the report needs to be rearranged and made more readable and useful.

Activity 4

Rearrange the data so that all data and labels are visible
- Add a run-time calculation, with a label, to show the sum of CostWeek of all students for each teacher.
- Add a run-time calculation, with a label, for the sum of all the student's CostWeek.
- Put your name and today's date in the report footer.

If Mr B Gibson is at the end of your report it should look like this. The last teacher in the report has a total for their students' CostWeek and then the report ends with every student's CostWeek.

Review and revise

You should now be able to:
- open and create a query and attach it to a report
- create a query based on relationships between tables
- understand and make use of the logical conditions AND, OR, NOT and LIKE
- understand and make use of wildcards
- add a query to a report.

Producing labels and business cards

Background

The practical sessions so far have produced reports that contain listings of records. Either you have a report that contains all the records in the database (resulting from a filtered sort) or you have a subset of the database (resulting from setting some search criteria).

But there will be times when you do not want the layout of the report to be a listing. One such situation will be when you want to sort (or search) the records and produce a set of mailing labels. In this session, you will investigate how to change the report to print as labels, not as a standard page.

Producing labels is not something that you choose from the print dialogue box. You create labels, just as you create a query or a report, and then print them.

Label layout

Printed labels can come in a variety of formats. The format determines the size of the labels and how many are across the page.

First, open up your database software and find out where you can access the labels option. It will most likely be within the menu or panel connected to reports. Look for something like the examples on the right.

Choose to start the sequence of producing the labels to see just how many options you have – probably quite a few.

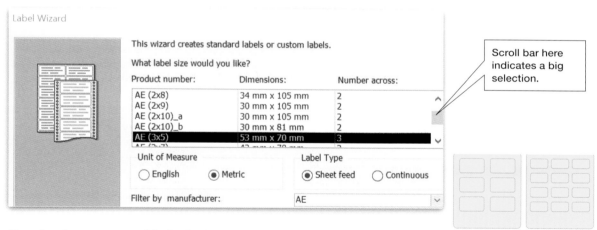

Producing a set of labels from a subset

When you collect your school end-of-term report, there might be a printed sticky label on the envelope. From your knowledge of sorting database records, it should be easy for you to imagine the filter that was used. Student records will be sorted by the name of the student within the tutor groups. This sort will probably match the order in which the reports themselves are printed.

Producing labels is a reporting option, not an option that you pick out of a print dialogue box. Because of this, you need to have already saved the filter or query that orders or selects records. This is attached to the labels in the same way that you would attach it to a normal report.

Labels for school reports

Miss Brown has written reports for all the music students. She needs to print labels for the envelopes into which these reports will be put.

Open the database **MusicStudents**. The first task is to create a query called **LabelsForReports**, which sorts all the records into the correct order and only displays the required fields.

Create and save a query based on **StudentDetail** that places the records in FirstName within FamilyName within TG. It displays only these three fields and AdNo.

Field:	TG	FamilyName	FirstName	AdNo
Table:	StudentDetail	StudentDetail	StudentDetail	StudentDetail
Sort:	Ascending	Ascending	Ascending	Ascending
Show:	✓	✓	✓	✓
Criteria:				
or:				

In some software, you have to select the data source first, rather than as the first step of the label dialogue.

Open the **Label** option in your database, making sure that the correct data source is selected.

Here you can see that the label wizard has opened with the query **LabelsForReports** selected. The first question you will be asked is about the size and layout of the label you need:

Tip

You may need to select, or open, the data source before closing the label option.

Choose the first in the list that offers you two labels across the page. Step through the dialogue boxes. You will probably be asked about such things as font size and colour. These can be amended later, so just accept the default options. The four fields from the query will be shown as available. You want them all, so choose them all:

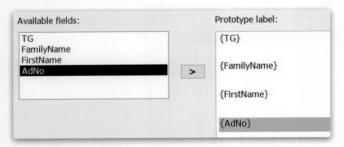

Tip

You should press **Enter** or **Return** after adding each field to create the layout shown.

In the design view, you can change the layout of the label. Rearrange the fields themselves and add labels (headings) alongside the fields. Keep moving between the design and preview views, checking and adjusting the label until everything is where you want it to be.

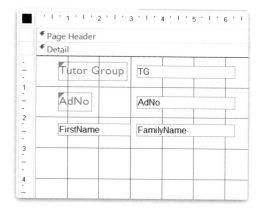

Rectangle control

The final 'page' of labels might look like:

Activity 1

You need to produce some labels to be used as identity stickers for students who are taking part in a piano competition.

- Create a query that uses StudentDetail and returns the FamilyName, FirstName and AdNo of students who play the piano.
- Use this query to produce a set of labels that display the three fields from the query, a heading **Pinetree Piano Competition** and a footer **Competitor**.
- Use fonts, styles and sizes of your choice. You should have six labels in total.

Save the labels as **ReportLabels**.

This facility is a useful one because, of course, you don't actually have to print on sticky labels. Paper and card is also possible – the label facility is just providing a template for multiple items to be printed per page. These items may be labels, but they could be tickets, business cards, identity cards – whatever your imagination leads you to.

If you produce something that is not on a sticky label, it would be a good idea to put a box or rectangle around the 'item' so that it can be cut out properly, as in the example on the previous page. You do this in the report design view. Select **Rectangle** from the control panel (the same panel where you find **Labels** for the headings) and place it around the text of the label to form a border.

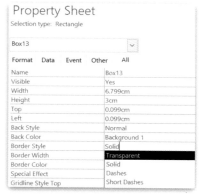

You will have to make the fill or background colour **Transparent**, so that the border line is all you see. You do this by looking at the **Properties** of the shape. You may need to select an option when working in design view to show the **Property Sheet**. Alternatively, right click on the shape you wish to format.

Creating business cards

Another task for you is to create business cards for all the orchestra members. You have put together a sample that Miss Brown is happy with. You now have to make the business cards. The sample you created looks like the one on the right.

This card is based on a size of 55 mm × 85 mm. It has a heading (Pinetree School Orchestra) and an image of a pine tree.

Pinetree
School
Orchestra

Peter Moritz
Xylophone

Activity 2

Create and save a query which:
- displays the student's name and their instrument
- has the criterion Orchestra = "Yes".

Open the label option in the reporting facility of your database and attach the query you created in Activity 2. If you can create a custom size label, then do so: 55 mm × 85 mm, with two labels across the page. If not, then choose a size close to this.

Place the three required data fields onto the label. Find an image of a pine tree (using Clip-Art or an image saved on your computer) and place it in the detail part of the label. Place a 'heading' label in the detail area with the heading **Pinetree School Orchestra**. Finally, place a rectangular box around all the elements of the label, which will provide an outline.

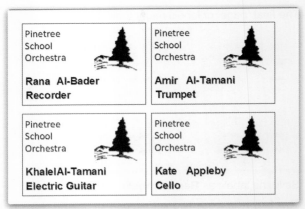

View the labels as they will be printed. Move between the print preview and the design, making any modifications until you are happy that they match the sample card. The top of the first printed sheet should look similar to the four labels pictured.

Activity 3

Following the success of the business cards, another proposal comes along. The music concert, which takes place towards the end of the summer term, is a big event. There are lots of people around and security has become an issue. In order to identify people, it has been decided that everyone should wear a security pass. The head teacher has come to you, asking for a sample to be made.

These are the requirements of the pass:
- Similar in size to the business cards.
- Should contain the heading **Pinetree School Music Concert**.
- Has a picture of a violin.
- All students except those in Y11 and Y13 will be involved.
- The student name in full and their Admission Number (AdNo) is shown.
- Contains another label with the word **Performer**.

Your task is to create this security pass.

The top of the last page of the printout will look something like this:

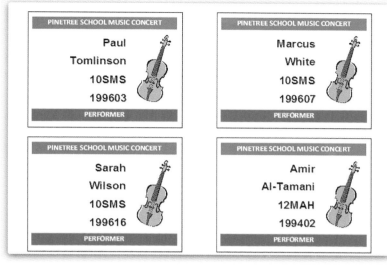

Review and revise

You should now be able to:

- create a query that is to be attached to a label-based report
- understand how labels are created
- attach the query to the label
- add an image to the label
- create a label set that matches a required outline.

Summarising data for use in other software

Summarising and exporting data

Sometimes data from databases needs to be used in other software. For example, a summary showing the total number of students in each tutor group can be found as a query, but may also be required as a table in a report or as a pie chart in a presentation. Perhaps the music store you investigated in Session 5.2 needs a summary of customers, totalled by area of the country, to go into a report.

This session will show you how to summarise data and also how to save the results of these queries in a format that can be used in other software.

Summarising data

Let's start with this example. At the start of each academic year, your head teacher holds an 'Information Evening' for parents and he or she requires information about the musical activity of students. The head teacher has specifically asked for a breakdown that totals the number of students in each tutor group. For the presentation to parents he or she needs a pie chart, and for an information sheet he or she needs a table.

Open the **MusicStudents** database you worked on in the previous sessions. Choose to create a query from the table **StudentDetail**. There are only two fields that you need to have in the query: AdNo and TG. You need TG because that is the field by which you are going to group students, and you need AdNo because you need to count up some field in the record (you could have actually selected any field to serve this purpose).

A new element needs to be introduced. The query needs to count records for you in a similar way that you asked a report to count them. In a report, you can introduce a field and a run-time calculation (see Session 6.9). Here, you are not planning on producing a report, so you need the counting to happen within the query itself.

In your panel for query tools, or a **View** menu, there will be an option to display **Totals**. This is another line in the query design like 'Criteria' and 'or'. Usually **Totals** is hidden, so selecting it from your toolbar just makes it visible and useable.

Choose settings like these:

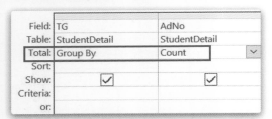

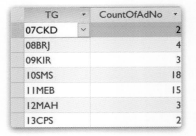

Run the query. You should see a results table like this:

Save the query as **TGSummary**.

Exporting the summary for other uses

You have two exporting requirements. The first is to export in a format that can later be inserted into a word processed document; the second is to export in a format that can be used to create a chart.

Exporting as text

When you export as text, the main point to remember is that you want to preserve formatting. In other words, you need the data to be in a table just as you see it in your database window, complete with field names.

TGSummary should still be open. Find the option for exporting data (it will be within the same menu that you found the import data option) under a drop-down menu for **File**, **Data** or **External Data**. Select the option which will export (save) text as an .rtf file (rich text format). Some software will default to this, but with some you may have to choose the file type for saving. Choose the destination folder for saving into, with the filename **TGSummary**.

Before you do anything else with the database, open the file you have just saved in your word processing software.

The field names (column headings) will need amending, but this file can be imported/inserted into a word processed document.

As usual, there is more than one way to create a chart from this data:

- Using the .rtf file, copy and paste the table from your word processed document to a spreadsheet and create a chart to copy and paste into a presentation.
- Using your presentation software, insert a chart and copy and paste the .rtf table from your word processed document into the data editor for the chart.
- Save the data from the query in a format that can be used by a spreadsheet and create a chart to copy and paste into a presentation.

Of these, it is the last one that concerns you here.

Export to spreadsheet

Other export options

Exporting for charting

Once again, **TGSummary** should still be open. Depending on the version of your database software you will have the following options:

- Export as a spreadsheet file, such as Excel, and open this in your spreadsheet software.
- Export as a text-based file and select delimited or a fixed width file. This can also be imported into spreadsheet software.
- Open your spreadsheet software and look for an option to import a database file. This removes the need to export.

Save **TGSummary** in your chosen format. Again, before you do anything else, open the saved file in your spreadsheet software. You should see something similar to that shown on the right.

This can now be used to create a chart for later use in a presentation.

You now have all the required information in formats that can be used by other application software. Close the query.

Miss Brown needs a list that indicates the different instruments that are played, and by how many students.

Create a query that groups the records by Instrument and counts the number of students (AdNo). You should have a list of 15 instruments, each with a number of students ranging from one (saxophone and tuba) to eight (piano). Save this query in .rtf format.

Tip

Rich Text Format (.rtf) files can preserve the formatting that was applied to the original version of the data such as: bold, underline, or cell shading.

Summarising and mixing Count and Sum

When you were selecting **Count** from the **Totals** options, you will have noticed that there are a number of other built-in functions that can be used (just the same as can be used as built-in functions for a report). It is possible to mix these within the same query, giving multiple summarising criteria.

Miss Brown, the head of music, is also required to have information ready for the parents' evening. She has a report almost prepared, but she needs to add a table, which:

- counts how many male (M) and female (F) students there are from each tutor group
- totals all the lessons for each of these M and F groups.

The query you require will need to:

- display TG, Gender, a count for Gender and a sum of LessonWeek.

Real world

In .csv files each row of data in the original is exported as a line of text with the data items separated by commas, so a table can be recreated – perfect for exporting to a spreadsheet – but formulae are not exported, just the resulting value.

Set up a query to have these settings:

Field:	TG	Gender	AdNo	LessonWeek
Table:	StudentDetail	StudentDetail	StudentDetail	StudentDetail
Total:	Group By	Group By	Count	Sum
Sort:	Ascending			
Show:	☑	☑	☑	☑
Criteria:				
or:				

TG	Gender	CountOfAdNo	SumOfLessonWeek
07CKD	F	1	1
07CKD	M	1	1
08BRJ	F	2	2
08BRJ	M	2	2
09KIR	F	1	1
09KIR	M	2	2
10SMS	F	8	8
10SMS	M	10	10
11MEB	F	9	16
11MEB	M	6	9
12MAH	F	2	7
12MAH	M	1	4
13CPS	F	1	3
13CPS	M	1	3

Run the query. It should look like the example to the right.

This result is needed as a table for a report, so it needs to be exported as a text file. Remember that the file type is .rtf because the formatting is to be preserved.

After you have saved the file, open it up in your word processing software to check that it has been saved as you expected it to be.

Once again, after the headings are edited, this can be imported into a word processed document.

Activity 2

The final piece of summary information needed by Miss Brown concerns the individual part-time instrument teachers. She needs a summary (count) of their students and a summary (total) of the lessons they teach. The results are needed for inclusion in a presentation as a table. This table is to include all the music teachers except Mr A Atkinson, who works full-time at the school.

Create the query and save the resulting data in a suitable format that Miss Brown can use. Set the criteria of the Teacher field to '>0'. This is because Tiffany Lu has not taken up an instrument yet so she is a student in the database without a teacher. If you do not do this your table will contain a row with no teacher name and a student count of 1.

Review and revise

You should now be able to:

● use the summary functions within a query
● mix criteria and summary functions to achieve a specific requirement
● export data in an appropriate format for later use in other software.

6 Practical review

What have you covered?

In these eight practical sessions you have:

- discovered how to create a record structure, assigning data types to fields
- imported data from a separate data source
- applied validation routines to fields
- created relationships between tables in a relational database
- created data entry forms for entering new record details
- explored the layout of a report and come to understand how to use the various parts of it
- investigated the use of run-time calculations, placing them in different parts of the report
- compared the application of filters and queries
- built queries using logical AND, OR, NOT conditions and incorporating wildcards
- discovered how to create labels and then apply this technique to other scenarios
- seen how data from searches can be exported so that it can be used in other application software.

Using your database software, open a new database - **BanknoteCollection** - and import the file **Banknotes. csv** that is on the digital download into a new table: **Banknotes**.

Some practice questions

1 Check the field names and set the field data types to:

PickNo	Text	Standard catalogue number – primary key
Date	Date (short: dd/mm/yyyy)	Date of issue
Cashier	Text	Bank of England Chief Cashier
Denomination	Text	Face value of banknote
Colour	Text	Main banknote colour
Replacement	Boolean (Yes/No)	Replacement and not a new issue
Condition	Text	Grade
Value	Currency	2 dp – Collector's value
Printed	Integer	Quantity issued (in millions)

2 Create a data entry form: **NewNotes** to enter new records to the table **Banknotes**

3 Using the form **NewNotes**, insert the following two records:

PickNo	B285	B292
Date	17/03/1960	27/04/1963
Cashier	O'Brien	Hollom
Denomination	1 Pound	1 Pound
Colour	Green	Green
Replacement	Y	N
Condition	UNC	UNC
Value	32	10
Printed	68	388

4 Create a new record structure **ChiefCashiers** with the following field names and data types:

FamilyName	Short text	Primary key
FirstName	Short text	
BankStart	Integer	Date started work at Bank of England
CashierStart	Integer	Date became Chief Cashier
CashierEnd	Integer	Date left Chief Cashier position

5 Using the file **ChiefCashiers.csv** on the digital download, import the data into this new table.

6 Create a one-to-many relationship between **Banknotes.Cashier** and **ChiefCashiers. FamilyName**. Check that the relationship is correct, for example O'Brien should have seven records connected.

7 Produce a report which:

- shows only the records where Denomination is 10 Shillings.
- contains a new field called P and P, which is calculated at run-time.
- calculates the field P and P as Value × 1.15
- displays P and P as currency (dollars) with two decimal places
- shows the fields – PickNo, Replacement, Condition, Value, P and P
- has the records sorted into ascending order of PickNo
- has the heading – **10/- banknotes for sale**
- has today's date in the bottom left, and your name in the bottom right, of the report footer.

Save the report as **TenShillings**.

8 Return to the report from Question 7 above.

Two new run-time fields are to be introduced, which appear at the end of the report:

- a field with the label **Total banknotes for sale** will display a count of the records in the report
- a field with the label **Average price** of **available banknotes** will display the average value of the Value field.

Save the report as **TenShillingsAverageValue**.

9 Produce a query that finds the total number of banknotes printed for each cashier when Replacement is No.

Save the results of this query in a format that can be used in a word processed document.

10 Banknotes are stored in special plastic pages of a folder. New labels to identify a selection of the banknotes are needed. Produce labels from all the data, which:

- are arranged in three columns
- are only for records where Denomination is 1 Pound
- shows – PickNo, Date, Cashier, Condition, Value
- displays the field name as well as the data
- includes today's date in the bottom left corner of each label.

Save the labels.

Progress check

Aiming for good progress

- You will be able to import data from another source into your database software.
- You can add, amend and delete records from the data set.
- You can create a data entry form.
- You can sort records with one criterion.
- You can search records with one criterion.
- You can apply a wildcard search to the data set.
- You can add a summary field to a query (SUM, COUNT).
- You can create a report with a query attached.
- You can create labels for the whole data set.

Aiming for excellent progress

- You will be able to import data from another source into your database software, whether the incoming data includes field names or not.
- You can add, amend and delete records from the data set.
- You can create a data entry form.
- You can create relationships between database tables.
- You can sort records with more than one criterion.
- You can search records with more than one criterion and with wildcards.
- You can create a query with multiple summary fields.
- You can create a report with a query attached.
- You can create a run-time field and introduce it into the appropriate place in the report's layout.
- You can export data in a format that can be used in other application software.
- You can create labels for a specific subset of the data set.

7 Systems analysis and design

Why this unit matters

Organisations use data in varied and complex ways. Each part of an organisation has functions and processes that relate to others. For example, the registration data that a teacher collects in class feeds into a whole school management system; this data needs to be managed and organised. The process of deciding how this should be done is known as **systems analysis**. A systems **analyst** needs to understand how a particular business works and what it wants to achieve so that she or he can set up a computer system that will work for the company.

Your practical task

Quality Foods is a large supermarket whose customers are complaining about waiting times and the way they are dealt with by checkout staff. Mr Grodzik, the manager, has hired a systems analyst to investigate the number of customers who visit the store and how to increase the use of technology at Quality Foods. He has also asked the systems analyst to have a look at the store's methods of monitoring stock levels.

Mr Grodzik is hoping for a system that will speed up the checkout process and reduce customers' waiting time, and automate much of the stock control process.

You, as part of the analysis team, will help the systems analyst prepare documentation during the design, implementation and documentation stages of the project. You will also refer to the supermarket scenarios throughout the theory sessions.

How will getting the system right impact on my job? (Checkout operator)

What steps will Quality Foods have to take to make sure that the move from one system to another will be successful? (Mr Grodzik, Quality Foods manager)

What this unit covers

THEORY

Sessions

Theory review

PRACTICAL

Sessions

PRACTICAL REVIEW

By the end of the theory sessions you will be able to:

- describe the purpose of each stage of the systems life cycle
- describe the different methods of researching a situation
- state the need for recording, analysing and problem identification
- state the need for, and be able to produce, designs to solve a problem
- select appropriate verification methods
- describe the development of a system from the given design
- describe the testing process and its outcome
- describe, and be able to justify, the choice of an implementation method
- identify the components of user and technical documentation
- explain the need for, and choose, a suitable evaluation strategy.

In the practical sessions you will develop and apply skills in:

- developing the skills introduced in earlier units
- developing, amending and testing a spreadsheet model which simulates a real life situation
- drawing recommendations from a fully working model.

Background

As businesses grow, they may need to look at how they process the data that helps them to do their work. However, developing new systems can be very expensive in terms of time and people, and therefore money, so the way an organisation approaches this task is of vital importance.

Systems of any kind have a life cycle: they are created, they develop, they mature, they may eventually lose their efficiency and be replaced. Information systems have this cycle – known as the **systems life cycle**. This session will introduce this cycle and its major stages. The way in which data is collected in order to analyse the effectiveness of a system is also examined.

The systems life cycle

The role of the systems analyst is to analyse how systems work and to suggest how to improve them. This may involve changing systems from manual paper-based systems to automated computer-controlled systems. Or, it may involve suggesting ways to improve existing computer-based systems. In most cases, the way people work will change in some way.

The system life cycle sets out the stages that take place when a system is designed and developed. There are many ways to represent the cycle with varying amounts of detail and different numbers of stages. The diagram below shows the cycle with the six major stages:

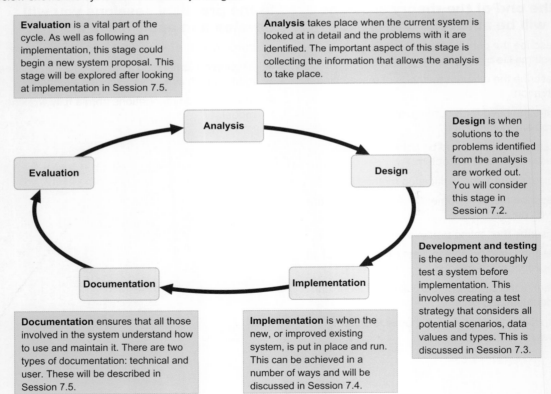

Evaluation is a vital part of the cycle. As well as following an implementation, this stage could begin a new system proposal. This stage will be explored after looking at implementation in Session 7.5.

Analysis takes place when the current system is looked at in detail and the problems with it are identified. The important aspect of this stage is collecting the information that allows the analysis to take place.

Design is when solutions to the problems identified from the analysis are worked out. You will consider this stage in Session 7.2.

Development and testing is the need to thoroughly test a system before implementation. This involves creating a test strategy that considers all potential scenarios, data values and types. This is discussed in Session 7.3.

Implementation is when the new, or improved existing system, is put in place and run. This can be achieved in a number of ways and will be discussed in Session 7.4.

Documentation ensures that all those involved in the system understand how to use and maintain it. There are two types of documentation: technical and user. These will be described in Session 7.5.

Each stage involves specific tasks, but it is important to realise that progress from one stage to the next is not automatic. At some part of each stage, questions will be asked as to whether the requirements of the system are being met. If not, it may be necessary to return to the previous stage and rework the outcomes of that stage.

Collecting data for analysing the current system

There are four main ways to collect information about the system as it is being used at the moment. Each has its own advantages and disadvantages. The systems analyst must balance the mix of these methods, depending on the number of people who may be able to supply first-hand information, the amount of time available and the detail required from these people.

The four ways to collect information are: interview, observation, questionnaires and using existing documentation.

Activity 1

Discuss with your peers and use internet research to find out about the following data collection methods. Complete the table below, adding a description and at least one advantage and one disadvantage for each method.

Interview	
Description	
Advantage	
Disadvantage	

Observation	
Description	
Advantage	
Disadvantage	

Questionnaires	
Description	
Advantage	
Disadvantage	

Examination of existing documents	
Description	
Advantage	
Disadvantage	

Activity 2

Based on your findings in Activity 1, decide which would be the best way to collect information in these situations.

Situation	Method
A small group of people have detailed knowledge of the present system.	
Only a few people have limited knowledge of how the present database is constructed.	
You need to understand how information and documents move around the organisation.	
Many people have views about how effective the present system is and who can provide answers to a number of specific questions.	

Recording and analysing information about the current system

Having carried out an analysis, it is necessary to bring it together in such a way that the present system can be described fully. It is vital that the input, processing and outputs of the current system are identified, understood and properly recorded. A systems analyst will ask questions about the input, processing and output.

Input	Processing	Output
• Where does data originate? • What does it consist of? • What is its format? • How does data enter the system? • Is data entry manual or automatic? • Who enters the data?	• What data processing takes place? • Is this processing manual or automatic? • What algorithms are used? • What checking procedures are in place? • What updating procedures are there? • Who does the processing? • How is data stored? • What format is the data? • What does it consist of? • How secure is it? • Who has access to it?	• How is data used? • How is it displayed? • What format is it displayed in? • Who uses it?

The analyst has to ensure that they have answers to all these questions, as insufficient information collected can lead to an inaccurate picture of the current system under investigation. This makes it possible for the systems analyst to identify the strengths and weaknesses of the present system. Strengths may be built upon; weaknesses are problems that need solutions.

Hardware and software choices

The outcome of this stage is a report outlining the requirements that any new system should fulfil. The report may also offer possible hardware and software combinations that the organisation should consider.

Hardware choices will consider:
- Will the system connect to a network or server?
- How many computers are required?
- What type of devices will be used? Desktop, portable?
- Are there any specific input or output devices needed?

Software choices will consider:
- Will the system require any specially written software?
- Will off-the-shelf packages be ok?
- Are there any licencing issues to be aware of?
- Will the software need to be used in multiple languages?

> ## Review and revise
>
> You should now be able to:
> - name the main stages of the systems life cycle
> - describe the purpose and outcome of the analysis stage of the systems life cycle
> - explain the key components of the analysis stage

SESSION 7.2 The systems life cycle: Design

Background

Once the systems analysts have fully investigated the existing system, the scale and nature of the problems they are dealing with will become apparent. The design stage is where solutions to the identified problems are considered and developed. This may result in a single self-contained solution or, more typically, a number of smaller interlinked 'modules', which together may provide a solution.

The design stage

The design stage is about identifying modules that will make up the solution to the problem. The analyst creates modules to address the problems identified in the analysis stage. For each module, it is necessary to consider the processing that is required and how they will connect, always reflecting on the 'terms of reference'.

The most significant element of this stage is that of file structure. The analyst has to work out the content of the data tables that will be needed. This requires very careful consideration because the entire system depends on the database not only holding the necessary information, but that it is held in the correct format. Look back to Sessions 6.3 and 6.5 to review the importance of data types. As well as table structure, key fields and data types, the analyst needs to consider how these tables will connect together and to any other related system in the organisation (see the diagram and notes about development on pages 319 and 320).

At the end of the design stage the systems analyst will have decided on the:

- **data structures**
- **file formats**
- input and output formats
- module specifications
- relationships that need to exist between the different modules (and systems) in the organisation.

> ### Real world
>
> It is also possible to extend the use of technology at the checkout to include a facility for the customer to pay by credit or debit card. This type of checkout is referred to as electronic funds transfer point of sale (EFTPOS).

Applying the design stage to the supermarket

The systems analyst agrees with Mr Grodzik that the introduction of technology is important. A solution that uses barcode scanners at the checkout is being considered. This new **point of sale (POS)** system should provide a number of advantages for Mr Grodzik and his customers.

> ### Tip
>
> Refer back to Session 5.4, where POS and EFTPOS were discussed.

Activity 1

Use the internet to find out what hardware will be needed at the POS. You could also refer back to Units 2 and 3. Prepare a list of hardware requirements that the systems analyst might recommend for the proposed solution.

Activity 2

What extra items of hardware need to be added to your list from Activity 1 to enhance the POS into an EFTPOS?

Activity 3

Making more use of technology at the checkout has advantages for Mr Grodzik and for his customers. This table lists one advantage for Mr Grodzik and one for the customer. How many more can you think of?

Advantages for Mr Grodzik
Stock control is efficient, so lower amounts of products need to be stored in the warehouse.

Advantages for the customer
Quicker checkout time

Language

Verification

A method for checking data entry for transcription errors – where there is a mistake when entering or copying data. This is a check for the accuracy of data entry. There are two methods of verification:

1. A visual check – is the data that has been typed in the same as that written on the sheet of paper?
2. Double entry – the data is typed in twice; check to identify any differences.

Design tasks

The design team will need to look in detail at many of the following tasks as part of the design stage – some of these you have already explored, for example, hardware, and some will be described in this session or later sessions within this unit.

Designing	Producing	Selecting and defining
• Data capture forms • Screen layouts • Output reports • Other printed outputs • File structures and tables • A testing strategy	• System **flowcharts** or **pseudo code** to describe the system • Data flow diagrams • Diagrams that describe the relationship between each module in the system, and with other systems	• Hardware requirements • Software requirements • **Validation** rules • **Verification** models

System flowcharts

A system flowchart is a diagram of the flow of data or the sequence of steps needed to complete a process. System flowcharts are explored in Session 7.4, but can you follow the system flowchart below?

The systems analyst working for Mr Grodzik proposes that the new system will need to take into account the following flowchart:

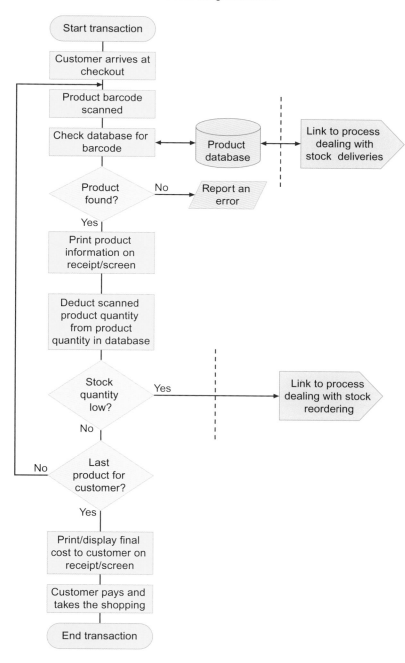

The flowchart indicates that if the product barcode is not found in the database then an error is signalled. Why might the barcode of the product not appear in the database?

The flowchart on the previous page shows that the electronic point of sale system links to other systems in the store: stock reordering and deliveries. If a flowchart was drawn for the whole stock control system then you would see links to other systems, for example, to accounts.

The analysis team will need to consider the design of the database that will hold the system's data. They will need to make decisions about:

- the fields (including the key fields) that are necessary in each data table
- the data to be stored in each field
- the length of each field
- the links between each data table.

Store managers need to be confident that the data in each data file is correct. It would be a problem for supermarket staff if, when the barcode for a can of tuna fish was scanned, it was found to be recorded as a can of chilli beans. Customers and checkout operators could lose faith in the system if the product price cannot be found when the barcode is scanned. This means that verification and validation checking must be thoroughly tested (see Session 7.3).

Screen and report layouts

The systems analyst has to design suitable layouts for the way information is displayed or captured, when, for example, new products are introduced, or prices for existing products change.

This is the screen design for the storeperson, who records deliveries of products. It's important that entry boxes, titles and buttons are clearly designed to meet the users needs.

Report layouts also need to be considered and designed. These might be used to create paper and electronic receipts, stock inventories or customer lists.

> **Language**
>
> **Data capture** is a phrase to describe the way in which data is collected, for example, on a questionnaire, by a touch sensitive screen, a Chip and PIN device or a voice recognition system.

Quality Foods – Stock Delivery

Barcode   505244900213

Boxes   20   Checked ✓

Units   40

Quantity   80

Clear   Submit

> **Tip**
>
> Remember: Capture only data that the system actually requires. In this case, the storeperson need not enter the date or time because the system will pick these up automatically. Make sure you click on the **Submit** button so that the data is captured. Simply completing the boxes will not save the data into the system.

Activity 5

Design the screen layout for the person who is responsible for updating the database with new product information.

Hint: the database requires a number of data items to be entered for each product. Think about what the customer needs to know and also what the people working in the store need to know.

Validation

Data **validation** is very important. The designers will have to be sure that they have designed appropriate validation routines that will test the data input to the system. They will need, for example, to check for complete barcodes and design a manual entry system for the checkout operator if the barcode cannot be read because it has become blurred or has creased.

> **Language**
>
> Validation is a software check that ensures that the data that has been entered can be used by the system. It is a check to see that the data entered lies within specified limits or fits a particular format.

Various fields in the records of the Quality Foods products database will need validation checks applied to them. Does the barcode have 13 characters? Is the sales price greater than $0.00? Is the sales price greater than the cost price? Does the product have a description?

There are eight commonly used validation checks. The designers will need to select the most appropriate data validation for the system on which they are working.

Validation		
Check	**Description**	**Example**
Range	Tests to see that the data falls within defined values.	All exam marks should be in the range 0 to 100 in an exam marked out of 100.
Length	Tests to determine that the data that has been input contains the required number of characters.	Credit card numbers have the same number of digits all over the world. If a number is entered with more, or fewer, digits then an error message appears.
Invalid character or type	Checks to see that there are no invalid characters in the data that has been entered.	A monetary value should only have numbers. Any currency symbol would be regarded as an invalid character.
Format	Data must be input in a specified format.	Dates should be entered in a specific format: mm/dd/yyyy or dd/mm/yyyy, for example.
Presence	Checks that the data has been entered.	The computerised checkout will not function unless the checkout operator has logged in and entered their ID number. In electronic forms, you may find that certain fields are 'required fields' and that transactions cannot be completed until all the data has been entered.
Consistency	Checks to see that fields match each other.	When booking a return journey the departure date/time must be earlier than the return date/time.
Check digit	The individual digits within a long number are used in a calculation to produce an extra digit, which is appended (added) to the end of the number.	Helps to identify three types of common errors: • Transposition – numbers change place when typed in: 23456 could be typed in as 24356. • Mistyping – where a number is entered incorrectly: 133398 is entered instead of 133598. • Missing numbers – 4099 is entered instead of 40996.

Activity 6

Review the range of validation checks. Some of the examples relate directly to the case of Quality Foods. For each of the other validation checks, give an example of how they could be applied to the electronic point of sale system that is being developed.

Review and revise

You should now be able to:
- list many of the tasks involved in the design stage
- follow a procedure that is represented diagrammatically
- design a suitable screen layout for data capture
- explain the purpose of verification and validation.

The systems life cycle: Testing and development

Background

When the design has been developed and the analysts have Mr Grodzik's approval, the next stage is to create, test and develop it to make sure that it works and performs as expected.

Checking that the new system works well is important; otherwise people will ask why the costly changes occurred in the first place. The systems analyst must be prepared to make sure that the new system solves all the problems it was meant to solve.

Once the system has been thoroughly tested it must be installed in the store and implemented (put into use) by employees and customers. The system will 'go live'.

The user interface

During the design stage, the data and hardware requirements were considered. In the previous session you investigated the hardware needed for the EFTPOS system. If the other aspects of this proposed system are considered, the list could be expanded to include:

Input devices:
- the scanner at the checkout
- hand-held scanners for counting and recording stock – these might also be used to record special offers or price reductions
- the POS/EFTPOS terminal
- a Chip and PIN reader.

Output devices:
- a display screen for the checkout operator
- a display screen for the customer
- a printer for itemised receipts
- a portable barcode printer attached to the hand-held scanner (so that on-the-spot reductions can be made as a product nears the end of its shelf-life).

The analyst must also check that:
- any messages and user instructions are clear
- all displays are easy to read
- the display is accessible to all customers – it may need to be adjustable
- the outputs are directed to the correct device, for example, that the receipt is sent to the printer.

> ### Language
>
> The Human-Computer Interface (HCI) refers to the way in which people actually use the system: how they enter data, how the system displays or outputs information. This takes place through the **user interface**.

Testing: modules and the whole system

Each module of the new system needs to be tested to make sure that it works as intended. Once the analysts are sure that each module is functioning independently, they will need to check that the modules work together as one system. During this phase analysts will check, for example:

- Data compatibility – are the outputs from one module recognised by another – are the formats the same or different? The system flowchart in Session 7.2 shows two links to other 'modules'; stock deliveries and stock reordering. It is vital that the output from the flowcharted module is acceptable as input to these other two modules. Imagine writing a document in your word processor, saving and emailing it to a friend. Later you find out that your friend's word processor could not open the file because it was saved as a file format unknown to your friend's word processor. This must not happen in the new system, data needs to be able to flow seamlessly between required modules.

This same requirement is needed between systems. Your system may produce files that are needed by another organisation. For example, financial information will be needed at particular points in the year by various government agencies – your system's output needs to be acceptable input to their computers.

- Hardware compatibility. A mini SD card will not fit into a CompactFlash card slot of a camera; this sounds obvious because these are relatively common-place devices, but the same principle applies across the entire system that is being created. A digital print shop would not do much business if the self-service machines only accepted CompactFlash cards. The analysts should have identified the variety of memory cards that customers (the users) would arrive at the shop with. In Mr Grodzik's supermarket there should not be, for example, issues with hand-held scanners linking to the Wi-Fi network.

- Memory and speed issues. You are probably familiar with the term 'denial of service' which means that a system has been flooded, or overwhelmed, by the messages that it is trying to process. Just think of the problems websites offering sale of tickets for big/popular festivals, events and concerts sometimes have. This can be equally as inconvenient as our email and telephone messaging inboxes getting full, although of course on a much, much smaller scale. In both cases the system breaks down. This could be an issue in the supermarket – can the checkouts cope with the volume of transactions and is the data transferred correctly?

In all cases, once individual modules have been thoroughly tested, the whole system needs to be just as thoroughly tested.

The testing strategies used may lead to a decision to restart or amend the design process. The team may have to look at new hardware, or may need to amend file structures, or even make changes to the input and output methods.

Testing data entry

The purpose of test data is to make sure that:
- inputs to the system are valid
- outputs from the system are accurate
- outputs are presented clearly.

The data that is used to test a system will fall into four categories:

1 **Normal test data.** This is data generated by the systems analyst that follows the expected formats and types, and will produce the outcomes for which the system has been designed. For example: is the quantity entered for a stock delivery > 0? Does a barcode have the correct number of characters?

2 **Live data.** Testing with normal data is not the same as testing with actual data that is within the current system. This phase of testing will still generate the same outcomes as with the normal test data, but using live data should test all eventualities that employees encounter in their daily use of the system.

3 **Extreme test data.** The system must also process data that is at the extremes of acceptable (or normal data). For example, an employee in the supermarket enters zero as the number of a product on the shelves because the product has sold out. This is extreme, but acceptable. Does the system respond as designed?

4 **Abnormal test data.** This test data is to ensure that the system rejects certain data entries, for example, a negative stock level, a price of $0.00, a barcode with the wrong number of characters. All these items of data are invalid and should be rejected.

Test plans

When testing a system, a test plan is a structured way to logically test all aspects of the design. Each test is carried out against the following criteria:

- **Test number.** 1,2,3 etc.
- **Description of test.** A simple description of what element is being tested.
- **Expected outcome.** All being well, what should happen?
- **Actual outcome.** What has actually happened?
- **Remedial action.** If the test failed, what needs to be done to rectify it?

> **Tip**
>
> There is no exact format for a test plan, or test table. Just try to ensure tests are logical and record what should, what does, and what needs to happen if a test fails.

Activity 1

The checkout receipts presented to customers contain a line of data that shows:
- the store code (four digits from 4001 to 4999)
- the checkout operator code (eight digits from 00000001 to 00009999)
- the ID code for the checkout (two digits from 01 to 30)
- transaction code (five digits 00001 to 99999).

Complete the three columns in the table below by deciding what kind of test data is being used and whether the data should be accepted or rejected. In the cases where the data is rejected provide a reason.

Store	Operator	Checkout	Transaction	Test Data	Accepted?	Data rejected because...
4394	00001424	07	08969	Normal	Yes	
1004	00001424	AB	08969			
4999	00009999	01	00001			
4455	00006565	28	10001			
4476	8766	15	09876			

What if the test data does not produce the right outcomes?

There is the possibility that the test plan could result in unexpected outcomes. Validation routines might not work correctly, but larger errors may be detected such as errors in processing the data. This may point to an error in the initial analysis.

Whatever the reasons for errors being detected, or the severity of the error, the analysts need to move back a few steps and rework the analysis and the design. They must work through the testing stage again, using the same data that caused the errors to be detected.

This cycle of testing, checking, refining, retesting, rechecking must continue until the analysts are convinced that the system will handle all data correctly and accurately.

Testing file and record structures

The analysts will have to devise a testing plan which rigorously tests each field in a record structure. Look back at the record layout for the **StudentDetails** table of the orchestra database at the beginning of Session 6.5. The start of a testing plan may look like this:

Test #	Field name	Data type	Test data	Test type	What testing	Test okay?
1	AdNo	Number	199702	Normal	Data is acceptable	Yes
2			999999	Extreme	Data is acceptable	Yes
3			19972	Abnormal	Data rejected	Yes
4			1992)2	Abnormal	Data rejected	No
5	First Name	Text	Harriet	Normal	Data accepted	Yes

This plan would need to test for all conceivable combinations of data for each field, and ensure that the test ran okay. You created a data entry form for this record structure in Session 6.7 and had some validation and data entry checks such as drop down lists attached to some fields. You would need to have checks over as many fields as possible. Remember that a visual check is a verification only and so even for fields such as the student name there needs to be at least a presence check.

A test for AdNo could be that 100000>AdNo<1000000. This would also have meant that test 4 would have passed. Maybe the programmer has only tested that there are six characters present.

Review and revise

You should now be able to:
- identify the processes of testing and analysis
- describe the need for data validation and construct a testing plan for data.

SESSION 7.4 The systems life cycle: Implementation

Implementation

When the system has been tested fully and meets Mr Grodzik's requirements, the next stage is implementation. Quality Foods should be ready to open its electronic point of sale checkouts. Implementation means that the old system is replaced by the new system.

Implementation can happen in any one of four ways:

1 **Direct changeover.** The old system shuts down and the new system is implemented immediately, without running two systems together.

2 **Parallel running.** The old and new systems run alongside each other for a set period of time.

3 **Pilot running.** The new system is used in one area of the organisation before full implementation is put in place across the organisation.

4 **Phased implementation.** There are two methods.

    a Individual modules of the system are introduced one at a time, leaving older modules running until they are replaced.

    b Some orders are processed on the new system; the rest are processed on the old system.

The choice of which type of implementation to use will depend on certain factors, for example, if:

- a quick change to the new system is needed
- any loss of data might have serious consequences
- it doesn't matter if errors in the new system are present because the old system can still be used
- time is not an issue.

Method of implementation	Advantage	Disadvantage
Direct changeover	• Benefits are available immediately. • Costs are reduced because only one system is being used.	• If the new system fails then there is the possibility of massive loss of data.
Parallel running	• If something fails in the new system, the old one is running as a backup. • Employees have time to learn how the new system works.	• There are two systems running so costs are increased.
Pilot running	• If the new system fails, only one area of the company is affected. • Costs are less than that experienced in parallel running, since only one area needs the extra attention.	• More expensive than direct changeover because there needs to be an evaluation period before moving to the next phase.
Phased implementation	• If the newly introduced module fails then there is only that area that needs attention. • Each area becomes fully functional before moving on to the next.	• More expensive than direct changeover because there needs to be an evaluation period before moving to the next phase.

As you can see, deciding which implementation method to employ is a critical decision.

Pilot running would be a good changeover method for a small business where the employees have the time available to use both systems. A restaurant owner may ask a few of its table staff to use new hand-held wireless devices to take orders while the remainder use their old-style notebooks and pens to take orders. After a suitable time period, which covers their prolonged busy times, the new system can be evaluated. If the trial was judged successful then the whole restaurant would move over to the new devices.

Activity 1

Consider the other two implementation methods: direct changeover and parallel running. Think of a situation for which these would be the most suitable method of changeover and explain why that situation is suited to this method.

Phased implementation would be preferable for a complex system. For example, your school probably has a very intricate way of collating all the information about students in the school. Aside from personal registration details there is information held about your examination entries, previous assignment scores, parental reports, detentions, credits, sports teams and so on. If your school was starting to implement a database solution to this data collection it would make sense to target one area only to get started: registrations and the setting up of tutor groups and class sets. Once that was working satisfactorily, the next phase (or module) could be recording of detentions, credits and other rewards, and memberships of teams. Later a reporting module may be added on. This continuous expansion is progressive and requires one phase to be completed before moving on to another.

Activity 2

Write a report for the systems analyst leading your team, indicating which implementation method you would recommend to the supermarket to reduce the impact of failure of the barcode scanners at the checkouts. Comment on the advantages of using this method in comparison to others.

Training

Regardless of the method of implementation that is chosen, the staff using the new system will need training and support, especially if they have never used a computerised system before. Training may involve giving staff time off to complete studies. This may disrupt the normal work patterns of the organisation. It could involve bringing 'experts' into the company to instruct the staff while they work. This would help staff to become aware of the changes in their work, allowing them to see the advantages and potential disadvantages for themselves. Some staff may find the changes too challenging and may choose to find work elsewhere. Others will enjoy working within the new system.

Some employees may find changes in their jobs (such as the checkout operators), but some employees may find that parts of their jobs disappear (such as products no longer needing individual price stickers). This does not automatically mean that their workload has been reduced. Technology also creates new jobs. Mr Grodzik will need some people to maintain the database and perhaps to develop more aspects of the system within the store. In some systems, **employment** related to hardware maintenance will also be created.

Review and revise

You should now be able to:

- describe the different models of implementations
- describe the advantages/disadvantages of each method of implementation
- identify a method of implementation for a particular situation.

The systems life cycle:
Documentation and evaluation

Background

As a system is being developed it is important that the management team and the systems analysts prepare documentation that will support the users and managers of the system. This documentation should be produced at each stage of the systems life cycle, because each stage may involve different people, and each module of the new system may have been developed by different members of the team. Detailed documentation means that everyone will know what has taken place.

Technical documentation

Technical documentation about the way the system was developed, and about the way it works, is essential for the continued maintenance and operation of the system. It will help analysts and programmers to make decisions about repairs, upgrades, updating and error checking.

This documentation includes a number of sections or reports, some short, some lengthy. They need to explain the workings of the entire system that has been created, as shown in the following table.

> **Real world**
>
> The life cycle begins with a review of existing documentation. A description of how the old system works is vital in helping to plan for future development. It allows users and managers to evaluate the impact of the system based on their experience of the system in practice.

Sections	Description/what is needed
Purpose and limitations of the system/program	A description of what the new system is designed to solve. Readers of the report need to know what the system can (and cannot) do. For example, the system will only read barcodes on products. The checkout will not weigh and price fresh fruit; this must be done elsewhere within the store, at which point a barcode is created.
Hardware and software requirements	A complete list of all the hardware used in the system, including the file storage requirements is needed.
	The software requirements will detail all the programs needed to run the system and include detail of any software that has been specifically written or amended for the system.
	The minimum system requirements must be listed, to help when buying hardware in the future.
File structure and a list of variables (field names)	The relationship between data files is very important, so a description of the use and data type of all fields in every file or data table is needed. The relationships between the tables and different files in the system are also required.
Input and output formats	Example input and output forms/displays/reports will help to illustrate how data is to be entered into the system and also how the system will present the results of processing.
Validation rules	Details of the validation routines applied to the data in the system are needed so that the analysts and programmers can test any future modifications they make to the system using appropriate normal, abnormal and extreme data.
Programming language	Any future developer will need to know the programming language used so that changes can be made successfully or problems investigated successfully.
System flowcharts/ algorithms and program listings	For every 'module' there will be a flowchart from which the program will be written. Fully annotated flowcharts and program listings will enable a developer to investigate problems and make changes quickly and easily.
Sample runs/test runs	These illustrate how the system will work with given data inputs, and the way the system responds to and processes that data.
Known bugs/*possible errors*	These must be dealt with in turn, as they appear.

Note: The documents in the table listed in *italics* could also appear in the User documentation (see page 320) but will not be included in both.

Systems flowcharts

As demonstrated in Session 7.2, flowcharts are an important method of representing the flow of data through the system.

There are five basic symbols used in a systems flowchart. They are:

In addition, organisations will have conventions about how to show on a flowchart the movement of data between other parts of the system. For example, in Session 7.2 the dotted line represents the boundary between the activity at the POS, the Stock delivery and Stock reorder parts of the system.

User documentation

While technical documentation is really useful for those who will support and maintain the system, some documentation is needed for the people who are going to use the system.

User documentation focuses on the needs of the user.

Description	Used for
Tutorials including: ● how to load/run/install software ● how to save a file ● how to print data ● how to add records ● how to delete/edit records	It is essential that help is provided for all stages. From software installation to day-to-day running of the system, everyone involved at Quality Foods needs to feel supported and know there is the support available when needed.
Error messages and error handling	Inevitably, users will come across situations that are not normal. Maybe a barcode is torn, squashed or faded and cannot be read properly or a message appears saying a new price is invalid. Users need to be told the meaning of error messages and what to do if a message appears.
Troubleshooting guide and helpline	Situations that are not common can also occur: paper gets stuck or jammed in the printer when printing a customer receipt, a barcode is scanned and the wrong description/details are retrieved. Hopefully these situations could have been foreseen by the analyst and a solution described in advance. If a completely unexpected problem appears, the user needs to know who to contact for help.
Frequently asked questions and a glossary of terms	A collection of FAQs is a popular way to foresee user questions about any aspect of the system, not just potential problems. A glossary will define the key terms that appear throughout the system, from on-screen text and button titles to error messages and software-specific terms.

Activity 1

You have been asked to contribute to the FAQ section of the user guide. Think of three more questions that might be frequently asked by the checkout operators at Quality Foods. For each, write the question and then a description that will help to solve that problem.

Evaluation

Evaluation actually takes place during each stage of the cycle, as the analyst and team work out what is required, how to solve problems and implement and test solutions. This means that each stage is evaluated as the system is developed. This could mean that work may go back a stage – or even back to the beginning. At each stage there is a measure of whether the system is developing along the required lines.

There is also a distinct evaluation stage that comes at the end of the entire development cycle. The evaluation may take place after a month, six months or some other timeframe determined by the natural business cycle of the organisation.

As with all other stages of the systems life cycle there will be a report. There are two considerations:

1 Why do we need to evaluate the new system?

Organisations need to establish how well the new system works in order to be able to report to the systems analysts. They want to know if the new system is an efficient and appropriate solution to the earlier identified problems. Do the users find the system easy to use?

2 How do we make an evaluation?

● Make a comparison between the new system and the one it has replaced. The analysts will have test results showing how the new system is performing. The aim is to decide whether the new system is performing as expected. There should be demonstrable improvement in terms of the way tasks are carried out. Is the performance more efficient?

● Once the system has been in operation for a short time period it will be possible to identify the limitations of, and quite possibly improvements to, the system. Often, new possibilities emerge that were not originally envisioned, simply because it is the new system that is opening up new possibilities. Any limitations identified might suggest that the new system is not flexible enough or that the initial design did not factor in enough adaptability.

● Equally important are the views of the users who are using the system on a day-to-day basis. Is the system easy to use? Have they identified any problems? Are they comfortable with any change in working pattern?

> **Real world**
>
> Evaluations will be a necessary part of the development cycle for any system, simple or complex, from the delivery system of a family run courier service to the introduction of a loyalty card scheme at countrywide petrol stations, from one-person businesses to government departments.

Future developments

All systems have a life span and, as mentioned at the start of Session 7.1, the evaluation stage could prompt another cycle of development. Technology is changing all the time, very rapidly. For example, how soon will it be before Mr Grodzik considers the introduction of a set of self-service checkouts? Or, having seen how successful this development has been, he may wish to expand the use of technology into other areas of the store. The whole life cycle will begin again, perhaps starting with a look at the documentation you have created during this development cycle.

Activity 2

During the course of this book you have created a number of spreadsheets and databases. Choose one of these and then write an evaluation of it. Your starting point ('terms of reference') will be the initial task outline, as either stated in the session activity, or set by your teacher. Use these headings:

● Purpose of the spreadsheet/database.

● How easy is the spreadsheet/database to use?

● Does the spreadsheet/database do everything that was requested (give a star rating)?

● Do you think that the spreadsheet/database can be improved in any way? What could be added or changed to make it better?

Activity 3

Refer back to the spreadsheet that you created in Session 5.8 for Excelsior Academy. You have been asked to put together a small user guide that can be passed on to the person who will use the spreadsheet. This only needs to be a short list of bullet points indicating how to load the spreadsheet, what cells need data (visitors, prices of drinks, the various expenses). You could also explain how, before the event, the spreadsheet could be used to calculate the prices to charge, based on expected attendance and the level of profit required.

Review and revise

You should now be able to:

● describe the structure and purpose of technical and user documentation

● produce elements of the technical and user documentation

● explain the process of evaluation

● evaluate a piece of software

● state why an evaluation triggers a need for further development.

7 Theory review

What have you covered?

In these four theory sessions you have:

- discovered the stages of the systems development life cycle
- identified and explored the stages of systems development
- outlined the fact-finding process and described advantages and disadvantages of each method
- understood the purpose of validation and verification
- identified why evaluation is important in helping to secure an effective system
- explored the different models of implementations, identifying suitable situations for each model of implementation
- described the structure and purpose of technical and user documentation.

Some practice questions

1 The systems life cycle can be described as having these stages:

(Analysis) (Evaluation) (Implementation)

(Documentation) (Design)

Put these in the order in which they would be carried out by the systems analyst.

> See Session 7.1

2 Four methods of fact finding are listed in the column on the left. Draw a line to connect each method with its correct description on the right.

Interview	Collecting a significant amount of data from a large number of people
Questionnaire	Using reports written by previous investigating teams, looking at training/instruction manuals
Observation	Having one-to-one discussions or using a focus group
Existing documentation	Watching people using the existing system to find out how it works in practice

> See Session 7.1

3 A systems analyst is designing a system to help the manager of the school kitchen. One of the important inputs to the system comes from the teachers who take morning registration each day. The kitchen manager needs to know how many students will be having a cooked meal and how many have a packed lunch. For those having a cooked meal it is important to know how many need the vegetarian option. The kitchen manager also needs to know the names of the teachers and whether they will be having a cooked lunch. The teachers will submit this information by filling in an on-screen form on the school intranet.

Design a suitable input form that the teacher can fill in.

> See Session 7.2

4 State *one* item of technical and *one* item of user documentation.

> See Session 7.5

5 Verification and validation are two processes applied to data that the system needs to use.

a   Give a one sentence description of each of these processes.

b   Give one difference between these processes.

> See Session 7.2

6 Drivers at Harriet's Parcel Service receive details of packages to deliver. The details need to be accurate so that the delivery can be made successfully. For each item of data identify a validation check that will have been applied to make sure that the data is accurate.

a Address

b Contact telephone

c Date of delivery

d Number of packets to this address.

See Session 7.2

7 A teacher has designed a spreadsheet that she uses to record the scores (as a percentage) that her students achieve in tests. After building the spreadsheet she needs to test it in order to make sure that it works as she intends it to.

She is going to enter for a student's score, some normal, abnormal and extreme data.

For each of these types of data:

a Give the data that she should enter.

b Explain what this data tests.

c Describe how the spreadsheet should respond to this data being entered.

See Session 7.3

8 Colin's Coin and Banknote Shop has just had a new computer system developed for stock control purposes. The shop is a small business, and Colin is the only person who works there. The systems analyst who has produced the system tells Colin that the new system is ready to be implemented.

a Name the best method of implementation for this system.

b Give two reasons for your answer.

See Session 7.4

Progress check

Aiming for good progress

- You can describe the different stages of the systems development life cycle.
- You can describe the different ways in which information can be collected.
- You understand the need for validation and verification, and can identify checking methods.
- You understand why evaluation is important in helping to secure an effective system.
- You can describe the different models of implementations.
- You can describe the purpose of technical and user documentation.

Aiming for an excellent progress

- You can describe the different stages of the systems development life cycle.
- You can describe the different ways in which information can be collected, and you can describe the advantages and disadvantages of each method.
- You understand the need for validation and verification, and can describe checking methods.
- You understand why evaluation is important in helping to secure an effective system.
- You can explain the way different models of implementation are applied, identifying and justifying a model of implementation for a given situation.
- You can describe the structure and purpose of technical and user documentation.

SESSION 7.6 Developing questionnaires and describing an existing system

Background

Understanding the process of systems analysis is very important, as it helps you to consolidate all that you know about the hardware, software, skills and techniques that you have developed. In this session you will consolidate and extend some of your word processing skills by creating a short questionnaire and preparing a report about the inputs, processes and outputs of an existing system.

Questionnaires

Quality Foods, the supermarket chain you have been studying as an example in the theory sessions of this unit, would like a simple short questionnaire to use to gather information from its customers about how they would feel about the introduction of an electronic point of sale (POS) system. The information they receive from the questionnaire should help them to decide whether or not they need to introduce the new system across all their stores.

The questionnaire they want you to develop needs to contain these questions:

Question	Possible answers				
1. How often do you shop at Quality Foods?	Every Day	Between two and six times a week	Once a week	Once a month	Less often
2. What is the approximate value of your normal shop?	More than $100	Between $50 and $100	Between $30 and $50	Between $10 and $30	Less than $10
3. What length of time in the checkout queue is acceptable to you?	More than five minutes	Around four minutes	Around three minutes	Around two minutes	Around one minute
4. We are thinking about introducing scanners at the checkout to speed up the checkout process. Are you in favour of the introduction of barcode scanners at the checkout?	Yes		No		No opinion/ Unsure
5. What can we do to improve your shopping experience at Quality Foods?					

Activity 1

Prepare the questionnaire and include the five questions above.

1   Set your page orientation to landscape.

2   Ensure that the questionnaire fits on one page.

3   Include the name of the supermarket in the header: sans-serif font, size 24 point, centred.

4   Include your name on the left-hand side of the footer and the filename and date on the right-hand side of the footer: sans-serif font, size 10 point.

5   At the top of the questionnaire include the following text:

For questions 1–4 place a tick or cross next to the answer that best fits your response. (serif font, size 14 point, colour red, centred)

6   Think carefully about the layout of the questionnaire – leave plenty of white space.

7   Choose a suitable serif font – size 11 point, colour black.

8   If you choose to use a table to lay out the questionnaire, ensure that there are no borders around the text. Only have borders where the customers will make responses.

9 The first four questions require only a tick.

10 The questionnaire will be filled in by hand – make sure there is enough space for the customers to enter their response to the final question.

11 At the bottom of the questionnaire include the following text:

Quality Foods would like to thank you for your participation in this survey. Please place your completed questionnaire in the box at the entrance of the store. (serif font, size 14 point, colour red, centred)

An example of a questionnaire is shown here.

- Notice the response boxes.
- Notice also that each question is numbered and that there is white space around each question.
- The text next to some of the response boxes has been right aligned to draw the customer's eye to the box.
- This questionnaire could have been developed in a table with only certain cells bordered, or with text and text boxes.

12 Save and print your questionnaire following the normal naming conventions, version 1.

It would probably be useful to add two more questions to the questionnaire.

13 Add a question: **What age range do you fall into?**

14 Make the responses: **Under 25, 25 to 34, 35 to 44, 45 to 54, 55 and over**

15 Add a question about gender.

16 Save and print your questionnaire following the normal naming conventions, version 2.

Preparing a report

Reports are useful business documents that present information in a structured and accessible format. For the purposes of the next activity you need to produce a report about the inputs, processes and outputs of the current checkout system at Quality Foods.

1 Open the systems analyst's notes in your word processing package (it can be found on the digital download – **SystemAnalystNotes.rtf**) and highlight the inputs, processes and outputs in the text by using the highlighting function.

   a Highlight the text – then press the highlight button. Choose a different colour for inputs (cyan), processes (magenta) and outputs (yellow). This will allow you to begin to group the inputs, processes and outputs together and create your report. The last paragraph might look like this:

If there are more customers the transaction process begins again. If it is the end of the day, or the end of the checkout operator's working time, the checkout operator presses a 'Total transactions' key on the checkout. This calculates the takings for the day – a printout is made. The cash from the checkout is taken with the printout to the cash office where the money is checked to ensure that it matches the total of the transactions on the printout.

  b Header: **Inputs, Processes and Outputs from Current System** – sans-serif font, 12 point.

  c Footer: Your name on the left, page number in the centre, date on the right – sans-serif font, 10 point.

  d Paragraph one heading: **Purpose** – sans-serif font, 14 point, bold.

  e All body text – sans-serif font, 12 point.

  f Paragraph two heading: **Inputs** – same format as paragraph one heading.

  g Paragraph three heading: **Processes** – same format as paragraph one heading.

  h Paragraph four heading: **Outputs** – same format as paragraph one heading.

2 When you have completed your report, save it as you usually do and print a copy.

3 Email the report as an attachment to your teacher. Use Cc to copy yourself into the email.

Review and revise

You should now be able to:

- develop resources to research a situation
- collect information about a current system
- create and open documents using information from different sources
- enter and edit text
- place and manipulate different forms of information
- format the page layout to meet requirements
- appropriately use headers and footers
- ensure the consistency of page layout
- create and format a table
- send and receive documents and other files electronically.

SESSION 7.7 Designing data capture forms and reports

Background

Systems design is an important stage in the cycle of systems development. The information that is gathered during the systems investigation will have identified the things that need to change in the new system. You know already that the design team must design the inputs and outputs of the new system, which is the purpose of this session.

Quality Foods

You are going to look again at the example of Quality Foods. You have already identified the inputs, outputs and processes. There are three outputs from the system.

1. Display Price	Price is shown on the checkout for the operator and on a small display screen for the customer	Needs to contain only the name of the item and the price
2. Message to shop floor staff	Short text message showing name of product, location in store, number to put on display	Showing name of product, location in store, number to put on display
3. Print receipt	Checkout receipt: 8 cm wide, length depends on the number of items sold	Needs to show a store logo, the address details of the store, the name of the item, the barcode details, the price; the total should be shown, together with any payment details and change given

Activity 1

The customer display screen is 10 cm by 3 cm.

1   Design an appropriate customer display using a text box in your word processing software. You need to show the name of the product (maximum of 12 characters) and the price (maximum of seven characters including the currency symbol and the decimal point). The characters should be:

- sans-serif
- large enough to read
- all upper case
- fit into the text box
- the name should be to the left of the screen
- the price should be to the right of the screen

2   Test your design using these product details:

Product	Price
Black-eyed peas	75 cents
Pasta sauce	$1.99
48 pack cola	$10.99

3   Save your work as usual. Print a copy for your file.

Examples

A customer buys a pack of cherry tomatoes at a price of 87 cents. The display would show:

CHERRY TOMS	$0.87

The customer also buys a multi-pack of tinned tuna for $4.00. The display would show:

TUNA	$4.00

Checking the size of a text box

As you draw a text box in your word processing package you could:

Right click on the text box and select: **More Layout Options ...** or **Format Text Box ...** Select the **Size Tab**.

Enter the sizes: height = 3 cm, width = 10 cm.

Click **OK**.

Activity 2

Design a text message for the shop floor workers. Their hand-held displays are 5 cm wide and 1 cm high. They show one line of text, sans-serif, 14 point.

- The name of the product is restricted to seven characters.
- The location is made up of six characters:
  A = short for aisle followed by the aisle number (up to nine)
  B = short for bay followed by the bay number (up to nine)
  S = short for shelf followed by the shelf number.
- The number of items to be placed on the shelves (maximum 48).

Test your design using these details:

Product	Location	Items
Baked beans	Aisle five, Bay seven, Shelf eight	48
Tiger cat food foil tray	Aisle nine, Bay one, Shelf one	24
English muffins	Aisle one, Bay two, Shelf three	48

Developing your text message

You could develop your text message using your spreadsheet program. This will enable you to validate the message details.

- Put the name of the product in one cell so that the text can be checked to see if it is between one and 12 characters in length.

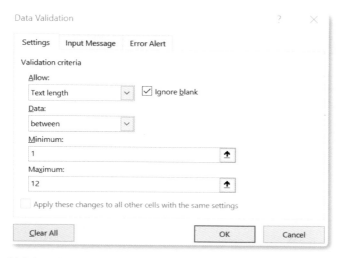

- Validate the number of items by checking that the number is equal to or less than 48.
- Have separate cells for Aisle, Bay, and Shelf and validate the number so that it is between one and nine.
- Consider an appropriate error alert to give the operator a clue about the acceptable range (up to 12 characters, for example).
- Your spreadsheet may look like this.

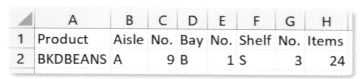

	A	B	C	D	E	F	G	H
1	Product	Aisle	No.	Bay	No.	Shelf	No.	Items
2	BKDBEANS	A	9	B	1	S	3	24

> ### Tip
> It is useful to practise adding validation settings to cells within this session so that you can see the practical application of validation that you have read about in Session 7.3.

- You should test that your validation works and use print screen to copy and paste the image of your error messages into a text document.
- Save and print your spreadsheet and your text files.

Activity 3

While producing a checkout receipt that will calculate the total cost of items, you could use a spreadsheet program to develop the design. In order to prepare your receipt you should:

1 Source or develop a logo for Quality Foods Supermarkets.
2 Use your town/village as the location of the store.
3 Use your name as the manager.

continued

Session 7.7 Designing data capture forms and reports

PRACTICAL

See from this sample design where cells have been merged. Cells A1 to I4 have been merged for the receipt heading. Cells A5 to I5 contain **QUALITY FOODS SUPERMARKET**. Cells A10 to C10 contain **CAULIFLOWER** and other items. Cells D10 to H10 contain the barcode for the product. Cells A16 to H16 have been merged.

4 Design an appropriate layout for a receipt.

5 Ensure that it is no more than 8 cm wide when printed.

6 You will need to vary the size of your font to ensure that all the data can be shown.

7 Your font should be sans-serif.

Entering numbers as text

You may find that if you enter the barcode as 000002108436 that the spreadsheet program automatically strips out the leading zeroes. You can force the spreadsheet program to look at the data as text by putting a single apostrophe in front of the first 0 ('00001424).

When you have finished your design, test it with the following data:

Product	Barcode	Price
PITTA BREAD	505244900213	$0.25
COFFEE	505085453605	$2.28
PASTA SAUCE	000002108436	$0.17
BUTTER	503658920001	$1.15
CANNED FRUIT	505141314362	$0.35

Save and print your spreadsheet.

Email a copy to your teacher and Bcc yourself as a recipient to the message.

Review and revise

You should now be able to:
- design an appropriate customer display using a text box
- check the size of a text box
- design and develop a message for shop floor workers
- design validation routines
- produce a checkout receipt
- design data capture forms and screen layouts
- design reports layouts and screen displays.

SESSION 7.8 Developing and interpreting a model

Background

Data models allow us to explore different ways to solve data problems. Data models should always be accurate and tested to ensure that the inputs, processes and outputs are correct. The analysts developing the system for Quality Foods wanted to create a model to show the number of customers coming though the store doors and how queues and waiting times are affected. During this session you will create a spreadsheet model, practise and develop skills that have already been introduced, but you will put them to use in a modelling exercise.

Building a model

Locate the file **CheckoutQueue.csv** in the digital download and open it with your spreadsheet software.

You should see a list of headings in column A and across row 1 a set of timings, 15 minutes apart. Adjust the widths of the columns so that all the labels can be read properly. It should look like this:

	A	B	C	D	E	F	G	H	I	J	K	L	M	N
1	Time		09.00-09.15	09:30	09:45	10:00	10:15	10:30	10:45	11:00	11:15	11:30	11:45	12:00
2	New customers to checkout													
3	Waiting from previous 15 mins													
4	Total customers waiting now													
5	Time required (mins)													
6	Checkouts needed													
7	Checkouts in use													
8	Time available (mins)													
9	Customers completed													
10	Customers waiting													
11	% waiting to next 15 minutes													
12														
13														
14	Time per customer		minutes											
15	Total checkouts													

The Labels in row 1 indicate 15-minute intervals from 9 a.m. (column C) until 12 midday (column N). Column A contains the labels to indicate information that is helpful in determining the length of queues and the number of checkouts that are being used.

To begin with, you will create a model based on what is happening now. Once you are satisfied that this model works, you will make adjustments so that you can see how the number of checkouts, the queue length and customer transaction times can change.

Before the analysts started their investigation Mr Grodzik was asked to collect numbers of people moving through the store and arriving at the checkouts at intervals of 15 minutes. He did this over a period of 10 days and came up with these average figures:

Time interval	09:00–09:15	09:30	09:45	10:00	10:15	10:30	10:45	11:00	11:15	11:30	11:45	12:00
Customers	75	90	100	100	115	115	120	120	125	100	100	120

Start typing in these figures from cell C2 across row 2. Save the spreadsheet with your own filename.

In the store there are 22 checkouts and while doing their investigations, the analysts observed that on average it took three minutes for a customer to pass through the checkout. In cell B14, type **3**; in cell B15, type **22**.

When the store opens at 9 a.m. there are no customers waiting from the previous 15-minute period, so into C3, type **0**.

Rounding

Rounding off a decimal is a technique used when limiting the number of decimal places to be displayed rather than having a long string of decimal places, or even one that goes on forever. Rounding off data in a calculation is also important, but remember that it can introduce an element of error, as you lose precision.

The three rounding functions should be used carefully and their effects fully considered.

This table indicates the use of the functions and their effects. The syntax is to round the original value to a number of decimal places – in this case to one decimal place.

Original	=ROUND(Original,1)	=ROUNDDOWN(Original,1)	=ROUNDUP(Original,1)
1.10	1.1	1.1	1.1
1.11	1.1	1.1	1.2
1.12	1.1	1.1	1.2
1.13	1.1	1.1	1.2
1.14	1.1	1.1	1.2
1.15	1.2	1.1	1.2
1.16	1.2	1.1	1.2
1.17	1.2	1.1	1.2
1.18	1.2	1.1	1.2
1.19	1.2	1.1	1.2

=ROUND has the kind of effect that we might consider as 'normal'. Mentally, we round things to the nearest value, $ or km or hour, so the effect of this function is easy to see.

=ROUNDDOWN and =ROUNDUP adjusts a value down or up as needed, irrespective of the place value being considered. Some examples:

How many vans are needed to deliver 83 packages if each van can carry 20 packages? ROUND and ROUNDDOWN (and INT) would say four, but you still need a van for the remaining three packages, so ROUNDUP would be used – returning an answer of five.

A shopkeeper is working out the amount of tax to add to a product's price. The tax amount should be the nearest cent below the calculated answer and ROUNDDOWN will be used. A $123.00 product taxed at 17.5 per cent would have $21.52 added to the price (actual calculated amount $21.525).

Activity 1

You are going to enter functions or formulae into five cells in column C, based on the following descriptions:

1   Cell C4 represents the total number of customers now waiting at the checkout – the new customers (C2) and those waiting from the previous 15 minutes (C3). Type a formula into cell C4 that will add these two cells together.

2   Cell C5 will display the total time needed for the customers in C4 to pass through the checkouts. This will be found by multiplying the customers in cell C4 by the average time to serve one customer (B14). Type in a formula that makes this calculation. Use an absolute cell reference for the average time.

3   C6 will tell you how many checkouts are needed. This is found by taking the people waiting (C4) and dividing by the customers that can be fitted into 15 minutes (15/B14). You also need to consider rounding. Type this into C6:

=ROUNDUP(C4/(15/$B$14),0)

4   Cell C8 is going to indicate how much time is available across all the available checkouts. This calculation will be the total checkouts (B15) multiplied by 15 (the number of minutes in the interval). Enter a formula into cell C8 that will achieve this. Use an absolute cell reference for the number of checkouts.

5 Cell C9 will indicate how many customers the checkout operators were actually able to deal with.

- If the value in cell C8 is greater than the value in cell C5, then the number of customers in cell C4 should be displayed.
- If not, then the number of customers dealt with is found by dividing the available time (C8) by the average time per customer (B14). Use an absolute cell reference for the average time.

Use an IF function in cell C9 to represent this decision.

6 Cell C10 displays the number of customers that could not pass through the checkout and are waiting into the next 15-minute interval. This will be the number of customers waiting (C4) minus the number that did pass through (C9). Type in the formula to achieve this calculation.

When you have completed these successfully, the spreadsheet will contain these values in columns B and C:

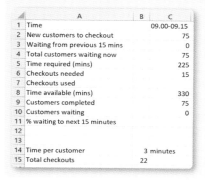

	A	B	C
1	Time		09.00-09.15
2	New customers to checkout		75
3	Waiting from previous 15 mins		0
4	Total customers waiting now		75
5	Time required (mins)		225
6	Checkouts needed		15
7	Checkouts used		
8	Time available (mins)		330
9	Customers completed		75
10	Customers waiting		0
11	% waiting to next 15 minutes		
12			
13			
14	Time per customer	3 minutes	
15	Total checkouts	22	

Checkouts in use

Cell C7 needs to contain a formula that works out how many checkouts will be in use in order to deal with the customers waiting – up to the maximum number of checkouts indicated in cell B14. If the number of customers exceeds the total that can be dealt with – that is, when a queue starts to develop – customers find themselves waiting into the next 15-minute interval.

Type this formula into cell C7:

=IF(C6>$B$15,$B$15,C6)

This breaks down into:

If the number of checkouts needed is greater than the maximum available, then display the maximum, otherwise display the number of checkouts needed. If you have typed this correctly you should have the value 15 displayed in cell C7.

Does this model work so far?

The accuracy of the model needs to be checked. If you have 75 customers, can they all pass through the checkout in the 15 minutes (cell C10 indicates no one is waiting)? And will only 15 of the 22 checkouts be needed to achieve this (cell C7)?

Each checkout operator will be able to deal with five customers in the 15-minute interval (15 minutes divided by a three-minute average). If there are 75 customers, divided by five customers per checkout; it gives an answer of 15 checkouts.

Activity 2

1 Change the Time per customer in B14 to four minutes. Remember to press Enter or move the cursor to another cell so that the value takes effect. Are all the customers dealt with? How many checkouts are needed?

2 Change the Time per customer to five minutes. All 22 checkouts are used and nine customers are waiting to the next time interval. Is the model working correctly? Can you work out how many checkouts would be needed for all these customers to be dealt with?

3 Change the Time per customer back to three minutes. Save the spreadsheet.

Completing the model

Cell C11 indicates what percentage of the customers who are at the checkout have to wait in the next time interval before being checked out. Type into C11: =INT(C10/C4*100)

Cell D3 needs to show the customers from the previous 15 minutes, those in cell C10. In cell D3 type in: =C10

Replicate the reference in cell D3 into the cells E3 to N3.

Replicate all the functions and formulae in cells C4 to C11 into columns D to N so that the complete set of information is calculated for all the time intervals.

Save the spreadsheet.

Interpreting the information in the model

Having replicated all the functions and formulae across all the time intervals, you should have noticed something quite dramatic. Everything progresses well for the first hour and then queues start to build so that by 11:15 a.m. 29 per cent of the customers arriving at the checkout have to wait into the next 15-minute time interval before being dealt with. It seems also that the queue, once it has developed never goes away; it shrinks a little – down to 18 per cent at 11:45 a.m. – but then grows again. From 10:15 a.m. all the checkout operators are working non-stop but are not coping with the volume of customers.

For Quality Foods this is an unacceptable situation and one that prompted Mr Grodzik to launch the investigation. He felt that he might lose customers who were not prepared to wait.

Activity 3

Change the value in B15 to find out how many more checkouts need to be available so that there is never a queue. With this new number of checkouts, how many of the 12 time intervals would actually require all of them to be operated?

You should have noticed that when you use two more checkouts (total 24) you have a small queue of five people at 11:15 a.m. but that the queue disappears after that. Mr Grodzik would have to buy two new checkouts and employ two new checkout operators. This might be a relatively small cost but these checkouts are only used for four of the 12 time intervals.

If three new checkouts are employed (total 25), all queuing disappears but that checkout is only used for 15 minutes of the whole morning.

Mr Grodzik may be of the opinion that a queue of five people for 15 minutes is acceptable if he can save on one checkout and operator.

Employing new technology at the checkout

Mr Grodzik's idea was that the introduction of scanners at the checkout would also improve the store's stock control. Scanners will also mean that customers will be able to move through the checkouts quicker.

Knowing that the spreadsheet models the movement of customers through the checkouts accurately, you can use it to investigate what could be possible if scanners were used.

The analysts predict that customers could now pass through the checkout in two minutes.

Change the value in B14 to reflect this, with B15 set to 22 again.

Activity 4

Reduce the number of checkouts now until you find the lowest level where there are no queues developing. How many do you need?

Reduce employment or increase custom?

Discovering that the number of checkouts can be reduced (in this case by five) can be an uncomfortable position to be in. It might immediately signal to Mr Grodzik (and the checkout operators) that he can cut the number of staff he needs. This is only one way of interpreting the information that the model is presenting.

What about using the same number of checkout operators and increasing the number of customers in the store? New technology does not only mean cutting costs – it also improves efficiency and productivity.

Set the number of checkouts back to 22, with two minutes as the average time.

Now look at increasing customer levels to predict how many more can pass though the checkouts before queues start developing again.

To help you change the customer numbers easily it is a good idea to add a new element to the spreadsheet – a kind of customer calculator.

- In cell A17 type a label: **% increase in customers**.
- In cell A18 type a label: **Multiplier**.
- In cell B17 type: **1**.
- In cell B18 type: +1+B17/100.
- Format cell B18 to have two decimal places.
- In cell C2, where there were 75 customers, type: =ROUNDUP((75*$B$18),0).
  The value in C2 should be 76
- Now type 10 into cell B17, the value in cell C2 should change to 83 because you have asked for an increase of 10 per cent over the original value of 75.
- Replicate the function in cell C2 across row 2, remembering to edit the number value so that it remains the same as it did originally. Cell D2 should display 99.

1 Save the spreadsheet.

2 Now that you have created an increase of 10 per cent in customers for the whole morning are there any queues developing?

3 Keep on increasing the value in B17 until you arrive at the percentage increase just below that which causes queues to develop.

Recommendations for Mr Grodzik

It is not the job of the analysts to tell Mr Grodzik exactly what to do in situations such as this. The analysts present their findings and make recommendations.

You have seen that with the current system:

- There is an unacceptable level of queuing by customers as the morning develops.
- It would be necessary to open two new checkouts to eliminate these queues.
- There is a cost associated with opening two new checkouts (equipment and operators).
- The three new checkouts are only needed for 50 per cent of the time.

If new scanners were used:

- The number of checkouts needed so that the current customers can pass through without queues drops to 17.
- The level of customers that could pass though the current number of checkouts increases by 32 per cent.

Mr Grodzik will choose the new scanners – that was the plan. He now has to decide how to use his employees. He will want to increase the number of customers but maybe not have as many checkouts. Releasing employees from the checkouts means that they could be used for other purposes:

- There could be openings for a new IT department, or at least working with software development.
- If the number of customers increases, it will result in more sales. This might lead to a need for more people involved in the reordering and stores side of the organisation.
- Perhaps Mr Grodzik could offer a completely new service, home deliveries, for example.

Review and revise

You should now be able to:

- develop/build a model which simulates a real life situation, using a spreadsheet
- understand that changing variables in the model changes predicted outcomes
- realise the need for the accuracy of formulae and functions
- have an understanding of the need to carefully interpret the information the model presents
- realise that the analyst's job is to present and recommend a solution, it is the client who makes the decision to proceed with it.

7 Practical review

What have you covered?

In the three practical sessions for document production you have:

- practised skills introduced in Units 1 and 3
- developed resources to research a situation
- collected information about a current system
- placed and manipulated different forms of information.

In the two practical sessions, using spreadsheets, you have:

- practised skills introduced in Units 3 and 6
- devised appropriate testing strategies
- added validation checks to a cell
- changed the display and format of cells within a spreadsheet
- imported, placed and manipulated images and different forms of information from an external source
- applied some evaluation strategies.

Some practice questions

You work for a company that delivers products ordered via the internet. In the coming year, the company must face a potential problem. Will its delivery vans be able to deliver all the orders it receives or will the director need to buy another van? The outline of the company's problem and details of the orders it is dealing with can be found in **HarrietParcel.rtf**, which is on the digital download, along with **HarrietParcel.csv**, which covers the beginnings of the delivery model.

1. Using a suitable software package, load the file **HarrietParcel.csv**.

2. Adjust the column widths so that all the data labels are visible.

3. Place the current delivery figures for Monday to Friday found in **HarrietParcel.rtf** in cells B3 to F3. Copy these figures into the second week, cells G3 to K3.

4. In cell B12, create a formula that multiplies the contents of cells B10 and B11.

5. In cell B4, you are going to work out how many deliveries have been made on Monday. Use a function that will display the deliveries according to this criteria:
   - If the sum of cells B2 and B3 is greater than the content of cell B12, display the content of cell B12.
   - If the sum of B2 and B3 is not greater than the content of B12, display the sum of cells B2 and B3.

Use relative cell referencing and absolute cell referencing.

6. In cell B5, create a formula that calculates the contents of cells B2 plus B3 less B4.

7. In cell B8, you are going to use a function to work out what per cent of next-day deliveries was achieved.

   If the content of B5 is greater than 0, then display the sum of cells B3 less B5 as a percentage of B3, otherwise display 100.

8. In cell B7 you are going to use a function to work out what percentage of deliveries has been made by the second day. If the content of B4 is greater than or equal to the content of cell B2 then display 100, otherwise display cell B4 as a percentage of B2.

9. Replicate the formulae/functions you have created in steps 5 to 8 across to column K so that you have figures showing the number and per cent of deliveries made for the full two-week period.

10. In cell C2, place a relative reference to Monday's deliveries that were not done and replicate this reference across to cell K2.

11. Copy the entire contents of cells A1 to K12 and paste them into cells A15 to K26.

12. Place the value 170 in cell B16.

13 Change the formula in cell B18 to reference B26, and not B12, and replicate this new formula across cells C18 to K18.

14 Change the contents of cells B17 to K17 so that they have the projected daily figures that Harriet has provided.

15 Save the spreadsheet model as **HarrietParcelProjected**.

16 Use the projected part of the spreadsheet model to answer these questions:

   a Is Harriet still able to maintain a 100 per cent delivery rate for within two working days?

   b Is Harriet still able to maintain a 90 per cent delivery rate for the next working day?

   c If Harriet chooses to stay with a maximum of 40 deliveries for each van, how many extra vans does she need to buy so that her target of 90 per cent delivery for the next working day is achieved?

   d If Harriet decides not to buy any more vans and to stay with the 24 she has, how many extra daily deliveries will each van need to make to achieve the 90 per cent next-day target?

17 Consider the pattern of deliveries not done, the likely costs of buying a new van and of paying her drivers for extra deliveries.

18 What **advice** would you offer Harriet?

Progress check

Aiming for good progress

- You can create a layout for a spreadsheet model.
- You can edit, copy and paste values in a spreadsheet.
- You can create, copy and replicate formulae and functions in a spreadsheet.
- You can adjust values in a spreadsheet model in order to arrive at a specific outcome.

Aiming for excellent progress

- You can create a layout for a spreadsheet model.
- You can edit, copy and paste values in a spreadsheet.
- You can create, edit, copy and replicate formulae and functions in a spreadsheet.
- You can adjust values in a spreadsheet model in order to arrive at a specific outcome.
- You can suggest answers to What if? questions, based on the outcomes a model presents.
- You can give reasons, or justify a position, for a suggested answer to What if? questions.

8 Safety and security

Why this unit matters

The advent of the internet and connected devices means we are not only using and connecting with technology personal to us, but also to systems around the world with limitless boundaries.

Along with the many benefits come potential dangers and the most important defence is knowledge and understanding. Only by knowing the potential physical risks, how we should protect our personal information, and the ways internet-based systems process it, can we ensure we receive the benefits and avoid the dangers.

I love online gaming; I play action games on my PC and strategy games on my tablet. My favourite games are the kind where I can compete against other children my age and chat to them in the vast online worlds we build. We had a talk at school about the fact that my friends online might not actually be my own age. Is this true and should I be concerned?

I've just started a great new job in the city. It's office based using lots of computer equipment. I've just been told I have to complete a health and safety training course next week before I start work. I use computers at home all the time, so how can there be so many dangers?

We use email almost every day, contacting our friends and family all around the world. A friend also recommended an online shopping site and I've signed up for regular emails containing the latest offers. Recently though I'm getting more and more emails from people and organisations with email attachments. What's the best way to deal with them and what are the risks?

Your practical task

You have applied for a new job at a large security firm. Peak Security advises new businesses how to protect the information they process and also how to keep their employees safe in the workplace. As part of the application process you have been asked to write a report in response to a hypothesis. The organisation uses this report to help judge how knowledgeable potential employees are in an ever-changing business. The hypothesis is: The dangers of using technology and online systems clearly outweigh the benefits.

What this unit covers

THEORY

Sessions

8.1   Physical safety in an ICT-based environment

8.2   eSafety

8.3   The security of personal and commercial data

Theory review

PRACTICAL

Sessions

8.4   Producing a word processed report in response to a hypothesis

Practical review

By the end of the theory sessions you will be able to:

- describe the potential physical safety risks to those using computer equipment
- identify the potential security risks of sharing personal information online
- describe how our internet browsing habits have changed and how we can protect ourselves online
- describe strategies to minimise the potential risks when using email, including spam and email attachments
- describe our use of social networking, online shopping and gaming and identify the potential dangers
- describe how secure websites keep data secure on their own networks and cloud-based data
- define the term hacking and describe the risks associated with it
- describe how computer viruses are transmitted and identify the risks to individuals and networks
- summarise continuing developments in computer security methods.

In the practical sessions you will develop and apply skills in:

- writing longer responses to a given question or hypothesis
- word processing
- using document production skills to create a professional looking report.

Physical safety in an ICT-based environment

Background

Many countries have regulations that support and encourage the safe use of computer systems. These regulations often include advice about safety risks and methods of prevention. During this session you will look at the common problems and injuries associated with poor ICT working conditions and how they can be reduced or eliminated. This knowledge will also allow you to evaluate your own use of IT equipment.

Potential safety risks, their causes and strategies to prevent them

Safety risk	Prevention strategies
Possible electrocution from spilling drinks near electrical equipment or touching live cables	• Do not allow food and drink near computers. • Use a residual **circuit breaker** to prevent overload and to cut the power supply in the event of an accident or electrical fault. • Ensure that plugs are wired safely and that cables are fully sheathed (with no bare wires showing at all). • Ensure that there is an approved fire extinguisher (CO_2 or dry/fine powder-based): a water-based fire extinguisher could cause electrocution.
Overloaded sockets that can cause fires	• Check ventilation so that equipment cannot overheat. • Do not overload power sockets with too many devices that require more electrical current than the socket is designed for. • Reduce voltage requirements – LCD screens, for example, use less electrical power than CRT monitors.
Fires or personal physical damage due to overheating equipment	• Ensure the room is properly ventilated. • Avoid over-charging portable computers. • Avoid resting computers on your legs for too long.
Tripping or falling due to trailing cables	• Use cable ducts or clips to keep wires together safely. • Tuck wires behind desks or other furniture to keep them out of the way. • Use wireless connections when possible to remove the need for wires altogether.
Physical injury from poorly placed and unstable equipment	• Heavy equipment should be placed on stable, strong desks, tables or shelving units. • Ensure that there is enough space on desks, tables and shelves for the equipment to be placed there. • Do not put equipment in places where it could be pushed or fall off, for example, on the edge of a desk, table or shelf.

Activity 1

Look at the photograph and identify the safety issues that need to be resolved.

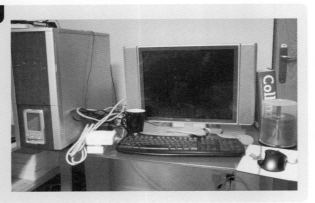

Real world

Every organisation should have a specific member of staff trained to deliver training and inform employees of potential dangers in their place of work. They will often work with a government organisation which provides support and information, such as the Health and Safety Executive in the UK.

Activity 2

How will the risks described in this session vary in different situations? Consider the following organisations and the computer equipment they use. Outline the common potential dangers and those particular to them:

- an office
- a hospital
- a library.

Activity 3

Your school will have a set of health and safety rules in relation to IT equipment. Try to find out the following:

- your designated safety officer
- the official guidance provided by the government in your region
- any rules specific to your school and its computer equipment.

Activity 4

Evaluate your own use of ICT equipment in your school and at home. For each use, describe the following:

- the potential risks
- what strategies you should employ to avoid dangers.

Review and revise

You should now be able to:

- describe the potential safety dangers in a range of environments including your own
- suggest strategies to prevent the issues described in this session
- evaluate your own use of IT equipment to minimise potential risks.

SESSION 8.2 eSafety

Background

In this session you will consider the potential dangers to our personal data when using internet based systems. This is often referred to as **eSafety** and as you will discover, it is not simply a **virtual** problem that only exists online. Many of the topics in this session relate to protecting our private data, make sure to refer to Session 4.7 that discusses data protection and the need for legislation.

The need for eSafety has arisen to meet the need of new internet users, both young and old, concerned about the level of information they share online, and the increase in criminal and inappropriate behaviour shown where people socialise online. You will consider what we judge to be personal information and how potential dangers can be spotted and averted in the following areas:

- internet browsing
- using email
- social networking
- online gaming.

Personal data

From internet shopping to chatting to friends, role-playing games to organising a new passport; you share almost every aspect of your lives online. Any piece of information unique to you and the things you do is personal data and you should protect it in the same way you protect a wallet or purse. Such personal information should be kept private and confidential and may include:

- your place and date of birth
- family names and maiden names
- home addresses and telephone numbers
- government issued social security or national insurance numbers
- medical history
- your social calendar.

> ### Activity 1
>
> Investigate the following situations where you would need to sign up for an account. List as many pieces of data as you can that might be asked for:
> - signing up for online 3D gaming world
> - applying for a driving licence
> - joining a gym or sports centre.

Much of this information is the same that any organisation would require to create a bank or online shopping account, start a new job or request a passport. If shared, the data listed could be used to illegally do any of these things in your name and potentially commit a crime in your name.

As an adult, many websites require you to enter personal data in order to use a service, and judging the security level of such sites is covered in the next section. Children though, should be particularly careful about the data they share online; in addition to the applicable items already discussed the following should be kept confidential:

- school locations and travel routines
- photographs, including those showing school uniforms
- favourite places to play with friends
- family circumstances
- holiday details or locations.

> ### Tip
>
> As children we try to tell the truth at all times, but in the case of social networks and young adults it is recommended that you avoid using any personal information. Create a full alternate version of yourself, an **avatar** as it were.

Having access to this sort of information can, in the hands of a **cyberbully**, lead to online abuse and in the worst circumstances physical danger as a child's location can be found out.

Think about all the online systems you may sign up to during your life.
- Which ones must you tell the truth in order for the application to be successful?
- Which ones shouldn't you take too seriously and use non-personal data?

Internet browsing

Remember, the internet as a general rule is not regulated and it is possible for anyone to create a website on any topic. Young learners in particular, when surfing the internet, should put the following advice into practice:
- Your teacher will recommend lots of websites and they will check them first to make sure they are suitable. They are also a good source of advice if you are unsure about a website you have discovered.
- Family friendly **software filters** can be installed at school and at home, which will filter inappropriate material.
- Government sites are a trusted starting point; sites they recommend should be OK but always check.
- Make sure you talk about your browsing habits with a parent or guardian.
- Your internet browser can be set up to block certain sites or web domains.
- Make sure the safe-search option is turned on within search engines and streaming services.
- Think really carefully about your search keywords as many words can have two meanings.
- Inappropriate sites can be reported to your **ISP** and possibly removed, so pass any concerns on to a parent or teacher.
- If a website asks you to confirm your age, that means it contains age-appropriate content and shouldn't be accessed if you are underage.

1 Evaluate your own web surfing habits out of the classroom. Is there anything you should now be doing that you didn't do before?
2 Conduct a survey of your class, and wider if possible, to see how many students already follow the advice listed and see if they offer any additional tips of their own.

Using email

Many of the problems of traditional paper mail: unsolicited '**junk**' mail and fraudulent letters relating to banking opportunities, have continued with email. Steps can and should be taken to minimise the risks:
- Update your **contact list** to ensure you are receiving mail from known addresses.
- Never open mail from an unknown source, even if they claim to be a long lost friend.
- Never email personal data; it could be **intercepted**.
- Always be wary of email attachments, unless you are expecting it from a known contact.
- Always scan attachments before downloading and opening.
- Avoid having the preview window turned on within your email software, this means you can delete messages without having to read them first.
- Unsolicited requests for money or financial information must always be deleted.
- If in doubt, delete any message and contact the sender directly, it can always be sent again if it is important.

Spam messages

Spam is junk mail that you didn't ask for that fills your email inbox. Opening a spam email and following a link could infect your computer with a virus or confirm your address to the spammer. The idea behind spam is that by flooding the internet with so many emails; only a very small percentage of readers have to be misled into following the link, download an attachment or respond to a request for information, in order for it to become profitable. One of the most effective ways to block spam email messages is through education. If we know what to look for, we can quickly spot a spam message, report it and delete it.

1   Investigate some of the most common email scams of recent times and try and categorise them into groups.

2   If we are all aware of the risks, why do emails still cause so many problems for users?

Social networking

To many, social networking leads the way in how the internet is interacting with our social and professional lives. Here are just a few of the many ways they are used today:

- personal communication
- sharing events with friends and family
- trying to meet new people with similar interests
- gaming
- sharing photography, music, art and video
- local and international news
- citizen journalism
- product and service marketing
- following public figures, celebrities and cultural events.

The potential dangers of social networking are very similar to those discussed so far; not sharing personal information, avoiding unfamiliar links and downloads and making sure parents are aware of your activities online. The majority of the potential risks arise when making new friends anywhere in the world that you will have never met and therefore cannot be sure of their **profile**.

As a class discussion with your teacher, discuss which of the potential social networking dangers you were aware of and how much of the advice given, you follow. It would also be wise to have the same discussion at home with your family.

Online gaming

The popularity of computer and console games has exploded in the last few years with the introduction of online multiplayer gaming. Personal, financial or confidential data should never be shared and real names should not be used. In a make-believe world of dragons and robots there is no need to share real data. A popular addition to online gaming is VoIP, discussed in Unit 4; this allows gamers to chat to each other whilst playing. This system is totally unregulated though, and users should be aware that some users simply use the feature to shout verbal abuse at other players.

Prevention strategies

The following strategies apply to any internet-based platform including social networking, gaming, using email and website browsing.

Potential Danger	Useful strategies
● Unwanted contact from another social network user	● Block their username from your contact or friend list. Most reputable social networks have this function. ● Report them to the owners of the network or website used.
● Reading unsuitable and adult language	● Always take part in groups, discussion and online activities designed for your own age group. ● Avoid unmoderated forums, these allow comments from anyone about anything with no rules or guidelines. ● A moderated forum will contain administrators that check messages and block unwanted material. ● Do not use inappropriate language on any platform.
● Losing control of confidential information	● Never share confidential information, especially images, about yourself or others online; it's almost impossible to know who you may be really talking to.
● Physical danger or abuse	● Never arrange to meet anyone online unless this has been arranged specifically with the involvement of a parent or legal guardian and a safe, public place has been arranged.
● Financial risk	● Never give out financial data, credit card or bank account details. ● Be aware of in-app purchases within games and mobile applications, these can quickly add up if the user is unfamiliar with payment methods. ● Avoid online gambling sites and apps. They are age-restricted, not suitable for children, and will try and attract new customers with free credits.

Activity 7

Write a list of rules that could be given to a ten year old child, just starting out playing online games. Offer friendly but informative advice for someone of that age.

Tip

Remember there is very little privacy online. When posting any messages or media online, ask yourself: 'Would every member of my family be happy to see or read this?'

Review and revise

You should now be able to:

- identify the potential security risks of sharing personal information online
- describe how our internet browsing habits have changed and how we can protect ourselves online
- describe strategies to minimise the potential risks when using email, including spam and email attachments
- describe our use of social networking, online shopping and gaming and identify the potential dangers.

The security of personal and commercial data

Background

In this session you will consider how large organisations keep data secure and the methods used to fraudulently obtain confidential data.

Keeping our own data private and secure using complex user IDs and passwords (See Session 4.7) is important but the owners of the systems we log into must also keep our data secure. Many large organisations are asking users to use two-factor authentication to access their systems. This makes 'hacking' a system much more difficult but systems are still vulnerable to other methods of attack.

Website security

When you log into a website that uses confidential data, you need to know it is the genuine site and not a fake (see Pharming). Anyone can create a website about anything, even creating a copy of your online banking site to gaining access to your username and password. A **digital certificate** is used to verify the identity of a website and is issued to the owner of the website by an independent and recognised **Certificate Authority**. The digital certificate contains unique identifiers, dates and details of ownership and their **public key**. When an internet browser makes a secure connection to a banking site for example it will check the certificate and inform you of any issues and potential dangers. If any are reported, the page should be closed and reported if possible.

Activity 1

Take note of the web browsing software you have access to in school and at home and investigate how they represent secure and dangerous websites to their users.

The secure connection between the browser and the website server providing the website is made using a Secure Sockets Layer (SSL) security protocol. SSL encrypts data so that it cannot be intercepted and understood by anyone else. A secure connection cannot be made unless the digital certificate and the public and private encryption keys are checked against the Certificate Authority by the browser. Ignoring such a warning from your browser could result in your personal details or credit card details being taken by a fake website and then used to make purchases in your name.

Hacking

A hacker tries to access a controlled system without permission or login details and will employ a variety of methods to either force their way into a system by trying multiple passwords, or find a poorly protected 'back door'. A hacker's reason for doing what they do is often varied and controversial but may include:

- pure curiosity, just to see what can be accessed
- financial benefit, the information accessed and taken may have value or be valuable to others
- personal beliefs about the rights of any organisation's control of information.

Real world

- Two-factor authentication is an extra layer of security, designed to check the identity of anyone logging into a system.
- When logging into a secure system, a second code will be sent to a pre-registered device, normally a smartphone, you have access to. Access will only be granted once this additional code has been entered.

Real world

Many organisations are described as cloud computing based systems, storing data 'in the cloud'. Remember this doesn't mean your files are only available wirelessly. It means they use a server farm (see Unit 4) to remotely store your data and have taken steps to ensure you can access this from any internet access point. This can cause potential problems though, as many people still use basic user names and passwords that they can easily remember and then systems can be easily hacked and compromised.

Tip

How to recognise a secure website: Most browser software will use a padlock icon combined with colour coding to represent a secure connection. The colour red is usually used together with a warning to announce a certificate has a problem.

The potential effects of hacking depend on the type of data being accessed. Access to personal home computers can lead to financial records being taken or malicious damage being done. The larger the business; the more tempting the hack. Financial centres, multinational companies and military powers have always had to defend against attacks.

You can minimise the risk of hacking by using firewalls and strong passwords. Firewall software stops external programs from accessing the network and causing damage, whilst allowing the user to control access and permit certain programs to send and receive data. A firewall can also prevent access to unauthorised sites, and logs or records, all traffic (incoming and outgoing data) on a network.

Tip

The only real way to prevent an external hacking attempt on a computer is to have no external communication systems of any kind; no internet access, wireless or wired connection to any other computer network. Or to simply turn off the power!

Activity 2

What might be the potential dangers if computers in the following organisations were hacked?
- a power station
- a hospital
- a large stock market centre

Computer viruses and malware

A computer virus is a small program designed to invade a compatible computer system and damage it. It is a piece of programming code that replicates itself with the purpose of then transferring itself to another computer.

These programs can:
- create new unwanted files
- move or delete essential files and other programs
- cause a computer to slow down by using up memory
- cause the computer to constantly restart, shut down or stop working
- corrupt your data files so that you can no longer open them
- install **malware** without your knowledge
- spy and record the work you do on a computer and transmit it to a criminal.

The most common ways for a virus to invade your computer are by:
- opening an email attachment
- installing illegal software or software promoted as free
- downloading files from the internet
- sharing files with friends and family on a USB stick.

Phishing

Phishing involves sending an email that looks as though it comes from a legitimate (and often powerful) organisation such as a bank or a law firm. If the recipient clicks on a link inside the email, he or she may be taken to a fake website and be asked to provide personal and financial details that could lead to identity theft, or money being taken from their account. Some phishing emails simply ask the recipient to send personal or account details by replying to the phishing email.

Pharming

Pharming is another type of scam, redirecting users from a genuine website to a fake version of the site in order to collect access credentials such as usernames and passwords. This is achieved by infecting a user's computer or network with a virus which instructs the computer to open the fake website even after the correct address is entered. Extreme versions of this attack can even attack an external server, not your computer, meaning anti-malware software or the user would not notice the site was fake.

Smishing

An extension of phishing, the process of imitating a well-known organisation has also extended to mobile phones. Smishing text or SMS messages bombard thousands of users with messages, with apparently urgent requests to confirm login details or contact a website in order to steal personal data. The voicemail equivalent of this is sometimes referred to as **vishing**.

Card fraud

Credit and debit cards are a common target for criminals. Gaining access to the name, account and security numbers on a card can allow fraudulent purchases to be made. Card fraud methods include:

- Shoulder surfing: simply looking over your shoulder to see the PIN being entered at a ATM or payment device.
- Card cloning: also known as 'skimming' this involves creating a duplicate of a card using a small device that captures the personal details stored on it. This device could be placed on an ATM or payment machine.
- Key logging: this form of spyware involves recording card details being entered into a website or application.

Protecting your computer from viruses

Anti-virus and Anti-malware software

One of the most important things to do with any computer system with online access is to install anti-virus software. It is designed to scan your computer's memory, websites, downloads, email attachments and connected storage devices to look for potential viruses. If the software detects a virus, it will destroy and delete it, or put it into **quarantine** (isolating the virus to an area where it cannot access, and possibly harm, the rest of your computer system).

Anti-malware software performs the same process but is an umbrella term that includes more recent pieces of malicious software in circulation, including spyware, ransomware and more complex programs designed with criminal intent.

It is essential that both anti-virus and anti-malware software are kept up to date, as the only way to identify and protect the system from the latest threats is to be aware of them. Most systems can be set to update themselves every day.

Tip

Most anti-virus software is updated daily and new versions of the software are installed automatically, ensuring that your computer will be protected from new viruses as they appear. Most anti-virus software companies will also provide a free version of their software for home users.

Working smart

You can also protect your computer from viruses by being very careful and asking yourself the following questions when browsing and emailing. If your thoughts start to seem like the ones below then simply stop, proceed no further and delete any files.

The email doesn't tell me what the attachment is for.

This new mobile phone advertisement is too good to be true!

My sister is sending me holiday photos but she hasn't been away for a while.

Do I know who sent me this email attachment?

This software sounds just like the one I wanted but its free!

This free movie download has only just arrived in the cinema.

Security methods are changing all the time. Investigate some of the newest technology that may be used in the not too distant future to securely identify us.

Review and revise

You should now be able to:

- describe how secure websites keep data secure on their own networks and cloud-based data
- define the term hacking and describe the risks associated with it
- describe how computer viruses and malware are transmitted and identify the risks to individuals and networks
- summarise continuing developments in computer security methods.

Real world

Viruses are not just limited to desktop and portable computers. As modern smartphones are now able to install additional apps (software applications) not pre-installed by the device creator, an increasing number of mobile device viruses are being created to act in the same destructive way. This has also led to mobile device anti-virus apps.

Real world

As the number of smart devices increases in our homes, many are now also concerned about the potential of malware infecting our smart televisions or even electric vehicles.

8 Theory review

What have you covered?

In these three theory sessions you have:

- identified potential physical safety risks to those using computer equipment and strategies to prevent them
- considered the risks to potentially sharing personal information online
- evaluated your internet browsing habits and considered strategies to minimise the potential risks when browsing and using email
- considered your use of social networking, online shopping and gaming to identify the potential dangers
- discovered how secure websites are authorised to keep data secure on their own networks
- investigated the term hacking and the risks associated with it
- considered how computer viruses are transmitted and the damage they cause
- summarised continuing developments in computer security methods.

Some practice questions

1 Match the physical accident on the left to the potential cause on the right:

Tripping over	Handling overheating equipment, poorly ventilated
Electrocution	A piece of hardware has been placed in an unstable position, a LCD monitor at the edge of a desk for example
Impact related injury to the body	Computer cables hanging from a desk or trailing across a walkway
A burn to the hand	Handling exposed or bare power cables

See Session 8.1

2 Give five pieces of health and safety advice that might be offered in an office that uses computer equipment.

See Session 8.1

3 Which of the following pieces of personal information would it be OK to share when using a social network:

	OK to share	Not OK to share
First name		
Home address		
School details		
Favourite colour		
Surname		
Mobile phone number		
Favourite movie		
Parents' place of work		

See Session 8.2

4 What are the main differences between a family friend you see regularly and an online friend from a social network or online game?

See Session 8.2

5 Complete each statement below using one of these words: Spamming, a virus, hacking, pharming, phishing.

a. You receive an email that appears to have come from your bank. The email states that your information needs to be updated or validated. You recognise that this is an attempt at _____.

b. _____ occurs when your email inbox is flooded by unrequested advertising for all sorts of products and services.

c. A colleague warns you against opening an attachment that has been sent to most people in the company where you work. He tells you that the attachment carries _____ that damages and even deletes files.

d. You realise that you have been a victim of _____ because some files on your computer have been deleted and some emails that you know you have not seen, appear to have been opened and read.

See Session 8.2

6 State whether the following statements are true or false.

	True	False
It is impossible to track an internet bully or stalker.		
No damage can come from email attachments.		
Social networking is a great way to chat to people around the world.		
I should always reply to an email from the bank marked as urgent.		

See Session 8.2

7 What is a digital certificate and how does it relate to a certificate authority?

See Session 8.3

8 A hacker may try to access a system by repeatedly trying thousands of different passwords until one works. Why should this affect your choice of password?

See Session 8.3

9 Pooja is worried that her computer has a virus. She has heard that email attachments can often spread them. State two other ways in which a computer virus could have found its way into Pooja's computer.

See Session 8.3

10 Anti-virus software should have been installed on Pooja's computer, so you look for an icon on her desktop that might indicate whether this has been done. Describe the terms anti-virus software and icon.

See Session 8.3

Progress check

Aiming for good progress

- You can discuss health and safety issues connected with ICT equipment.
- You recognise what is classed as personal data and why you should protect it.
- You can outline tips for safe internet browsing.
- You can describe viruses, hacking, phishing, smishing, pharming and spam.
- You understand how social networks are used around the world and some of the dangers they present.
- You can describe the term online multiplayer games.
- You can describe the security used by websites that process personal data.
- You can describe what a hacker tries to do.
- You can describe the dangers of allowing a computer virus to install itself on your machine.
- You realise the importance of virus protection software and the dangers of spyware and malware.
- You understand the need for questioning online information and examining your own usage.

Aiming for excellent progress

- You understand health and safety issues connected with ICT linked scenarios and possible prevention strategies.
- You can describe examples of personal data and the potential dangers of losing access to it.
- You can give advice on safe internet browsing and dangers to be aware of.
- You understand the terms viruses, hacking, phishing, smishing, pharming and spam, the damage they can do, and how to prevent them.
- You understand the many positive and negative aspects of social networking.
- You can provide sensible advice for those playing online games.
- You understand the process by which website certificates are checked and authorised.
- You understand the reasons given for hacking and the many dangers it presents.
- You understand what a computer virus is, how to protect against it and the damage it can cause.
- You can evaluate your own use of all the systems outlined in this session and describe detailed strategies to use them to their full potential.

Producing a word-processed report in response to a hypothesis

Background

Helen, the head of human resources at Peak Security always asks potential employees to write a written report as part of their application. Rather than asking a range of simple questions with specific answers she likes to provide a hypothesis that requires the applicant to come up with a range of thoughts and ideas.

What is a hypothesis?

A hypothesis is a statement or proposed explanation based on limited evidence. It is meant as a starting point for further research in order to provide a well-balanced response that should either prove or disprove the original statement made. The hypothesis you have been asked to respond to is:

"The dangers of using technology and online systems clearly outweigh the benefits"

Planning a response

Sometimes the best way to tackle a report is to create a visual plan, or mind map, of all the elements and expand it to include ideas and thoughts on each of the topics. The diagram below is **incomplete**; it is a starting point to work from.

> **Tip**
>
> Once a mind map is complete, numbering the many parts can help in deciding their order in your draft report.

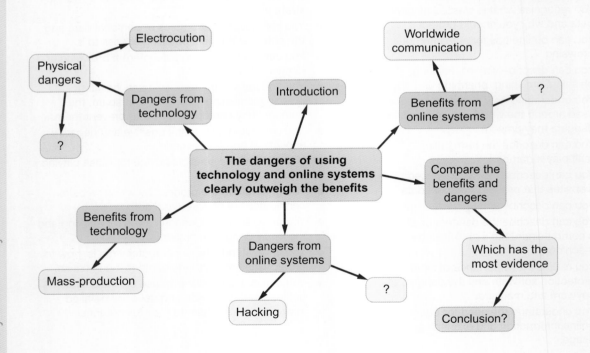

Activity 1

Plan your response as a mind map. Use the one shown as a starting point and complete and expand it with your own ideas and thoughts.

Background reading

Background reading is essential before writing any long response to a question. Having broken down the question in Activity 1, your ideas can be used for research starting points. In Unit 1 you developed a range of internet searching skills and can use the following:

- Keyword searches
- Boolean logic searches

Activity 2

Using your ideas from Activity 1 to build a list of keywords and topics, carry out additional research to help write your report. Many of the topics are included in this book but recent news articles and journals can provide additional detail.

Writing a draft report

If a document or report is important then a draft version is a good idea. It should be created with only the written content in mind, so don't worry about formatting or how it looks at this stage. Once complete it should be printed and checked. You can annotate and highlight any issues as required.

Activity 3

Using your plan and the research collected, write a first draft of your report. Once complete; print, proofread and also ask a friend to check it.

Report Presentation

As a professional application, your report needs to look formal, well presented and be checked completely for any errors. Using the document presentation skills built throughout this book; create a final version of your report. Before handing it on, make sure you have done the following:

- a spelling and grammar check
- clearly displayed the title and your name
- made clear and appropriate font, formatting and styling choices
- included an introduction and conclusion
- proofread it one last time.

Activity 4

Using the notes from your draft version, create the final version of your report. Once complete, ask friends to read it and collect any feedback they may offer in order to improve it.

Review and revise

You should now be able to:

- understand the need to research, compare and contrast multiple sources of information in order to create a balanced response to a question or hypothesis
- write an essay style, well-constructed response to a particular question in a report format
- use a range of formatting and paragraph tools to improve the look of a document
- use software tools and proofreading to make sure a document is fit for its intended audience.

8 Practical review

What have you covered?

In the previous theory session you have:

- discovered the nature of a hypothesis and how to deconstruct it
- considered the need to research, compare and contrast multiple sources of information in order to create a balanced response to a question or hypothesis
- written an essay style, well-constructed response to a particular question in a report format
- used a range of formatting and paragraph tools to improve the look of a document to a professional standard
- used software tools and proofreading to make sure a document is fit for its intended audience.

Some practice questions

1 Define the term hypothesis.

2 Write a hypothesis that could be stated for each of the eight units in this textbook.

3 Create a mind map of the statement below; breaking the question down into as many parts as possible.

Studying a university course, you have been asked to write a response to the following statement:

'Tablet computers, smartphones and smart watches will replace all home computers in ten years' time'

4 Identify where in your breakdown additional information would be useful and carry out internet research.

5 Write a draft response, print and proofread.

6 Create a professional looking report that presents the original statement and your response to it.

Progress check

Aiming for good progress

- You can describe a hypothesis.
- Given a topic, you can plan a written piece of work using a mind map.
- You are able to research a range of topics using suitable keywords.
- You know how to check a document using software tools and proofreading.
- You can create a professional looking written document.

Aiming for excellent progress

- You understand the term hypothesis and how it should be responded to.
- Given a topic, you can plan a detailed response that considers all points that may be considered using a mind map.
- You are able to research a range of topics using advanced search tools and specific keywords.
- You know how to thoroughly check a document using software tools and proofreading.
- You can create a professional looking written document that considers the prospective audience.

Glossary

actuator A device that takes a signal from a computer and converts it into motion or controlled movement, for example, switching a heater on or off, controlling a motor.

ADC Analogue to Digital Converter. A device that converts analogue signals, like that produced by a sensor, to a digital signal, which a computer can process.

algorithm A sequence of instructions which will perform a particular task. A computer program is an example of an algorithm.

alignment Formatting text lines or paragraphs horizontally so that the text is placed to either the left or right margins, or centred.

alphanumeric A data type where the data can be any keyboard character is acceptable – this data type is often referred to as text.

analyst An ICT professional who is responsible for carrying out the systems analysis.

animated gif A combination of multiple GIF images, or frames, that then appears as an animated clip or short movie.

anti-virus Application software that scans files for the presence of, and will remove or isolate, computer viruses.

applications programs Software that will carry out specific tasks on a computer such as word processing or using a database.

apps Short for 'Applications'. A term used to describe mini-programs designed to run on a computer or mobile device. Apps may be linked to the internet to provide constantly updated weather, sport and entertainment features.

Artificial intelligence biometrics Coupling the latest advances in biometrics with artificial intelligence to create systems which will recognise individuals based on for example, fingerprint or facial recognition.

ascending In order of small to large.

ASCII A method of coding English characters where each letter is given a number between 0 and 127, this allows transfer of text between computers very easily.

aspect ratio The proportion of width to height of an image. An important aspect of resizing an image so that the original proportion is maintained.

ATM Automated Teller Machine. Remotely connected to a bank's computer system, it can dispense cash and provide account information.

attribute Providing additional information about an HTML element.

augmented reality A way of combining live video with computer-generated data and visualisations, for example, layering real time information over your camera display so that if you point your viewfinder down a street you could find out information on all kinds of things, from restaurants, to historical/tourist information.

avatar The representation of a real person in the online world, this may be an image to represent them in a discussion or a 3D model in an online game.

backing storage Devices that allow large amounts of data to be stored outside the main memory, for example, CD, DVD, memory stick.

barcode A row of vertical stripes of different thicknesses, often with numbers, that can be read by a computer. Used to identify products.

batch processing The method of ordering a series of computer requests by creating a job queue that is then processed one at a time.

Bcc Blind carbon copy. Sending a copy of an email to someone other than the main recipient. The main recipient (and cc recipients) will not know that the Bcc recipient has had a copy of the email sent to them.

bias Showing too much favour towards one viewpoint without due reason.

BIOS Basic Input Output System. Start-up code that enables the operating system to be loaded and the computer to start successfully.

bluetooth A short range (approx. 30 m) wireless technology used in computers, mobile/cell phones and portable devices.

BMP (Windows Bitmap) Uncompressed images created in the Microsoft Windows operating system. File sizes are often too large for internet use.

Boolean Data that can have one of only two values – true/false.

Boolean operators Using AND, OR and NOT to combine criteria to search for information or filter a data set.

boosters (amplifiers) Used to extend the range of a wireless network by connecting to and amplifying network signals.

break-even The point at which expenses are equal to income, meaning that profit is zero.

CAD Computer Aided Design. Software packages used in design and engineering to plan and analyse anything from kitchens to automobiles and architecture.

call centre A large office environment designed to process large numbers of telephone requests and centralise business and customer communications. Used in the banking and products and service industries.

cascading style sheets (CSS) Allows the creation of formatting rules that can be applied to any webpage to create commonality and save time.

Cc Carbon copy. Sending a copy of an email to another person other than the main recipient. All recipients will know that they have received the email.

cell padding The setting of a fixed space within a cell between the content and the border.

cell spacing The setting of a fixed space between the cells of a table.

Chip and PIN system Used in credit and debit card transactions; a combination of a computer chip containing account information and a secure PIN number to access it.

circuit breaker An automatic switch designed to protect a circuit or device from an overload or short circuit that would damage it and potentially hurt any local user.

citizen journalism The process of any individual taking part in recording, commenting and reporting on news and information. For example the use of smartphones to record and share news events live as they happen, at the scene.

clients Computers that are connected to a network and access shared material.

cloud computing The use of online based systems and programs that save information and files on a remote server rather than a local computer. This allows a user to access the same programs and files through an online portal, anywhere they have internet access.

CMOS Complementary Metal Oxide Semiconductor. A type of IC that holds data, such as BIOS, and which has its own power supply.

CMS Stands for 'Content Management System'. A software tool, often based online, that allows a user with minimal technical experience to build and edit web content.

coaxial cable A type of cable that has an insulated central core and a conducting shield to prevent electrical interference, used primarily in radio transmitters, network connections and cable television systems.

collaborative learning Allows multiple users from any location with an internet connection the ability to work simultaneously on the same documents, often connected with cloud computing.

Command Line Interface (CLI) The type of user interface where the user needs to type in a single line of text, which is a direct command to the operating system.

compatibility Ensuring that the different parts of the system fit or work together as required, for example is the output from one part of the system accepted as input to another?

compose To create a new email message.

compression To reduce the file size of a computer document or group of documents so that they can be stored and transferred more easily.

computer generated The creation of an object or character completely within a computer system without the need for a physical object.

computer system The combination of hardware and software that enables information to be input, processed and output in a suitable format.

conditional function A function where its outcome is dependent on whether a condition is true or false.

contactless payment The ability to pay for goods and services easily by waving a debit or credit cards containing RFID chip over a reader at the point of sale.

control application A system in which a microprocessor is managing or regulating the operation of a system.

copyright The legal protection given to the creators of text, images, music and software to prevent their work being used illegally.

corrupted A file containing errors that were created while transmitting, processing or accessing it. Errors can sometimes be corrected but this depends on the amount of corruption.

criterion (pl criteria) The field content to be examined when selecting a record with a filter.

crop Removing unwanted parts of an image.

CRT Cathode Ray Tube. A type of computer monitor similar to a television in the way it works; using an electron gun and glass tube.

cryptography Protecting information by transforming it (encrypting) into something which is unreadable unless you know how it has been scrambled

.csv Comma Separate Variable file format. Data is stored as a text file with all the data items separated by a comma.

data modelling Using numerical data to model, predict and analyse situations, for example the profitability of an organised event.

data protection act Places restrictions on organisations that deal with personal data on how they can process and transfer it.

data structures The way in which the collected data is organised, stored and connected so that it can be managed and processed as required by the proposed new system.

default An option, setting or value that is used if no user input is added.

delimited A way of separating data items that are written as a long string of text. The comma in a .csv file indicates to software reading it that the commas show where a data item begins and ends.

deskilling When workers have to retrain for a new job but that new job requires a lower skill level than the job they had been doing.

desktop publishing Application software that allows text and graphics to be combined to produce professional-looking material for publication, for example newsletters, flyers.

digital certificate Used to confirm the online identity of a user or organisation by checking their Public Key, usually linked to secure websites.

disks Magnetic or optical storage devices.

document sharing The ability for more than one user to access and edit the same document, often online.

downloaded Transferring a file from one location to another, typically refers to the transfer of a file across the internet, for example from a webpage or an email attachment, to the user's own computer.

drives Component of a computer that allows CDs or DVDs to be played.

eBooks An electronic version of a printed document. Many devices now have the ability to view eBooks; from mobile phones to tablet computers and specifically designed eBook readers that can mimic the look of a traditional book using electronic paper.

Ecommerce Business carried out on the internet, allowing products to be bought and sold from any internet-connected location.

EFTPOS Electronic Funds Transfer At the Point of Sale. The ability to pay for goods and services electronically, allowing direct computer access between banks and service providers.

electronic funds transfer The process of transferring currency electronically between two banks.

email accounts The technical information, settings and data related to one particular email address.

embed Taking an element from one website, usually in the form of coding, and placing it into another so that the original element can be viewed. Often used to view online videos.

encrypted The process of scrambling a piece of information so that it can only be read by the owner of the encryption key.

encryption key A piece of information or data that allows an encrypted message to be decoded and read.

POS Point Of Sale. Using technology for the efficient recording of the sale of goods or services to a customer by scanning barcodes, retrieving information and updating data files.

ergonomic design The development of furniture and equipment which will help to relieve health related problems such as RSI.

ergonomics The study of the relationship between workers and their environment especially the equipment they use.

eSafety A term used to include all aspects of personal safety when using electronic systems.

facsimile Or fax for short, the ability to scan and send a document using traditional telephone lines to another facsimile, or fax, machine.

field A single item of data, such as a name, an account number, the stock level.

file extension A label (usually three letters), attached to the end of a file name which indicates to the operating system what format the data is stored in.

file formats The way in which data will be organised in a specific file, considering, for example key fields (primary, foreign), data types.

files Collections of data or instructions; a program, an image, a database, a document.

file size The amount of storage space required within a computer system to save a document or file.

filter The set of criteria that is applied to a data set.

firewall A piece of hardware or software that provides a controllable barrier between a network and external access. This is to protect against hackers or other software from gaining unauthorised access to your computer or network.

flat file database A single collection of structured data.

flexible hours A work time arrangement allowing the employee to change their working hours to fit around their own needs rather than be tied to a rigid timetable.

flowcharts Diagrams describing the operations involved in a process or system. Special symbols are used to represent various activities or devices.

footer A 'reserved' area at the foot of a document between the bottom edge and margin of the page.

foreign key A field within a record that contains the primary key to a record in another table, creating a relationship between the two tables.

formula (pl formulae) An expression that you create to carry out a particular calculation such as =B4*C4*$0$1.

forum A type of, or part of a website that allows users to post comments and reply to other users comments.

function A pre-determined routine for a calculation, such as SUM.

GIF (Graphics Interchange Format) A file type limited to 8-bit often used for diagrams or cartoon-style images.

gigabytes Equivalent to 1000 megabytes of computer information or 1 000 000 000 bytes.

GPS Global Positioning System. A global system of navigational satellites developed to determine the precise position of a vehicle or person.

Graphical User Interface (GUI) The type of user interface where the user controls the operation of the computer by using a pointing device to select icons on screen.

hacking Gaining unauthorised access to a computer system.

hardware The physical components of a computer system, for example mouse, monitor, printer.

header A 'reserved' area at the top of a document between the top edge and margin of the page.

hit counter Code embedded in a webpage, which tracks information such as how many times the page has been viewed, where the page viewers are or even what OS they are using.

homepage The first or main page of any website. Also referred to as the index page.

house style A set of visual rules that documents from the organisation should refer to in respect to colour, fonts and imagery.

HTML Hyper Text Mark-up Language, a coding language developed to design the layout webpages.

HTML element An individual coding component that combines tags and content to create elements such a title or block of text.

https A more secure way of handling data on or through a webpage than the standard http:// Apart from the 's' in https:// your browser may display a small picture of a padlock in the address bar. This gives users the confidence to use websites, for example, online banking.

hyperlink A piece of text, image or graphic that web clicked takes the user to a specified webpage, resource or website.

icon A small graphic or logo representing a piece of software, a particular command or function or a brand.

identity theft Stealing the personal details of another person and using them online to fraudulently obtain goods or services. For example, stealing credit card details and using them to buy expensive products.

immersive technology Term given to technology that enhances 3D gaming or simulators to provide a more realistic, or immersive, experience.

inference engines Software that interacts with a knowledge base in order to find a response to a particular question.

integer A whole number, one which has no decimal or fractional part.

integrated circuit (IC) Another name for a chip, an IC is a small electronic device that can be used for a number of purposes, including memory and processor. The most complete integrated circuit is a microprocessor: a computer on a single chip.

intercepted email Having the contents of an email viewed unlawfully by a third party before it reaches the intended recipient.

internet A wide area network (WAN). A global network allowing anyone connected to it to access information located anywhere else across the network, provided they have permission. Sometimes referred to as a network of networks.

IP addresses The unique identifiable address provided to every computer on a specific network.

ISP Internet Service Provider, a company that provides users access to the internet, usually for a regular fee.

job sharing Two (or more) people share the responsibilities and pay of one full-time job.

JPEG (Joint Photographic Experts Group) A file type designed for flat, rectangular images. They have lots of compression options and the quality of images can be selected when saved.

key field See Primary key.

knowledge base A database created by experts of a particular field or industry.

legislation Rules and regulations in relation to a specific subject and normally issued by government.

link Known as a hyperlink, a clickable word or image in a webpage that causes another webpage to be loaded. Text is usually underlined. The pointer on screen will change to a small pointing finger.

linux A free and open source operating system that competes to be a genuine alternative to commercial operating systems like Windows and Apple.

logical conditions When examining the values of multiple fields the connection between them is made using AND, OR. A field's content can be negatively compared using NOT.

main memory Memory chip(s) physically located very close to the processor, which holds programs of data that the processor needs immediately. Also referred to as central memory.

malware Short for malicious software. A piece of software designed to secretly pass on information about your computer when in use. This may include passwords or personal details.

media player A device that can play a variety of media files, from films to music or digital photographs. Usually connected to a television or display.

memory chips These are integrated circuits which can be used to either store or process data. RAM and ROM chips are memory chips. See also *integrated circuit* (IC).

merged cells The combination of multiple cells within a table into one single cell.

microprocessor A special kind of CPU used in PCs, smaller computers and small computerised devices such as washing machines.

moderator Often a named user within a forum or any web-based discussion that monitors and if required edits comments and if required can impose sanctions.

motherboard The main circuit board of the computer and is also known as the mainboard or logic board, holding all the vital electronic system components.

multimedia The combination of sound, images, video and animation to present information.

nested function Having one function inside another.

nested IF Having multiple IF statements with each other in order to make multiple decisions based on true, false outcomes.

nesting The coding of one HTML element inside another.

networked When a set of computers are linked together to allow sharing resources such as files, printers, an internet connection

network administrator A managerial role, leading a network team in the development and running of a network.

Network Interface Cards (NIC) A hardware device required in any computer wishing to connect to a network.

online processing Used in network or internet-based booking systems to provide user access to a database. Examples include cinemas and travel ticket systems.

open source A type of software that is freely available and its users are encouraged to suggest or submit modifications and developments, which then become incorporated into the software.

operating system A systems software program that controls the entire operation of the computer as well as allowing interaction with the user. Popular operating systems include Windows, Apple OS and Linux.

operators When examining a field's value a comparison is made using =, < >, =<, =>, <, >.

palmtops Now called netbooks, smaller versions of laptops, but with limited functionality. Palmtop is a term that is now better applied to PDAs (personal digital assistants).

password A personal identification phrase or collection of characters that in conjunction with a password will allow access to a system.

.pdf Portable Document File format. Converts documents into a format that can be viewed exactly as they would be printed.

peripheral devices Any piece of hardware connected to a computer, outside of the CPU and working memory.

personal data Any piece of information that can be used to identify you online. This may relate to you, your personal circumstances or past history.

pharming An attempt to steal personal or confidential information by redirecting users to a fake website without them knowing it.

phishing The use of fraudulent electronic communications to try and trick readers into providing usernames, passwords and banking details.

PIN Personal Identification Number, a secret number of normally four digits used in secure systems such as banking and security alarms.

plugin An additional piece of software that enhances another application, such as a web browser, with additional features.

PNG (Portable Network Graphics) Similar to a GIF file but can support 16 million colours and higher quality images.

pointing devices A device used with a GUI to control a cursor or pointer, for example, mouse, joystick, trackball.

primary key A field in a record that contains a unique data value and is used to identify that record.

processing Performing or carrying out a task

processor An integrated circuit where the main components of the CPU, excluding main memory are combined as a single unit.

profile In respect to social networking, a term to describe the public face of a user through the images and personal details they share online.

programs A complete set of instructions that can be executed in order to carry out a task

proofreading Visually checking a document for errors, either graphical or text based.

prototype A first working version of a system, piece of software or hardware, designed to represent a final product with all its main features.

proxy server A server that allows multiple computers to connect to the internet but can filter their access and cache pages for quick access.

pseudo code A readable type of code that uses key words and structures which are similar to, but without the strict rules of, those found in programming languages.

public key An electronic document with a digital signature that identifies a user or organisation. See also Digital Certificate. Normally issued by a certificate authority.

quantum cryptography A method of encrypting transmitted information with a key generated by using photons instead of a mathematical algorithm.

quarantine A feature of anti-virus software. When viruses are detected in a file the anti-virus software will place the virus into a safe area where it cannot continue to have an effect. This is done because sometimes the action of deleting a virus causes damage to files.

query A filter that you have previously saved so that you can easily access the subset of records again.

QWERTY A keyboard with keys placed in the traditional typewriter positions with the keys to the left of the top letter row being QWERTY.

RAID (Redundant Array of Independent Disks). The use of multiple hard drives to protect data in the event of a problem. The same data can be saved to two drives at the same time; keeping a redundant backup.

real number A number that has decimal places.

real-time processing An online processing system that requires instantaneous access or responses. Examples include air-traffic control and ATM machines.

recipient The person that the email message is to be sent to.

record A collection of related fields. A set of information about one item that the file is about, such as a book, a car, a student.

record structure The collection of fields and their properties, such as data type or size, which make up a record.

relational database A database that has links (relationships) with data held in different tables.

resolution The number of lines, pixels or dots within a standard area. Used in computer monitors and printing, the higher the resolution, the higher the quality or detail.

RFID Stands for 'Radio-Frequency Identification' and it used to track any object a unique RFID tag is attached to using radio waves.

routers A device that connects different networks. This may be two LANs or a home computer and the internet.

RSI Repetitive Strain Injury. Aching muscular injury occurring from carrying out an action such as texting or using a mouse continuously over a long period of time.

.rtf Rich Text File format. A text file which retains some, but not all, of the formatting done in the word processor.

rules base A set of interface rules that an interference base uses to apply reason to a question.

run-time calculations A field that is added to a report (or query), which displays a value calculated as the report (or query result) is being compiled.

sans-serif A simplified font face style not using serifs on characters, for example, Arial, Tahoma, Verdana.

satellite navigation See *GPS*.

search Selecting a specific set of records from a file/table according to some criteria using a filter.

secondary storage See *backing storage*.

secure webpage Used to describe a webpage or site that meets agreed standards to prevent unauthorised access or tampered by those other than the user. A key element of online banking, shopping or site that uses usernames and passwords.

serif A font face style, which has a small finishing stroke (serif) attached to the ends of characters, for example, Times New Roman, Perpetua.

server A network-enabled computer that provides services to other computers on a network.

server farm A collection of computer servers in one, usually secure, location with the purpose of running a particular online service or system.

smart watch Used to describe any wrist-worn device that allows additional functionality such as mobile phone connectivity or fitness activity monitoring.

smishing A combination of 'SMS' and 'Phishing' which uses mobile phone messages to trick readers into providing usernames, passwords and banking details.

software The programs, instructions and data that enables the computer to carry out a task.

software piracy Copying and/or distributing software without having the legal right to do so. This is illegal.

sort Rearranging all records in a table into another order according to some sort criteria.

spam The use of email systems to send large quantities of unwanted advertisements for goods and services to multiple addresses at once. Often linked to criminal business methods, computer viruses and identity theft.

stand-alone A computer that is not connected to a network and used as an isolated work station, it does not share any resources such as files, storage or printers

storage A device into which data can be placed, held, and later retrieved.

streaming The instantaneous viewing of a video (or listening of a sound file) from an internet based source without having to download the file first.

strong password Describes a password that includes a combination of combination of letters, numbers and symbols that would be difficult to guess or calculate.

style Used to define style attributes with HTML coding, colour or font options, for example.

style sheet hierarchy The order in which CSS styling is applied to a website document.

subset A selection of records that are returned as a result of applying a filter.

syntax The rules that describe how a statement should be written. The key words, together with how conditions, commas, brackets and other required elements are to be arranged so that the software will understand what is to be done.

systems analysis The study of an existing system to discover any problems within it and building a solution that meets the requirements of the customer.

systems life cycle The various stages that are to be completed to create or modify a system. The stages form a cycle because after a period of time the system will need modifying or replacing and the process has to be repeated.

system software The name given to software such as operating systems and utility programs that control and maintain the computer system.

tablet computer A slim, lightweight, portable computer which is a new type of internet-enabled device that works in a similar way to smartphones, with touchscreens and downloadable apps.

tags A web design coding term used when specifying different visual elements from horizontal lines to paragraph breaks.

teleworkers People who use ICT technology to enable them to work from home rather than travelling to an office.

text wrapping A formatting technique which makes text surround an image.

third party software Software freely provided or sold to accompany a piece of software or hardware but not created by the original manufacturer or developer.

TFT A flat panel display screen used in computers and televisions.

touch screen An input device that allows the user to control a process or select icons by touching the screen.

transactions Term to describe the electronic movement of currency between one organisation, business or person to another.

tuck shop Common name for a small shop selling sweets and snacks, especially in a school.

two step verification Used to add an additional code or security question to any standard username and password system, making it more difficult for a hacker to access.

.txt A text file that is stored without any of the formatting that you may have done to the text with the word processor.

URL Uniform Resource Locator. The string of text, usually starting with 'www' that refers to the location where a webpage is stored.